I0824460

"A must-read book for policy-makers, especially in the defence and foreign affairs spheres. This thoughtful, clear-eyed and outspoken work proves how Putin's Russia employs multi-frontal warfare in a way that we are likely to see more of in the coming years and explains why the war in Ukraine will be seen as one of history's paradigm-shifting conflicts. If this important book is heeded, Bob Seely's time on the ground in Ukraine will have been put to phenomenally good use."

ANDREW ROBERTS, CO-AUTHOR OF *CONFLICT: THE EVOLUTION OF WARFARE FROM 1945 TO GAZA*

"Packed with insights personally drawn from the battlefields of Ukraine and ably weaving them together to demonstrate how Russia is blazing a trail in new ways of war, Seely's book is an indispensable guide to conflict in the twenty-first century for the public and policy-makers alike."

PROFESSOR MARK GALEOTTI, AUTHOR OF *FORGED IN WAR: A MILITARY HISTORY OF RUSSIA FROM ITS BEGINNINGS TO TODAY*

"Bob Seely, with his unique blend of experience as a journalist, soldier and MP, delivers a sharp, insightful look at the Kremlin's approach to warfare. In the age of Russia's shadow war against the West, this is a must-read."

ANDREI SOLDATOV, EXILED RUSSIAN SECURITY SERVICES EXPERT AND AUTHOR OF *OUR DEAR FRIENDS IN MOSCOW*

"Piercing, unflinching and grounded in original Russian sources, this book lays bare the Kremlin's doctrine of war as statecraft, revealing not just how Russia fights but how it thinks."

DR JADE MCGLYNN, POST-DOCTORAL FELLOW AT KING'S COLLEGE LONDON AND AUTHOR OF *RUSSIA'S WAR* AND *MEMORY MAKERS*

"This is no dry academic tome – on page one you find Seely in a deadly position as he is hunted by a Russian drone in eastern Ukraine. He explains through stories of real people how the Russian state has reinvented warfare for the twenty-first century, not by abandoning past doctrines but by fusing them into something far more dangerous, flexible and continuous: a new form of total war. In this book, Seely puts together his ideas gained through decades of experience, giving us the opportunity to understand the strategic drivers of the horrors on the ground and the future horrors that await us if we do not wake up to what is happening. If you ever wondered what was really going on with Putin's Russia and its relations with Europe, you need to read Seely's book – he completely nails it."

ADAM HOLLOWAY, FORMER SOLDIER, FOREIGN CORRESPONDENT AND MEMBER OF PARLIAMENT

"Bob Seely has combined fine scholarship with journalistic skill and political analysis to provide a superb account of Putin's war in Ukraine. It will be the go-to book for anyone who wants to understand the war's genesis, Putin's motives, the new dimensions of conflict that the war has originated and their dangerous implications for democracies now pitted against Putin. Seely's book is not written from an ivory tower as a military handbook. It is a first-hand account, sometimes composed at a brisk pace while some of the 900 bombs Putin drops on Ukraine each month are literally raining down around him. There are also vivid descriptions from the front line, and these moving and powerful stories help us understand the courage and resilient stoicism of Ukrainians and that for them this is an existential struggle – a war for survival."

LORD ALTON OF LIVERPOOL, CHAIR OF THE JOINT PARLIAMENTARY COMMITTEE ON HUMAN RIGHTS

"This book combines in-depth research on the history and philosophy of warfare with vivid, personal reporting from the front line in Ukraine and sobering strategic perspectives on security and defence in Ukraine, Europe and the United Kingdom. By confronting the reader with the realities of war, *The New Total War* leaves no room for denial."

NATALIYA ZUBAR, CHAIR OF THE MAIDAN MONITORING INFORMATION CENTRE, KHARKIV, UKRAINE

THE NEW TOTAL WAR

BOB SEELY

FROM CHILD ABDUCTION TO CYBER ATTACKS AND DRONES TO DISINFORMATION

RUSSIA'S CONFLICT WITH UKRAINE AND THE WEST

First published in Great Britain in 2025 by
Biteback Publishing Ltd, London

ISBN 978-1-78590-948-1

10 9 8 7 6 5 4 3 2 1

A CIP catalogue record for this book is available from the British Library.

Set in Minion Pro and IvyPresto

Printed and bound in Great Britain by
CPI Group (UK) Ltd, Croydon CR0 4YY

CONTENTS

CHAPTER 1

KOLESO, KHARTIIA AND THE NEW TOTAL WAR

'A historical struggle for our existence'

– Solomiya Khoma, Ukrainian Security and Cooperation Center[1]

I am sitting in a bomber drone 'bunker' in the basement of an abandoned farm a few kilometres from the Russian front line in eastern Ukraine. On my left is a 21-year-old pilot, call sign Koleso (wheel). He's guiding his airborne Vampire drone onto tonight's target, a Russian trench. The Vampire strikes fear into Russian soldiers. They've nicknamed it Baba Yaga, after a Slavic folklore tale about a haggard witch who flies around at night, frying and devouring the young. It's not a bad description.

As his drone nears the target, Koleso moves the camera from looking ahead to looking down, constantly checking two of his screens. On the right is Ukraine's battlefield software, called Kropiva (nettle), which charts his course and has identified the targets. In the centre is the video feed from the drone's thermal imagery camera. Its green crosshairs sit over grainy black-and-white images of woods and fields. It picks up the trunks and thick branches of the birch and conifers but not the late autumnal leaves, giving the impression of deep winter out in the woods. The light reflected off the ground looks as if snow has already fallen.

Koleso prepares to kill his enemy.

The unit I am with is Khartiia, one of Ukraine's new regiments, which sprang up after the 2022 Russian invasion and is designed to be a model of best practice. To get to the bunker, we meet late at night in the empty car park of a small service station between the eastern Ukrainian city of Kharkiv and the front line. After a final, sparsely manned checkpoint, we drive into the 'drone zone' – the 10-kilometre band where small, so-called 'suicide' or kamikaze drones are most likely to operate, hunting for targets and detonating on them, making movement a tense game of Russian roulette. In the rear of the zone, you'd be unlucky to be struck, but the nearer you are to 'line zero', the busier the sky. Electronic warfare tools can confuse a kamikaze drone into veering off target by just enough to miss, but it's a risk best avoided.

We drive fast along the potholed, abandoned roads that punish the car's suspension, past vehicles destroyed by drones in previous days and weeks. We take a sharp left. The road thins. To our right are orange lights from the nearest Russian villages just over the border. After a few more twists and turns, we park in between overgrown bushes by the side of a barn. It's pitch black and very silent. Red headtorches are turned on as we walk up a path in single file, following the boots of the soldier ahead. A password is exchanged and we file into the empty farm outbuildings ahead. Hidden under a rusting canopy is a pick-up truck with repair tools. Stacked up alongside the walls are spare batteries for the drones and the bombs that they are dropping.

The outbuilding is home to a three-man team; as well as Koleso, there is Kosak (Cossack) and Sonic. Under the canopy, Kosak, a burly man with a tattoo stretching from his right arm around his shoulder, is making minor repairs to a Vampire drone with a hand grinder, known locally as a *bulgarka*. Glints fly in the dark, reminding me of the hand-held sparklers we light on Bonfire Night in the UK. We are escorted down a steep brick stairway into the basement, where the team lives for days at a time. It's a tight space, with just enough room for three mattresses laid out on the floor. The walls, whitewashed many years ago, are faded, but there are pictures on display, an old armchair and a couple of friendly cats, who come in for company and occasionally try to steal the team's food. As forward positions go, it's homely.

From here, the three-man team launch repeated missions with their drones. Pilot Koleso sits in one of the corners with his screens on a couple of tablets in front of him. The team has a target list, to which late priorities are sometimes added. Tonight, they are visiting destruction on a series of trenches covered with tree trunks and thick branches (known locally as *brindage*) under which Russian soldiers live. Koleso's co-pilot tonight is a dispatcher in battalion headquarters. Their conversations are brief and occasional as Koleso glides the drone towards the target. They talk in a chat room on gaming software – no billion-dollar contract here for communications. Ukrainians have innovated all the way through this war, from communications to drones. Even the bomb has had a homemade stabiliser added, in the shape of an empty plastic fizzy-drink bottle with its bottom sliced off. Other bombs, stacked up outside the basement, have 3D-printed tail fins.

Koleso hovers his drone over the target for perhaps fifteen seconds. To be under or near it must be petrifying. The Vampire is noisy, and below it Russian soldiers are huddled, desperately hoping that the anti-tank mine it is carrying is not intended for them, not tonight. Ukrainians are aware of the psychological effect of drones in general and the Vampire in particular. It adds to the suffering inflicted on their Russian invaders.

Koleso adjusts the position just slightly and then hits the release. We see the bomb, a TM-62 anti-tank mine, green and flat and about the size of half a dozen large dining plates, fall 60 metres to the earth. As it lands, a white and grey-tinted explosion envelops the centre of the screen as the trench target is incinerated. Khartiia has just added another couple of unlucky soldiers to Russia's dead and seriously injured, a total that as of spring 2025 ranged from estimates of 600,000 to an astonishing 900,000.

Koleso lifts the drone slightly before pulling it back. The camera points towards the enemy on the return journey to ensure that it is not being followed.

Shortly after the drone lands, orders come through for no movement above ground, drone or human. The skies over our stretch of the line are closed. There are enemy drones hunting for our positions. We hold still. Drone teams are some of the highest-value targets in this war, and the Russians will throw artillery, drones and even missiles at us if they find our position. Bomber drone positions need to be close to the front line but not on it. The team's neighbouring position was hit a couple of weeks before. I ask the senior officer with us, call sign Acoustic, what happens under incoming fire? I assume we hunker down and wait for it to pass? No, Acoustic tells me. When one drone hits, more, plus artillery and mortars, will be on their way, so you 'bug out' fast, pile into a car and drive like hell to outrun the other drones, which will give chase like electronic flying zombies.

Thirty minutes later, HQ tells us the skies are clear. The Russian drones have moved on. We leave the basement and watch Sonic continue his night's work. He carefully loads two bombs – they look like mortar rounds – to the underside of the drone. We return to the basement as he arms the weapons for Khartiia's team to resume their deadly work.

• • •

For frontline soldiers, the tactics and tools of Russian warfare have been clear. But talk to others involved in this two-decades-long conflict, where Ukraine has fought for its survival and Russia has rethought and redeveloped its tactics of total war, and the answers are different.

This has been a war fought using cutting-edge drones, with tactics changing every couple of months, but also one of First World War-style trenches and panic-inducing artillery bombardment. It has been a war not only of algorithms and bots peddling disinformation but also of assassinations, blackmail and bribery. It has been a conflict in which the Russian state has abducted children. It has been a war in which special forces, spies and organised crime work together to stage coups. In the West, it has been a conflict that includes assassination and, increasingly, sabotage. The Kremlin has funded the hard left and right in Europe and elsewhere; it has used Western lawyers and banks to facilitate some of the largest financial thefts in history whilst intimidating the media into silence. Russia has groomed, cultivated and manipulated politicians and celebrities in Europe and the US to do the Kremlin's bidding, either wittingly or by being, as Russian revolutionary Lenin once called them, 'useful idiots'.

In Podil, a dockside area of Kyiv near to the city's onion-domed centre, Solomiya Khoma and Serhii Kuzan monitor the tactics of their enemy in Ukrainian territories that Russia seized, either in 2014 or at the beginning of the 2022 invasion. They work in a small office without electricity – Russian missiles are systematically destroying Ukraine's electricity grid. Serhii reels off a list of tactics used by the Russians: 'Mass torture and murder, filtration camps, forced passporting [forcing people to take Russian passports to access basic services such as healthcare], the public destruction of Ukrainian books and the active work of Russian occupation administrations to change the outlook of the Ukrainian population to a pro-Russian one.'[2]

Solomiya explains that this is Ukraine's war of survival. Ukraine was by no means the perfect state and internal corruption, significantly manipulated by Russia, helped damage its ability to defend itself. But its people want to be free to form their own nation and are dying in large numbers to defend that idea. If they lose, it is the meaningful end not only of their state but also of their identity as a people, which will be subjected to forced Russification. In the past, Ukraine's language was repressed within the Russian Empire. The Bolsheviks crushed initial attempts to form a Ukrainian state in 1917, aided by divisions amongst Ukrainians. In the 1930s, a full decade before the Holocaust, the Soviet Union's leaders forced a deliberate policy of mass starvation on Ukraine to compel the collectivisation of its peasant farmers and destroy Ukrainian identity in the process. Between 4 and 7 million died. The Holodomor, as it is now known, was covered up by the Soviet Union and its Western 'fellow travellers' for decades. 'For centuries, the Russians have been engaged in the deliberate extermination of Ukrainian identity: from the physical destruction of millions of people to the banning of language, religion, culture and history,' says Solomiya. 'Our goal is to end this struggle now and not pass it on to future generations.'

In telling the story of the conflict in Ukraine and Russia's new way of waging war, this book presents a series of fundamental ideas. These are outlined in the following pages.

INTEGRATION IS KEY

Russia has created an integrated, flexible and innovative form of warfare based on the use of the full spectrum of state tactics and tools – the 'unification of everything'[3] – in the service of aggressive state power. This reflects the idea that, according to the head of the Russian armed forces, the 'very rules of war' have changed.[4] Some of these tactics or tools would not be understood as instruments of warfare in the West, but critically, they are, regardless of category, interpreted as tools of 'contemporary military conflict' in Russian military doctrine.[5]

Russia's new form of warfare is an updated form of total war, in which *all* the tools of state power can be used in conflict, military or otherwise, to gain advantage over the adversary. This is an evolution of the old idea of total war based on industrial strength, mass armies and popular will. Russia has developed this idea now more than any other nation in recent history. This integration has sometimes been called hybrid warfare, although the term has become so overused as to have limited value. Whilst Western nations talk about integration, Russia does it.

RUSSIA'S NEW TOTAL WAR IS THE INTEGRATION OF THE TWO RUSSIAN WAYS OF WAR OF THE TWENTIETH CENTURY

The first way of war is what soldiers call 'traditional' or 'conventional' war. That's the war we see in films and books, the war of armies and tanks, planes and warships. Yet the Soviet Union had a second way of war, which they practised in the last century – revolutionary, subversive, politicised conflict. That was the war of spies and blackmail, assassination, propaganda and disinformation, of fake organisations, political 'fronts' and paramilitary groups, of politicians and opinion-formers being knowingly or unknowingly manipulated by their adversaries, of the use of economic and other forms of power, including language and religion. This second way of war, also known euphemistically as 'active measures', a term invented by the KGB, has not necessarily been seen as a way of war in its own right. I believe it should be, especially given its likely prominence in this century.

In Russian, the word for 'war' is *voina*,* whilst the revolutionary, subversive form of conflict has often been referred to as 'struggle' or *bor'ba*.† Russia's new way of war is the integration of military *war* and political *struggle* into a seamless whole.

IT'S NEW ENOUGH TO BE NEW

This way of war *is* substantially new. However, it has its roots in Soviet and Russian historical experience, thinking and behaviour. Many of the tools of this new total war were initially developed and integrated in the Soviet Union. Some tools, related to language and religion, have their provenance in the Russian Empire. However, whilst it has similarities with the past, this new way of war is not just a repeat of its predecessors. The level of integration is greater than before. Some of the tools are new.

The integration of military and non-military tools sits *within* Russian military doctrine. It is a new approach to conflict, with much more focus on the human mind as the ultimate battlefield

* Phonetically pronounced as 'vayna' with the stress on the last 'na', so vay*na*.

† Phonetically pronounced as 'bar'ba', with the stress on the final 'ba', so bar'*ba*. These terms are used by Soviet and Russian military theoretician General Makhmut Gareyev, former deputy Chief of Staff for the USSR armed forces and former president of the Russian Academy of Military Sciences.

even during periods of 'traditional' war. This new warfare is more ideologically flexible than before. During the Cold War, Moscow aligned with and used the hard left worldwide; now it allies with both the political hard left and the hard right, as well as unscrupulous commercial structures and media influencers, to aid its aims. There is more emphasis on non-military tools and tactics and the level of creativity is higher.

In this way, whilst Russia's new way of war is inspired by the past, it is not a facsimile of it.

THE CONFLICT IN UKRAINE STARTED IN 2005 AND HAS GONE THROUGH THREE CLEAR STAGES

By rooting this book in Russian thinking and theory, I show that the conflict in Ukraine has been ongoing for nearly two decades. Putin has aimed to pull this country of nearly 40 million people back into Russia's sphere of influence, stifling Ukraine's genuine independence and trying to create a Russian vassal state with a veneer of independence.

The first stage of the Ukraine conflict took place between 2005 and 2013, after the democratic revolution of late 2004, known in Ukraine as the Orange Revolution, and the defeat of Russia's presidential candidate. From then on, Putin began a systemic campaign of primarily non-military methods to undermine the Ukrainian regime. To do this, he used economic, political, cultural, religious and informational tools, including supporting political parties run by agents of influence; intense espionage; the corruption of police, security agencies and the armed forces; and the use of influential businessmen to buy up parts of the Ukrainian economy.

The second stage of the conflict began in early 2014, as the FSB spy agency – heir to the infamous KGB – 'curated' a string of violent uprisings in multiple Ukrainian oblasts (counties) using Russian political-front organisations and paramilitary groups. They aimed to collapse Ukrainian state authority. Most of these uprisings failed although two, in the oblasts of Donetsk and Luhansk, succeeded.

The third stage of the conflict was signalled by the large-scale invasion that began in February 2022. Even then, this was not a conventional invasion but a show of force in which spies, special forces and agents of organised crime working with Ukraine's pro-Russian fifth column planned to seize the presidency, Ukraine's Parliament and other key buildings. The aim was to carry out a *coup d'état* whilst the Ukrainian Army was pinned down in the east of the country.

The conflict against the West has gone through phases that have broadly mirrored these stages. Putin's infamous 2007 speech in Munich rejected the post-Cold War settlement. Sabotage and political warfare against Europe and the US started after the 2014 partial invasion of Ukraine, with a significant increase after the 2022 full invasion. Conceptually and emotionally, Putin and the Russian regime have been in active conflict with Ukraine and the West since the first decade of this century.

RUSSIA'S NEW WAR BLURS 'WAR' AND 'PEACE'

By combining the traditional with the subversive, Russia's new war blurs the meaning of 'war' and 'peace'. This blending of traditional categories will be a significant feature of 21st-century conflict. The wide array of integrated tools in Russia's way of war enables a perpetual struggle, so that even outside periods of traditional, military warfare or threat of warfare, the Russian state remains in conflict with the idea of Western liberal democracy. Fighting against the West and weakening it through divisions, schemes and machinations, as well as waging war in Ukraine and threating war elsewhere, is an end in itself.

The father of military theory, Carl von Clausewitz, said – and I paraphrase – that war is the continuation of politics by other means. It is a truism that many are familiar with. Russia closely aligns its military and political ends. However, for Putin, politics is also an extension of warfare in the Darwinian struggle of nations.

This view of international politics evolved in the last century. The name associated with it was that of another German, Erich Ludendorff, the country's military leader for much of the First World War and an early Nazi sympathiser.[6] For Germans who shared his outlook, 'peace' signified nothing more than a period of non-military conflict and preparation between war in the permanent zero-sum game of the struggle for power. This idea was also adopted by revolutionary Russia's early leaders, who believed communism and capitalism could not co-exist. One would eventually defeat the other. They were right, but not in the way they hoped.

So, the idea of permanent struggle is not only Clausewitzian (war is politics by other means) but also Ludendorffian (politics is war by other means). Russia's new way of war – its new total war – is, therefore, a recipe for permanent conflict, whether that conflict is political or military. This is the thinking of those who rule Russia. It is a doctrine for eternal conflict.

ADVANCED INFORMATION THEORIES ARE AT THE HEART OF THIS WAY OF WAR

Information warfare is a vital part of this type of war. It is designed to create conflict and confusion, to manipulate emotions and to present rival realities – or, as one Ukrainian told me, 'messing with people's minds so they don't know what's true or not'.[7] Information warfare encompasses a variety of techniques from the interconnected fields of psychological warfare, propaganda, indoctrination and disinformation.[8] Research into psychological forms of manipulation goes back decades and formed part of Soviet top-secret research programmes.

TOTAL WAR IS DESIGNED TO BE EFFICIENT (EVEN IF THE RUSSIAN MILITARY ISN'T)

This new form of total war is designed to be used in a unified manner to become more than the sum of its parts, thus allowing Russia to challenge the US and NATO despite its shrinking resources. Force is used to achieve political aims, and Russia escalates to the use of force when the original tools and tactics are insufficient, as occurred during 2014 and 2022.

This form of war is also designed to be efficient. Why physically attack a country when you can carry out a coup or corrupt its leadership through oil deals or cheap loans? The tools and tactics used depend on the type of conflict, the aims of the conflict and the 'permission set' that soldiers, spies and other state officials would be allowed to use. There are different tools for different rules.

RUSSIA HAS EVOLVED THIS NEW WAY OF WAR TO ACHIEVE ITS GOALS WHILST LACKING THE SUPERPOWER RESOURCES OF ITS RIVALS

The Russian state wishes to dominate nominally independent former Soviet states. It aims to develop and defend its anti-Western value system, especially against what it perceives as indirect forms of conflict, such as democratic revolutions and popular protest – the so-called 'colour revolutions'.[9]

The roads to the strategic neuroses of Vladimir Putin and his security cabal meet in Kyiv, the ancient citadel of the first eastern Slavic civilisation. They aim to control Ukraine, feeling that Russia is less of a great power without Ukraine and that the West is physically and psychologically closer than is comfortable. A democratic Ukraine threatens Russian autocracy by presenting a rival path of development. Western nations have underestimated Putin's obsession with Ukraine – and this is a strategic error. Putin's obsession with Ukraine is near-existential for him and his Russian regime. As ex-CIA director William Burns has written, 'It is always a mistake to underestimate his [Putin's] fixation on controlling Ukraine and its choices.'[10]

RUSSIA'S NEW TOTAL WAR ALSO HELPS TO CONTROL ITS CITIZENS

A Russia at war with Ukraine or in conflict with the West enables not only political control but the justification and opportunity to reimpose a Russian state identity that is hostile to the West. Russia's total war and its confrontation with Ukraine and the West is an external manifestation of an internal battle over political identity and values – about how the nation defines itself. War and conflict become a means of control, whilst a new image and character for the Russian state is created. War stifles dissent; war justifies and makes real the propaganda that many older Russians have experienced for much of their lives. Putin, who once sardonically joked about the 'old Russian entertainment' – the search for a national idea – is imposing a new national identity built around xenophobic nationalism, political authoritarianism and religious orthodoxy.[11] The 'war against NATO' in Ukraine – a war Putin defines as being fought against 'Nazis', 'fascism' and the US 'Antichrist' – makes the Russian population much more pliable for what the regime has in store for it. The forging of a new national Russian identity in opposition to the West, underway since the early 2000s, has become more marked since 2014 and more virulent since 2022.

RUSSIA'S STRATEGIC OUTLOOK AND CULTURE HASN'T CHANGED

The influences that have shaped Russian thinking about conflict and its place in the world – its strategic outlook and culture – have not fundamentally changed from the Soviet days.[12] There was a temporary thawing from the late 1980s to the mid-1990s, after which the door of strategic change slammed shut.

Since then, Russia has recreated its sense of permanent struggle with a re-energised and reimagined integrated theory of war fit for Russia's battles this century. By combining the conventional with the subversive, Russia's new way of war results in a blurring of the tools of war and peace – and even the notion of war and peace as distinct terms. The wide array of integrated tools enables Russia's perpetual struggle with Western nations, so that even outside periods of traditional military warfare or threat of warfare, the Russian state remains effectively in conflict with the West, and by doing so, reaffirms its identity in conflict with Western liberal democracy. Russia's new war is a whole-state concept of conflict; it is a strategic art, not simply a military one.

RUSSIA'S NEW WAY OF WAR IS A BLUEPRINT FOR AUTHORITARIAN DICTATORS TO CHALLENGE THE FREE WORLD

Due to Russia's deep history of creative thinking about war, the current conflict is an indicator of how authoritarian states will challenge the West for global supremacy. The Russo-Ukraine conflict is becoming part of a wider global struggle for the future of humanity between open and closed societies, between democracies such as the US, the UK and their European and global allies and authoritarian states such as Russia, China and allies like Iran and North Korea (both of which are supplying equipment to Russia and in North Korea's case, soldiers too). It is as yet unclear what influence US President Donald Trump will have on this wider ideological struggle or whether he will move the US to a more neutral or a pro-Russian camp. We should remember that the destruction of the Western alliance, by whatever means, remains one of Russia's great strategic goals.

Russian forces have started to conduct sabotage operations in Europe to create 'sustained mayhem' according to the head of Britain's domestic security agency, MI5.[13] Our enemies are either in non-military conflict with us already or are strategically shaping the world for a more violent clash of nations and civilisations. As Vladimir Putin himself declared in late 2024, 'A serious, irreconcilable struggle is unfolding for the formation of a new [world order].'[14] Russia is building its military beyond its needs in Ukraine. Other states in Eastern Europe may be in danger.[15] We in the West are spending billions to support Ukraine. Our generals tell us we may ourselves be at war with Russia in the next decade. The Russian people have *already* been told that they are at war with NATO in Ukraine. As the Russian revolutionary Leon Trotsky once said, 'You may not be interested in war, but war is interested in you.'

Ukraine is, for now, the physical battleground in that struggle. If we can grasp the new nature of modern conflict and react to it, the West and the international order we created will survive. If we fail, the next few decades will witness the twilight of democracies.

This book is intended to be an investigation into the style of conflict that will be, at least in part, waged to undermine our beliefs, our power and our influence. Some, possibly many, of the tactics being used by Russia are being or will be used by China, Iran and other states dedicated to attacking the current global order. The Russian permanent struggle template is, therefore, also a global one. It is a blueprint for the wars of the twenty-first century. It is a toolkit for the conflicts that are coming – or the conflicts that are arguably already here.

• • •

I want to describe and explain this form of warfare because too few people, including diplomats, soldiers, politicians and journalists, understand it. If Western leadership doesn't understand what it is up against, our nations are in peril.

There are several reasons for our collective ignorance at this dangerous time. First, in the West, war is seen as something limited in time and space – it has a start and end date. It is difficult for us to understand the idea of permanent conflict. Second, conflict possesses characteristics we associate with 'war'. So Western minds don't 'get' some of the tactics of warfare associated with not only Russia but other twentieth-century revolutionary regimes. We may see child stealing, assassinations or economic conflict as 'bad things' that happen in and around war but we don't consider them part of conflict strategies – and certainly not a core part. Whilst a narrow definition of 'war' may still be about 'traditional' war – the war of tanks and planes manned by uniformed men and women – warfare and especially conflict, in the Russian leadership's mind, has a much wider definition.

Third, the act of violent war, whether we like it or not, remains the ultimate human theatre. 'Traditional war' contains life and death, love and hate, courage and bravery, as well as treachery, cowardice and deceit. We are moved by the tears of refugees and innocents; we seek timeless heroes and villains. We are naturally drawn to action because it contains such powerful images and stories, some of which are contained in this book. All this is hardwired into human nature. But it can stop us from seeing the real strategies and tactics of conflict.

Let me give you an example: as of the winter of 2024, what was Russia's main effort? Most people would assume that it was on the battlefield. However, arguably Russia's main effort was to target the will of the Ukrainian people so that, exhausted by war, they will reluctantly sue for peace. Russian forces have been targeting morale and will by using missiles and devastating glide bombs to strike major cities, particularly Kharkiv, whilst at the same time degrading Ukraine's electricity capacity. As of early 2025, 900 bombs are being dropped a month – not including the many more that are hammering Ukraine's front line.

Imagine a family living in one of Ukraine's great cities such as Kharkiv, in a cold apartment in a freezing continental winter, surviving on limited electricity with bombs hitting the city several times a week, with air raid sirens multiple times a day, with their frightened children partially schooled in bunkers underground. How long will that family stay if they can move somewhere safer in Ukraine or to Western Europe, never to return? Under the stress of bombs, the cold and an imploding economy, the Kremlin is trying to break Ukrainian will to set conditions for a Russian victory, made more likely by a US administration that has appeared at times dangerously agnostic and a European leadership whose actions rarely match their rhetoric. Already, 8 million Ukrainians are internal refugees and a similar number have fled the country. As one senior Ukrainian military officer put it:

> Is this their main effort? I believe yes, yes. Because for them it's much more important to kill many civilians, to destroy our civilian infrastructure, to cut the access to resources, water and electricity, heat and so on and not just to destroy the army … Because this is a hybrid war … [The] Russians are doing this war in different spheres, as well as in cyberspace, as well as in promotion of disinformation and fake news.[16]

This war has ebbed and flowed and we cannot predict future events. Western conventional wisdom, so often wrong on Russia, wrote off Ukraine in 2022. Ukrainians won the decisive battle for Kyiv and when Russian lines in north-east Ukraine collapsed in 2022, an ecstatic population believed a quick victory was possible. Since the initial disaster, the Russian Army has regrouped and the Russian regime has developed a three-pronged strategy to pursue the war. Whilst in many senses illegal and immoral, this strategy has been slowly succeeding and has put Russia in a more commanding position both for when it comes to negotiations and the war's continuation. We overestimated Russia in 2022. We underestimate it now.

Russia's three-pronged strategy has sought to attrite (wear down) Ukraine. It can be succinctly explained as hold the line, make life hell, break the link:

1. Russia is holding its line – it's done this by building up very significant defences, thousands of acres of landmines and many kilometres of deep trenches and dug-in positions. From there, it has been making grinding progress on the frontline battlefields, willing to see the slaughter of many thousands of its own men for a smaller but still significant number of Ukraine's volunteer army.
2. Russia is making life hell for Ukrainian civilians by bombing

cities as well as destroying electricity supplies. Putin wants to freeze Ukrainians into surrender.

3. Russia is working to damage the relationship between Ukraine and its Western backers, without which Ukraine would be unable to fund or fight this war. This includes the use of an array of tools of political warfare, including information and disinformation campaigns and the manipulation of politicians, not only in Europe but also in the US and globally.

Whilst Russia's military weaknesses have been well reported, we should be aware that it fits our narrative to highlight Russian failings and portray the conflict as David versus Goliath, with an assumed eventual victory for a Ukrainian David. But the Russians are learning and improving. Russia has maintained a recruitment rate of 30,000 soldiers a month, enough to maintain its forces despite its extraordinary casualty rates and the horror of relentless, so-called 'meat assaults', where small fire teams of five or six are relentlessly sent towards Ukrainian lines. Russian troops are still willing to fight, whether through the threat of rape or death, financial inducements or misplaced patriotism repetitively instilled through two decades of propaganda.

Russian industrial production is also now kicking in. They are learning the art of drone war, which is making the battlefield even more lethal. Russia is building a brutal military machine, which is learning through fighting and dying. We should be in no doubt that at the end of this war, Russia, in terms of drones and electronic warfare tactics at least, will have a significant advantage facing NATO forces in the Baltic republics.

• • •

So, what are my qualifications to write on this subject?

In 1990, I was working for a national newspaper during the dying days of 'Fleet Street', as it was then known. For the first time, I had money in my pocket. A friend working for then MP David Alton (now Lord Alton) told me about Ukrainian priests who were being sent to the Chernobyl nuclear disaster site without protective clothing as punishment for their religious beliefs. The power station blew up in 1986, radiating deadly fallout into the atmosphere and across northern Europe. To work there without protective clothing was a slow death sentence from the inevitable cancers that would follow.

When I started as a journalist, I had just missed the collapse of the Berlin Wall and the Eastern European revolutions, but I wanted adventure and I wanted to see this country, the Soviet Union, which had for so long threatened us. Intrigued and fascinated, I arrived in the western Ukrainian city of Lviv, then still part of the Soviet Union, during Easter 1990, just as the banned Greek Catholic church was allowed to celebrate Easter for the first time since the Second World War.

Crossing the border and arriving in Lviv, I felt as if I had stepped into a black-and-white 1950s movie, so little seemed to have changed. The city was not so much stuck in time as trapped in history. There were the very priests I was planning to meet, conducting the first church services in this part of Ukraine since it was conquered by Stalin's Soviet Union. The unique sights and sounds of that Easter – the chanting Orthodox liturgy, the charismatic radiance of those priests, the faded but still splendid baroque majesty of St Peter and Paul's Church – enthralled me. Around the priests seeking sacramental blessings were petite *babushkas* (grannies) wrapped in shawls. They reminded me of my mother, whose German and Slavic ancestry came from nearby. In the nooks of their elbows, the ladies carried wicker baskets with painted eggs covered by embroidered linen napkins. Some wore the traditional Ukrainian linen tops called *vyshivankas*. They queued on ancient, pockmarked streets to enter the candlelit cold church. The only animation and colour in that drab Soviet world seemed to come from the ebullient priests and the faithful, chatting away in a sing-song rural Ukrainian.

From there, I went to Kyiv and started filing stories, thanks to the support of the then *Times* Moscow bureau chief. A few months later, I was back permanently as a stringer – a junior foreign correspondent – for the newspaper, covering not only Ukraine but also the wider collapse of the Soviet Union. I was twenty-three. I stayed for four years. Since then, I have returned regularly.

As a young reporter, I feared the events that have come to pass decades ago. I first wrote about Russian determination to control its neighbours in 1995 in an article for the *Wall Street Journal*.[17] I witnessed at first hand Russia's 'managed conflicts' in Georgia and Moldova. I wrote of the strategic mistake of partitioning Serbia and how Russia would use it as an excuse to do the same, which it did in short order in Georgia and later Ukraine. I've long been fascinated by the fusion of different forms of conflict and I've tried to understand them from informational, military and political angles, having been a foreign correspondent, a reservist soldier on permanent service for a decade and then a Member of Parliament. In addition, I devoted a decade of academic study to Russian warfare for my PhD from King's College, London.

Before the 2022 invasion, I argued that Putin would, in his remaining years in power, attempt three things: first, destroy Ukrainian independence; second, rebuild and reshape Russia as a virulently anti-Western nation and a core leader of the global anti-Western alliance; and third, try to break NATO and with it, Western power.

I didn't pretend to know when these would happen or how, but as the military build-up around Ukraine continued in 2021, I argued that common sense suggests that dictators don't like to back down.

Putin has tried to crush Ukraine. He has created a brutal, militarised Russia. He has not yet tried to take on NATO. However, unless we relearn the art of deterrence, I fear it will be only a matter of time. Ukraine's defeat, should it happen, will pave the way for an extraordinarily dangerous confrontation. Therefore, it is in our practical as well as our moral interest that Ukraine succeeds. Polling from Ukraine shows that Western support has a material effect on Ukrainian willingness to fight. Holding back Putin's brutalised Russian Army at the gates of Kharkiv is better for us and Ukraine than blocking him in the NATO-member Baltic republics or at the Polish border.

I am a believer in the extraordinary achievements of the Western world, especially my own nation, but since the end of the Cold War, we have lacked strategy and we have become divided. We have failed to understand how others, especially our adversaries, view us and the world. Our leadership has at times been weak, short-termist and self-absorbed, more intent on advertising our own 'progressive' virtues than dealing with a hard world. Faced with determined dictators in Russia and elsewhere, Western nations have been hesitant and unsure. An alliance of the indecisive is facing an axis of the ruthless. The West urgently needs to relearn the art of deterrence and the art of strategy. It also needs to relearn the values that made it great and be willing to defend them.

Now that Ukraine is at war, there is a tendency to brush its problems under the carpet. I am not blind to its faults. The hidden domination of the secret services, the growth of organised crime and the interconnection between oligarchs and politics have acted as a significant drag on progress in Ukraine. Before 2014, its elections were rigged for Moscow's candidate. In many ways, Ukraine was an easy 'mark' for the Putin regime, with its deep well of knowledge in the dark arts of political and economic warfare, perfected over the lifetime of the Soviet Union. However, whatever Ukraine's faults as a state, one should be clear that there is no moral equivalence between the actions of Putin's Russian state, which have been murderous and barbaric, and Ukraine's. Those that claim such equivalence are the Kremlin's modern 'useful idiots'.

Slowly from the 1990s and more quickly from the 2000s, as new generations came of age, there has been a slow but definite refusal in Ukraine to follow Russia down the path of its new authoritarianism. The two 'brother' nations, Russia and Ukraine, decisively went their different ways. Of the two paths, Putin, in partnership with his FSB internal security agency and other malign forces, took the road well travelled by Russian leaders: strangling civil society and creating an authoritarian state with a veneer of sham democracy. Putin liberally murdered his opponents along the way and created a state based on the trinity of an unrepentant secret service, a corrupt bureaucracy and exceptionally violent organised crime. Ukraine, slowly at first, took the road less travelled in the East Slavic world. It has become a vibrant, if messy, democracy. In doing so, Kyiv rejected Moscow's rule as well as Moscow's rules.

What has distinguished Ukraine from Russia has been the growth of civil society. People from all walks of life see themselves as free and organise themselves outside the control of the state – but nevertheless influence it by their actions. Ukraine's volunteers, military and civilian, have shown the true value of a free society. They are the greatest proponents of freedom in our era. At critical moments – in the 2004–5 Orange Revolution to protest and overturn the rigging of the country's presidential elections, in the 2013 Revolution of Dignity to oppose the country's reabsorption into the Russian economic and political space, in the first invasion of 2014 and during the desperate days of the 2022 invasion when Russian forces were at the gates of Kyiv – these volunteers saved the nation from the Leviathan facing them. They did so in 2005 and 2013 by taking to the streets, and from 2014 onwards by manning the patriotic volunteer brigades that fought Russian troops in the east of the country, making with their own hands much that Ukraine's hollowed-out army needed, from drones to camouflage nets and uniforms. Critically, and somewhat remarkably, civil society was protected by some senior members of the Ukrainian security service, the *Sluzhba Bezpeky Ukrainy*, or SBU, who refused to countenance a violent crackdown in 2005 and probably in 2013 too. Those decisions, perhaps surprising ones, changed the course of Ukrainian and Russian history.

As of 2025, some 45,000 Ukrainian soldiers have died, along with tens of thousands of civilians and more than 300,000 Ukrainians injured. This roll call of the dead and maimed suggests that this is the worst of times for Ukraine. But *if* the nation survives, sees off one of the world's largest and most brutal armies and builds a defensible state, generations yet unborn will say that *this* was their finest hour. The eternal heroes in this nation's founding story will be those men and women who stayed to serve and stood to be counted.

So, there has been a stoicism amongst many, if not all, Ukrainians, especially those that are fighting or otherwise playing their role. They have the qualities that the British were once admired for: a good-natured and understated determination, a desire to 'Keep Calm and Carry On'. There is a fatalism mixed with bloody-mindedness, which explains why air raid sirens are so often ignored. There is a surprising positivity too, manifesting itself in the close comradeship of conflict, despite the fact that many will not finish this war as they started.

Most understand that Ukraine may never have another chance to form a state. Russian rule under Putin, if it does return, will be nasty, brutish and rapacious. This is 'a historical struggle for our existence', as Solomiya Khoma frames it. And in that clear choice, there is a sense of comfort in accepting their fate and doing the best they can with it. Finding humour in the darkest of circumstances is not new for Ukrainians. One of the 150 or so interviewees for this book, a three-time injured drone pilot with the call sign Pisok (sand), told me of the time he'd been injured alongside his former commander. Pisok's injuries had been mild, but his commanding officer had both hands and one of his legs blown off. Yet Pisok reassured me that 'even now he is laughing and telling jokes'. Turning away from me, he reflected, 'We need to live *this* life.'

• • •

My aim for this book is that it is useful, useable and used. It is aimed at different audiences, including interested readers who want to know the story of the war but also want something beyond the headlines. It is also written for military comrades. It's for students, civilian and military, in universities, military academies and staff colleges the world over studying war, strategy and international affairs.

This style of war, in its complexity and breadth, is the war of the twenty-first century. In five years, I believe the infantry soldier's primary weapon will be a day sack of drones thrown into the air to keep stag (guard) on a company outpost, or as reconnaissance or to help assault an enemy position. For commanders, they will need to understand why the idea of a safe 'rear area' for HQs to function and troops to rest may be a thing of the past and why armour is increasingly vulnerable. It is a truism repeated by soldiers in Ukraine that a $1,500 drone will destroy an armoured personnel carrier (APC) worth a million dollars whilst a handful of them can 'kill' a $2 million tank.

All, including our political leaders, need to understand that conflict starts, as Russia's Chief of Staff has written, in undeclared ways and potentially years before the 'traditional' war begins. The tragedy is that too few, in Ukraine itself, Europe or the US, saw the coming storm. One of the greatest tricks the Kremlin ever pulled was to fool Ukraine and the West into thinking it wasn't at war.

To make the book readable for all, I alternate between the story of how the Russian state developed this new form of war and the experiences of Ukrainians – between the story of ideas and the stories of people.

I explain why there is confusion in the West about what war is and how Russian thinking about strategy has developed over two centuries. I tell the story of the rise of Russian fascism – for that is what it is. I look at the characteristics and tactics of Russia's new way of war. I show the development of Russia's subversive espionage war and argue why we need to see it as a way of war in its own right. I examine how Putin merged this with traditional war to make a single blueprint for integrated conflict, using all the tools and tactics of his authoritarian state, and how he may have personally helped to mould it. I then explain how Russia plans conflict and the order in which it does things to achieve its effects.

I tell the story of the drone war and the war to steal Ukraine's children. I tell the stories of the war against the cities, Russia's attempts to destroy Ukraine's will to fight and the soldiers on the ground, in the trenches and manning the aid defences. I talk to a widowed sniper who twice a week walks to the edge of no man's land to kill Russian soldiers and who unburdened her grief by telling me the most harrowing thing she has done in this war was to bury her fiancé, a man who was not only her love but also her commanding officer. I show the human side of the conflict as well as its theory.

The serving Ukrainian soldiers I talk to are almost always referred to by their call signs, out of respect for their military roles but also for security reasons. When I use a full name, it is used because that person is in the public eye. When I use a first name only, I am doing so because revealing either their full name or their call sign could potentially help their enemy, especially if they are working in special or secret military units. Please assume all are pseudonyms.

Finally, the book is dedicated to a specific audience, one that I have already mentioned: the volunteers of Ukraine. I have written it so that they can better see and understand the overt and covert wars being waged against them to destroy their identity, their language and their nation. I thank them for letting me tell their stories, and I thank the army, national guard, secret service (SBU) and military intelligence (HUR) units and individuals who let me visit them and spend time with them. In return, I am telling the story of Russia's conflict through the eyes of Ukraine's volunteer army. Their blood, toil, tears and sweat have saved their nation three times since the turn of the century. They may yet be called to save it once more. Their forebears would have been proud of them. Their descendants will be.

Slava Ukraini – Glory to Ukraine.

CHAPTER 2

REINVENTING CONFLICT: WHAT IS WAR?

'Wars have become fuzzy at the edges.'

– Hew Strachan[1]

Nearly two decades ago, the great military historian Sir Hew Strachan questioned whether we still knew what war was – a seemingly bizarre statement. He asserted, 'One of the central challenges confronting international relations today is that we do not really know what is a war and what is not. The consequences of our confusion would seem absurd, were they not so profoundly dangerous.'[2]

Wars, Strachan continued, had become 'fuzzy at the edges'. What did he mean?

By definition, war has always had explicit assumptions attached to it. It is fought between recognisable armies with recognisable soldiers using recognisable kit fighting a recognisable enemy in a specific timeframe. It is 'war' as popular imagination would recognise it. However, some aspects of modern warfare have been marked by an indefinability that has spawned new ideas. Whilst 'warfare', the means by which war is fought, has been defined by its ever-evolving nature, as humanity seeks new tools and technologies with which to wage it – from bows and arrows to tanks and jets – the *idea* of 'war' as a violent clash of wills was seen as static. However, both are now in a state of flux.

Definitions of war have encompassed 'traditional' state-on-state violence, conflicts fuelled by organised crime or between groups competing for control of natural resources.[3] They include paramilitary violence driven by political organisations and Russia's so-called 'controlled' or 'managed' conflicts in former Soviet territories, where violence and chaos are turned off and on at will by the Kremlin. 'Information war' and 'psychological war' have become critical handmaidens to conflict and sometimes even standalone components of conflict in their own right.

Some military scholars, in examining Russian warfare prior to 2022 and even 2014, have questioned whether future conflicts could be waged without armies. The lead characteristic of this new generation of warfare is that it may not primarily depend on armies or organised military violence to achieve its goals.[4] This new 'warfare' might be devoid of actual 'war' or at least without the conventional armies to accompany it. This aligns with the Russian view of modern conflict, which sees the mind as the primary battlespace and psychological and informational warfare techniques as critical to 'new generation' warfare. The definition of warfare, therefore, is up for debate. As historian Jeremy Black argues, 'There is no agreed definition today among the multitude offered, and none that works across time and cultures.'[5]

As discussed, Clausewitz, the Western father of military theory, defined war as an extension of politics.[6] Physical force was the integral 'means of war' to enable the exertion of that will.[7] In this way, he saw the violent clash of wills as being at the heart of war. The centrality of violence to the definition of war is today affirmed in NATO and US doctrine, where warfare 'remains a violent clash of interests between organised groups characterised by the use of force'.[8]

Clausewitz did not see war as being *isolated* from politics. Although he lived before the rise of modern ideologies, he recognised the political nature of conflict or what the great British military historian Michael Howard calls the 'primacy of the political aim' – namely, the truism that wars are fought to achieve objectives.[9] However, in the West, I believe that we have lost sight of this simple but vital fact thanks to a combination of intense professionalisation and technological dominance. We have separated the military and the political too much. For more than two decades from the 1990s, Western nations came to believe that the application of advanced military force could solve complex political problems, as if hitting the button that said 'military action' meant that politicians – a distrusted class – could hand a problem to soldiers – an admired and trusted class – who would effectively solve that problem. It fed a liberal internationalism that faltered in Iraq and Afghanistan, even against tribesmen, because we believed force alone could impose our solution, despite the fact that most wars end in a negotiated settlement. Disconnecting war from its outcomes encouraged our leaders to see war as an end in itself, rather than as a means to a (political) end.

In Russia, Clausewitz's linkage of war and politics has never been forgotten. He found a receptive audience over a century ago with Vladimir Lenin and the leaders of the Russian Revolution and he remains highly influential to this day. Russia's new way of war is political – or *Clausewitzian*, as military academics would say – in two ways. First, some of the tools are indeed those of politics and political violence. Why invade a former Soviet state, for example, when you can collapse it from within by organising an assassination, or an uprising that leads to a coup, or insert into the leadership an oligarch who does your bidding – or use a combination of tools, which may include some military violence that helps support the other elements in your strategy? Second, it is closely geared to outcomes. Conflict is the means; the political end state is the purpose.

An additional obstacle to our understanding Russia's new total war is the definitions that the Western mind places on war and conflict itself. Westerners have done much collective thinking about the nature of conflict in recent years, but I believe that collectively, and despite some notable exceptions, our understanding of the subject remains too constrained. Conflict is seen as a fundamentally military topic and therefore the preserve of the professional soldier, rather than something that encompasses the wider state and involves our non-military leaders. Looking briefly at Western definitions, US doctrine recognises two states of warfare, traditional and irregular – sometimes also referred to as conventional and unconventional forms of war. The former is defined as a violent struggle 'for domination between nation-states or coalitions and alliances of nation-states', whilst the latter is defined as a violent struggle between state and non-state actors for population control.[10] One seeks direct domination of nation states; the other seeks control over populations. Both are binary and too restrictive.

The British Army's definition of war is found in the Oxford English Dictionary, where the 'core'[11] definition of war is, 'A state of armed conflict between different countries or different groups within a country.'[*12] By this definition, the 2014 annexation of Crimea by Russia was not a war, despite being a successful seizure of territory

* The UK's Development, Concepts and Doctrine Centre – the British Army's 'think tank' that produces military doctrine – only provides its own definitions when the *Concise Oxford English Dictionary* (COED) does not. Therefore, the definition that appears in the COED is, by definition, *the* UK military definition.

using an armed force. Neither was the period from 2005 to 2013, when the Kremlin was engaged in a predominantly non-military struggle to regain control of Ukraine. Both definitions hinder us in seeing the true picture. The dictionary's secondary definition of war – 'a state of competition, conflict or hostility' – is a broader definition into which Russia's new way of war could more comfortably fit.

Some academics have attempted to define ideas of traditional warfare. Martin van Creveld defines it as 'armed conflicts openly waged by one state against another by means of their regular armies'.[13] This ties into the idea of 'regular' equipment and 'regular' soldiers against 'regular' enemies, i.e. forces belonging to recognised states. This definition of traditional warfare doesn't just reference ideas about kit and soldiers but is also an intellectual and cultural exercise reflecting a society's assumptions, covering such things as rules of engagement, the goals of violence and an adherence to the dominant conventions of the day – fighting according to a nation's thinking about war and the values and standards associated with conflict.[14] In the West, this reinforces a binary idea of warfare. Other definitions of war and conflict continue to be offered by academic institutions such as Uppsala University.[15] However, all define war as something separate from peace and involve state forces or irregular forces in opposition to state forces.

However, what may be considered 'traditional' or 'conventional' in one state may not be in another. Western researchers and writers stress the unconventional nature of much recent Russian military activity, but it's only unconventional by Western standards. Seen through the prism of Russian actions of the past 250 years, 'unconventional' behaviours have arguably been very conventional, whether that is the Russian Empire's use of language to suppress identity or the Bolshevik use of disinformation or paramilitary violence.[16]

As well as problems defining exactly what war is, there are some practical issues too. Soldiers prefer training for and thinking about traditional ideas of high-intensity warfare, rather than more complex, politicised struggles, which require nuance and understanding of an adversary's culture and behaviours.[17] Soldiers who embrace the more creative forms of warfare are rare. In the UK, this is despite a remarkable tradition of unconventional, innovative or creative forms of warfare. This ranges from irregular insurgents such as Elizabethan privateers, licenced to raid Spanish ships and share profit with the crown, to Roger's Rangers, a British eighteenth-century light infantry operating against the French in North America, to Lawrence of Arabia in the First World War and the Special Operations Executive in the Second World War, designed by British leader Winston Churchill to 'set Europe ablaze' with partisan fighters.

That experience broadened after the Second World War, as the British, and to a lesser extent the US and France, developed a cottage industry of writing about and practicing what became known as counter-insurgency warfare, the art of defeating insurgent anti-colonial movements, often socialist in ideology and backed by the Soviet Union. Works by RAF officer Robert Thompson, French Algerian War veteran David Galula and Brigadier Frank Kitson all described insurgency and low-intensity warfare alongside the style of warfare needed to oppose it.[18] All three argued for the primacy of political action, the centrality of civilian support and co-operation with local partners. 'The *sine qua non* of victory in modern warfare is the unconditional support of the population,' wrote Roger Trinquier, a veteran of the Second World War, France's Indochina wars and the Algerian War.[19] Arguably, this has remained true since. In the mid-1970s, Andrew Mack produced a seminal piece on the

Vietnam War, 'Why Big Nations Lose Small Wars: The Politics of Asymmetric Conflict', which explained why might alone was not enough to win wars – namely, because insurgents target the political will of their opponents.[20]

Since the collapse of the USSR and the nominal end of the Cold War, the conflicts in the Balkans, Iraq and Afghanistan have helped spark a new generation of military writing by authors such as General Rupert Smith, Australian-born US military adviser David Kilcullen and former British infantry soldier Rob Johnson, amongst others.[21] Their work has tended to examine the difficulty of supporting political stabilisation and development whilst fighting an enemy without uniforms, hiding in and supported by elements of the civilian population. Some of the definitions given for this new form of war include 'hybrid warfare', 'fourth-generation war' and 'three-block war'.

The term 'hybrid warfare', probably the most common, was coined during this time by Frank Hoffman, using Lebanon's Hezbollah as his model, a group which combines political action with violence.[22] The term has also been used to describe Russian warfare and it is a useful, if vague, term in that it helps us to understand the variety of tools that Russia might use. Hoffman himself defined hybrid war as incorporating 'a range of different modes of warfare, including conventional capabilities, irregular tactics and formations, terrorist acts including indiscriminate violence and coercion, and criminal disorder'.[23]

There were other attempts to describe these new and more fluid forms of warfare. William Lind and others coined the concept of fourth generation warfare in an article in the *Marine Corps Gazette* in the late 1990s.[24] Former US Marine Thomas Hammes further argued that the future might belong to advanced networked insurgencies, as a type of warfare that 'directly attacks the minds of enemy decision makers to destroy the enemy's political will'.[25] The three-block-war idea, meanwhile, was coined by former US Marine Corps Commandant Charles C. Krulak to describe the modern need to be able to fight multiple styles of unconventional warfare – peacekeeping, humanitarian and mid-intensity war in the same battlespace at the same time.[26]

WESTERN CONFUSION OVER RUSSIAN WARFARE

Yet despite these important contributions to the debate, conflict is still seen as something that soldiers engage in, as a military exercise, not a political one that encompasses the whole state. Russian war, meanwhile, is a 'complex and politically led form of contestation' that takes the nature of conflict outside the Western comfort zone, in the words of British academic Mark Galeotti.[27] To understand Russian warfare, we need to redefine our definitions of what conflict is. 'For a long time we thought of them as entirely separate: diplomacy and politics on the one hand and warfare in the other,' Galeotti argues.[28] But Russian doctrine, he says, questions that separation. 'What this doctrine is saying is no, let's just appreciate that in fact we are talking about a whole spectrum of capabilities.'[29]

The evidence of our inability to define Russian war is in the many different attempts at defining it – well over twenty to date. However, very few come close to a valuable definition. They focus either on one aspect of new Russian warfare without seeing the whole, such as 'grey zone war',[30] or they take a characteristic of one element and define it through that, such as 'ambiguous war'[31] or they give Russian warfare a designation or moniker so broad as to be meaningless, such as 'special war'.[32] Other definitions have included terms which themselves are almost impossible to define and would take pages to do so: non-linear war,[33] the Gerasimov doctrine (named after Russia's armed forces Chief of Staff Valerii Gerasimov),[34] measures short of war,[35] guerrilla geopolitics or military persuasion.[36] The list is a long one. Yet which of these definitions best suits Russia's conflict in Ukraine and against the West? Russia would simply bracket all of these in what it would call 'special operations', conducted by special operations forces. Prior to the 2022 full-scale invasion, Western thinkers understandably focused on the non-military aspects of Russian warfare, hence the idea that 'new-generation warfare', to give it a name popular in Russian circles, may not depend on the use of military violence to achieve its goals or as its primary tool – namely, that warfare may no longer include actual war.[37] Since the invasion of February 2022, we have focused on the military elements of Russian warfare, perhaps to the detriment of understanding other tactics and tools of Russian warfare, which are equally important to the final outcome.

Yet whilst Western thinkers try to pin a definition on Russian war, Russia's thinking about war has not changed. It has fought all three stages of the war according to a single definition and understanding of conflict. The use of military power does *not* preclude the use of non-military tools of warfare. And the use of non-military tools does *not* preclude the use of military force. They exist on a spectrum – a full spectrum of state power ranging from soft power to hard power, from culture to nuclear weapons, to be used to exert will, purpose and power over others. Russian warfare is integrated, using the tools Putin and his team believe are necessary to deliver the political end state he wants, depending on the circumstances.

CHAPTER 3

STORIES FROM THE FRONT: THE DRAGON SKY DRONE SCHOOL

'They killed my cousin yesterday,' Viktoriia said.

I was in the UK, on my way to the airport to fly to Poland and then travel overland into Ukraine. I had just texted my Ukrainian friend to see how she was. We hadn't chatted in a while.

Her answer jumped out at me. I responded as best I could. 'I'm so sorry. Where? How?'

Volodymyr, she said, had been a policeman in Kherson, the frequently shelled city on the north bank of the wide Dnipro River in southern Ukraine – its citizens are effectively used for target practice by Russian soldiers. He had been helping to evacuate the elderly. What he didn't see was a drone approach slowly and hover above him before releasing a small explosive charge.

A low-definition drone feed video of the killing had appeared on Telegram social media channels – popular amongst Russian military bloggers – showing white crosshairs above a white police car in what appeared to be a courtyard. The drone had dropped its device and then had zoomed in. There was a small explosion on top of the bonnet, just where it met the windscreen, and a small flash of flying shrapnel. A man crouched and fell to the ground. A pool of blood, near black in the video, quickly spread from his head and neck. Like most videos on the internet where a human being has been killed, it was disturbing and upsetting.

A few Russians were celebrating his death on Telegram. 'They laugh and write how cool it was to hit him in the head,' Viktoriia wrote despairingly. 'Why are they laughing and happy? I am heartbroken.'

She sent me a photo of Volodymyr's son, a sweet-looking boy of about ten. Volodymyr was thirty-eight, with a wife and two young children. His parents couldn't attend his funeral. They were in a Russian-occupied part of Ukraine. They grieved alone.

Whilst Russia's new way of war takes its strength from the integration of *all* the tools of state power, there are some changes on the conventional military battlefield too, which will dramatically alter how wars are fought. The most significant by far is the explosive rise in the use of cheap, mass-produced drones to reconnoitre, target and kill. In the next couple of years, this situation will again be profoundly changed when the same drones are linked by artificial intelligence so they can deliver a swarm effect. This will make war much more lethal, not only for soldiers in trenches but also for individuals living in towns and cities, such as Kherson. Instead of 1,000 drones flying along the 600 miles of the front line – the situation in early 2025 – there will be many times more. Human armies are facing a battlefield saturated by drones. Indeed, in time, drones may replace humans entirely because the battlefield will have become so lethal. Humans will have become a dangerous liability in drone wars.

'The drone battle will be much more intense, and we'll use many more,' Colonel Pavlo Khazan, an officer in the Electronic and Cyber Warfare Directorate of the Ukrainian armed forces, told me. 'We are already using machine learning for targeting.'[1] In civilian life, Khazan was an environmental engineer with a background in physics and a PhD in statistics. Prior to his current role, he led Ukraine's unmanned systems (drones). 'In the nearest time, we will have the "system" of drones; not the drone alone, but squadrons [or swarms] of unmanned systems in air, ground and water,' he says.

The skies, seas and land of Ukraine are a testing ground as well as a battleground, and it's not just drones in the sky. Ground drones are being used as firing platforms or to transport ammunition, food and medicines and carry wounded soldiers. On the sea, Ukraine's army of cheap sea drones has, with the help of its Neptune missiles, rendered Russia's Black Sea Fleet unusable, a revolutionary achievement in terms of warfare. A nation without a navy and armed primarily with drones has intimidated a navy of nearly fifty surface ships and sent it scurrying to the far side of the Black Sea. I saw one of these naval drones being built one night in a factory in western Ukraine; imagine a grey speedboat with an aerodynamic cover, hiding a guidance and communications system, and packed with explosives and a detonator. Relatively simple but deadly.

A few years ago, drones were the preserve of a very small number of major power air forces, led by the US and Israel with the UK, France and Russia behind. The Kosovo conflict in 1998–9 proved to be a watershed for reconnaissance drones, with the US, UK, France and Germany either using US Predator drones or flying their own national drones.[2] However, whether tactical, medium altitude or high altitude, these were expensive – effectively slow-moving planes without pilots, flown in relatively uncontested skies. The Iraq and Afghanistan wars, together with the search for Al-Qaeda's leadership, saw the US, and then other nations, develop armed drones. Drones became an important part of what soldiers call ISTAR (intelligence, surveillance, targeting acquisition and reconnaissance) – that is, the process of building up intelligence (information and analysis) on potential targets, putting them into the targeting cycle and then striking them. This is also sometimes referred to as 'find, fix and finish'.

Since then, aided by advances in commercial technology, drones of all sizes have proliferated. The first state-on-state war in which armed drones played a highly significant role was the 2020 conflict between Azerbaijan and Armenia, a relatively little-known war in the West. Azerbaijan was armed with Israeli and Turkish drones, of which the Israeli Harop and the Turkish Bayraktar TB2 played a prominent role.[3] They destroyed Armenian static armour and positions.

Turkey then sold the Bayraktars to Ukraine before the 2022 Russian invasion. Several dozen proved invaluable during the defence of Kyiv, especially as Russia failed to use its significant air defence and electronic warfare capability effectively. The Turkish drone spawned a Ukrainian war song called 'Bayraktar', sung by members of its army in homage to their favourite weapon. Only the UK-supplied anti-tank NLAWs came anywhere near in terms of public popularity. Bayraktars, hero of the moment in 2022, are used much less now due to Russia's improving air defence systems.

However, critical to the Ukraine War – and probably all future wars – is the dynamic evolution of small drones known as first-person view drones (FPVs). These are flown by a single individual or small team to reconnoitre or attack targets, using a small screen or wrap-around vision goggles. At their most basic, they are commercial quadcopters, with a battery on top and a bomb underneath.

FPVs were first seen in the conflict against the ISIS terror group in Iraq and Syria. I was serving in UK forces at the time and we saw how ISIS pioneered the use of FPV 'bomber' drones for reconnaissance, attacks and propaganda – all using the same machine. ISIS would take a commercial, Chinese-made drone and attach a modified warhead with a carriage and release system. The warheads would generally be cheap and plentiful Soviet-era rocket-propelled grenades. ISIS would also attach a camera and transmitting capability. The drone would reconnoitre enemy positions, drop a bomb and record the propaganda video of panicked Kurdish Peshmerga – normally very brave troops – diving for cover. It was adaptive, cheap warfare.

In the course of this dramatic process of change, drones have got smaller and pilots, certainly those flying tactical drones, are much closer to the battlefield. While in the West, drone flying has been done at a distance – even from different continents – in Ukraine, drone pilots sit in trenches on or close to the front line, as I experienced with the Khartiia Brigade. This follows the evolution of how drones have been used. They have gone from being a recon and a strike capability for air power to becoming a support and strike weapon for infantry soldiers – in effect, becoming flying eyes and flying grenades.

Call sign Dekstor is an example of someone who is up close to the enemy in an ultra-tactical, highly lethal position, sharing the same woodland with his Russian adversaries. I talk to him in a wood not far from Kharkiv. When in position, he's perhaps 100 metres behind the Ukrainian line – in military terms, what's called the FLOT or forward line of own troops. There is perhaps 100–150 meters of no man's land and then the Russian line, or FLET (forward line of enemy troops). Russian infantry assaults mean that Ukrainian soldiers need to be on permanent and high levels of alert to prevent their positions being overrun. The drones are their tactical reconnaissance.

Dekstor weaves his small drone between trees to hunt for Russian positions 700 metres or less from him. His skill is akin to that of civilian hobbyists who fly racing drones around circuits in woodland. As he describes his drone work, I think of those stealthy spy drones or droids in the *Star Wars* movies, moving autonomously through forests. From more than 50 metres away, Dekstor's drone can't be heard, but within that range, it makes a familiar, high-pitched, variated buzz as it weaves, sometimes fast, sometimes slow, through the woods. The sound is more muffled in summer due to the thick vegetation. I ask if Dekstor would prefer his drone to be silent. He shakes his head. He appreciates the 'psychological effect' that drones inflict on an enemy in this deadly cat-and-mouse game. The Russians hold completely still in the undergrowth or shallow trenches when they hear a drone sneak up on them. Once found, their position is reported and – depending on how close they are to the Ukrainian positions – an officer will generally order either a 120 mm mortar or bomber drones to hit the Russian positions and, as the military euphemism goes, 'finish' their targets.

I wanted to understand more about drone warfare after meeting Dekstor, so I returned to a town in central Ukraine to attend a drone pilot course and talk tactics at the Dragon Sky Drone School.

Sitting in a white van, I am watching Dragon Sky's students take turns flying kamikaze drones into a 'Russian target', in this case a net about a mile away. These military students, many from Ukraine's 3rd Assault Brigade, are perfecting their skills in the art of drone warfare. Call sign Lito (summer) is one of their teachers. Before the invasion, Lito was a musician, the lead guitarist in an indie band led by one of Ukraine's best-known female singers. After the invasion, he joined the war effort and now teaches at the drone school. It's at places like this that Ukraine's ad hoc drone tactics are being slowly formalised.

His student just misses the target. 'He added throttle in the last moment,' Lito explains. 'Drop it in like a basketball into a hoop,' he advises. Drones have an accuracy rate of 40 per cent, and given the relatively small size of the explosives, hitting the target is important.

Ukrainian teachers delineate FPVs into three types. The first type conducts reconnaissance; these are Chinese or, increasingly, Ukrainian-made quadcopters, which have a range of perhaps 5 to 10 kilometres. Their optics, communications and range are improving on an almost monthly basis.

The second type are drones that drop bombs (bomber drones) between 1 and 10 kg in weight. Social media carries plentiful images of Ukrainian drones sneaking up on Russian targets, often tanks or troop-moving armoured personnel carriers, hovering over them and dropping small but deadly charges through vehicle hatches before scooting away. A second or two later, before the Russian troops are able to throw the device out, the charge explodes and a light flares momentarily out of the hatch. Inside, anyone not killed by the blast would be by the ball bearings ricocheting around the interior like lethal pinballs. Sometimes the blast will start a violent chain reaction in the turret that ignites the tank's shells, resulting in the 10-tonne turret exploding 100 metres or more into the air from the force of the explosion. Both these recon and bomber FPV varieties are designed to survive missions, i.e. to be flown back to base, although their average life expectancy tends to be half a dozen missions at most. Their size is indicated by the diameter of their four propellers. A 7-inch drone carries a payload of perhaps 1.5 kg; a 10-inch drone carries a charge of 2 to 3 kg. A Vampire with five larger blades can carry a 9-kilo anti-tank mine or two smaller but still lethal warheads.

Finally, there are single-use FPVs, which generally have the capacity to loiter in the air and hunt for targets, chase them and explode on impact. These are the so-called suicide or kamikaze FPV drones (also known in the West as 'loitering munitions'). They have come of age in 2023 and 2024. They can have the same quadcopter design or, with increasing frequency, can resemble small flying missiles. They look like massive fat grey cigars, with optics (an 'eyeball') at the front, short wings on the side and a propeller at the rear. The Lancet drone being used by Russian forces is a good example. It is an increasing danger to Ukrainians and evidence that Putin's forces are adapting, despite assumptions to the contrary.

A visit one afternoon to an artillery position held by Ukraine's 92nd Assault Brigade in eastern Ukraine brought the point home and showed me the extent to which drones are changing battlefield behaviour. The unit is hidden deep in a forest. It's a grey, drizzly day and the journey there takes us along several miles of rutted, waterlogged forest tracks that even our four-wheel drive struggles to gain traction on. We were there to look at artillery equipment and to talk with the soldiers, but shortly after we arrive, a Russian drone begins to circle above our wood and we are hurried under the camouflage netting so as to minimise movement and visibility. We wait for the best part of an hour, chatting away under the netting, waiting to see if the drone will identify us.

To pass the time, I talk with Ruslan – not his call sign, as revealing it would be valuable for Russian forces who monitor comms 'traffic' – whilst we wait for the drone to either instigate an attack or fail to see us. We talk artillery. Although self-propelled artillery resemble tanks, albeit with much bigger turrets, their purpose is very different. The tank is designed to be fast and mobile and to dominate the battlefield. Its gun fires on a much flatter trajectory. It is designed primarily to destroy other tanks – although in this war, is it also being used as fire support for infantry troops. Self-propelled artillery, on the other hand, is not designed as a short-range weapon or to destroy other tanks but to launch shells on targets from 10–35 kms away. At the start of the 2022 invasion, the 92nd was equipped with the Soviet-era Gvozdika (Carnation) 122 mm self-propelled guns but has since received German-supplied US Paladin guns. Ruslan jokes when comparing them: 'It's like the difference between driving a Zhiguli [an old Soviet-era car] and a Mercedes.' He and the team burst out laughing – a bit of good-humoured morale boosting never goes amiss.

We get the call that the drone has moved on. I'm relieved. In their last location, they were hit three times. Identification would have meant an unpleasant hour or two in a trench under Russian bombardment. With the Russian drone gone, they now have a short window of opportunity to use the gun. They fire up the Paladin, which is hidden 50 metres away in a deep trench, under more netting. It drives up and out, churning out black and grey fumes and spitting out dark brown clumps of earth sideways from its tracks as it negotiates the muddy path for 75 metres or so until it reaches a small opening in the forest – the tips of the branches have been shot off on the surrounding trees. It stops. A target is programmed into the weapons firing system and the gun is raised. The barrel adjusts slightly and then fires with a deafening thud and a shock wave that passes through the body. 'Keep your mouth open to equalise the pressure!' Ruslan shouts. The gun fires a second round thirty seconds later, and then the weapon is driven back into its trench as we wait to see if another drone will come looking for us. We thank them and say our goodbyes as the deadly game of cat and mouse continues. As I leave, I wonder at what point the drone in the sky will become a permanent presence.

Back at the Dragon Sky School, Lito tells me that, properly crewed, a drone team consists of upwards of five people: a lead pilot and second pilot to spot the things the lead may miss, an explosives technician to prep and arm the device, a second drone with pilots to photograph the 'kill' and provide additional 'eyes on' and a driver. For longer missions, a third drone carrying a transponder might also fly, increasing range and link quality. In reality, drone teams are often made up of three people: two pilots and the armourer. The types of warheads are evolving too. In a side room at the Dragon Sky School, littered with initiation boards, sensors, detonators and plastic explosives, a technician with the call sign Dyadya Sasha (Uncle Sasha) talks me through his work designing warheads: incendiary, shaped charge and the most common, high-explosive fragmentation. Additionally, some units are beginning to use a thermite mix of metal powder and metal oxide, which creates a molten stream that pours from the drone onto targets.

Outside, in a dry and dusty field, I strike up a conversation with Pisok (sand), who I introduced in Chapter 1. Pisok is a wiry 31-year-old from Zaporizhzhia, once the capital of Ukraine's seventeenth-century Cossack republic. One of Ukraine's drone 'top guns', he talks me through drone piloting. Quiet, unassuming and thoughtful, he reminds me of the type of colleague I most respected back in my army days. I only later find out that he has been injured three times. Like many Ukrainian soldiers, he wears his courage lightly. In civilian life, Pisok was a salesman. He's sold metal, iron and agricultural products in his time. But he's always loved flying drones, and his face lights up when he talks about them, rattling off the names of Chinese-made drones he's owned.

In 2022, Pisok was a volunteer serving alongside the 73rd Naval Special Operations Centre, conducting what are best described as partisan-style sabotage operations. 'We'd come from the market with bags, looking like civilians, and then be planting bombs in the fields for them,' he says of the Russian occupiers. He was injured by a mine himself. Whilst in recovery, he decided to return to the Azov Brigade – he had served with them in 2014 – where his commander told him, 'You're flying drones.' He enjoys reconnaissance and using drones to help get his wounded colleagues to safety, but he also has fifty 'kills' to his name – the first in May 2022, when he destroyed two tanks.

For most of the first year of the drone war, Russia had little to fight back with, making life easier for the Ukrainians. However, the arrival of Russian FPV drones has changed the dynamic, especially during troop rotations when Ukrainian soldiers are most exposed. When Ukrainian drone teams are found via Russian electronic warfare (EW) or drone reconnaissance,* Russian forces will put a valuable missile such as an S-300 on them – drone teams are high-value targets. It's one of the reasons they are taught to use as little transmitting power as possible to reduce the heat signal and to disperse equipment and people over perhaps 50 metres to lessen their attractiveness as a target.

But this is just the tip of the iceberg when it comes to how drone tactics on ground, sea and air are evolving. At the beginning of the war in Ukraine, Kyiv's advantage in drones was in part thanks to the 'band of brothers' volunteer units, who helped establish Ukraine's reconnaissance drone army. But 2023 saw a change in drone use, with the evolution and counter-evolution of tactics. When I ask Lito whether tactics change every six months, he shakes his head and corrects me: 'In drones, it's every three months.'

That chimes with what soldiers elsewhere told me. Call sign Segar

---

* Electronic warfare uses the electromagnetic spectrum to block the enemy's ability to control their drones, missiles and other military equipment.

ran a three-man 82 mm mortar team in Bakhmut for a Ukrainian HUR unit. In December 2022, he used a tablet loaded with the Ukrainian targeting platform Kropyva but relied on a human forward observer to help confirm targets and fire for accuracy. By January 2023, the forward observer was replaced by a drone. From then on, Segar ran his team using two hand-held tablet screens. On one, he still had the Kropyva targeting app giving him terrain, weather and other details. On the other, he had his own drone video feed, which enabled him to correct his fire in seconds. 'No need to wait; the targeting cycle is now super quick,' he said.[4] 'I'd see the splash,' referring to the impact of the mortar, 'correct it and be firing by the time it would take the TOC [tactical operations command] to be even telling us where the splash was.'

Tactics and technology evolve in parallel. Soldiers take advantage of emerging technology and find ways to use it, but at the same time, Ukraine's armed forces are shaping the direction technology goes. When I spoke to Colonel Khazan, he said, 'Tactics also dictate what technology we'll use, because tactics, for example, dictated the new technology of bombers: UAV [unmanned ariel vehicles], FPV drones or UGVs [unmanned ground vehicles or land drones].' He was speaking about Ukraine's need to develop drone bombers, including the new long-range ones that in September 2024 destroyed two vast arms dumps in Russia hundreds of miles from the Ukrainian border, in one case setting off a mushroom cloud that could be seen by satellites. That attack, near the Russian town of Toropets not far from the Estonian border, destroyed 750,000 shells – around three months' supply of artillery ammunition for Russian forces. The advances in drone technology have allowed Ukraine to use drones as a replacement for, or a complement to, artillery, a trend which is only likely to increase. 'Unmanned systems are eating from the artillery pie now, becoming more and more effective on the battlefield,' Khazan said.

Using these Ukrainian-made drones to replace Western-produced artillery as well as Soviet-era shells makes logistical and economic sense. A tactical bomber drone that can drop two bombs and may survive half a dozen missions or more costs approximately $2,500. Western 155 mm artillery shells cost up to $5,000 apiece and need a gun costing millions to fire them and to be kept in good order. Individual regiments have shown me their data, and the kill rates for kamikaze and bomber drones are extraordinary compared to the rates for all other weapons in this conflict. Artillery, and mortars especially, are no longer the biggest killers on the battlefield. An infantry unit without drones and protection against them is a sitting target.

In 2024, the Russians developed a dangerous advantage in reconnaissance drones. Russian drones had a constant presence behind Ukrainian front lines, keying up strikes with missiles and kamikaze FPVs. A Russian ZALA reconnaissance drone was combined, I was told, with the Lancet kamikaze drone – the ZALA identifying and 'lighting up' a target with a laser whilst the Lancet locked onto it. Ukraine did not have enough anti-aircraft missiles to shoot down these small but valuable targets and so answered this advance by using their own cheap FPV drones to attack the Russian reconnaissance drones – effectively using FPVs as a slow-moving air-defence system. They did so in three ways. First, by using a kamikaze drone to explode a shaped charge over a Russian drone whilst it was flying, destroying both. Second, by firing a net at the Russian drone to bringing it crashing to earth.[5] Third, by attaching a metal stick to a Ukrainian FPV drone and using it to literally prod the rear of the larger Russian drone, thus triggering its parachute and bringing it down gently. The third approach allows Ukrainians to recycle Russian drone parts from ZALAs or other often-used recon drones such as Orlans.

Ukranians, as of early 2025, have been focused on how to overcome the EW 'walls' constructed by Russian forces along the front line. That may mean using drones linked to their pilots by ultra-thin fibre optic cables to overcome electronic blocking or the development of technology to enable a drone to visually lock onto a target once seen, thus negating localised EW jamming.

The question that the Ukrainians – and every other armed force – will face in the next year is how to protect soldiers on the ground, or in tanks and armoured personnel carriers, on a battlefield saturated by drones?

'It's a very big challenge,' admits Khazan. Defence against enemy drones, he says, has been evolving in two ways. First, by developing electronic warfare protection and second, by providing advance warning to enable soldiers to find physical protection. 'So the Ukrainian Army should have this system to detect the enemy drone and to protect electronically or to protect physically – to understand that the drone is flying and you have to hide yourself somehow.' I saw both with the Khartiia Brigade. Before entering the worst parts of the drone zone, we put on electronic defence. Whilst there, we saw how Russian drones are permanently monitored.

On the ground, both Ukrainian and Russian troops are working to make themselves less attractive targets. Both are now walking further to the battlefield rather than use armoured vehicles. This means that if a drone strike occurs, it can at best hit one or two soldiers, rather than a military vehicle carrying six or eight soldiers plus crew. In the spring of 2025, Ukrainians began constructing anti-drone netting on 5-metre-high poles alongside and over some of their most vulnerable supply routes.[6] Shotguns are a close-range and last-ditch defence, with pellets and buckshot enabling soldiers to hit the target more easily than with rifle rounds. Ukrainians are also experimenting by firing anti-drone nets from them.

The Russians, meanwhile, are making greater use of motorbikes and quad bikes to move around the front line more quickly, even outrunning drones on straight roads. Crews are also turning their armoured vehicles, be they tanks or APCs, into what have been nicknamed 'turtle tanks', building bizarre-looking metal frames around them to take the initial impact of a drone strike.

Ukrainians are also using drones for tasks ranging from mine laying to tactical logistics and rescuing injured soldiers. Pisok tells me his most rewarding work is doing just that. 'We had two tanks damaged, but we knew that our "tankies" were alive. They had crawled under the tank.' He received orders to get water and medicine to them. 'I used the drone with bomb system to fly to the tanks and drop water and drop medicine to them.' He then flew an FPV armed with water rather than a charge into the earth by the tank. 'We had no communication with them, but we saw the medicines had been taken,' he says with satisfaction. He and his team put together a rescue plan to get them out. They survived.

At the end of the drone course, as with all military courses, there are group photos and jokes exchanged, as instructors and students josh with each other. There are many exclamations of *Slava Ukraini* (Glory to Ukraine), with fists tightened and pumped to the chest, and the response *Heroyam slava!* (Glory to the heroes!) Pisok speaks to the group. Whether you are from the border guards, interior ministry troops or the army, he tells them, 'We fight for our Ukraine, for our home, for our family. We are united by one thought, the thought to free our Ukraine. Let's fly with victory wings. Glory to Ukraine.'

CHAPTER 4

REINVENTING RUSSIAN STRATEGY: THE SEARCH FOR A SINGLE TRUTH

'There is one truth and one only ... this ancient and familiar doctrine.'

– Isaiah Berlin[1]

AUTOCRACY AND THE ENDURING STRUGGLE BETWEEN WESTERNISERS AND SLAVOPHILES

Autocracy exists in Russia not only as a political concept and practice but also arguably as a characteristic, indeed even a celebration, of its identity. Russia, in whatever guise, has experimented rarely and unsuccessfully with democracy or limited government, briefly between 1906 and 1917, and for two decades after the collapse of the Soviet Union. Its political development has had a dramatically different trajectory from that of European states. Whilst the countries of Europe accepted some form of contractual understanding with their subjects, no such thing happened in Russia.[2] The tsars engaged in 'social revolution from above' with landholding and wealth dependent on royal favour, entrenching a 'deep authoritarianism'.[3] There are echoes of that system today with the emergence of

Russian oligarchs, whose wealth and position have been dependent on connections at the 'court' of Putin.

Although autocracy has been a defining feature of Russian political life, it has at times been a highly contested one within the country's small political and governing class. Putin himself has joked about the subject of identity, describing how an old Russian pastime has been the search for a national idea.[4] For three centuries, a struggle has been waged intermittently between two competing Russian political identities: Westernisers, who saw Russia as backwards and who looked to the West as a model to be emulated or improved upon, and Slavophiles, who celebrated Russia's unique path and either excused or indulged its separation, even its backwardness, in relation to the West. In both cases, the country's political identity was bound up with its relationship with the West.

Russian Slavophilism, argues scholar Peter Duncan, should be seen as both a restatement of traditional culture and a rejection of the West.[5] He suggests that the political battle for Russia at the end of the 1980s and throughout the 1990s should be interpreted through the prism of this historic Westerniser versus Slavophile contest. I agree. The death in prison of opposition leader Alexei Navalny in 2024 was not just the murder of a single, courageous individual but the final shuttering of this latest period of battle, with a resounding and violent victory for extreme, virulent Slavophilia. Hostility towards the West is a critical element of this identity.

Where and how did this fissure in Russian identity evolve? Russia emerged as a European power during the eighteenth century after defeating Sweden in the Great Northern War. Before that, it had been largely isolated from Catholic and Protestant Europe. Under Peter the Great, Catherine the Great and during the Napoleonic Wars, Russia 'closed the political, military and cultural gap with

Europe to its narrowest point in Russian history'.[6] Whilst the 'broad consensus' that passively accepted or actively supported autocracy was maintained for much of the eighteenth century, the idea that Russia could represent both tradition and progress began to break down in the nineteenth century.[7] The political, economic and technological gap between Russia and the rest of Europe began to widen thanks to the impact of the ideas of the French Revolution, as well as the industrial and scientific revolutions underway in Britain and elsewhere. It provoked a crisis amongst Russia's elites: should Russia 'catch up' with and hopefully surpass the West or reject it?

In her brilliant study of the different routes to national identity, Liah Greenfeld argues that both Slavophilism and Westernism arose out of the same font of inferiority in Russia. Slavophilia produced excessive self-admiration, whilst Westernisation produced self-revulsion.[8] Russian philosopher Pyotr Chaadayev, who lived in the first half of the nineteenth century, was an outspoken example of an early Westerniser. In his *Philosophical Letters*, he famously argued:

> We are alone in the world, we have given nothing to the world, we have taught it nothing. We have not added a single idea to the sum total of human ideas; we have not contributed to the progress of the human spirit, and what we have borrowed of this progress we have distorted. From the outset of our existence as a society, we have produced nothing for the common benefit of all mankind … we have borrowed only empty conceits and useless luxuries.[9]

Compare that assertion with the closing address by Russian industrialist Mikhail Khodorkovsky during his 2010 political 'show trial' nearly 200 years later:

> We were able to build a hydrogen bomb, and even a rocket, but we still can't make our own first-rate modern televisions, our own cheap, competitive, modern cars, our own modern mobile phones, as well as a whole lot of other modern goods. But then we have learnt how to put on a beautiful display of obsolete models of foreign companies ... A state that destroys its own best companies ... a state that holds its own citizens in contempt, a state that trusts only bureaucrats and the security services, is a sick state.[10]

Chaadayev explained Russia's backwardness by its disconnection from Europe. The Reformation, the Counter-Reformation, and the scientific and industrial revolutions that had spread both reform and technological advance had scarcely touched the Russian Orthodox world. For his arguments, Chaadayev was declared insane – perhaps the first time, but not the last, that criticism of the Russian state has been equated to mental illness.*

Whilst Russian Westernisers despaired, Slavophiles revelled in Russia's mystical uniqueness, seeing in it a glorious contrast with the corrupting rationalism of Europe. Nikolai Karamzin, in his 1818 *History of the Russian State*, argued that autocracy embodied the Russian tradition and urged rulers to 'stand fast and not follow the path of constitutional monarchy'.[11] Konstantin Aksakov, a Russian critic and writer, believed liberal political rights to be an object of ridicule rather than aspiration, just as neo-fascist Russian philosopher Aleksandr Dugin does today.[12] Aksakov concluded in his 1855 'On the Internal State of Russia' that politics had no interest for the people.[13] He argued, as increasing numbers of secular and religious Slavophiles were to do throughout the nineteenth century, that Russian

* This was a tool used by the USSR against dissidents in the twentieth century.

society was based on communal rural life, the *obshchina*. Russians themselves had a unique spiritual connection with God and therefore played an equally unique role in the development of humankind. This exceptionalist 'Orthodox messiah complex' is also seen in modern Slavophilia – hence Putin's claim that Russians are more moral than Westerners.[14] Aksakov argued that the importation of impure foreign ideas risked destroying Russia. The people, he said, 'seek moral freedom, the freedom of the spirit, communal freedom – life in society within the confines of the People'.[15] Russians, he said, were the only truly Christian people. These ideas around the uniqueness of Russia, the martyrdom of Christ-Russia, the corruption of the foreign and the purity of the Russian peasant and the commune are echoed today. They combine the spiritual and temporal in a quasi-messianic belief, whereby Russian Orthodoxy aligned with Russian nuclear weapons – so-called atomic orthodoxy – protects the country against the Antichrist in the guise of the US.[16]

Inside Russia, a state doctrine was developed in the first half of the nineteenth century for Tsar Alexander I by his adviser, Count Sergey Uvarov.[17] Its three pillars were Orthodoxy, autocracy and nationalism. Outside Russia, Tsar Alexander I established an anti-reformist Holy Alliance with fellow absolute monarchies Prussia and Austria. In 1845, Russia codified political crimes to make criticism of the tsar or his government a criminal offence.[18] The code, historian Richard Pipes has commented, 'is to totalitarianism what the Magna Carta is to liberty'.[19] Yevgenia Albats, a historian of the KGB, the Russian infamous secret service, argued that lawless Bolshevik practices found their roots in Tsarist legal precursors, such as the 1871 and 1881 edicts that gave police the right to arrest people without evidence of guilt for acts that are not criminal, based on unverifiable information.[20]

A Slavophile faction representing 'a romanticised view of Russian military history' also existed in the armed forces at this time, consisting of a 'deep-seated reaction against Western influences and a vague search for a native military method'.[21] Author and military scholar Richard Harrison argues that despite the theoretical weakness of this group, its 'strongly nationalist appeal' meant that it was influential in the later Tsarist period: 'Ironically the nationalist school would come to enjoy its greatest success under the ostensibly "internationalist" Soviet regime, which assiduously promoted the idea, particularly after World War II, of a distinctly Russian-Soviet military tradition.'[22]

Russia's loss of the Crimean War against Britain and France in 1856 acted as a driver for a more virulent and revanchist form of Slavophilia. Defeat at the hands of Western nations resulted in Russia turning away from Europe and towards Asia. This 'turn to the east' and the expansion of the country's empire in Central Asia was fuelled by, according to Dietrich Geyer, a 'psychological hunger for compensation'.[23] Fyodor Dostoevsky, whose political outlook was a 'mystical version of nationalism deeply stained with xenophobia,'[24] said, 'In Europe, we were hangers-on and slaves, whereas we shall go to Asia as masters. In Europe, we were Asiatics, whereas in Asia we, too, are European.'[25]

The link between military failure and (forced) political change is a powerful one. Defeat in Crimea, in the Russo-Japanese War of 1905, in the First World War and in the Soviet–Afghan War in the 1980s spurred change or were precursors to state collapse. Following the breakdown of its relationship with the West in the past two decades, Russia has again engaged in a turn to the East.[26] This has been supported by the 'Western rejectionist' philosophy of Eurasianism developed by twentieth-century ultra-conservative philosophers such as the late Ivan Ilyin, the 'court' philosopher of President Putin.[27]

The division between Westernisers and Slavophiles became more entrenched and by the late nineteenth century, Westernisers' hopes of progress, Greenfeld argues, 'gave way to resentment, the rejection of the West based on envy and the realisation of the all-too-evident, and therefore unbearable, inferiority'.[28] The Russia intelligentsia became saturated with ideas rejected by the West.* German idealism, French Comtean positivism, Darwinism and anarchism struggled against ultra-conservative 'mystical monarchism, Slavophil nostalgia, clericalism, and the like'.[29] From the 1880s, in the words of the philosopher Isaiah Berlin, 'a vast, now unreadably tedious, mass of books, articles, pamphlets began to flood upon the Russian intelligentsia.'[30] Reaction to these works continued in the established xenophobic or xenomanic – foreign hating or foreign loving – trends. Russia was either

> destined to obey unique laws of its own – so that the experience of other countries has little or nothing to teach it – or, on the contrary, that its failures are entirely due to an unhappy dissimilarity to the life of other nations … which Russians ignore at their peril.[31]

Critically, both trends sought, in trying to solve the ills of Russian society, integral, organic solutions and all-encompassing concepts, which mirrored the need for spiritual and/or intellectual wholeness

* A popular but somewhat disputed term, defined here as a secular educated class of people, detached or alienated from mainstream society, who define their role as importing or explaining external ideas.

and unity. Nicholas Berdyaev, in his work on Russian intellectual life, *The Russian Ideal*, argued that the roots of Russia's twentieth-century totalitarianism lay in the need of the Russian intellectual classes to offer, as the solution to Russia's ills, a single, holistic concept:

> The Russian Intelligentsia has always been bent upon working out a totalitarian and integral view of life in which truth shall be combined with justice. By means of totalitarian thinking they sought the perfect life and not only perfect works of philosophy, science or art. One might even say that this totalitarian character is a definite attribute of the Intelligentsia.[32]

So, by the end of the nineteenth century, Russia was torn between two flawed identities: an idealising of Russia or an idealising of the West, an exaggerated self-love or an exaggerated self-loathing. Both were rooted in an overriding sense of inferiority and both sought to escape reality in a proto-totalitarian intellectual and spiritual utopia.

This search for an integral whole helps to inform our understanding of the integration and unification of Russian warfare today. The concept influences those in power who make policy. It is not the only factor, but it remains a deep one. For example, Putin's former adviser Vladislav Surkov has argued that the essence of Russian culture is the search for a holistic truth. Surkov is the architect of Putin's managed democracy, as well as being highly influential in the redevelopment of non-military ways of conflict. In one article, he answers the question of what Russian culture is by echoing the holistic ideal, paraphrasing Putin's favourite philosopher, Ivan Ilyin, who said, 'Russian culture is the contemplation of the whole.'[33] This was an idea, Surkov observed, that was 'astonishing in its brevity and profundity'.

Twentieth-century Western Sovietologists speculated on the extent to which communism found resonance in enduring Russian political and social identity. Theories sometimes veered towards the bizarre, such as the notion that the tight swaddling of infants in traditional peasant Russian households created intense and destructive rage, as the mollycoddled child was unable to express itself through movement.[34] Slightly less eccentrically, German scholar Klaus Mehnert linked the authority of the Soviet state, beyond Soviet propaganda and police tyranny, to Byzantine theocratic tradition. 'Both priest and Party functionary have in turn been credited with possession of the sole, absolute, indivisible truth – the former through the revelations of God, the latter through the no less infallible medium of "scientific" knowledge,' he wrote.[35]

More recent works have explored the link between Russian identity, martyrdom and the 'cult of suffering'.[36] The mathematical psychologist Vladimir Lefebvre postulated that Russians accepted autocracy based on their profoundly different assumptions about the nature of society compared to that of the US. In *The Algebra of Conscience*, Lefebvre argued, 'The difference between Western society and Soviet society is much deeper than is usually assumed. This difference touches upon fundamental structures connecting the categories of good and evil.'[37] Studying Soviet émigrés and their US counterparts, Lefebvre used mathematical models to explain moral experience. He argued that Americans evaluated compromise between good and evil negatively but tended to compromise in situations of confrontation with a partner, whereas Soviets evaluated compromise between good and evil more acceptingly but were uncompromising towards partners in confrontation.[38] He further argued that ethical systems similar to that of the Soviets were connected with authoritarian regimes or extreme religious philosophies.

In this way, can autocracy be seen to be wired into Russia's social as well as political DNA? A 1981 Brookings Institution report argued that despite large-scale repression, the Communist Party retained the support of large segments of the Soviet population.[39]

The restatement of autocracy witnessed in Russia today should be seen not only within the context of Russia's historic tradition of autocracy but also as part of the struggle for power amongst Russian elites. Post-1991, the struggle between Slavophile *derzhavniks*,* loosely translated as 'strong staters', and Westernising liberals continued. Both sat within this historic tradition of either rejecting or copying the West. The failure of democratic reform and a series of manipulated ethnic conflicts on Russia's periphery through the 1990s strengthened the *derzhavniks* at the expense of the Westernisers. Westernisers faced a solidifying alliance between 'right-wing' nationalists and 'left-wing' communists – ostensibly at opposite ends of the political spectrum but who shared a common heritage in hostility to the West, an adoration of communalism (not communism) and a sense of Russian messianism and exceptionalism. Both the West and their Russian supporters were presented as inimical to Russian tradition and a threat to it.[40]

These anti-Western ideologies shared a perception that Western values were being imposed on Russia, hence the need to defend spiritual and moral values and the need to arm the state to counter those threats.[41] During the 1990s, Western observers underestimated this sense of threat to 'Russian values' felt by those who embrace the illiberal, Slavophile view of the country. They also underestimated the power that Putin began to wield, in which the KGB, now the FSB, linked arms with a corrupt bureaucratic class and the new

* The term later evolved to *siloviki*.

organised crime networks, which had become an integral part of the Russian state.

After 2000, the events of the previous twenty years could be interpreted as the re-establishment by President Putin of a Russian autocratic model. Its architect, Vladislav Surkov, said:

> The new democratic order has its origin in European civilization – but in a specific Russian version of that civilization. It is viable to the extent that it is natural – that is, national. Our democracy is viable if it does not reject Russian political culture but is part of it, developing not in defiance of but together with it.[42]

Surkov states the obvious: that Russian political development owes more to authoritarianism than democracy, to which he paid lip service. However uncomfortable it is for Western nations, Putin and his team have returned Russia to an autocratic leadership, ancient and familiar to many Russians.[43]

BOUNDLESS BORDERS

There are two other enduring themes that have shaped Russian strategic thinking, which we should briefly examine. These are the relative lack of defined borders and its desire for greatness – what one might call a sense of geographical and psychological boundlessness.

Russia lacks geographically defined borders over much of the south and west of the country. Whilst this has aided diaphragmic territorial expansion – expanding, sometimes contracting, then expanding again – it has also made the Russian state vulnerable to land invasion. As the late military theorist Vladimir Slipchenko commented, 'Russia is boundless.'[44] The country's most defining shared experiences have been of brutal invasion by a succession of nations and peoples from the thirteenth century onwards. From the east, the Mongols and from the north and then west, the nations of Sweden, France and most recently, Germany. From the south, there was a limited insertion from Great Britain and France during the 1853–6 Crimean War. The Russian Civil War also saw insertions from Poland and the UK following the First World War.

Russia's borderless expanse has produced an 'almost obsessive perception of a general threat towards Russian sovereignty and territorial integrity'.[45] This has fed not only a heightened sense of vulnerability but also an appetite for achieving security through expansion – hence the Russian framing of the war against NATO as a defensive one for Putin.[46] Russia wants military 'breathing space' between it and the West. Scholars have noted the tendency of the Russian state to combine both a 'defensiveness bordering on paranoia … with assertiveness bordering on pugnacity'.[47] Vladimir Putin and his regime comprise a particularly impassioned version of this.

Its borderless expanse has also, at times, shaped Russian military thinking through the development of attritional warfare strategies.* These were most famously utilised by Field Marshal Mikhail Kutuzov, whose tactics of withdrawal, scorched earth and guerrilla skirmishing combined with the Russian winter destroyed Napoleon's forces in 1812. A similar attritional fate had befallen Sweden's Charles XII in the Great Northern War.

The most recent geopolitical shock to the Russian state took place in the late 1980s and early '90s, with the collapse of both the Warsaw Pact alliance and the USSR. Moscow not only lost its advanced

* The early wave of Soviet military leaders rebelled against attritional warfare of the kind practised by Kutuzov, preferring to seek destructive warfare. See Chapter 5 for more on this debate.

position in eastern and central Europe – its buffer against Western threats, real or imagined – but with the dissolution of the USSR, much of the territory it had conquered in three centuries of imperial expansion. All fourteen of the non-Russian republics of the Soviet Union declared independence. Rarely has so large an empire collapsed so quickly. Former Warsaw Pact states and three former Soviet republics (Lithuania, Latvia and Estonia) joined NATO and the EU. This brought both alliances significantly closer to the heart of Russia. In Estonia, NATO troops in Tallinn are just 228 miles from St Petersburg.

However, it may well be that the Russian leadership believes that the most profound threat facing their country is not the physical one but the psychological, political and cultural threat to their concept of Russia as a state separate from the West and a state in confrontation with the West and its values. Arguably, the most significant threat that the Russian state believes it faces today is that from indirect political conflict such as from grassroots democracy campaigns or so-called 'colour revolutions', which it presents as Western-backed, indirect warfare, undertaken to undermine Russia's stability, sovereignty and spiritual and moral values.[48]

The Russian sense of exceptionalism and the desire to be a great power has in part been a by-product of Russian imperial expansion, driven by insecurity and the borderless geography of Eurasia. Great-power status has been expressed in part through the domination of Ukraine (as well as Belarus), the denial of Ukraine's separate identity and the historical narrative of Russians and Ukrainians as one people, translated into the Russia imperial narrative of the 'gathering of Russian lands'.[49]

Historically, Russia's sense of physical greatness has been reinforced by its sense that Russians are in some way chosen for a purpose.[50] This sense of unique purpose had been transmitted both by orthodoxy and communism. The concept of Russia as the *true* Christian kingdom was initially articulated by the Orthodox monk Filotheos in 1523 or 1534. In a letter to the Tsar's deacon, Filotheos claimed that, following the fall of Constantinople, Muscovite Russia was the only true Christian state – the Catholic Church in Rome being deemed heretical – and Moscow therefore should be regarded as the third and final Rome.

Sweden's Maria Engström argues that the idea of the Russian people as the chosen nation fighting against the Antichrist led to the identification of two enemies of Muscovy: an *external* Antichrist in the lands beyond Muscovy and the *internal* Antichrist. Resistance to the state, especially during periods of instability, was the internal Antichrist at work. Engström sees in modern Russian messianism the concept of the *Katechon* – of Russia as the self-appointed shield against the Antichrist, a concept discussed in conservative circles in the past two decades.[51] The influence of this idea, she said, is enduring: Russia as the shield of Europe against the Muslim East, Russia as a protector of the Slavs and the Orthodox faithful in the nineteenth century and Russia (in the guise of the Soviet Union) as protector of the working class and the saviour in the battle against Nazism in the twentieth century.

This century, this idea has been expressed in the notion of Russia as a restraining force against the unipolar power of the US – for example, in Putin's speech at the 2007 Munich Security Conference, which signalled the end of co-operation with the US and, effectively, the start of a new Cold War.[52] As Surkov states, 'When the hegemony of the "hegemon" was not disputed by anyone and the great American dream of world domination had almost come true … the Munich speech suddenly sounded sharply.'[53]

The deep-seated desire to remain a great power is not just a reflection of the current Russian administration but can be seen in its recent history. Anatoly Chubais, the man who led Russian privatisation in the 1990s, also articulated that Russia's imperialist mission for the twenty-first century was to be the natural leader of the former Soviet countries – the 'recognised' leader of half the world. In this expectation of dominance over the former USSR, including Central Asia, there are echoes of Dostoevsky's appeals to imperial glory in an earlier turn to the East.

Ukrainians I interviewed for this book believed that Putin needed to regain Ukraine to feed a great-power conception of Russia. Putin 'dreams of an empire', said one, 'and the empire is either the Russian one of the nineteenth century or the Soviet one of the twentieth.'[54] Without Ukraine, Putin's ambition becomes impossible to achieve.

The loss of Ukraine has had a profound influence on Russia's perception of itself. As Alexander Bogomolov and Oleksandr Lytvynenko explain, the 'very idea of a Ukrainian nation separate from the great Russian nation challenges core beliefs about Russia's origin and identity'.[55] Of all the elements in the collapse of the USSR, the loss of Ukraine is most painfully felt. It goes significantly deeper than merely reversing 300 years of Russian expansion. Russia without Ukraine meant the loss of millions of fellow Slavs, a significant proportion of its industrial output, some of its richest agricultural land and many of the symbolic locations in Russia's national story, especially Kyiv. Both Russia and Ukraine take their founding story from the Kyivan Rus, the first eastern Slavic state. However, these myths are not shared but contested. One of the Tsar's original titles was 'autocrat of all Rus'. Its implication was that Muscovy alone was the true successor to the old Kyivan state.[56]

After the collapse of Kyiv in the thirteenth century, following internal disputes and external pressure from the Mongol invasion, the city and the lands around it became part of the Polish–Lithuanian Commonwealth. Ukraine began to be absorbed into the Russian Empire only in the 1650s, when the Zaporizhzhian Cossacks aligned with the Tsar against the Polish–Lithuanian Commonwealth. Control of Ukraine solidified Russia's transnational status as leader of the East Slavic nation. As Bogomolov and Lytvynenko state, 'In time, these myths of common national origin were complemented by the myth that Russian language and culture are a legacy shared by all Eastern Slavs and the myth of the perpetual incremental growth of the Russian state, otherwise known as "the gathering of Russian lands"'.[57]

This idea of 'the gathering of Russian lands' to make Russia 'whole' remains relevant today. Russia's founding myth is exclusive, not inclusive. As a result, the Kremlin recognises neither an independent Ukraine's narrative that it has sought independence over a protracted period nor Ukraine's claims to the Kyivan Rus and the Ukrainian symbolism connected with it.[58] Slavophil Russia cannot share a foundation story with Ukraine as a separate entity without accepting Ukraine as just that – a separate entity. Hence the Kremlin's need to believe that Ukrainians and Russians were and are one people. It justifies the war.

In pursuit of this historic claim, throughout the nineteenth century Ukrainian language and culture were slowly eradicated, leading to the 1876 Decree of Ems. The decree instituted a ban on the import and publication of Ukrainian books, the prohibition of Ukrainian language on stage and the removal of Ukrainian language books from school libraries, as well as other restrictive cultural measures.[59] This confirmed to Ukrainians that Russia's historic policy has been, according to one Ukrainian I interviewed, 'to eradicate Ukrainian sovereignty, language and culture'.[60] In the Soviet era, whilst the Ukrainian Soviet republic gave a semblance of autonomy, Ukraine and Ukrainian cultural symbols were treated with deep suspicion. In the 1920s and 1930s, the Stalin-era purges and the Holodomor – the organised 'terror' famine imposed on the Ukrainian peasantry – took some 4 million lives.[61]

Yet despite this, for the first decade after independence, Ukrainians elected former Soviet and Communist Party managers to political authority rather than Central European-style nationalists, suggesting both an innate conservatism and that the simplistic Ukraine-as-victim trope does not explain the complex relationship between it and Russia. However, since the 2014 war and especially since 2022, Ukrainians have significantly shifted to a markedly more pro-EU and pro-NATO stance, combined with a distrust, and now hatred, of the Russian state. Modern attempts to frame Ukrainians and Russians as one people have been actively opposed by Ukrainians, who now appear to separate their past from Russia's and see in their history, especially in the case of the Zaporizhzhian Cossacks, a proto-democratic republic subsumed by Muscovite autocracy.[62] The civilisational divide now runs between Ukraine and Russia, not between Eastern Slavs and Europe.[63]

Putin, for his part, believes that Russia without Ukraine is Russia fragmented. Russia and Ukraine, he believes, are together 'a single whole'.[64] Those words are from the opening line of Putin's article on the historical unity of Russia and Ukraine, published on the Kremlin's website in the summer of 2021, in which he laid out the historical reasons for the invasion that would take place the following February. He argued that Russians and Ukrainians were one people, separated by political errors but also by deliberate efforts by outsiders to divide them. This natural unity was not only political and economic but also 'spiritual'. Attempts to split the two amounted to an anti-Russia project. True sovereignty for Ukraine was only possible with Russia due to the spiritual, human and civilisation ties, for, in Putin's words, 'we are one people'. In a 2013 piece, Putin noted approvingly that neither communists nor anti-communists in the Russian Civil War had countenanced an independent Ukraine. 'Both the White movement and the Reds fought among themselves to death, millions of people died during the civil war, but never raised the question of secession of Ukraine,' he said. 'Both Red and White proceeded from the integrity of the Russian state.'[65] Russians could slaughter each other, but they would always agree on Ukraine.

So, to summarise, the themes that have shaped historical Russian political culture and its thinking about security remain: the heightened sense of threat, the defence of autocracy and the desire to retain great power status. However, they have also evolved. The acute sense of threat remains, but the Kremlin arguably believes that the threat is now predominantly the threat of political and psychological invasion rather than physical assault. Under Putin, authoritarianism has been re-established in Russia after its brief and flawed flirtation with democracy, but it is in a different guise from both Soviet totalitarian socialism and Tsarist autocracy.[66] Finally, the desire to remain a great power is still as potent as ever, both to dominate its neighbours and re-establish itself as a rival to the West. The ideology that drives this thinking is now not socialism, but a deep illiberalism and a nationalist hostility to the West as a way of defining modern Russian identity.

The loss of Ukraine – especially given its potential to be a rival and alternative model for East Slavic society – is intimately linked to Russia's sense of itself as a great power, its own perception of threat and its reborn autocracy traditions. All are threatened, potentially fatally, by a functioning, independent Ukraine. The growth, albeit initially slow, of Ukrainian democracy is an existential menace to Russian authoritarianism, whilst a genuinely independent Ukraine represents a 'threat to Russia's conception of itself' as the one and only eastern Slavic state.[67] A free Ukraine broke the whole.

CHAPTER 5

STORIES FROM THE FRONT: PANOUSHKA THE WIDOW SNIPER

'I will fight and avenge his death.'

– Panoushka[1]

At least twice a week, Panoushka and her small team are dropped off deep in the 'drone zone'. They walk for at least an hour and then hide at the edge of a tree line or in a building, meticulously camouflaging themselves and changing nothing that might give away their position. For several hours at a stretch, she will, in an almost zen-like state, watch the scene in front of her, waiting for her targets to wander into her sights. When one comes into view, she will kill it. Panoushka is a sniper and one of the best in the business. She shoots her enemy from up to 1.6 kilometres (one mile) away, risking her life almost daily. But for Panoushka, the most difficult thing she has done in the past year was to bury her partner.

'For that moment, I had to be a warrior – not just a woman who had lost the love of her life but also a soldier who had lost my brother in arms,' she told me.

Panoushka's fiancé was Lieutenant Colonel Oleksandr 'Sasha' Hostishchev, commanding officer of Tsunami. Tsunami is a unit composed entirely of police volunteers. Ukrainian policemen are exempt from conscription, but through a small number of units such as Tsunami, they have been able to play an active role in the war, improving the police's reputation in the process. Sasha was the driving force behind Tsunami. I had met him some eighteen months before. We ate with him and his men before he invited us back to stay in his billet. We drank brandy late into the evening and talked about the war.

The irony is that of the two, Panoushka was always the more likely to be killed. Sasha had fought in 2014 and was now leading his men from the operations room, whilst she was on and around the front line. Yet by a terrible piece of bad luck, he was killed during a rocket attack on the unit's rear base in Odesa, hundreds of miles from the front. 'Of course we would discuss that one of us might die, but I was always convinced that if someone would not survive this war, it would be me,' Panoushka told me.

I had arranged to meet Panoushka in a town near the front line in eastern Ukraine to express my condolences. I wasn't expecting a long conversation, especially given her role. However, we talked all day about her life as a sniper, the characteristics required for the job and the tactics she used. We talked too about her life with Sasha and how they combined domesticity whilst living and working around the front line together. We discussed his death and how she was saved by her comrades. It was a window into lives consumed by war.

Panoushka sat upright and explained herself very clearly and, for the most part, without emotion. She was a Latin teacher for eight years in the city of Lviv before working in Kyiv and then joining the Ukrainian Army in 2022. Her call sign does not translate precisely, but it is a diminutive, almost ancient term for a Ukrainian child from a wealthy or privileged class – 'little heiress', perhaps. Call signs are chosen by comrades and often as a term of endearment or army humour. Lviv is the cultural capital of Ukraine and Panoushka's colleagues clearly thought that with her well-pressed uniform and slim and careful appearance, she fitted the description. Like many women in this culturally conservative country, she makes an effort to look her best. When the war started, Ukrainian women cut back on restaurant spending but not on beauty products. 'There are many fears in the war. I don't want to be another one for my colleagues by looking scary. It's also important to look nice for the enemy,' she jokes, before emphasising that the only make up she wears on operations is camouflage cream.

I had visited Sasha in early September 2023 at his regimental command post in the basement of a building just outside Kramatorsk. I'd seen very similar places during my days in Iraq and Afghanistan.[2] It was a small, cramped room with folding chairs and wooden desks, around which wound a messy soup of cables attached to laptops, where officers and soldiers from different roles – intelligence, current operations and artillery – sat. At the head of the room was the commanding officer's desk. Unlike in Afghanistan, where there was little chance of our heat signal being picked up by the enemy, being identified here could invite a missile attack, so the basement was insulated with padded metallic sheeting, which also kept the room warmer in winter. The practical purpose of operations rooms such as these is to bring together all the different elements in a unit or command, so that informed decisions can be made by the commander or those they delegate to.

We sat with the team and watched the tactical war play out, as Tsunami soldiers fought through streets of rubble-strewn houses in the village of Klishchiivka, clearing it of Russian soldiers. Sasha talked via Discord gaming software with his front line, mortar lines and drone lines. What occasional conversation there was between the junior officers was quiet and succinct. The team 'walked' their mortars onto the immediate target, a shell of a house containing three Russian soldiers lying flat and still, as if they were willing themselves to blend in with the rubble and ruins around them. A few more words were passed between Sasha and his teams and then moments later, a Ukrainian mortar landed. After the puff of white-grey smoke dissipated into the air, the Russians were no more. There was neither pause nor celebration. Sasha's men edged forward to the next Russian position. And so the battle continued, house by house, day by day.

A week later, the regiment told me that Klishchiivka had been recaptured. Over that summer, Tsunami had retaken a little over a kilometre of land, with more than fifteen lives lost and more injured. Soldiers often discuss the cost of war – 'blood and treasure' is the old phrase – and the cost to Tsunami in their area of operations, just south of the razed city of Bakhmut, in the summer of 2023 was a man's life and some injured for roughly every 100 meters. They had many miles yet to travel.

Whilst all this was happening, Panoushka herself had been in training and then serving with other units prior to her transfer to Sasha's Tsunami unit. She had had some experience shooting as a hobby whilst a teenager and was from a 'patriot' family. Her own father had fought in 2014 and 2022 and had only retired due to his age. Although Panoushka has two children, they were growing up and were able to live with her former husband. When the war started, she wanted a frontline role and wondered how to get one. 'I understood that a woman with a machine gun is 100 per cent in the rear or on the staff [a desk job]. I wanted to fight. I wanted to be directly involved. So, I thought what exclusivity can I offer the army?' She signed with special operations, and had a bet with her commander that she could pass the sniper's course. She was given three weeks to learn to shoot a target one mile (1.6 km) away.

'My instructor said that it would never work. I replied, "We are in the army and this is an order, so I have to do it."' She won her bet. Another course followed. She moved from the US-made Barrett sniper rifle (very large as rifles go) to a slightly smaller and more manageable Italian Victrix, still nearly two-thirds her height with a silencer attached. 'And that's how my story began,' she told me.

Panoushka works in a pair with another sniper and an escort to protect them. They take up positions that have been identified earlier by reconnaissance teams and then analysed and developed by the snipers themselves. She prefers to work out of buildings because of the extra height, but due to intense artillery damage, that has become more difficult. The teams move at dawn and dusk, during a thirty- to forty-minute window when the day drones are coming in and the night drones have yet to come out. The pair rotate through their operation, however long that is. 'When I'm "on" the rifle, my colleague is sleeping or resting,' Panoushka explains.

So what makes a good sniper? Eyesight is no longer key, she says – the rifle's sights adjust for that – but composure, endurance and attention to detail are essential. This is, she adds, an 'intellectual' form of war. Anything from opening a window in a damaged building to moving a downed tree trunk can give her and her team's position away to enemy snipers. After a couple of hours looking through her sites, she will know the land ahead of her intimately.

'By the end of my shift, I'll know which way a branch is moving or which bush is growing towards me,' she said.

'The sniper's work is a little bit romanticised,' Panoushka continues. 'Having twenty rounds doesn't mean twenty kills, and sometimes we can sit there for several days and, you know, have no targets at all.' Additionally, not every shot hits or results in a kill. There is a discussion in sniping circles about whether an injury is more valuable than a kill because of the additional work for Russian soldiers tending to their wounded – provided, of course, the Russians bother to do so. They have often tended to leave their wounded as well as their dead.

Drones, as we have already seen, have made life more dangerous and difficult. Their sound is now a permanent battlefield feature. Speaking about an operation in Toretsk, eastern Ukraine, in late summer of 2024, Panoushka said, 'Honestly, there wasn't a moment when I didn't hear the sound of a drone.' She distinguishes them by their sound: the more stable the sound, the larger the drone, whilst the more 'dynamic' the sound, the lighter and smaller the drone. For days after her 48-hour mission, she was still hearing their sound in her head. 'It's like, when you go to the mountains or to the sea and you constantly hear this noise of water, like waves, or you're in the mountains and there's some mountain river. It's constantly in your ear and when you leave, you're looking for this sound.'

Every rotation, she says, seems to be more challenging and finding Russians within range takes longer. 'It's difficult to find an adequate position from which you can work, and if such a position is located, then you must be very, very careful not to burn it.' That's because sometimes Russian and Ukrainian soldiers find themselves next to each other, literally. Once, she said, Russian and Ukrainian teams were living cheek by jowl, unbeknown to each other, in neighbouring flats in the same drab and damaged Soviet-era apartment block. They had been using different entrances. When one of the Russians went out onto the balcony for a smoke, they saw each other. Because a few civilians were still living in the building, both were confused. Both were dressed in civilian clothes. The Russian did not realise that the Ukrainian was a soldier, but the Ukrainian saw the Russian's radio and antenna showing from his pocket. Both then clicked. In the race to reach for their weapons, the Ukrainian's sharper thinking gave him the edge. He shot the Russian at close range.

Luck has kept Panoushka alive too. She was leaving one position with her team when a Russian drone arrived overhead. They ran to a nearby tree. 'It was a big tree,' she recollects, 'with a big crown, and we all hid under it, under this tree, and the drone was hanging over us, hanging and hanging, and we sat there for two minutes.' They quickly realised that staying there would attract more drones and potentially mortar and other artillery fire. They started running, zigzagging between houses and gardens.

The drone followed as if they were in a dystopian movie. 'We started running. You stand; it stands. And you run and it runs, and it's just hanging behind you, and it's watching.' Why didn't the Russians strike? The drone turned out to be a reconnaissance drone, and perhaps the Russians were not as coordinated as they should have been or could not get artillery or an armed drone onto Panoushka and her team quickly enough.

'At moments like this, I understood that it wasn't supposed to be my day to die.'

In early March 2024, she returned to Lviv to spend time with her parents and children over her birthday. She had planned to return and celebrate with Sasha, but her parents asked her to stay longer. 'I called him and said, "You know we had New Year together and Christmas and your birthday together, so I would like to stay in Lviv with my parents."' She asked him to join them, but he stayed at the base to work on a new rotation plan for the unit.

That evening, Odesa was hit with Russian missiles. These were becoming so common that Panoushka paid little notice. A while later, her phone rang. Did she know Sasha had been injured? She rang the regiment's second in command. It was serious. Doctors were fighting to save Sasha's life. Panoushka had a premonition – 'a sense that the worst had happened' – but she didn't want to take any phone calls or hear updates. She drove immediately to Odesa, on the Black Sea coast. She hoped that Sasha would still be alive, that somehow when he saw her, she, through the power of her love, would fix everything. 'I wasn't ready to hear any news,' she said. 'I had a fantastical hope that he will wait for me.' As she drove, she was aware that texts were arriving on her phone. An hour from Odesa, more started arriving again. She briefly looked; they were condolences. One came from her brother. At that point, she recollected, 'I realised that I had already known that Sasha had gone and that it no longer made any sense to lie to myself.'

That night, Panoushka opened the door to their apartment in Odesa. She saw Sasha's semi-automatic weapon in front of her in the hallway, propped up and loaded, as always. At that moment, she began to comprehend 'how much pain and what hell was awaiting' when she awoke the next morning, to say nothing of what she would endure in the weeks and months ahead: the burial, the loneliness and going back to the war without him. 'Honestly, my first instinct was just to shoot myself. I thought, "I know how to kill. It's one second, that's all."' She stared at the weapon. But she had second thoughts: 'I am a Christian and I believe in life after death. According to the Christian tradition, if you commit suicide then you go to hell. Those who fight for our state, they go to heaven. The purpose of my suicide was to be with him for ever, but if I went through with suicide, I would not be with him because we would be on different sides [in the afterlife].'

The funeral and its preparations fell to her. Overwhelmed by events, she found herself reading his old text messages, as if he was still alive. It was her colleagues who stepped in and grounded her.

'There is an important moment when you are on a mission and you are about to lose control of yourself,' she explained. Panic or fear can overwhelm. In that case, to refocus, she had been taught to ask herself, 'Who are you? Where are you? What is your mission?' Her comrades – her 'brothers', as she frequently described them as we chatted – helped her. 'They told me, "You are not only a woman who has suffered loss; you are an officer-sniper of the special operations forces. You are at war. Your mission is now to look after this man."' She repeated this mantra in the days before the funeral 'probably a million times'. Her task for the moment was to set aside her feelings and ensure the best funeral she could. 'I had to be strong and I had to keep everything under control.'

'I was not just protecting a person,' she told me. 'I was protecting an amazing commander, a great person. I didn't want to be that person, but fate made this my responsibility.' She paid immaculate attention to detail. She held up the funeral cortege for an hour because the wrong belt had been fitted around Sasha's waist. 'I postponed my personal feelings to perform probably the hardest task in life but to perform it to my best abilities, to carry him through to the last path and to do it as worthily as he lived.'

Forgiving she was not. 'At his funeral, I said that as long as I live, I will fight and avenge his death.'

The funeral was in Odesa and Sasha was to be cremated in Dnipro. After the funeral and in the four hours between saying goodbye to the body and waiting for the ashes, Panoushka's grief returned. 'For these four hours, I was so exhausted. I hadn't slept and I hadn't eaten,' she remembered. 'I refused to calm down. I said,

"There is no point in delaying this moment because it is impossible to avoid the grief.'"

A priest had given his blessing to sprinkle some of Sasha's remains on the Dnipro River, where he had loved to fish when he was younger, and to keep some for a grave so the regiment could have a physical memorial of their commander. On the river, Panoushka struggled to collect some of his ashes in her hands to scatter them. Days passed before she washed them. 'His ashes were under my fingernails. It was, like, a little crazy,' she said.

When Panoushka spoke, she was occasionally moved to tears but remained poised, sitting upright and wiping her eyes with a napkin. She explained that she still found it difficult to talk without being overcome. She recollected her life with Sasha. As we sat and drank coffee, she recalled that Sasha had initially been furious that she had signed up to be a sniper. They had quarrelled as she went through training and didn't see each other for months. He eventually mellowed, accepted her decision and then asked her, 'Aren't you tired of not seeing each other all the time? Let's take you with us [into the Tsunami Regiment] so that we can be together more? How about it?'

Panoushka accepted but with conditions. 'Give me your word', she told Sasha, 'that you won't go behind my back and block me from operations.' So they made a deal. He promised that he would not prevent her from going into the fight. And she promised not to work as a marksman, which is more dangerous work than that of a sniper.

She said Sasha told her, 'I know how adventurous you are, but please, each time I sign an order for your mission, remember that it's an order signed by me.' He understood what the consequences might be, she said, but he always signed the orders committing her to battle in respect of her wishes. He told her, 'I am not only a commanding officer; I am a person who loves you. I am also human. There are things that are very difficult to deal with, so, like, let's… let's not shake my nervous system too much.' She kept her word. After every mission, she would ring when safe to tell him, '450, the code for I'm fine. All is well.' Then she would go to headquarters to see him 'no matter how dirty or smelly I was'. Once or twice, she told him off when he stepped over the line. She was once mildly injured with two other comrades, when they were all cut by razor wire. Sasha rushed to the local hospital where she was being treated, only to have her give him a dressing down: 'If you don't do it for others, why do you do it for me?' Normally, the second in command would have gone to the hospital, not the commander.

For a while, the pair lived a life of domestic contentment a few miles behind the front line. They had a house not too far from Kramatorsk, abandoned by the owners but still in a good state – the place that I had visited when Sasha had hosted me. When they lived there, Panoushka could focus on her missions. She had his support. He even helped with the dreaded staff work, the bane of every officer.

'I would go on a mission, shoot a Russian, and I would come home where someone was waiting for me, took care of me, and loved me. That's what it was like.' They talked about anything other than the war and created, for a brief period of time, a haven of domesticity, despite the maelstrom of chaos and death a few miles from them. 'You understand that you are living in someone else's house, using someone else's dishes, sleeping on someone else's bed, but you somehow create your own little life and, well, this family.'

The bizarre normality of their situation had struck her the previous New Year's Eve. Sasha's favourite New Year dish was an Olivier salad (known sometimes in the West as a Russian salad, with ham, egg, peas and other vegetables in mayonnaise). 'We always eat it on the New Year,' Panoushka recalled. 'Some people say that it's part of our Soviet past, but he loved, *loved* that salad.' As a treat, she was going to make it for him, but he had signed an order committing her to an operation.

'Do you really have to go?' he implored her. 'Yes, you signed the order yourself,' she replied. The mission turned out to be a difficult one. Their position was given away, and for two hours of Russian bombardment, Panoushka huddled in a shallow trench with a wooden plank little thicker than her rifle above her, hidden by branches and leaves. Sasha watched from the screens in his operations room as the Russians tried repeatedly to kill his fiancée. They only escaped when a neighbouring Ukrainian unit engaged Russian positions to draw fire. Sasha was at headquarters with a senior officer. Struggling to hide his relief, he addressed her formally, using her first name and patronymic, and asked, as he always did but with special care this time, if everything was 'normal'. She replied, 'I've completed the mission. Now we need to get home if you want me to cook that Olivier salad for you.' It was their final New Year together.

After the funeral, the forty days of mourning, sorting out their property and the other practical things that take place following a death, Panoushka struggled. She sought mental health help, but lacking the experience of warfare, the psychologist found it difficult to connect with her. Back on rotation, it was her colleagues – her brothers – who again came to her aid.

'The easiest thing is when I have my brothers with me. My comrades have the same thoughts as I do. They have also experienced difficult moments as I have. They do not ask stupid questions; they will not say banal phrases that are not necessary,' she said. 'But I know that they are here and I can rely on them.' These 'modest people', she said, got her out of bed, forced her to train and took her for coffees.

Panoushka says she has not become addicted to war but enjoys the sensation of returning from her missions. The feeling of euphoria when surviving after danger, she said, is unique, a point made by Winston Churchill more than a century before when he said that nothing in life was so exhilarating as to be shot at without result. She finds comfort too in the brotherhood in arms around her: 'We experience this new form of human coexistence. They are not your family, they are not your friends, but with them you experience the most intense things, and you are sincere with them because it may be your last seconds.' She described this as living a 'common story'.

Having experienced death, how does she feel killing? 'First of all, I don't want to take it just like that. Like, I've never "killed" anyone in my life. Secondly, even among snipers it is not customary to discuss the numbers.' But, she continued, there was a simple equation. 'Either I do it or the Russians will come and kill my family, for example, or take my house. So, it's a very obvious choice.' Fight them here, she says, or fight them in Kyiv and Odesa and Lviv and see her family flee. Like many Ukrainians who are fighting, she does so now so that her teenage son will not have to do so when he turns eighteen.

'When some people say, OK, you are as bad as they are and that they're still human beings and they have families, of course. But if you start thinking about that, I remember all people I loved and who had families. And they are no more.' Panoushka paused and then explained, 'It doesn't occur to me to have pity on my enemy. For me, it's more important to analyse my mistakes, what could have been done better.'

Now, Panoushka shares a new digs, a safe distance from the front, with her comrades and four dogs plus a cat – the animals are all rescued from frontline locations and she is working to rehouse them. The cat and one dog have new homes waiting in the west of the country, but Panoushka is still looking for homes for the other dogs. When we visit, the woolly Alsatian lookalikes jump up to greet us.

When she can, she visits Sasha's grave. She lights a candle not only for him but also for twelve other souls whom she has lost. Not people, she stressed, whom she had merely 'crossed paths with' or heard about, but people she knew well: 'People who were in my life before the war or during the war, who became my close friends. I buried thirteen such people. Thirteen people whom I will never meet again, I won't drink coffee with, I won't celebrate any holidays with or invite to my birthday. There are so many of us. I, as one small person in this society, lost thirteen close people. It's a pain you will carry for the rest of your life.' These are thirteen out of the 45,000 Ukrainian dead.

Panoushka dismisses comparisons with Soviet female Second World War snipers, some of whom were propaganda creations. Whilst her father's side of the family fought reluctantly with the Red Army, her mother's side fought with Ukrainian partisans and were sent to Siberian camps as punishment after the war. Even with her extensive military experience, she sees Russian warfare in the round. 'It's a hybrid war and I think that this battlefield is a small area of this war, one part of it, yes,' she says. 'The bigger part, I think, is informational and political warfare. All wars are political.'

Panoushka's is fundamentally an existentialist approach to life. She defines herself by her actions and 'a small but certain role in this fight for my country'. She is working with Sasha's family and regiment for permanent recognition of his work, but her grief remains.

'Time does not heal. It does not heal anything,' she says. 'Time just teaches you how to deal with certain manifestations of this grief. Because you have to live it, and the longer you deny it, it will then catch up with you more painfully. You just have to go through all this. And you just learn to have this immunity with time.'

Panoushka finds peace in her work. 'I'm always told that I'm comfortable to work with because I am very calm.' When she looks through her scope for between two and five hours at a time, with her fellow sniper resting in a corner and her reconnaissance squad around her, time fades. Psychologists call it 'flow', when you lose yourself in your task. 'For hour on hour, I feel like the time is just disappearing. It's just me, my optics and my sector. And then I forget about everything.'

CHAPTER 6

REINVENTING THREAT: REIMAGINING THE WEST AS THE ENEMY

'Ill will towards Russia has been deeply rooted in the West since the days of yore.'

– General Makhmut Gareyev[1]

SOVIET COLLAPSE: CONSERVATIVES AND INNOVATORS

The swift collapse of the Warsaw Pact and then the USSR itself in 1991 was accompanied by a wider collapse in the certainties on which the state had been based – the 'theoretical and ideological constructions of the Soviet era'.[2] After the deluge, those who debated how to rebuild Russian military capability divided into two camps: 'conservatives' and 'innovators'.[3] They debated the threats facing Russia, the resources needed in manpower and technology and the changing nature of conflict. They speculated as to the weapons of future wars and how to offset the West's scale and scientific advantage. Conservatives, broadly speaking, remained adherents of traditional Soviet military thinking. Innovators championed radical ideas. Conservatives, broadly, saw little change in the fundamental nature of warfare. Innovators predicted fundamental change. Conservatives supported a continuation of strategic consistencies. Innovators were more likely to question them.

The debate took place across institutions and publications over a number of years. It saw an 'intense political struggle'[4] between different institutions: between the Military Academy and the Security Council and between the General Staff and the Ministry of Defence.[5] It also took place under the presidency of Vladimir Putin, a man schooled in the KGB's tradition of subversive conflict. Elements of that debate, especially around the future of Russia, its values and its relationship to the West, echoed the dividing lines between Slavophiles and Westernisers. Ultimately, the debate was the struggle to establish an agreed view of the world and Russia's place in it. Establishing a doctrine, an expression of that viewpoint and the means of setting the direction of development, was the prize.

At this point, I need to briefly mention the role of doctrine. Before I started my PhD in Russian warfare, my eyes would glaze over at the thought of doctrine and definitions. However, they are important. Military doctrine in Russia is highly influential. It, and the art of strategic thinking, have little direct comparison in the West. Doctrine is critical for this book and I explore it in this and other chapters because it tells us about Russia's evolving style of warfare. Understanding Russian military and other strategic doctrines is to understand Russian fears, Russian concepts about conflict and how it will fight current and future wars. Understanding the Russian security 'mind' means engaging with its doctrine. Anything else is guesswork.

The late General Makhmut Gareyev,* one of Russia's more intellectually influential recent generals, defined doctrine in Russia not

* General Makhmut Gareyev (1923–2019) was the former head of the Russian Military Academy.

only as a 'system of officially accepted conceptual points of view' covering security, conflict and military development but also a preparation of the country and the armed forces for 'undertaking military and other forms of struggle in defence of the country'.[6] Doctrine in Russia, Gareyev said, was a 'declaration of policy'.[7] It's also representative of a collective view of the past. In 1963, Marshal V. D. Sokolovsky described it as being 'based on the entire life-experience of a state' – showing a specific sense of strategic thinking, rooted in and drawn from history.[8] It, and Russia's National Security Strategy, are statements of the political and military elite's understanding of the world. Military strategy sat below it and was focused on the practical, akin to where military doctrine sits in the West.

Senior NATO adviser Steve Covington has argued that there is no Western equivalent to the Russian tradition of strategic thinking. 'It is virtually impossible,' he said, 'to create a single system of strategic thought in the West that approximates the Russian approach.'[9] This culture, he added, reached from the General Staff – the brain of the army – into other security and government ministries, melding with Russia's centralised and autocratic system to allow military thought to merge with political authority, creating a single, holistic culture for security decision-making – again, the idea of a single whole.[10] The General Staff itself has a significant role. It produced 'original works of international standing' in the 1920s and '30s before many senior members of the armed forces were killed in Stalin's purges and produced them again in the 1980s.[11] These ideas influenced not only Russian but also Western ideas about 'operational art', the art of combining different military elements into a single, coherent, sustaining vision. The General Staff also plays a role in analysing future war – a function that was strengthened in 2004, according to

Norwegian defence academic Dr Tor Bukkvoll.[12] This role is seen to be as important as current military planning.[13]

The most powerful conservative voice was arguably that of Gareyev, who wrote prolifically until his death in December 2019, especially in the influential journal *Voyennaya Mysl'* (*Military Thought*), the in-house publication of the Military Academy, which he headed. The most influential innovator was the late Vladimir Slipchenko, who argued for radical change up to his death in 2005. Whilst this chapter quotes a number of Russian and Western sources, it will, for the sake of clarity, predominantly use Gareyev and Slipchenko to show the intellectual lines of dissent between 'conservatives' and 'innovators'.* Much of the debate was not held in public, but there are a limited number of articles and publications to give a sense of the direction of travel.

Above all, Russian military 'conservatives' were the defenders of the Clausewitzian tradition – they saw warfare and politics as intimately linked. They held traditionalist views of the threat facing Russia, with Slavophile sensibilities regarding the uniqueness of Russian identity. They harboured a xenophobic suspicion of the West, which they presented as Western hostility to Russia. As Gareyev said, 'Ill will towards Russia has been deeply rooted in the West since the days of yore.'[14] The threat, they believed, was both physical and psychological. They were the inheritors and the purveyors of an anti-Western worldview. Some believed the trope that the Soviet Union had been brought down due to the machinations of the West, whose plots, according to lurid KGB imaginations, had infected grain harvests and crashed the Soviet currency.

* To these two groups, Tor Bukkvoll adds a third group: modernisers. The modernisers are less radical than the innovators. The innovators, he argues, wanted Russia's armed forces to go through reforms similar to those undertaken by Western militaries.

The threat faced by Russia was one of the issues of contention. Gareyev complained in 2007 that the then military doctrine was too focused on narrow military threats. He argued for a doctrine based on military *and* non-military threats, presupposing a sense of permanent threat and therefore a permanent struggle against the permanent adversary, the West.[15] Since then, that sense of a Russia under attack has only become more acute. 'The new [US] administration … has declared war on us everywhere,' Ministry of Defence adviser Andrei Ilnitsky said in 2021, claiming that the historic and current policy of the West was to 'exterminate Russia as a species'.[16]

Conservatives have worried intently about the loss of power over former Soviet/Russian Imperial lands, believing that the US was 'seeking to oust Russia from the entire post-Soviet space, tear the Commonwealth of Independent States (CIS) countries away from it, drag them into the infinitely expanding NATO system'.[17] Of the non-military threats to Russia, Gareyev cited indirect and political tactics such as pro-democracy protests, which became known as 'colour revolutions'. They showed, he said, that the main threat to Russia's political sovereignty was in 'methods of political and diplomatic, economic, informational impact, various subversive actions and interference in the internal affairs of other countries'.[18] This included threats to Russian values and patriotism and demanded a countervailing need for 'spiritual and information security'.[19]

These claims have been repeated by Putin and those around him. In 2014, at a Russian Security Council meeting, the Russian leader argued that colour revolutions were used 'as an instrument of geopolitics and redistribution of spheres of influence' i.e. pulling former Soviet republics out of Russia's orbit.[20] Ukraine's 2004–5 Orange Revolution was one such example, which Russians alleged was funded by Western intelligence.[21] Close Putin ally and then chairman of the National Security Council, Nikolai Patrushev, argued in June 2020 that the West's strategic goal was a colour revolution in Russia and the overthrow of the Putin regime. Work towards these ends, he said, was 'constantly intensifying'.[22] These comments by Russia's political, security and military leaders explain the perceived psychological threat posed by the West to Russia's sense of patriotism and identity.

On the other side of the argument were the innovators. They focused on narrower military issues, such as the use of force and the nature of the future of traditional forms of war. Amongst the innovators, the late Vladimir Slipchenko's major contribution to Russian military thought was through his delineation of war into generations. He argued that by the 1990s, humanity had reached the sixth generation of warfare.[23] The first five were war with spears and swords, war with gunpowder, war with rifled weapons, war with automatic weapons, tanks and air and fifth, nuclear war. The sixth generation was the emergence of non-contact warfare using weapons such as long-range cruise missiles, of which the 1991 Iraq War and the 1999 Yugoslavia war were examples. Speaking about the latter, Slipchenko explained, 'There was no battle … one side strikes from the air and the other cannot repulse the attack; it has nothing with which to repulse it.'[24]

Slipchenko argued a series of outcomes. First, that the military capabilities of great states needed to be reoriented towards non-nuclear, non-contact weapons such as cruise and ballistic missiles; second, that land forces will not be needed in future wars, or certainly not to the same extent as they had been; third, that Russia would not face land attack again; fourth, that Russia needed to reorientate its armed forces for two purposes, strategic strike and strategic defence; fifth, that new airfields would be needed on the periphery of Russia to aid interception of attacks; sixth, that the military-industrial complex would need to be reorganised to prioritise the new, non-contact war; and seventh, that Russia needed to be ruthless in reorientating its defence posture.[25]

Whilst there has been acceptance of elements of Slipchenko's agenda, other elements, such as the abolition of ground forces, have had few supporters.[26] Events in Yugoslavia, Iraq and Afghanistan since the early 2000s have undermined Slipchenko's predictions. Whilst contactless operations such as drone attacks against terror groups became normalised, the need to hold ground with infantry troops remained. 'In Somalia, Bosnia, Chechnya, the hand of a fighter reaches not to a "mouse" ... but to a knife tested for millennia,' commented one military academic.[27] Conservatives in Russia criticised Slipchenko's acceptance of non-contact war as defeatist, claiming it implied an acceptance of US tech domination. Arguing that future wars would be contactless condemned general forces 'to passivity and inaction' argued the conservative Gareyev.[28]

Slipchenko also arguably downplayed the political aspect of warfare. Andreĭ Kokoshin, former secretary of the Russian Security Council, noted that whilst advanced sixth-generation US forces were able to defeat a fourth-generation army in Iraq, the US was unable to impose a political victory.[29] Whilst the military objective may have been easily won against conventional Iraqi forces, the political outcome was lost due to the US's inability to cope with the Iraqi insurgency. US military forces could defeat a regular army but not control a population. It therefore failed to use military power to achieve its political aims. Indeed, its dependence on military power may have made it blind to the political importance of winning hearts and minds – or at least subduing them.

Some practical changes in the Russian armed forces since have been driven by moderate reformers. Their victories included the reorganisation of the army based on brigades rather than divisions – although this has since come under criticism in the Ukraine War – the partial scraping of the mobilisation system and the introduction of non-commissioned officers and a dramatic reduction in the number of officers.[30] Slipchenko's ideas also influenced concepts such as network-centric warfare, where information, communications and intelligence dominance is translated into battlefield success. Much of the reform agenda was driven through by Anatoly Serdyukov when he was Minister of Defence. Whilst his work 'won him the loathing of most of the officer corps,' his successors have continued some of these processes.[31]

To show the tenor and wide breadth of the debate in Russia, I am going to look briefly at three examples of the arguments covering types of weapons, concepts of war and the role of violence in war.

First, weapons. Military academics Sergei Chekinov and Sergei Bogdanov wrote a series of articles between 2010 and 2013 exploring ideas around traditional and non-traditional developments in war and warfare, including a focus on the use of psychological weapons.[32] Whilst elements of their work are speculative – they raise the possibility of weapons capable of causing earthquakes or typhoons – they stressed the centrality of information dominance in what they refer to as 'new-generation warfare', without which victory would not be possible.

Chekinov and Bogdanov said that future war would consist of powerful information technologies simultaneously engaging mass media and cultural and educational institutions, as well as undermining a nation's stability using social media.[33] Arguably, this is already happening; recent examples include the Russian Internet Research Agency's meddling during the 2016 US presidential election – and US security agencies were clear that Russia *did* interfere.[34] More generally, they predicted that prior to an outbreak of war, tools of 'information, moral, psychological, ideological, diplomatic, economic' effect would be utilised under an integrated, single plan.[35] The importance of non-military tools was stressed by Putin himself in 2012, when he described it as a complex of instruments and methods to achieve foreign-policy aims without the use of force.[36] Putin himself defines soft power as something void of force. According to Joseph Nye, 'Soft power is the ability to obtain preferred outcomes by attraction rather than coercion.'[37] In Russia, soft power is very much about manipulation. In the West, it is about the power of attraction. Indeed, Putin claimed that soft power had been used aggressively by the West to support 'extremism, separatism, nationalism, manipulation of public consciousness, direct interference in the internal affairs of sovereign states,' repeating the claims made by Gareyev and others.[38]

The question now is: are Putin's operations in the West – using tools such as sabotage, assassination and political corruption – a form of non-military conflict that might continue indefinitely, or are they shaping operations in the expectation of military violence – 'traditional' war – between Russia and NATO states? Or is it both? Does manipulation of Western politicians and narratives in Western states make traditional military conflict with Russia less likely as Russia feels it is better able to defend its interests by controlling our perception, or does it make Putin dangerous because his espionage networks will embolden him to take greater risks?

Turning to how Russians have conceptualised warfare in recent decades, Russia's former armed forces Chief of Staff General Yuri Baluyevsky and his colleague Colonel Musa Khamzatov argued in 2014 that the two decades of conflict between 1990 and 2010 should be framed as a battle of mass consciousness. The decade after 2010, they argued, ushered in a new form of conflict, which they described as wars of 'managed chaos'.[39] Turmoil was created for 'regime change' – remarkably similar to the KGB's political warfare in Moldova, Georgia and Ukraine. More recently, Ministry of Defence adviser Ilnitsky has developed the concept of 'mental war', designed to ensure 'a change in the civilizational basis of the enemy's society'.[40] This concept of mental war is more evidence of how identity and values in Russia have taken on an intense, almost existential nature. It reinforces the way in which the West is seen as 'a source of Russia's economic and political turmoil' and why Russia needs to find ways to defend itself, spiritually and militarily, against this alleged source of turmoil.[41]

Third, the role of violence itself in war. Some of the thinking around integrated warfare had been conceptualised in the early years of this century by Vladimir Kvachkov, a decorated officer and Soviet–Afghan War veteran. Kvachkov's primary work, *Special Forces of Russia*, was published in 2004. It predicted significant elements of recent Russian doctrine, despite predating it by a decade. NATO's *Handbook of Russian Information Warfare* credits Kvachkov's theory of special operations as the basis for Russian military instruction and training materials.[42] Kvachkov is well known in Russian ultra-nationalist circles after he was accused of attempting to assassinate senior politician Anatoly Chubais in March 2005. Kvachkov was found guilty and imprisoned but later acquitted. On his release, he was rearrested and later found guilty for his involvement in a bizarre *coup d'état* in the town of Ekaterinburg in the Ural.[43] Kvachkov denied the charges but defended the 'right of Russian citizens to hold an uprising'.[44] Despite – or perhaps because of – his alleged behaviour, Kvachkov nearly won election to Russia's

Parliament, twice coming second in constituency elections to the state Duma.

In *Special Forces of Russia*, Kvachkov argued for a decisive step change in our understanding of war. The post-war world, he said, had ushered in dramatic changes, including a transformation of the well-known laws of war.[45] He called for a new military art based on new principles. Kvachkov radically rejected the necessity of armed struggle as the core element of war. It had become counter-productive, almost restrictive. He argued it prevented 'the possibility of achieving decisive military and political goals … by … other forms of confrontation'. A more subtle application of influence, military or non-military, could result in a greater chance of the desired political outcome.

He argued that a new type of warfare was emerging, in which the armed struggle had 'yielded its decisive place in achieving the military and political goals of the war to another type of struggle – the information war'.[46] Russia's armed forces, he said, had failed to recognise these new forms of warfare. He argued that the true aim of war 'is not the defeat of the enemy's armed forces or the seizure of his territory, but the post-war peace'.[47]

He argued that various forms of struggle could be used to achieve military-political goals without the use of armed force or in conjunction with it. Therefore, to some extent at least, war could be waged *without* the violent aspects of war, certainly without large-scale military force. Kvachkov used the term 'war' to describe conflict by non-combat means. The means could be political, economic, information, scientific, technical, moral, cultural, demographic and environmental.[48] 'War' also covered non-military tools as well as military. In this definition of warfare, the 'war' comes from the intent to defeat an opponent, not necessarily in the use of traditional military force.

Kvachkov's ideas about the role of violence in war link strongly not only to current Russian doctrine, with its emphasis on 'integrated' impact, but also historic Russian military thinking. Soviet military theory of the 1920s and 1930s outlined the idea of 'deep operations'. Deep operations were originally defined as a complex series of continuous and linked operations using manoeuvrable forces, allowing an army not only to break through an enemy front or contact line but continue the offensive to the final victory. By linking to an earlier era, Kvachkov is redefining 'deep operations' for this century. They no longer necessarily include large-scale force, but critically, he reinterprets deep operations around the idea of striking psychological blows or targeting 'will'. This was evident in Russian targeting of Ukrainian cities and electricity supplies in 2024 to undermine the country's will to resist. It is also evident in the tools of political and informational warfare being used against NATO states or in political or business leaders co-opted, controlled and corrupted by Moscow, either in the West or in former Soviet republics.

Finally, he stressed scale. Size is not an indicator of special actions – the most important thing is their impact. In this, he echoes modern Western special forces theory, whereby actions by small groups of soldiers achieve disproportionate strategic effects. However, in Kvachkov's thinking, this disproportionate effect includes, and may even be dominated by, non-military tools of war – effectively a mix of physical with cyber or informational skills. This is a development considerably beyond Western special forces doctrine.

GAREYEV'S DEFINITION

During the course of the debate, conservatives had accepted the idea that multiple tools of struggle could be used against the West.

Gareyev agreed that warfare had changed and that non-military tools were more powerful, accepting that the 'ratio' of military to non-military means of struggle – political and diplomatic, economic, information, psychological – had 'changed significantly'.[49] He argued for a unified approach – a 'single purpose and concept of action'.[50] These integrated and interlinked tools could be used as a strategic deterrence, with the aim of blocking aggression against Russia.[51] Whilst this acceptance of the power of non-military tools may seem 'innovative' by Western standards, it sits in the tradition of Bolshevik political warfare and Soviet permanent struggle against the West.

What makes it different in this generation, however, is the greater level of integration, the new tools used by Russia, the focus on non-military tools within military doctrine and the focus on the mind as the ultimate battlefield. This new approach is also notable for its ideological flexibility, aligning with both the political hard left and the hard right, and the use of unscrupulous commercial structures and media influencers. Finally, another key difference is its level of complex creativity, which still manages to confuse the West's so-called experts.

Despite this new, innovative approach to conflict, conservative theorists have tended to argue for a clear delineation between 'war' and 'struggle' – i.e. between traditional forms of military violence and subversive political conflict. 'If the use of any non-military means in international confrontation is war, then all of the history of humanity is continuous war,' Gareyev said, 'and thus we do not know when the Hundred Years War was, the Russo-Japanese War, the First or Second World Wars.'[52] To prevent this, Gareyev distinguished between 'war' (*voina*) and 'struggle' (*bor'ba*) – the distinction I identified for readers at the start of the book. He argued that confrontation 'in any sphere' without weapons is struggle, whilst 'the continuation of political violence with other means, with the use of armed strength – that is war'.[53]

Whilst this definition creates a grey area with regards to paramilitary violence and the staging of coups – which the Russians and the Soviets excelled at – Gareyev argued that whilst traditional war is 'war', all else is not. The non-military tools he refers to fall under the definition of 'struggle'. Gareyev's insistence on a continued delineation helps to identify the two ways of war developed by Moscow in the twentieth century: the *war* of the Red Army and the *struggle* of the KGB and the Communist Party.

Gareyev's delineation is a valuable one – there needs to be a distinction between ideas of traditional military violence and the violent and non-violent tools of subversive conflict, even if we accept that they exist on an integrated spectrum. *War* and *struggle* represent complementary themes in conflict, which between them produce a unity of effort.

There have been gaps in the debate. The most important were in the evolution of political warfare or 'active measures', which will be covered in the following chapters, and the development of top-secret forms of psychological manipulation known as 'reflexive control' (*refleksivnoye upravleniye*), which help underpin Russian ideas of psychologically based warfare.

Reflexive control is a core part of the game of geostrategic chess played by the Soviets and now the Russians. It has been defined by Timothy Thomas as 'a means of conveying to a partner or an opponent specially prepared information to incline him to voluntarily make the predetermined decision desired by the initiator of the action'.[54] In plain English, it is the act of leading a target willingly into a trap. Writing in the 1980s, Diane Chotikul argued that something similar to reflexive control had been practised throughout the Soviet Union's history and was, post-Second World War, rooted in cybernetic theories developed in the 1950s.[55] Cybernetics is defined as the science of control and communications in animals and machines.[56] Reflexive control has been treated as a highly confidential subject by Russia, potentially due to its importance in formulating Soviet and now Russian strategies.[57] After the collapse of the Soviet Union, there was a temporary thawing in relations, with some modest amount of shared work on the subject. That openness did not last.

Soviet authors saw reflexive control as a form of perfected intelligence and one that, unlike most military intelligence, covered not only understanding of the physical terrain and enemy but also the psychological and cultural terrain.[58] Colonel S. A. Komov, a prolific Russian writer on information operations, described reflexive control as 'intellectual' information warfare, with techniques including information overload, conflicting information, distraction, provocations, military exercises as a cover for pre-planned operations, presenting false information to the enemy (*maskirovka*), creating divisions within enemy coalitions, creating threats real or otherwise to force the enemy to reassess its behaviours, provocation, and media pressure by discrediting an enemy government in the eyes of its own population.[59] However one defines reflexive control, there is overwhelming circumstantial evidence that its tactics are being used again, against both Ukraine and the West.

Writing on reflexive control has also generated more speculation, including the idea that the Russians might use 'psychotronic generators' to send powerful electromagnetic signals through telephone lines, TV and radio or develop equipment designed to damage the central nervous system.[60] Whilst some have yet to come to fruition, others may have. For example, an incident in Havana, Cuba, in 2017 that left two dozen US diplomats needing medical treatment has been variously linked to a biological virus,[61] sonic waves[62] or targeted microwave weapons.[63]

THE PUBLIC DEBATE IN RUSSIA

It is impossible to separate the military debate from the wider conversation in Russian society and the state-encouraged drift to virulent authoritarianism. First, nationalist figures have been influential in military circles, especially conservative ones. Second, the Slavophile romanticisation of the Russian communal identity and the Russian peasant is arguably reflected in beliefs about the stoicism of the Russian soldier, which in practice is leading to the mass slaughter of those soldiers, sent to their deaths at the point of a machine gun in the gruesome 'meat assaults'. Third, ideas around Russian spiritual identity and the need to defend it against the corruption of the West have become part of the security debate, as we have seen.

From the 1990s, Alexander Dugin, the son of a senior military officer and one of the most politically influential philosophers on this issue, gravitated from the 'lunatic fringe' of Russian politics, standing for the National Bolshevik Party in the 1995 Duma elections, to become a figure of influence.[64] This has especially been the case in military circles, where his identification of liberalism as the enemy and the need for a Russian crusade against the West found a receptive audience. He has also advised politicians from Putin's United Russia Party. In over thirty publications, Dugin has developed a critique of liberal democracy in tandem with Eurasian geopolitical theory, which sees the world shaped by geography and a fundamental clash between Russia and the West, with Russia as the land power and Rome, the US and Europe as the sea powers. Dugin has decried the liberalism and individual human rights agenda associated with these Western sea powers as an 'idiotic, anti-natural and perverted ideology'.[65] He called for a new fascist order and a reawakening of the Russian state and its peoples after a period of decadence. This resurrection, he believed, would come forged in crisis and conflict:

> Fascism – this is nationalism, yet not any nationalism but a revolutionary, rebellious, romantic, idealistic [form of nationalism] appealing to a great myth and transcendental idea, trying to put into practice the Impossible Dream, to give birth to a society of the hero and Superhuman, to change and transform the world.[66]

Like the Slavophiles 150 years before him, Dugin found the source of Russia's mystical power in the simple Russian and with it, the sense of humanity wrapped in the Russian soul: 'The Russian Ivan as an individual is nothing, but the most Russian thing in him is everything. The idea is everything, the stage is everything, but the individual is nothing.'[67] This sense of the communal wholeness over the individual is echoed on the left as well as the right. Former Russian Communist Party leader Gennady Zyuganov, in his 1995 book *Za Gorizontom* (Beyond the Horizon), argued against Western individualism, promoting instead the Russian concepts of the commune (*obshchina*) and spiritual communalism (*sobornost*).[68]

This emphasis on communalism reflects some implicit assumptions about the Russian soldier's ability to endure hardship more stoically than their Western equivalents and their ability to survive in conflict.[69] Their 'moral strength' was a decisive advantage, 'to be constantly defended'.[70] A persistent assumption in Russian military debate is that this Russian stoicism compensated for the technological superiority of the enemy and has resulted in an acceptance of much higher Russian casualties in warfare. The lazy assumption about the willingness to endure suffering has been questioned by reformers. Academic and strategist Kokoshin pointedly said that military studies should be focused on Russian commanders who minimised losses rather than those who accepted them.[71] However, given the staggering level of Russian casualties in the Russo-Ukraine War, with near 900,000 dead by March 2025, this is unlikely. The greater the slaughter and the greater the lie, the greater the need to justify it.

The idea of the spiritual uniqueness of Russia is an argument that has been promoted by President Vladimir Putin, echoing not only Dugin but Slavophiles throughout history. A Russian, according to Putin, is characterised by being focused not on themselves but on the greater good. They are marked by a 'higher moral principle' compared to Westerners, whose culture prioritises external, personal success.[72] In the Russian world, according to Putin, 'death is beautiful and to die for one's friends, one's people, the Fatherland, is beautiful.[73]

Bound up with Russia's identity as a great power is the concept of sovereignty. President Putin has argued that Russia is one of the few 'sovereign nations' on earth neither dependent on others nor under the leadership of others, saying that 'Russia will either be independent and sovereign or will most likely not exist at all'.[74] This determination to be seen as sovereign has two elements: to stress difference and separation from the West and to stress uniqueness. As Putin wrote in a 2012 newspaper article, Russia draws 'strong support from that mentality, culture and identity that are ours and ours alone'.[75]

This is reflected in events that took place in Russia from the 1990s. That battle was broadly similar to those that had been played out before at critical periods in Russia's history, as discussed: between Westernisers, who wanted broadly to align with the West and saw Russia's future as part of it, and Slavophiles, who defined Russian identity as a rejection of the West and its values. Westernisers – for a variety of possible reasons, including the deeply entrenched nature of Soviet authoritarianism and the historic weakness of the Westernising tradition compared to the Slavophile tradition – lost that struggle for power. But this process was not begun by Putin. The revanchist seeds were sown before the era of reforms known as perestroika failed, but they were certainly watered by events that took place in the 1990s: two failed coups in 1990 and 1993, flawed privatisation, rampant corruption, the hollowing out of institutions, the general discrediting of democracy and the First Chechen War.

From the late 1990s and early 2000s onwards, elements of the new authoritarian state took shape. Its purpose was not only to provide stability to a country that suffered external decline and internal chaos in the 1990s but also to stifle Western-style democracy, attempting to reimpose an authoritarian political system familiar to many Russians. The media was brought under direct state control or under its controlling influence, as were energy companies, ensuring that Putin could use Russian gas 'as a major factor in foreign policy decision-making'.[76] KGB allies were brought into key positions of power. In the words of one KGB historian, the Putin regime 'slowly and systematically extended the state's control over society and tightened its grip on Russia's most important institutions'.[77]

President Putin formed a close alliance with the Russian Orthodox Church, as Russian spiritual and moral values were politicised.[78] The Russian armed forces worked to restore a full spectrum of capabilities, including nuclear, conventional and unconventional forms of war.[79] As soon as Putin was given the role of Prime Minister in 1999, a series of apartment bombings in Moscow, Buynaksk and Volgodonsk shook Russia. More than 300 Russian citizens were killed and over a thousand injured. The attacks directly led to the Second Chechen War and also helped ensure Putin's election as President in 2000 with over 50 per cent of the vote. Former FSB agent Alexander Litvinenko, who was later assassinated in London on the orders of Putin, believed the bombings to be a provocation or false flag operation organised by the FSB, as did US journalist David Satter.[80] An attempt by Sergei Kovalev, former Soviet dissident and member of the Duma, to establish a commission to investigate the bombings failed after two of its members were assassinated and the commission's lawyer was imprisoned. The conclusion, they argue, is that Putin was brought to power with the aid of the FSB plot to kill hundreds of Russians to create conditions of fear and panic in society.

Putin's time in power has been marked by the hunt for enemies, internal and then external, enabling increased state control. Putin has presented the Russian state as one surrounded by enemies, leaning on the idea of Russia being a 'besieged fortress', an old and powerful trope in Russian identity and history.[81] Russia expert Lilia Shevtsova argued that without the creation of external enemies in particular, the post-Soviet political model of control could not survive.[82] 'The dismemberment of Ukraine,' she wrote in 2014, 'exposes the mechanism of the Russian matrix, in which foreign policy is the main instrument of domestic agenda.'[83] From the Second Chechen War to the Ukraine conflict, war has enabled and extended Putin's control of Russia and has enabled the recreation of authoritarian Russia.

THE OUTCOME OF THE SECURITY DEBATE

The outcome of Russia's security debate was, unsurprisingly given the leadership and direction of the country, a victory for conservatives. Beginning in 2006, President Putin embraced the defence establishment and intelligence agencies' evaluation of the threat to Russia, even though it was, according to US expert Stephen Blank, 'a grossly exaggerated and patently self-serving assessment that began with a presumption of conflict and Russia's isolation'.[84] Blank attributed the rise in defence spending from 2004 onwards to this heightened threat assessment. Russian doctrine that has been published since, but especially after 2010, reinforces this viewpoint. I include and discuss it here because it says, in black-and-white, what the Russian state thinks.

Whilst all relevant doctrines – military, information security and foreign policy – articulated a sense of worsening international tensions, the National Security Strategy – both the 2015 version and the updated 2021 edition – were the most aggressive of Russian state documents regarding identity, security and Russia's view of both the West and Ukraine.[85]

Turning to the 2015 iteration first, not only does it repeat the central criticisms of the West seen in previous doctrines, but it repeatedly accuses the US, the West, and the Western Alliance of being too quick to use force to solve international problems, of destabilising the world by developing new weapons systems, of threatening Russia's national security by building up forces on its borders and of reckless policies in Ukraine.[86] Russia is portrayed as a purely defensive actor, with its independent foreign policy and freedom of action being stifled by the Western alliance, which was trying to contain Russia using military and non-military means, including an 'entire spectrum' of non-military tools, backed by 'special services'.[87] Consciousness was being manipulated and history falsified. Russian spiritual and moral values were being eroded and were in need of defence. In the National Security Strategy, Russia describes itself as being in a global struggle, encompassing its political culture, language and territory, with the Western states. However, this time the proxy wars were being fought not in Africa or Asia but in Ukraine and, via the internet, in the hearts and minds of Russian citizens.

The 2021 iteration of the National Security Strategy contained more of the same. Whilst references to the conflict in Ukraine had been almost entirely erased, the sense of physical and psychological threat had, if anything, increased. This updated strategy accused Western states of attempting to 'strengthen their hegemony' amidst growing global instability.[88] It warned of the increasing danger of the use of force and aggravating tensions near Russia's borders and forewarned of the escalatory risks of nuclear powers engaging in proxy, localised conflicts that could become global flashpoints.[89] These threats around nuclear war have become significantly more pronounced since 2022.

In the 'battle' over values, the document said that the Western liberal model was in 'crisis'.[90] It presented Russia as being the victim of hostile information campaigns, of sanctions against its athletes and prohibitions against its language. A number of states, it said, were trying to 'purposefully erode traditional values, distort world history, revise views on the role and place of Russia in it, rehabilitate fascism and incite interethnic and interfaith conflicts'.[91]

The 2016 Information Security Doctrine echoed and confirmed the Russian sense of being under attack. Whilst much of the 38-article document shared the language of modern states discussing crime prevention and terrorism online, there was also clear focus on information security as something protecting not only the technical infrastructure of Russia but also its psychological stability. For example, the doctrine accused the 'special services of foreign states' of using informational-psychological influence to destabilise countries, politically and socially, throughout the world.[92] It claimed that states were using information technology 'for military-political ends', to undermine and subvert the sovereignty as well as the political and social stability of the Russian Federation and its allies.[93] Russia was the target of propaganda aimed at its population and 'in the first instance, at the young, with the aim of eroding the traditional Russian spiritual/morale values'.[94]

WHY DOCTRINE SAYS RUSSIA IS AT WAR

Military doctrine also explains why Putin believes his country is already in a state of conflict with the West. Russia's military doctrine lists two types of danger it believed Russia faces; military risks (*voyennaya opasnost*), and military threats (*voyennaya ugroza*). A 'military risk'* is defined as a state that, in combination with other factors, *could* lead to a situation of military threat. A 'military threat' is defined as the *real* possibility of the outbreak of conflict between opposing parties.[95] A military 'risk' is therefore less dangerous than a military 'threat', although if they accumulate, they could become a threat. The doctrine cites fourteen external risks, four internal risks and five military threats. Prior to 2022, many of these risks and threats could have been seen to be 'active', as interpreted by the Kremlin, due to the physical and psychological threat presented by

* The official Russian translation uses the word 'risk', although it is also often translated as 'danger'. This book will accept the official Russian translation and use the world 'risk'.

the West. After 2022 and given the near hysterical mindset of the Russian regime, almost all of the risks and threats have, in their eyes, been triggered. This is why the Russian regime presents itself as being in conflict with NATO in Ukraine, because, according to its doctrine, it is.

Risk one is the expansion of NATO. This is clearly happening and it is happening on Russia's borders, with NATO having taken in Finland and Sweden. Ukraine, which Russia believes is an integral part of its world, also wishes to join NATO. Risk two is destabilising individual states. Whilst Western governments see Russia's war as a hugely destabilising action, Putin claims he is acting to prevent his adversaries destabilising Russia – i.e. 'switching' Ukraine to the Western camp. The Kremlin claims that risk three, the deploying of forces, is also underway, with NATO forces on its borders and also in Ukraine. Risk four, the creation of a strategic missile defence system, does not name the US per se but cannot be aimed at any other country. Indeed, given Russian bombing of Ukrainian cities, NATO states will only be keener to develop a missile defence system. Germany and Poland are both developing an air shield. Risk eight, military force in states next to Russia, and nine, conflict in states next to Russia, are also clearly happening.

That Russia's leaders may have brought this and much else on themselves is again not relevant. This is not *our* judgement call but theirs. The Russian regime is one which carries a sense of victimhood and aggressive entitlement.

In addition to the physical threat, these risks speak to the regime's fears of being a target of subversive, indirect warfare. This book shows repeated evidence that the Russian leadership believes that these risks and threats are live and not merely theoretical. Their existence reinforces my argument that Russia's security elites believe in the effectiveness of psychological and informational tools and therefore in their *critical* importance in modern warfare. Out of the five threats, at least three could, going by Russian interpretations, be in play. There has clearly been a drastic aggravation of the military-political situation (threat one), whilst Ukraine has attacked Russian chemical and oil facilities (part of threat two). Finally, there has been an increase in NATO activity, with some initial preparatory steps, in countries such as Finland and Sweden, for defensive mobilisation (threat five). There has also clearly been an intensification of military activity in Western states, brought on by the Ukraine War.

So, regardless of how Western nations interpret this in both the physical and psychological arenas, almost all the 'risks' and several of the 'threats' outlined in their own doctrine are, in the Russian mindset, now flashing red. The Kremlin believes it is in conflict with NATO because by its own interpretation of its own doctrine, it is.

GERASIMOV'S BLESSING

If the start of this debate was heralded by the collapse of the Soviet Union, the ending was signalled in an article by Russian Chief of Staff Valeri Gerasimov titled 'The Aim of Science in Prediction' and published in the newspaper *Voyenno-Promyshlennyy Kuryer* (*Military-Industrial Courier*) in early 2013. In the article, he explains the doctrine to his troops.

Gerasimov, echoing Kvachkov and others, argued that there had been a blurring of the lines between war and peace and that the rules of war had changed.[96] He additionally posed a question. He asked why soldiers should be interested in the Arab Spring – the series of uprisings against authoritarian governments, which was ongoing at the time in the Middle East – which superficially had little to do with traditional warfare? 'It is easiest to say that the events of the Arab Spring are not war and therefore, as soldiers, there is nothing to learn,' Gerasimov said. 'But maybe the opposite, it is precisely these events which are the typical wars of the twenty-first century.'[97] These new 'wars' showed, he said, how non-military tools of conflict were now, in some ways, more powerful than traditional military force.

Gerasimov dismissed, for practical intents, a hard delineation between war and struggle, implying that difference had become irrelevant. He argued that if this century's ubiquitous form of war *was* indirect operations such as colour revolutions, Arab Springs etc., then the Russian military has no option but to engage with this, regardless of whether soldiers believe it to be 'war' or not. This way of war 'cannot be considered exclusively military,' he argued.[98] That point is worth stressing. He accepted that the conventional military force may only have a supporting role in modern war, implying that war may no longer consist predominantly of a violent clash of wills – more evidence that Russian thinking appears to be bending, if not breaking, with Clausewitz insistence that warfare is a fundamentally organised, violent act. From that perspective, Russian thinking has been revolutionary and, in its practical doctrinal, years ahead of the West. Again, it is worth stressing that Russia's new theory of war did not preclude using traditional military force, as it was to do in 2022, but it did mean that war and conflict used an integrated mix of the two.

So, from the initial faltering steps in the 1990s to the intense debates in security circles in the 2000s, by 2013, on the eve of the invasion of Ukraine, Russia had finalised a new integrated theory of conflict. It was and still is a work in progress. As we will see, the Kremlin had been putting elements of that theory into practice in

Ukraine since 2005 and reforming its army after the short 2008 war in Georgia. But the key elements of the new Russia were coming together. The message that Gerasimov sent to his armed forces was that the Russian Army needed to be ready for and understand non-military forms of conflict, as well as ideas of traditional war, and be willing to find novel solutions against its foes.

CHAPTER 7

STORIES FROM THE FRONT: SARMAT, THE EASTERN FRONT AND RUSSIAN PRISONERS OF WAR

'The 300s [the injured] were stinking.
They smelt like they were rotting alive.'
– Russian prisoner of war Zayats

'We have a saying: "F*ck up and you're already dead,"' call sign Kos explained to me.[1]

Kos, two of his comrades and I are sitting in a makeshift but highly effective *banya* (sauna) in their rear headquarters, between the eastern Ukraine town of Kramatorsk and the frontline 'drone zone'. A DIY sauna off the front line is the oddest place I have ever interviewed in.

I am here to listen to Kos and his men in order to understand the trials of the infantry soldier. Kos is a company commander – he has perhaps 100 soldiers under him – in Sarmat, a unit that is part of the 56th Motorized Infantry Brigade. The name is taken from that of the Sarmatians, an ancient Black Sea tribe. In Ukraine, captains tend to command at this level, not the more senior rank of major as would happen in the West. It's a traditional infantry unit, with armoured personnel carriers to help troops get around the battlefield.

Apart from one month away from the front line, Sarmat has been fighting the Russians every day since the 2022 invasion, whether that's exchanging mortar fire, drone strikes or repelling 'meat assaults'. They have been in at least 1,000 'contacts' (battles) with the enemy. At just twenty-six, Kos himself is the survivor of over a hundred 'contacts'.

'Something falls on our position every day – drone, artillery, mortar, grenade launchers. We are always in the sh*t,' he laughs. Kos's dark humour and that of those around him is evident. The unit's military honours cover several of the more intense battles in eastern Ukraine. With a sense of irony, he explains how he always seemed to foresee where Sarmat would be sent next.

'I'll be sitting, wondering, hmm, I've heard that Vuhledar [a battle in eastern Ukraine] is really hot right now and BAM, a month later we'll be there. Then, I will be wondering what Wagner are doing in Bakhmut and how tough they are? Then, f*ck, a month later, we're there.' He rattles off his words in both Ukrainian and Russian, the latter especially when he is swearing. But the battle in the town of Pisky, he said, near the old front line just on the outskirts of Donetsk, was perhaps the worst battle he had ever faced. Some 6,000 Russian shells landed on 2 square kilometres of land.

Sarmat is a unit that roots itself in Ukraine's Cossack past. Kos is sitting underneath the unit's flag. On it is in the inscription, in Ukrainian and Latin, 'Through Me Flows Cossack Blood' and a skull wearing a military headset. The red and black was the emblem of the Ukrainian Partisan Army and is an example of the contested and bloody history of these lands. On the eve of the Second World War, Nazi Germany and the Soviet Union signed the Molotov–Ribbentrop Pact, agreeing the partition of Poland and the Baltic republics between them. The Soviet Union invaded Poland in September 1939, where there was a large ethnic Ukrainian population, and they began to impose violent communist rule. When the Nazis then invaded the Soviet Union in June 1941, the Ukrainian Partisan Army initially sided with Nazi Germany before later fighting both the Nazis and the Soviets, as well as Polish partisans. In Soviet days, possession of the flag was enough to get you arrested by secret police. Since 1991, the flag has been rehabilitated and, in Ukraine at least, now represents mainstream Ukrainian nationalism. For Putin's regime, however, the Ukrainian Partisan Army and its leader, Stepan Bandera, represent Ukrainian treachery and fascism – however ironic that sounds given the xenophobic nationalism of his government.

I had first met Kos in Kyiv the week before. He and his wife 'Nataliya' are both young officers in frontline roles. Out of uniform, they look like a fashionable couple. She is an elegant young intellectual. Kos, with his shaven head, beard and well-shaped, precise moustache with upturned corners, reminds me of a young Hercule Poirot, Agatha Christie's famous detective.

A week later, he invited me to Sarmat's rear base near Kramatorsk. Our *banya* and the location is out of range of the small kamikaze FPV drones that crowd the skies. Many units have their operations rooms in the town. Whilst we're safe from kamikaze drones here, the town is regularly hit with missiles, and, as in Kharkiv, the sirens are constant. There are occasional casualties, and should Russian collaborators identify times and places where people congregate, the outcomes can be deadly. Strikes on Kramatorsk Station and a restaurant have both produced mass casualties, with seventy-six dead and 200 injured across both attacks.

For people coming from Kyiv, Kramatorsk feels like a frontline city. Every second vehicle is a camouflaged pick-up truck or armoured vehicle moving at speed. However, for soldiers coming from the front, our base and Kramatorsk itself offer a haven of relative tranquillity. During their rotation and brief rest, Kos's lads sweat in the *banya*, drink alcohol-free beer and get thwacked by a *venik* (a bunch of branches tied together), which increases the heat of the sauna and improves circulation. A colleague of Kos's apologises that they have an oak-leaf *venik*, not the traditional birch. The regiment has standards, after all.

Kos shows me round his collection of buildings. It's basic and at times ramshackle, but he's proud of how he's looking after his men. There is a billiards room, a small food hall and, of course, the *banya*, heated by vast pots of water cooked on an ageing concrete and plaster stove built into the interior walls. There is also a chapel. Icons and religious artefacts have become commonplace. The unit has a chaplain, Father Vyacheslav from Vinnytsia in the centre-west of Ukraine, who, with his fine beard, looks every inch an Orthodox priest. He worries about Russian psychological operations targeting frontline troops on the internet using gambling and other apps, saying, 'Our enemy is doing everything to break our will.' However, he also gives thanks for the determination of Ukrainian troops. 'Soldiers tell me they were in situations where they were not supposed to live. But they keep believing and they tell me, "Something saved me; it was God because there was no other way for me to survive."'[2]

Kos's task has been to hold the line. Since 2023, fighting has been increasingly static but attritional. Sarmat has conducted a few assaults, but for the most part their role is to survive daily artillery barrages, repel assaults and rotate troops in and out of position. 'That's the most difficult thing right now,' says Kos, due to kamikaze drones prowling for targets.

To protect themselves, they are adapting tactics and the kit itself. They have fitted additional protection to the armoured vehicles, such as the side bars that US and NATO armour was equipped with in Afghanistan, as well as additional protection on the tops of vehicles – normally the weak point. Call sign Svarshchik (welder) shows me his own design for what looks like well-fitted chicken-coop caging around APCs. 'It works, we've tested it in battle,' he says, showing me a video of the vehicle surviving a hit from a Russian kamikaze FPV drone.[3]

The troops' APCs are hidden beneath camouflage netting and thinning tree canopies in the woods around the base. We walk carefully around them. Three of them are *trophinii* (trophy kit), captured and now used against the enemy. Their medic's quad bike is fitted with an angled seat for a casualty and thick rubber matting around the engine casing to give basic protection against 'petals', the small anti-personnel mines scattered around the battlefield. As we walk through the wood, jets fly overhead. I hit the deck, assuming a Russian bombing raid and bracing myself for an impact. They belly laugh and shout *nashi!* (They are ours!) I get up sheepishly.

• • •

The front is an intensely lethal battlefield, catastrophically so on the Russian side, where soldiers are driven to their deaths at the point of a gun. To understand the brutal experiences of a Russian meat-assault soldier, I talk to a prisoner of war who has agreed to chat.

Russian call sign Zayats experienced two months of cruelty before he was taken captive.[4] He now run errands around Sarmat's headquarters and makes himself useful by manning Sarmat's *banya*. His call sign means hare, as in the animal. Given Zayats's short legs, I assume Russian irony hasn't died yet.

Zayats was a bit of a boozer. A thirty-year-old from Bashkortostan, an ethnically Muslim area in the Ural Mountains, he was harmless when sober but a thief when drunk. He was in jail serving an eight-year sentence for theft in penal colony no. 7, in Ufa, a city just over 700 miles (1,150 km) east of Moscow, when army recruiters showed up on 29 June 2024. They offered 125,000 roubles ($1,400) for signing up and a pay cheque of 204,000 roubles ($2,300) a month – a lot of money in Ufa. Zayats, who hadn't been following the war, thought, 'I can either stay here or get out.'

'They were asking for specialist mechanics and drivers. I signed up as a mechanic,' he explained. He was given a bank account, a bank card and a pin code.

Two days later, he was on an Il-76 military cargo plane heading for Rostov-on-Don, the city out of which much of the war is being run. As soon as they landed, the bank card that gave access to his bonus was taken from him. 'You won't be needing this for the moment,' he was ominously told. He and the other recruits were lined up in the baking sun, still in the clothes they had been imprisoned in – flip-flops, trainers, tracksuits and the like. A soldier addressed them bluntly: 'No one forced you to come here. From now on, you are all assault troops.'

'I was in shock. I thought, "What the hell is going on?"' said Zayats.

Over the next twenty-one days they were repetitively drilled by black African trainers, most probably Congolese employed by the infamous Russian Wagner mercenary group. Zayats was told he was to be a medic, despite the fact that, in his own words, 'I didn't know anything about it.' The conscripts slept in mud 'coffins' cut into the sides of trenches. Woken at 2 a.m., they were marched 5 miles (8 kilometres) for breakfast and then back again for supper. 'Every day was the same: assault the trenches. All day, every day.' Three weeks later, the conscripts were moved forward to the village of Druzhba in Russian-occupied eastern Ukraine, where they were billeted in abandoned private houses. A local volunteer with a stutter brought on by shell shock gave them navigation lessons in nearby woods.

Zayats was mulling an escape but was put off by the fate of one soldier who had tried to do so a few days earlier, with brutal consequences. Recaptured, the soldier was dragged back, trussed up and held in the basement of a bomb-damaged hospital. Zayats and his cohort were ordered to the basement to witness the punishment. It was a scene from hell. The pitiful figure of the escapee faced them with his handcuffed hands above his head. On the other side of the darkened space were groaning, injured servicemen being treated by 'medics' no more qualified than Zayats. They were rebandaging infected, pustulant wounds but doing little else. The '300s', as Zayats referred to the wounded, 'were stinking. They smelt like they were rotting alive.'

Ahead of him, two instructors – one of which he believed to be an ex-Wagner mercenary, with the call sign Relax – began to beat the escapee to death, cracking him around the head with a pair of garden shovels, slowly at first before reaching a crescendo of blood-splattered violence. As he was hit, the dying man screamed for water. Zayats watched in horror as the two soldiers bludgeoned their victim. The following morning, when a hole in the ceiling brought more light into the basement, they cut down his blue-grey bloated body.

'I was in shock. I kept on thinking, "This is unbearable; how the hell can I get out of here?"' Zayats recalls.

In the following days, the troops were split into groups of five and taken to different positions and then into battle. Zayats and his cohort patrolled into a town past burnt-out houses. In the distance, they heard the sound of Ukrainian drones. Moments later, bombs were falling around them. The squad leader, call sign Hog, ordered the men to get to cover. Zayats dropped his weapon and instinctively started to run.

He remembers Hog shouting 'Zayats! Zayats!' and then the fizzle and crack of rounds around his head. He was shot above the collarbone but kept on running. 'I didn't know where I was running. I had an idea I was running towards bigger buildings and people. Most importantly, I was just surviving.'

Zayats kept moving for the rest of the day. He remembers crossing a railway line and then another burnt-out village. He changed out of his uniform for civilian clothes he found in abandoned homes. 'I hid in basements for more than a week, sleeping in cellars. My wound was smelling and bleeding. I ate pickled food I found in the basements.

'I ran at first and then I walked. I thought they were going to come after me,' he said, referring to his fellow recruits. On 29 September, out in the open countryside, he was making his way along a thick tree line when he heard first one generator and then another. A drone buzzed above him. Suddenly, three Ukrainian soldiers appeared, weapons pointing at him. 'I'm a 300 [injured]!' he shouted, putting his hands in the air. He carefully removed his shirt to show his wound. The Ukrainians treated him and took him in as a prisoner of war (PoW).

During our conversation, Zayats told me that he and his fellow conscripts were instructed to keep a grenade or last bullet for themselves. It seems to be common for Russian soldiers to be told not to be taken alive. I asked a Ukrainian interrogator, who has asked not to be named, why this was. 'They're convinced that they're going to be tortured by Ukrainians,' she told me. 'And if they're going to be exchanged, they *know* they're going to be tortured by the Russians back at home. So when somebody is captured, they are feeling pretty down.'[5]

On a human level, it's difficult not to feel sorry for people like Zayats, who haplessly find themselves effectively sentenced to death by their own state and driven to their deaths like slaves for a few extra feet of land. Those PoWs, the interrogator said, know they have been lied to. 'They've been told, "Oh you're going to serve somewhere in this border region or you're just going to protect some objects" – and then they are sent into the meat grinder.'

PoWs are important for Ukrainians because they give them some leverage over the Russians, even when the Russian Army care little for their PoWs. The day after we leave, our SBU contact rings to let us know they have taken five more PoWs. Common themes emerge. Some come from families who didn't support the war but need money. Others were pushed into 'serving' Russia by their families, sometimes for patriotic reasons, sometimes for the payout when they inevitably die.

'They don't want to go back to the families that send them to fight in the first place,' said the interrogator.

'They send them to die here for the money?' I ask.

'Yes, or if the father is a pensioner, he might say, "It is your f*cking duty to go and serve your country."' They believe, she said, the propaganda on Russian TV. Their attitude, she added, was 'How many f*cking Ukrainians have you killed today?'

Of those that come before Ukrainian interrogators, many, like Zayats, don't want to return home. They know they face jail for twelve years as deserters or being sent straight back to the front. About 60 per cent beg not to be exchanged, 30 per cent want to go home but 'promise' not to fight again and 10 per cent are Putin's loyal subjects.

'The 10 per cent are the guys who look you in the eye and say, "We came to fight Zelensky because Zelensky sold you to [Emmanuel] Macron, sold you to Europe, to European leaders,"' she said. 'They say, "He's already signed the contract that Ukraine now belongs to NATO and to the European Union." The 10 per cent, they believe, and they say, "If we'll be in the exchange, we'll come back because we are fighting for you guys. We are trying to set you free."'

The interrogator rolled her eyeballs.

As for Zayats, he was waiting to hear his fate – whether he will be allowed to stay in Ukraine or not – and figuring out his future. 'I don't want to go back, that's for sure. I could never kill anything,' he says earnestly, recollecting a time in his childhood when his older brother beat him when he refused to kill a chicken. 'As soon as I tried to cut the chicken's throat, I realised I couldn't.'

• • •

Whilst these forced Russian conscripts may be lied to or cheated, the bitter reality is that their presence in Putin's war machine is killing Ukrainians. Whilst the ratio of Russian to Ukrainian dead is high, perhaps ten to one, the Ukrainians too have many fatalities. It's not something that is talked about publicly, but I ask Kos how they survive given the extended time on the front line, which can seem an open-ended deployment that can all too easily end in injury or death.

'It's a complicated discussion,' he says. 'Basically, each trooper, each soldier, is surrounded by his brothers in arms, but being infantry, we are well aware that it [death] can happen to any of us any moment, any day. So right now, you can be alive and something just explodes and you're gone in a second. The soldiers who've been fighting a long time, they somehow – it's a very individual thing – but they adjust. They rewire their basic mentality to get used to it.'

Understandably, he doesn't dwell on it. The important thing, he says, is to learn from mistakes. He reckons 85 per cent of casualties are down to human error. 'We are all going to be there anyway,' he says, looking up towards the heavens, 'but every time a brother in arms dies, we need to analyse, we need to learn. How and why did this happen? Was it a mistake of some sort or was it because a projectile can just fly in from somewhere and it's just not your day?'

There is an old Soviet Army-era role: an ideological commissioner or *politruk*. They were responsible for the political education of the unit they were assigned to. In Ukraine's army today, this role has changed from mind control to mind support. It's now called an MPZ (*Moral'no-Psykholohichne Zabezpechennya*, which translates to moral-psychological support), reflecting the change to a focus on the well-being of soldiers rather than enforcing party or state propaganda. This is part of an overhaul of the mental and spiritual support chain within the army. However, if a soldier is struggling – or 'swimming', in Kos's words – the best remedy is often to pair him with those who've been at the front the longest. 'We'll just sit him down with older soldiers. "Son, sit with us, talk, what's on your mind? Have a cigarette." Stuff like that.'

'For us, we care about every person, every soldier we have. If you are losing one, it's a big loss for the whole unit. For the Russians, losing tens is just nothing,' said call sign Schumacher, who is the company's NPZ.[6] We are sitting in the rear headquarters, in a small, single-room dacha. It's a cold day outside, with few leaves left on the trees and a sharp wind, but it's warm inside. There's an ageing metal wood burner in the corner, a table covered with plastic sheeting for brewing coffee and tea and another with a bench on two sides. On the other side of the room is the normal rigmarole of a company office: battered laptops on a trestle table, maps on the walls in front of them, hand-written notes and sheets of telephone numbers on clipboards.

Schumacher warms to his theme: 'They can lose seventy, eighty men on one small piece of the front line and they don't care. They will bring another seventy, eighty tomorrow. They have no regard. They don't care how many people they lose.' He pauses and thinks about what he has just said and the relentless pressure on the Ukrainian lines. To break the silence, Kos makes a joke when I ask Schumacher's age. He is forty-two. 'You're not getting any younger, but you're running as a young one,' Kos jokes. Schumacher replies, 'I look in the mirror and see what's left of me. I want to cry and go to bed.' The team laugh at the banter, but the tiredness of these men is as visible as the bags underneath their eyes.

Schumacher turns to the problem of supply. 'Even before Putin, Russia never stopped producing ammunition. They can afford to send one drone per fighter. They can use two mortars against one fighter. The amount of stuff they have, it's virtually unlimited.' Since Russia has scaled up drone production, Schumacher says, 'the amount of the drones they have, it's through the roof'.

The changing nature of the violent element of this conflict raises questions about the usefulness of some NATO doctrine and training. One of Kos's colleagues, who asks not to be named, tells me, 'We can't fight as NATO fights because NATO have never fought a war like this.' He has a point. NATO has, certainly in practice, air superiority and technological dominance, but it's a generation behind in infantry tactics thanks to the drones now being used en masse at infantry level.

Of the NATO training courses, he said, 'They are trained to choose the right angles, the right positions, to storm buildings. Great, but we just chuck in six grenades. Choosing the right angles is useful for shooting terrorists in an airport, not Russians.'

There is also a sense of frustration that those traditional units that have weathered the Russian storm the most may not have had access to NATO training. It would, Kos says, have been good to improve skills, but for the infantry that has already been in the fight, not for green, 'unshelled' soldiers, to use Ukrainian parlance. 'Trained by European *Spetsnaz* [special forces] – great! But coming back as tough guys with no experience of actual combat? People die because of that. Guys already fighting would be eager to learn to survive better, but for green guys it's sh*t.'

Drones have created a new layer of lethality on the battlefield, over and above highly accurate artillery. Effectively every infantry unit is now a drone unit because the drone is now part of the infantryman's arsenal. Even a traditional unit such as Sarmat is producing drones for ISTAR tasks in their tech workshop, and they have land drones to supply frontline positions too. The drone technician is as common now in Ukrainian infantry units as the vehicle mechanic. Even SBU and HUR have their own drone units.

'Drones broke the status quo,' call sign Khersonets said, negating the individual skills and even the *esprit de corps* of a unit. 'The tank is a pile of steaming metal, the mortar is just dead crew, so is artillery – but the Lancet [a Russian kamikaze drone] can reach many kilometres. If you don't have proper electronic warfare, it's irrelevant how tough you are. You can be special forces or something, but any $400 drone will mince you.'[7]

Khersonets is a lanky, weathered-looking 36-year-old, with deep bags under his eyes, from the Ukrainian city of Kherson. He's a character well known to soldiers. Weary, cynical but grumpily proud, dismissive of anything out of his purview, suspicious of the generals who give the troops their orders. The kit is never enough, his first team was the best and most of his sentences are generously littered with a rich array of profanities – and in Russian and Ukrainian there are many more profanities to choose from than in English. Khersonets is the voice of the infantry sergeant the world over.

He fought in 2014 and 2015 and again from 2022 onwards. In 2015, he was in a coma for two weeks when a 120 mm mortar round hit the wall he was sheltering behind. Comparing fighting now with fighting in 2014, the quality of the soldier, he says, counted for more in 2014. Those fighting were heavily motivated. Russian artillery was lethal but lacked the precision of drones. 'I could bet anything that my guys could decimate any other company, have a smoke and move on.' Fighting through Russian positions for the best part of a year, he lost three out of twenty-six of his men. Most were injured but would return after treatment. 'We gave the Russians hell. Men were so concussed they could not pick up a bottle of water, but we stood our ground – that's motivation.' They assaulted positions in -16 degree temperatures and were sleeping back to back in basements to stop themselves from freezing. Of the command back then, he says, 'In the morning, no one gave a f*ck about us, and in the evening, no one gave a f*ck about us even more.'

Like most infantrymen, Khersonets is cynical about those considered 'special'. He remembers one attack in Svitlordars'k in 2015. A special forces company in modern Cossack armoured vehicles – or as Khersonets describes them, 'real f*cking robo cops' – arrived to storm a Russian position in the forest. Rather than reach the target on foot, they drove in. 'The furthest any of the Cossack [vehicles] got was 500 meters; everything else was f*cked.' He continues: 'We took the vehicles, cleaned out the bodies and finished the job the next day. My old commander – he's dead now – he said, "Having balls doesn't making you ballsy."'

CHAPTER 8

INVENTING RUSSIA'S NEW WAY OF WAR: CHARACTERISTICS, TACTICS AND TOOLS

'It is the unification of everything. The means of struggle, and the means of armed struggle, into a single whole.'

– Senior Ukrainian military intelligence officer, describing Russia's new way of war[1]

In the last two decades, the Kremlin has used an astonishing variety of tools in its conflict against Ukraine, the West and its allies: from nurturing pro-Russian fifth columns in former Soviet republics to information operations designed to disrupt US and European elections to two invasions of Ukraine, as well as attempted coups, cyberattacks and assassinations in Ukraine and Europe. Priests are used as military 'spotters' for Russian missiles, whilst the Russian Orthodox Church has declared holy war on Ukraine. Putin's missiles destroy Ukraine's energy system to target the civilian will to resist, whilst the Russian state abducts children from occupied Ukrainian territories in order to reprogramme their minds.

The tactics and tools of Russian conflict are physical and psychological. Conflict takes place in the trenches of eastern and southern Ukraine, in bombed cities across the country and in the minds of the Kremlin's targets in Ukraine and the West. Russia's new way of war is, according to Steve Abrams, 'limited only by the imagination' and includes anything from the traditional concepts of war to the subversive tactics of 'propaganda, kidnapping, murder, drug trafficking and the illicit support of terrorism.'[2] Above all, conflict is all-encompassing. As one Ukrainian, religious scholar Liudmyla Fylypovych, told me, 'War is everywhere, and most importantly, it is in our heads and in our souls.'[3]

In this chapter, I am going to return to doctrine to show what the Russian state believes the characteristics of modern warfare are and the tactics and tools it is using. However, although doctrine provides a strong guide, it does not reveal all the detail. For that, we need to carry out a detective hunt, cross-checking evidence from individuals, soldiers and members of the secret agencies, as well as politicians and academics.

The current Russian military doctrine, published in December 2014, is the third iteration since 1999.[4] It identifies ten 'characteristics of contemporary military conflict'. The first overarching characteristic is the integration of military and non-military tools. The doctrine refers to this as the 'integrated use of military force, political, economic, informational and other measures of a non-military character, implemented with the extensive use of protest potential of the population and special operations forces'.[5]

This is the key statement of Russian understanding of modern military conflict. It is 'integrated' and it combines military and non-military measures *within* military doctrine, i.e. as a part of conflict and the overall military struggle. From there flow nine further characteristics. They also reflect the thawing of the distinction between traditional war and other forms of conflict, through Russia's use of 'active measures' – subversive, political warfare, in other words. Two of the ten characteristics speak to both 'types' of war, four speak to the tradition of conventional war (*voina*) and four to subversive war (*bor'ba*). Traditional concepts of war and non-military forms of struggle are given the same importance. Thus, staging political rallies, establishing violent protest groups or organising assassinations now hold the same weight in Russian theory of conflict as drones and cruise missiles. What works, works.

A senior Ukrainian HUR official explained to me the idea behind Russia's 'whole-state' conflict. It was, he said, 'the unification of everything. The [combination of the] means of struggle or confrontation and the means of armed struggle into a single whole.'[6]

Over and above integration, the second joint characteristic is unity of action. Whilst this characteristic is common in military theory, it is arguably given greater importance in Russian military doctrine because of the flexible and integrated nature of Russian war and the linking of action with political outcome, regardless of the tools and tactics used.

The four characteristics of modern conventional war highlighted within Russian doctrine are the use of high-precision weaponry, the high speed of destruction and manoeuvrability of troops, the shrinking of decision-making time and a networked system of control. It effectively describes high-tech, networked war, where information quickly shared around the battlefield feeds quick decision-making and high-precision strikes. These characteristics are not only part of the general debate over the changing nature of warfare but also draw from military theoretician Slipchenko's work in the 1990s, based on the Iraq and Yugoslav wars. They are the chief lessons drawn by the Russian General Staff and Military Academy in their analysis of 'contactless', sixth-generation warfare. They are not particularly original findings and in all of them, Russia has been playing catch-up with NATO and especially the US. Only in the use of high-precision weapons are they beginning to come anywhere near Western power.

Next are the four characteristics of subversive, indirect and unconventional conflict, which were most notable in the Ukraine conflict prior to 2022 but remain important even after the full-scale invasion. Characteristic seven is the creation of conflict zones on the territory of warring parties – fanning political instability and organising conflict in countries that Russia wishes to pressure. Ukraine, Moldova and Georgia are all examples. Characteristic eight is the use of irregular forces in modern conflict, be they organised crime, separatists or mercenary forces. Characteristic nine references the use of indirect war. This covers not only Russia's development of tactics to counter forms of indirect war, including the perceived threat from colour revolutions, but also the indirect tactics it has used in Ukraine and against the West.[7] Characteristic ten notes the use of foreign-financed political and social groups, ranging from cultural, religious and history groups in former Soviet republics – the real aims of which have been to act as fronts for Russian influence – to the direct or indirect funding and support given to groups or individuals in Europe and North America.

THE UNSTATED CHARACTERISTICS

There are also several unstated characteristics, which are just as important in understanding the Russian form of total war but do not feature overtly in their doctrine.

Whilst integration of various tools is explicitly stated as the first characteristic of modern conflict, the implicit reason for this is the need to use Russia's declining power efficiently, especially given its ambitious agenda. If aims can be achieved without military violence, so much the better – as a result, Russia is agnostic about the tools it uses. Political warfare can be cheaper and more effective than military force. There is less economic cost and often less diplomatic and political cost too.

In light of British strategist Lawrence Freedman's assertion that strategy is the art of creating power,[8] Russia's new way of war helps the Kremlin create power by giving it a wider variety of tools to use than most states and hence more options at its disposal, especially when these tools are used together in an integrated way.

The recognition of efficiency as a core characteristic of Russia's new way of war explains the Kremlin's preference for non-military tools in the first phase of the Ukraine conflict (2005–13). Only when Russia had lost control of the political situation in early 2014 with the collapse of Ukraine's pro-Russian government led by Viktor Yanukovych did Putin choose to escalate by annexing the Crimea and launching a serious of controlled 'separatist' paramilitary uprisings in southern and eastern Ukraine, in which 10,000 Russian troops were eventually used. Then, only when the 'paramilitary' strategy failed to pull Ukraine back within Russia's sphere of influence did Putin choose to escalate again in 2022 with a larger invasion. Putin opted for that high-risk option only when he had run out of patience with other choices. Only if this strategy fails will Russia escalate again, potentially to the use of nuclear weapons.

Integration and efficiency presuppose other characteristics. A key one is synergy. Ukrainian think tank director Mykola Sunhurovskyi told me how the Russians create synergy by using multiple elements of war, which together produce 'a combined effect greater than the sum of their separate effects'.* The advantages, Sunhurovskyi said, 'are in surprise, in uncertainty, in asymmetry.'[9] So, one of the benefits of Putin's new way of war is that the tools used, when combined, become greater than the sum of their parts – or at least have the potential to do so. This then delivers a complex conflict that overwhelms adversaries because it is fought on so many fronts, a modern blitzkrieg with speed and surprise integrated across all domains – physical, virtual and psychological – creating confusion, disorientating perception and damaging decision-making.

A number of other Ukrainians I spoke to focused on the tactic of subversion. Yevhen Fedchenko, founder of the StopFake website, designed to expose Russian fake news, commented on the 'fusion of different means'.[10] By this he means the use by Russia of political parties with openly subversive, pro-Russian agendas, backed by oligarchs who were 'cut-outs' for Russian secret agencies. In this subversive form of warfare, think tank head Mykhailo Honchar noted, external aggression is minimised whilst internal decay is maximised.[11]

In the run-up to 2014, inner decay was nearly fatal to Ukraine's ability to defend itself. Prior to the 2022 invasion, infiltration of Ukraine's secret agencies and political parties, whilst not on the same scale as what took place before 2014, was highly damaging nevertheless, especially in the south of the country. In the West today, internal divisions, magnified on social media, are helping to fracture societies. Whilst the causes may not be the fault of Russia or Russian agents, divisions and vulnerabilities within societies, especially around multiculturalism, race and identity politics, are being ruthlessly exploited by them.

---

* As defined by Oxford Languages online.

Closely tied to subversion is the idea of confusion. One news website editor I interviewed characterised Russian conflict as the shaping of an artificial reality, 'messing with people's minds so they don't know what's true or not. It's basically ... eroding any feeling of what actually exists.'[12] Another interviewee specifically characterised Russian disinformation tactics as the cultivation of fakes,[13] whilst a third talked of an 'information ecosystem' designed to create a 'parallel reality'.[14] Academic Mykola Riabchuk talked of Russia's mastery of information networks on the internet. 'They place not only fake news – absolutely cynically – without any responsibility,' he said, 'but they place also fake opinions, they create some fake sites, which pretend to be analytical sites, and mix real analysis, real articles ... with fake and falsified and so on.'[15]

This sophisticated information war aims to confuse and rot society from within. People don't know what to believe. In such circumstances, some in the West, for example, have fallen for the idea that Ukraine is responsible for the Russian invasion or that if only it would stop fighting, the war would somehow end – which is true only in the sense that Russia would succeed in conquering the country and slaughter more of its inhabitants.

Despite its unpleasant absurdity, Russian propaganda was successful in eastern Ukraine during the first invasion in 2014 – in part because it was the culmination of a decade of work. One businessman I spoke to said many of the workers in his factories in Donbas believed the Russian narrative that Ukrainian 'fascists' would attack them. 'I myself spoke with my employees in Donetsk,' he told me. 'The transformation that took place in their minds was unbelievably fast. The speed at which people changed their minds and immediately absorbed those fears that were not there before. It was a strong machine that Russia used.'[16]

The creation of confusion is not by accident but design. Vladislav Surkov, a former senior Kremlin official and an alleged architect of Russian operations in Ukraine in 2014, has argued that Russia's techniques, which he described as its 'political algorithm', had succeeded in more than just meddling in elections and referendums. 'Russia interferes with their brains,' he said of his targets, including the West, 'and they do not know what to do with their own altered consciousness.'[17]

Finally, this way of war is an acceptance not only of the strength and merit of non-military tools of conflict but also the relative, historic weaknesses of the Russian Army. Political writer Włodzimierz Bączkowski noted back in 1938 that Russia has always brought its army into play only in the final phase of a longer process shaping the enemy through subversion and propaganda campaigns.[18] This is yet another reason why the Russian definition of warfare is much broader than in the West. It needs to be to offset the relative weakness of Russia's armed forces.

Doctrines and statements from Russia's military leaders all offer slightly different interpretations of the categorisations of tactics and tools, although there are multiple overlaps. Russia's military doctrine records the tools of modern conflict as political, economic and informational, in addition to military.[19] The 2016 document titled 'Foreign Policy of the Russian Federation', released by Russia's Ministry of Foreign Affairs, cites economic, legal, technological and informational tools alongside the tool of military power.[20] It also stated that 'soft power' had become integral to achieving its foreign policy objectives.[21] It defined 'soft power' tools as those of civil society, sub-categorising them as informational, humanitarian and 'other'. Again, it is unclear what 'other' implies, although it could include culture, religion, sport and use of government-controlled non-governmental organisations – so-called GoNGOs.

Chief of Staff Valeri Gerasimov said in late 2013 that 'methods of confrontation' had shifted towards political, economic, informational and other non-military tactics, supported by coordinated popular protests.[22] All of these measures, he said, were supported by covert military, information warfare and special forces operations. These suggest an array of espionage, cyber and specialised military tactics. Russian GRU military intelligence special operations cover an array of paramilitary and politicised violence that doesn't really have an equivalence in the West – certainly not on the same scale.

Ukrainians from different walks of life gave me examples of the different tools of Russian warfare. Liudmyla Fylypovych told me that the tools of war 'cover absolutely all areas of our lives: economics, social sphere, politics, culture, history, religion, philosophy, art'. In this, she echoes the 'unification of everything' concept. Kharkiv academic Ihor Rushchenko saw elements of Russia's warfare in the manipulation of mass consciousness through the economy, energy, infrastructure and a militarised society.[23] A former senior secret service director stressed the intermingling of criminality and the economy,[24] whilst think tank director Sunhurovskyi listed 'military, economic, political, legal, historical, semantic, cybernetic and the like'.[25]

The debate in Ukraine on the nature of the war has changed depending on what phase of the war they have been living through. Between 2005 and 2013, primarily non-military tools were used and the focus was on information and political operations. Russia corrupted the Ukrainian political system and hollowed out its defence and security agencies. But despite the political warfare aimed at them, few Ukrainians thought that they were in conflict with their neighbour. From 2014, with Putin's successful annexation of

Crimea, the Russian-controlled uprisings and the limited invasion in the east of the country, larger numbers of Ukrainians understood that they were at war. But even then, opinions were nuanced, reflecting the war's primarily non-traditional nature. Only after the invasion of 2022 did Ukraine grasp the magnitude of the Kremlin's hostile intent and the willingness of the Russian people to accept it. This point is crucial, because if there is no consensus within a nation as to whether it is in conflict and whom it is in conflict with, there can be no consensus as to its defence.

Taking into account Russian warfare theory, I believe that the tools of Russian warfare should be categorised into six broad areas:

- political (based on the 'active measures' tactics of the KGB and the Communist Party)
- cultural (including religion, law and governance)
- economics (including energy, food tariffs and the use of oligarchs and organised crime)
- military power (including the use of special forces for niche operations)
- diplomacy and public outreach
- information

Let's take a look at how Russia uses these tools both in Ukraine and the West.

INFORMATION WARFARE

During the chaos of the summer of 2014, Russia's Channel One reported on 12 July that Ukrainian soldiers had retaken the eastern Ukrainian town of Slovyansk from Russian militants. They entered the town and herded residents into its central square, where they executed a small boy and his mother by crucifying the boy and tying his mother to a tank, dragging her around the square until she was dead – an act of wanton brutality.[26] This degenerate and shocking incident appalled Russians. Widely reported, it marked a turning point in the Kremlin's curated conflict in Ukraine and led to a rise in recruits to the Russian-controlled *opolcheniye* (volunteer brigades) willing to fight Ukrainian troops. It also confirmed to millions of Russians that Ukraine's regime, echoing President Putin's accusations, was indeed a barbaric and neo-Nazi one. It was a manifestation of evil.

It also didn't happen. Neither the crucifixion nor the murder took place. What appeared 'real' in the eyes of the Russian media, the Russian public and the Russian consciousness was, according to Yevhen Fedchenko, a 'textbook' example of the 'construction of the fake', magnified and spread by state-controlled media.[27] The story of the crucified boy, which has since been categorically disproved, is just one example of how the Russian state continues to invest time and energy into mastering the power of information warfare, both as a standalone tool and an accompanying tool to maximise the impact of violence.

Information operations underpin and infuse Russian operations. The Russian military does not see them as an add-on, as Western militaries still generally do. They, along with elements of political warfare, are often the main effort used to deliver the political outcomes desired by Russia.

Russia's intense focus on information operations is not new. It is rooted in the Soviet Union's founding political culture. The Bolshevik Party mastered information warfare with brilliance to confuse and disorientate its rivals, not just in the sulphurous maelstrom of

Russian revolutionary politics but also during the wider struggle that saw them seize power in the 1917 Russian Revolution. In his 1902 essay 'What is to be Done', Lenin stressed the centrality of propaganda in installing a new consciousness in the masses.[28] In his 1905 'Lessons of the Moscow Uprising', he outlined how information was not only a tool to win over supporters but also a weapon to divide and undermine opponents.[29] In his 1920 work *Left-Wing Communism: An Infantile Disorder*, he stressed the need to use tactics such as 'practical compromises, tacks, conciliatory manoeuvres, zigzags, retreats and so on' to manipulate others.[30] The use of information and disinformation to win over, confuse, divide and demoralise was built into military and espionage operations from the 1920s, as were forgeries for propaganda purposes. The Communist International began to export revolutionary propaganda to colonial socialist movements from 1928. International radio broadcasts began in German in 1933 and then in English shortly afterwards. By 1942, the USSR was broadcasting in seventeen foreign languages and in sixty by 1962.[31]

Russian information operations are rooted in a deep understanding of human nature and aligned with tactics such as the reflexive control, which manipulate perception and corrupt judgement. Messaging is directed at specific target audiences. A message for one group is not necessarily used on another. Polish academic Jolanta Darczewska argues that whilst internal messages are often shrill and hysterical, the Kremlin tended, at least prior to 2014, to address the West in a more nuanced style.[32] Since 2014 and especially since 2022, the language of the Russian state has become more extreme, and arguably more of the tactics used inside the country are now used outside. Whereas before, the Kremlin might have taken something factually correct but manipulated it into something else, now it also produces entirely fake narratives intended to confuse. There is no truth per se, only choices about which narrative to believe.[33] Belief is a lifestyle choice, divorced from reality and fact. This is why the battle for objective truth is so important for Western civilisation and for open societies. It is Russia's intent for Ukraine to be seen as the aggressor and for people to believe that if only Ukraine would stop fighting, there would be 'peace'. Those who peddle this betray not only Ukraine but a fact- and truth-based world.

'Russian propaganda is sometimes so crazy, it says such impossible things, it doesn't have the effect of making people believe them, but it breaks down people's defences,' Russia expert Kadri Liik was quoted as saying in a 2015 *Guardian* article. 'It's not just lies, in the way of Soviet propaganda. It's more sophisticated. A kind of violence against the mind.'[34]

One of the few proven examples of the simultaneous release of confusing and contradictory narratives occurred during the shooting down of the Malaysia Airlines flight 17 (MH17) on 17 July 2014 by a Russian BUK missile, launched ostensibly by Russian separatists. In reaction to this ethical and PR disaster, the Kremlin prepared a list of 'lines to take' – key soundbites and wording used to make sure the person using them remains 'on message'. The MH17 'lines' were revealed in a cache of hacked and leaked emails, which featured in a report by myself and Ukrainian author Alya Shandra titled 'The Surkov Leaks'.[35] The document listed eight separate lines, which were concurrently fed to the media to generate a sense of confusion. These were:

1. It was a provocation by Kyiv, targeting the separatist areas of the 'Donetsk People's Republic' and the 'Luhansk People's Republic' (the two pro-Russian breakaway areas in Ukraine).

2. Kyiv carried out the strike and, backed by the West, is trying to blame Russia and Putin personally.
3. The Malaysia Airlines plane was deliberately directed through an area where anti-terrorist operations were taking place.
4. An audio recording of militiamen talking about being attacked by 'so-called' civilian airliners had been revealed, implying that MH17 was not a civilian plane.
5. NATO had carried out the strike as an excuse to intervene in Ukraine.
6. It was an act designed to hide Ukraine's strategic failure in the conflict.
7. It could be compared to the shooting of Archduke Franz Ferdinand in June 1914, with Kyiv trying to start a new world war.
8. Ukraine's own air defence, partially located in the occupied territories, shot the plane down, and there is evidence to show that these air-defence systems were readied shortly before it was hit.

These messages were articulated, wittingly or unwittingly, not only in the Russian media but also to media outlets in the West via influential voices.

The Russians have also experimented with new information techniques. One such technique is called *vbrosy* (literally 'tossed in'). *Vbrosy* is not necessarily fake but 'often involves rapidly spreading pieces of emotionally charged information through prepared channels to manipulate the audience's attention'.[36] It's information that travels quickly through a community and incites an immediate, visceral reaction. In Odesa in 2014, the Kremlin directly tried to exacerbate ethnic tension via a *vbrosy* campaign, with articles about the 'monster of nationalism' appearing in ninety-five social media outlets, media outlets and blogs. Journalists were often bribed to promote such stories.

Since the 2022 invasion of Ukraine, the Russian state has also significantly ramped up its use of nuclear intimidation, with the aim of increasing the level of fear in Western societies. Again, in some senses this is a return to the past. The Soviet Union regularly used such threats during the Cold War and Russia has done so occasionally since, for example against Denmark in 2015.[37]

Information operations are not only a tool of war at the operational or tactical level. President Putin's ambition is greater. At the strategic level, false narratives are used to shape Russian consciousness and Western perceptions. Information, in the form of history, news, educational broadcasting and popular culture, is being used to reshape and recreate Russian identity. This narrative perpetuates an apocalyptic view of the world, which sees the West as a deep military and psychological threat. The Russian nation has, for a decade or more, been fed a diet of propaganda and readied for conflict. Stalin is no longer criticised. Soviet-era massacres and crimes have been denied, as they were under the Soviet Union.[38] Speaking out against any of this carries dangers.

In relation to Ukraine in particular, information has been used as a weapon to demoralise and divide Ukrainian society, especially using Russian TV channels – which, until 2014, were widely available in Ukraine – to tell Ukrainians how dysfunctional their state is and how much better life was with Russia. TV has also been used to change the perceptions of Ukraine and Ukrainians from reliable allies to pitiful adversaries. Russia 'began preparations for this war at the informational level,' Roman Burko, one of my interviewees, told me.[39] 'Long before they attacked us, I heard the stories from my acquaintances, friends from Russia, that "we have programs on our TV channels in which they either ridicule or … humiliate Ukrainians"'.

These tools were employed not only in broadcast news outlets but also in modern TV fiction, coinciding with increased state influence over Russian television.[40] Prior to 2005, the archetypal protagonist in a Russian drama was an honest person fighting for justice, either inside or outside the system, in a crime thriller such as *Banditskiy Peterburg*. After 2005, a change took place. One of the first programmes on Russian state TV that signalled this change was the series *Sea Devils*, about Russian naval special forces. The focus of such programmes changed from, say, exposing corrupt officials to defeating Russia's enemies and defending Russian interests in the 'near abroad' – the former Soviet republics. In the words of one analyst, the messaging of the programmes, watched by millions throughout the former Soviet space, was clear: 'For the sake of justice, for the sake of peace, Russia has the right to interfere in the affairs of neighbouring countries.'[41] As well as being produced for a home audience, they were offered free or at discounted prices to TV companies in the former Soviet republics.[42]

Even before *Sea Devils*, the film *Brat II* (Brother II) became a cultural outlier for Russian nationalism. It contained the often-repeated line, 'You'll pay for Sevastopol.' This is a reference to Russia's loss of Sevastopol, when Ukraine (and with it, Crimea) became independent. Lines from the film, where Russians are the good guys and Ukrainians and Americans are the bad ones, have become etched in popular, anti-Western Russian culture. 'Are you gangsters?' 'No, we're Russians!' and 'Bunch of bastards' (about the Americans) are just two examples.[43]

The right to intervene was just one of many narratives developed by Russia in relation to Ukraine. The Ukrainian group StopFake, which works to highlight Russian state disinformation, identified eighteen narrative 'lines' propagated by the Russian state, of which the four most prevalent were:

1. Ukraine was the victim of an illegal *coup d'état* by a pro-Western junta
2. Ukraine is a fascist state
3. Ukraine is a failed state
4. Russia was not involved in the conflict in eastern Ukraine.[44]

These strategic narratives, since 2005, have fed a variety of goals with different target audiences at different times. These have ranged from creating division and dissatisfaction within Ukraine, recruitment to paramilitary groups, justification for Russian action and the undermining of international support for Ukraine. In Russia, they have helped to create a society ripe for mobilisation.

In some cases, this has evolved to entirely fictional news, such as the crucified boy. Former Member of Parliament and military commander Ihor Lapin asserts that the story of the crucified boy enabled the Kremlin to root the present Ukraine conflict in past battles against Nazi fascism. It was, he said, 'a skilful combination of information policy and instilling hysteria at home, so that people there would believe that they were going to Ukraine to fight against the Nazis'.[45] The result was a 'colossal patriotic upsurge', with a rise in volunteer enlistment.[46] StopFake's founder Yevhen Fedchenko added that the fake story 'was a very powerful recruitment tool for some people in Russia who went to sign up … to go to Donbas. Many other people who didn't sign up … were absolutely persuaded that that's exactly what the Ukrainian Army is doing.'[47]

To reinforce the rooting of the war in past Soviet glories, pro-Russian paramilitary rebels in the 2014–15 stage of the Ukraine conflict were referred to in the Russian media as *opolchentsy*, the word for peasant volunteers who supported the anti-Nazi partisans in 1941, and the Ukrainian soldiers as *karateli*, a reference to the pro-Nazi, anti-partisan squads extensively and negatively portrayed in Soviet literature and films.[48] In Putin's now infamous Kremlin speech accepting Crimea back into Russia, he described the instigators of Ukraine's pro-democracy revolution as 'nationalists, neo-Nazis, Russophobes and antisemites' who had resorted to 'terror, murder and riots'.[49]

To support the anti-fascist narrative in 2014, the Kremlin initially attempted to portray Ukraine as an antisemitic state, claiming that Russia was acting to save Jews. Here, the fake story was the mirror image of the truth. Antisemitic graffiti in Russian-controlled Crimea was presented as being in Ukrainian-held Kyiv and a story about a rabbi fleeing Crimea was presented as if he was fleeing Kyiv. 'These stories were not created for Russian audiences. The Russian audience is antisemitic itself – it was for Europe and the US audience,' said Fedchenko.[50] The only place where antisemitic measures were carried out was in Donbas, where pro-Russian rebel authorities initially wanted Jews to submit to registration.[51]

Fake stories were accompanied by the creation of fake think tanks and fake news agencies. One such example is the Kharkiv News Agency, run out of Savushkina Street in St Petersburg, close to the now dead mercenary leader Yevgeny Prigozhin's infamous 'troll farm', which attempted, along with the GRU, to manipulate the 2016 US presidential election.[52] It created a world of sometimes real, sometimes fake news mixed with conspiracy theories. These chimed with Russian state-controlled media, politicians and trolls peddling the same tune, where the war was manufactured by, according to journalist Karen Horn's analysis, the depraved 'NATO-Jewish-Gay-Fascists conglomerate sponsored by the US'.[53]

POLITICAL WARFARE

In October 2014, in a leaked email exchange, a Russian MP corresponded with a close associate of senior Kremlin adviser Surkov. They discussed how to bring the 'Russian world' to the Ukrainian city of Kharkiv. Options ranged from political protests (overt and legal) to sabotage operations (covert and illegal), leading up to an invasion from the Donbas or the nearby Russian county of Belgorod. Their planned legal tactics included rallies, a picket, a flash mob and a 'sticker war' advocating the boycott of the forthcoming local elections. They also planned to publish the 'personal data of enemies' on the internet and troll them on social media.[54] On the other side of Ukraine, in the south-eastern port of Odesa and at the same time, similar operations were discussed between pro-Russian activists. In an operation known as the 'Porto Franco' project, Moscow's planners looked at 'actions of direct influence', including street rallies and protests, inflammatory messaging and violent political agitation.

Some of the tools of political warfare are recognisable in the West. They are the instruments of politics: rallies, party political events, merchandise and street protests organised by local groups. Where they differ with Russian nations, however, is that illegal, violent and corrupting methods are also part of the toolkit in Russia. Political front organisations are linked to paramilitary groups. Assassins are used, as well as agents of influence. 'Political technologists', as they are called in Russia, bribe and manipulate. Organised crime is engaged as an important source of muscle. In the Crimea and eastern Ukraine in 2014, gangs provided street thugs – nicknamed locally as *titushky* – to support military objectives, stage protests or disrupt adversary protests.[55] In the FSB's plans for chaos in 2022, martial arts club members were to help as outriders for the Russian military.

The tools of subversive political warfare were originally honed and perfected by the Soviet Union. I will tell their story shortly. They came with a series of techniques and tactics: provocations, fabrications, agents of influence. All were often used in an intricate *kombinatsiya*, a word used to describe 'the Soviet fixation with complex operational initiatives, analogous to intricate chess moves'.[56] In 2014 and 2015, agents from the pro-Russian enclave of Transnistria worked with Moscow on the creation of a subversive campaign. Overt activity included a founding conference and appeals to the Ukrainian authorities for 'equal rights'. Covert plans saw pro-Russian terror gangs creating 'panic' by means of guerrilla attacks on civilian power, water, gas and transport infrastructure, as well as on the vehicles and homes of targets. These plans were eventually disrupted and then exposed by the Ukrainian SBU and police.

Russian political technologists worked closely with pro-Putin Ukrainian President Viktor Yanukovych to help him finally get elected in 2010. He repaid Russia by hollowing out state institutions, with endemic corruption at the local and national level. There were attacks on reformist politicians.[57] Local and national government was further infiltrated by Russian activists and agents.[58] Russian passport holders were promoted to key positions in the defence ministry and security agencies. The NATO/Ukraine relationship was undermined and Ukraine's armed forces were 'deconstructed through corruption'.[59] Before the Ukrainian Army faced the

Call sign Sonic arms his Vampire bomber drone. It is a delicate process. This drone has two bombs attached to the underside. The target is the Russian trench a few miles away, covered by leaves and branches known locally as *brindage*. The drone is nicknamed Baba Yaga by the Russians, after a haggard folklore witch who flew around at night frying and then eating the young. It's an apt name. © Annabel Moeller

The Vampire can also carry a single anti-tank mine. Here, Sonic prepares one. To make the mine's unwieldy shape slightly more aerodynamic, Sonic attaches the empty plastic bottle on the right-hand side of the table to the mine.

© Annabel Moeller

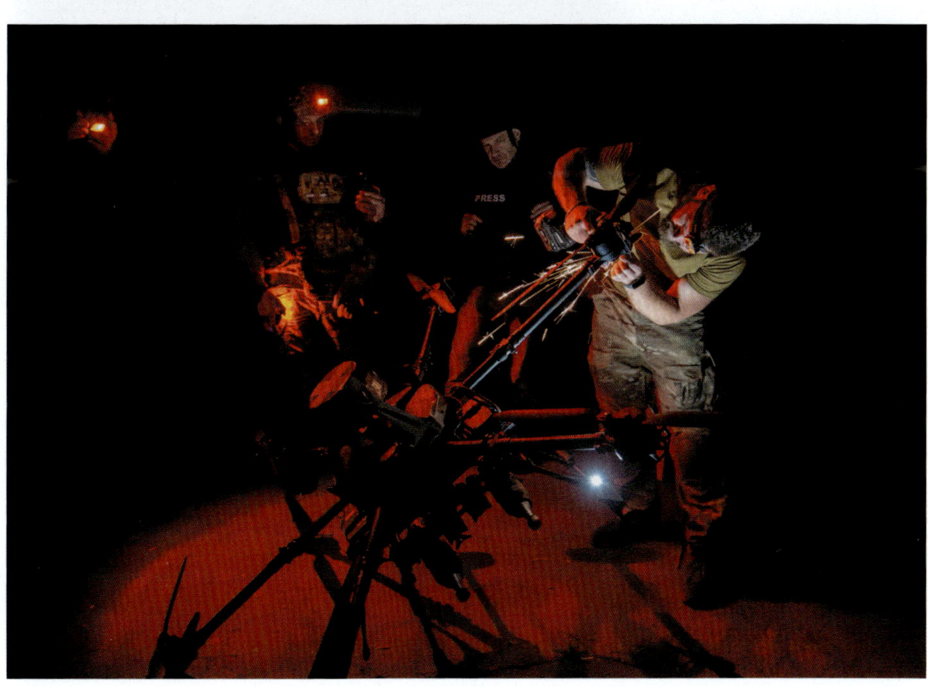

Call sign Cossack repairs part of his Vampire in preparation for the night's attacks. © Annabel Moeller

Sonic attaches tail fins, partially 3D printed, to a couple of bombs. The dugout's curious cat watches. © Annabel Moeller

I watch the pilot, call sign Koleso (wheel), manoeuvre his drone. We are underground in the bunker, with the drone now positioned above the Russian lines. He has been flying the relatively slow-moving drone for about ten minutes, communicating with the co-pilot in headquarters. © Annabel Moeller

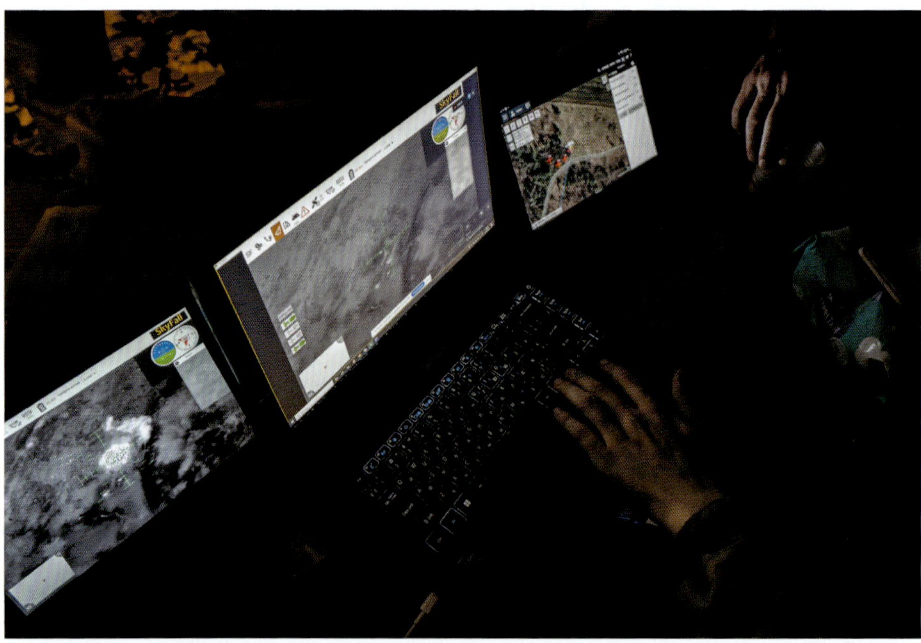

Koleso releases the drone's charge and it falls to the target. As the device lands, we see it explode on the left-hand screen. © Annabel Moeller

The artillery battery I visit plays a game of cat and mouse with Russian drones. When Russian reconnaissance drones are overhead, we stay under the camouflage netting. I chat with gunner Ruslan. He compares the new Western gun with the old Soviet gun the unit was initially equipped with. 'It's like the difference between driving a Zhiguli and a Mercedes,' he jokes, referring to an old Soviet car. © Annabel Moeller

As soon as the drone moves on, the team get to work. The gunners fire up the Paladin, hidden nearby in a deep trench under more netting. It drives up and out, belching fumes and churning the mud along a 75-metre track until it reaches a small opening in the forest. The team load and prep the weapon. © Annabel Moeller

The Paladin's 155 mm gun is raised, a target is programmed into the firing system, the barrel adjusts slightly and then fires with a thud and a shock wave that passes through the body. 'Keep your mouth open to equalise the pressure,' Ruslan shouts. The gun fires a second round thirty seconds later and then the weapon is driven back into its trench. © Annabel Moeller

The unit now has a permanent guard to shoot down Russian bomber or kamikaze drones. The Paladin has been hit – and repaired – three times. © Annabel Moeller

In the West, drone pilots could be hundreds if not thousands of miles away from their targets. In Ukraine, tactical drone pilots are either a few kilometres behind the front line or on it. Call sign Dekstor sits just behind Ukraine's most forward infantry line. From there, he flies his drone, looking for Russian positions. Once he finds them, they'll be targeted either by Ukrainian mortars or by kamikaze and bomber drones. © Annabel Moeller

Call sign Pisok (sand) is one of Ukraine's drone 'top guns'. He has been injured three times. Quiet, unassuming and thoughtful, like many Ukrainian soldiers, he wears his courage lightly. Pisok is most proud when he uses his drones to save the lives of his colleagues, but he also has over fifty 'kills' to his name. In civilian life, Pisok was a salesman. He's always loved flying drones and his face lights up when he talks about them. © Annabel Moeller

I meet Serhii and Solomiya during the summer of 2024 in Kyiv. They monitor Russian actions in the occupied territories. There was no electricity in the apartment block I met them in, thanks to Russian bombardment. © Annabel Moeller

Call sign Lito (summer) is an instructor at the Dragon Sky Drone School. Before the war, he was the lead guitarist in a well-known indie band. He talks through the theory of drone warfare. On the screen, a Ukrainian drone is about to drop its bombs onto a small group of Russian servicemen, who have just become aware of their fate.

© Annabel Moeller

Call sign Dyadya Sasha (Uncle Sasha) talks me through the various explosive charges that can be fitted to the drone. He explains that as well as carrying the bomb, the drone needs to have enough power to carry the battery. It's an ongoing struggle to find the trade-off between the ability to travel far and the ability to take more explosives and firepower.

© Annabel Moeller

The Dragon Sky Drone School classroom during the week-long course that teaches Ukrainian servicemen how to become drone pilots. © Annabel Moeller

I chat with call sign Kos, company commander of the Sarmat unit, in their rear headquarters. On the wall are letters and paintings from schoolchildren thanking the soldiers. Apart from one month away from the front line, the unit has fought every day since the 2022 invasion. At just twenty-six, Kos is the survivor of many of these 'contacts' (skirmishes or battles). © Annabel Moeller

Since 2023, crews on both sides have been building drone cages around their armoured vehicles. On Russian vehicles, these bizarre-looking metal frames have been nicknamed 'turtle tanks'. They are designed to take the initial impact of a drone strike. © Annabel Moeller

A Sarmat soldier sits on a piece of kit taken from the Russians in battle. These items, known as 'trophy' kit, are prized spoils of war and were particularly valuable in the opening months of the invasion, when Ukraine lacked enough military equipment. It's hidden by camouflage netting to prevent its discovery by Russian drones. © Annabel Moeller

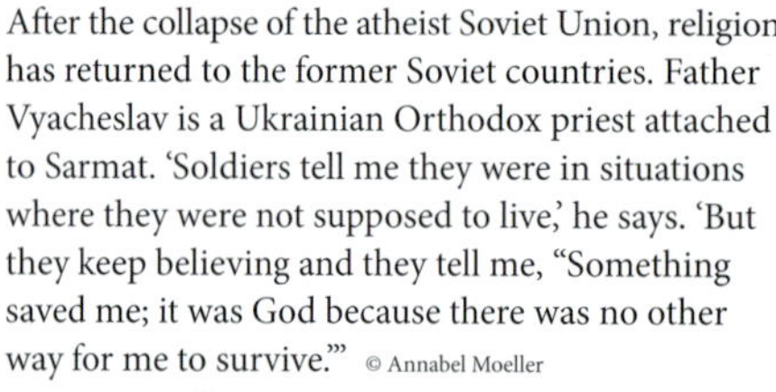

After the collapse of the atheist Soviet Union, religion has returned to the former Soviet countries. Father Vyacheslav is a Ukrainian Orthodox priest attached to Sarmat. 'Soldiers tell me they were in situations where they were not supposed to live,' he says. 'But they keep believing and they tell me, "Something saved me; it was God because there was no other way for me to survive."' © Annabel Moeller

Kos shows how a kamikaze drone detonates on a target. It's simple but effective. When the copper prod hits the steel coil on impact, the connection is made. © Annabel Moeller

Call sign Svarshchik (welder) is responsible for the drone caging around Sarmat's military vehicles. 'It works; we've tested it in battle,' he assures me.

© Annabel Moeller

battlefield, it was, said one interviewee, 'torn apart very diligently during the reign of Yanukovych'.[60]

One of the most significant outcomes of this was the removal of Ukrainian heavy weapons from the Crimea before the 2014 annexation.[61] A perfect example of the efficiency of modern Russian conflict: why destroy kit in war when, through bribery or espionage, you can have it removed or you can even buy it from your future enemy? It is a cynical joke amongst Ukrainian servicemen now that they are being bombed by their own weapons – a reference to the amount of military equipment, which, legally or illicitly, found its way back to Russia in the 1990s and 2000s. By the time of Russia's first invasion in 2014, Ukraine's Ministry of Defence was so incapable of providing equipment that there was little military supply to speak of. Provisions were made or procured by volunteers. Lapin says that 'clothes, bulletproof vests, plates for bulletproof vests – all this was done by hand ... Women sewed pockets for ammunition, our self-defence guys made plates ... and pasted them with cloth so that there would be no ricochets.'[62]

Russian political warfare also takes place through physical and reputational assassination. As to the first, not since Stalin's day has murder been so easily or casually used. In July 2006, the upper chamber of the Russian Parliament, the Federation Council, approved a law permitting the Russian President to use the country's armed forces and agencies outside Russia's borders to carry out extrajudicial killings.[63] The list of state-sponsored killings or attempted killings is an extensive one. In Russia, it includes politicians and journalists such as Galina Starovoytova, Boris Nemtsov and Anna Politkovskaya, as well as the death in prison of Alexei Navalny in 2024. In Ukraine, it likely includes the September 2004 poisoning of Viktor Yushchenko before he won the Ukrainian presidency.[64] In the UK, it includes the attempted murder of Sergei Skripal in March 2018 and the gruesome murder of Alexander Litvinenko, poisoned with radioactive polonium in November 2006.[65] Poison has become the new go-to weapon for assassination, including opioids, radioactive poisons and dioxides. They can leave little trace, but they also cause a very public execution. Either way, their use creates an air of menace around the Kremlin.[66]

Reputational assassination is carried out through the release or threatened release of compromising information, known as *krompromat*, for blackmail purposes. The collection and use of *kompromat* is one of the most ubiquitous and infamous staples of Russian political warfare. The word is derived from 1930s Soviet secret police jargon and arguably is a relatively unique feature of Russian economic and political behaviour. *Kompromat* is collected on one's political and economic activities, one's criminal activities, such as roles in assassinations or links to organised crime, and private and family life and affairs, including sexual behaviour.[67] This is why the FSB vet the prostitutes who work at the more exclusive hotels in Moscow and other major cities and why some of the major suites and rooms in the hotels are bugged for audio and video, especially those used by high-profile Western guests. Sexual blackmail is part of the toolkit.

Kompromat is collected on friends as well as enemies. As Russian novelist Yulia Latynina wrote, 'To keep *kompromat* on enemies is a pleasure. To keep *kompromat* on friends is a must.'[68] One of the defining moments in Putin's rise to power was in January 1999 when Russia's Prosecutor General Yury Skuratov, intent on exposing the wrongdoing of then President Boris Yeltsin, was shown on TV having sex with two prostitutes. The tape was rumoured to have been given to a notorious TV 'shock jock' by Vladimir Putin himself, then head of the KGB.[69] The release of the tape proved to the Yeltsin family that Putin would protect them. Later that year, Putin became Prime Minister.

On a smaller scale, individual targeting has also taken the guise of online and in-person trolling. The academic Mykola Riabchuk and the reformist politician Svitlana Zalishchuk have given accounts of their experiences of stalking, both in person and online. From 2014 onwards, Riabchuk experienced repeated attempts to discredit him and other Ukrainian academics at international conferences. At these conferences, Riabchuk would face the same questioning from individuals wearing the St George's ribbon – the ribbon, worn as part of a Russian campaign to mark the battle against Nazism, has become a symbol of support for the separatist eastern Ukraine campaign. Individuals would ask copycat questions, using Soviet-era tropes equating support for Ukraine with anti-Soviet and pro-fascist sentiment. Their goal, Riabchuk said, was part of a 'very long tradition of labelling "fascist" any opponent … who descends from the official line'.[70] Zalishchuk, meanwhile, was the target of online misogyny. She noticed the campaign when she began to encounter social media posts featuring a naked woman looking similar to her. 'I thought at that time, to be honest, that someone, probably, has been mistaken … so I didn't really pay attention,' she says. 'But now I understand that it was a deliberate way of discrediting my name.'[71]

New tools not available to Russia in Soviet days include the use of Western PR firms, political-campaign professionals and Western agents of influence. Whereas Moscow's partners were limited by ideology before, they now include a kaleidoscope of dissatisfied groups from the left and right. The result, author Peter Pomerantsev argues, was 'an array of voices, all working away at Western audiences from different angles, producing a cumulative echo chamber of Kremlin support'.[72] Supportive voices have included former German Chancellor Gerhard Schröder, who joined the board of Russian energy corporation Gazprom after Germany's 2005 election. He was quoted criticising German policy towards Russia in 2015, saying he 'sees no reason to fear a possible Russian threat in Eastern Europe'.[73] The use of Western PR has also enabled Russia to gain intelligence and influence in US politics, as evidenced by the Paul Manafort case. Manafort, at times, ran Donald Trump's 2016 US presidential campaign, yet the US Senate Intelligence Committee reported that he 'sought to secretly share' information on the Trump campaign with individuals closely associated with the Russian intelligence services.[74] The committee commented that Manafort's actions 'represented a grave counterintelligence threat'.

ECONOMIC WARFARE

These tactics have been used relentlessly and ruthlessly by Moscow in Ukraine and elsewhere in former Soviet countries since the break-up of the USSR. During the era of the Soviet domination of eastern Europe, subsidised gas delivered through Moscow's pipeline network was used to tie various countries to the Soviet Union, cementing Moscow's dominance.

Economic levers include not only oil and gas supplies but also trade and food sanctions, criminality, oligarch power, soft loans and asset seizures. However, gas prices were arguably the single most powerful overt tool in Moscow's armoury in the first stage of the Ukraine conflict and were ruthlessly used during the three so-called Russo–Ukraine 'gas wars' of the first decade of the twenty-first century.* Energy was fed to an unreformed Ukraine using debt financing. This created a dependence, which was then leveraged into political and defence concessions. As one energy researcher put it, 'How to solve debt dependence, and how to reduce gas prices? Russia says, "Well, there, we have the [Russian] Black Sea Fleet based in Sevastopol, let's ... extend its basing and we will write off your debts."'[75] Ukrainian politician Svitlana Zalishchuk agreed. 'Cheap gas was like a ransom for ... political loyalty.'[76]

Following the Orange Revolution, when a nominally pro-Western government came to power in Ukraine, Gazprom reduced gas flows by 125 million cubic meters and demanded an increase in price from $50 per 1,000 cubic meters to $230, in line with the international market.[77] Prices continued to rise steeply after the gas wars that took place in the first decade of this century, only to fall when the pro-Russian Viktor Yanukovych signed the April 2010 Kharkiv Pact, which extended Russia's right to lease Ukraine's Crimean military bases until 2042 in return for a 30 per cent drop in the price of natural gas. By spring 2014, when relations between Moscow and Kyiv had broken down following the annexation of Crimea, Russia unilaterally cancelled the deal and demanded a price of $480 per 1,000 cubic meters. The aim was to shatter the Ukrainian economy.

Ukraine was not the only state hit by political pricing of gas. In 2008, Georgia paid $235 per thousand cubic metres whilst Russia-friendly Belarus paid $46. Any state which attempted to move out of Russia's political and economic orbit was hit with higher prices and more frequent interruptions of service. Those that didn't, such as Armenia, Belarus and the Russian-controlled statelets of

* Three disputes over the supply and price of gas took place 2005–6, 2007–8 and 2008–9. An additional dispute took place 2013–14.

Abkhazia, South Ossetia in Georgia and Transnistria in Moldova, weren't.[78]

Gazprom's chief, Alexei Miller, an ally of Putin, has denied that the company is used by the Kremlin for political purposes, calling the accusations 'a good stereotype for western readers'.[79] Others disagree. Energy expert Karen Smith Stegen argues that the Kremlin's relationship with Gazprom and its senior executives is evidence that it is not simply a commercial company.[80] Irwin Stelzer from the US Hudson Institute says that 'to view Gazprom or any Russian energy company as anything other than instruments of Russian foreign policy is to be naive in the extreme'.[81] In April 2015, the EU accused Gazprom of overcharging customers and using its power to block rivals.[82] In response, Gazprom was forced to admit that it 'performs functions of public interest and has a status of strategic state-controlled entity' – confirming the fact that it is effectively a foreign-policy arm of the Kremlin.[83]

The use of food bans and tariffs has also been a tool of policy since the early 1990s. In August 1993, Russia imposed high tariffs on Moldovan goods after it refused to join the Commonwealth of Independent States (CIS), the ill-fated successor body to the Soviet Union. As Moldova's economy was tied heavily to Russia's, the tariffs caused significant hardship. In response, Moldovan President Mircea Snegur signed an array of CIS agreements in October 1993.[84] Two months later Russia lifted its tariffs. In October 2013, Russia suspended Lithuanian dairy imports. Lithuania at that point held the rotating presidency of the EU. The act was seen as the Kremlin's response to the encouragement given by Lithuania to other former Soviet states to establish closer ties with the EU.[85] In July 2013, Russia banned Ukrainian chocolate. The block was lifted after the Yanukovych government broke off EU Association Agreement negotiations, only to be reimposed in early September 2014.[86]

The role played by oligarchs was also a powerful factor in this tactic, especially prior to 2014. Essentially the 'oligarch' model saw the Russian government exercise informal power through billionaires, whose wealth was closely tied to concessions and contracts won through the Kremlin. Businessmen, often linked to both organised crime and Russian secret agencies, prospered through sweetheart deals and multi-billion lines of credit from Russia, the profits of which went to developing major businesses, which in turn channelled money to pro-Russian politicians.[87] The Kremlin has worked through oligarchs in many parts of the world as an informal but important part of Russian foreign policy.

Russia has also taken mineral rights and industrial equipment as the spoils of war. After the Crimea annexation, Russia seized a gas platform in the Sea of Azov (between Russia and Crimea) and nationalised the previously Ukrainian Black Sea oil and gas firm Chornomornaftohaz, gaining valuable rights to the northern Black Sea mineral reserves.[88]

Russia is also allegedly exporting significant quantities of coal from Luhansk, formerly part of Ukraine. The value of coal, raw material and rare earth deposits in eastern Ukraine runs into the hundreds of billions of dollars. For Russia, this war could still be self-financing. As well as being annexed and invaded, Ukraine is also being stripped of its assets.

CULTURAL AND RELIGIOUS WARFARE

In March 2024, the Russian Orthodox Church declared the 'special military operation' in Ukraine a 'holy war'. In uncompromising and apocalyptic tones, it stated:

> From a spiritual and moral point of view, the special military operation is a Holy War, in which Russia and its people, defending the single spiritual space of Holy Rus', fulfil the mission of ... protecting the world from the onslaught of globalism and the victory of the West, which has fallen into Satanism.[89]

Culture, including religion, governance and law, matters to Putin, be it Russian prestige at the Olympics, the use of music and poetry in newly conquered territory or Orthodox Christianity as an arm of the Russian state. Culture may not fire the bullets that kill – although Russian Orthodox priests in Ukraine have been accused of arms sales as well as storing weapons and target spotting – but historical narrative, belief and patriotism are core components of a Kremlin that wants to inculcate a new spirit of malleable patriotism.[90] They provide the ideological underpinnings for the Kremlin's permanent struggle against the West and its perceived corruption. Russia's spiritual and moral values, argues scholar Jardar Østbø, draw on anti-Western and Slavophile notions of the uniqueness of the Russian soul, traditional morality and collectivism.[91]

The Russian Orthodox Church has described Putin's leadership as a 'miracle of God'.[92] Putin, in turn, has described Russian Orthodoxy as one of 'the most important elements of our external politics, especially in relation to near neighbours in the former Soviet Union'.[93] Putin sees the church as a unifier of Russians both inside and outside the borders of the Russian Federation, with a concurrent boost to the Russian state's ability to lay claim to them and to give the church grounds to act in the name of Russians abroad. It is for these reasons that the church has been described as a 'known tool within the Russian hybrid warfare toolkit'.[94] Even in 2021, on the eve of the invasion of Ukraine, the Orthodox Church, riddled with Russian intelligence agents, had the approval of more than half the Ukrainian population, according to FSB social surveys.[95] In its infamous March 2024 statement, the church referred to Ukraine not as a separate state but as south-west Russia. The war in Ukraine was 'part of the national liberational struggle of the Russian people', whose spiritual mission was to block attempts 'to subjugate humanity to a single, evil principle'.[96] This directly refers to the idea in Russian Orthodoxy of Russia playing the role of martyr, battling the Antichrist in the guise of NATO and the US.

The Kremlin's attempts to use religion in its battle in Ukraine suffered a major setback in January 2019, when the head of the Eastern Orthodox church, Bartholomew I, signed a decree granting independence to the Orthodox Church of Ukraine. This act revoked the right of Moscow to appoint Kyiv's senior clergymen, a right in place since 1686. Thus ended a 'four-hundred-year quest' to ensure that no Ukrainian national church could establish itself.[97] It was a major spiritual defeat, which is now slowly overturning Moscow's influence over the parish churches of Ukraine.

Under the Yanukovych regime, the cleansing of history included plans to rewrite Ukrainian history textbooks to purge nationalist figures and seminal events, such as the Orange Revolution.[98] Other expressions of national identity, such as military parades, were banned.[99] In governance, Ukrainian officials were expected to comment on relevant 'Russian experience' when writing policy papers, presumably to mirror and match Russian behaviour to ensure that should Russia and Ukraine merge, different approaches to governance would be minimised.

Cultural warfare overlaps with information warfare to reshape consciousness and Russian national memory, as Jade McGlynn has shown in her work *Memory Makers*.[100] Control of the historical narrative matters to Putin because who controls the interpretation of the past helps to shape identity now. In the summer of 2021, Putin published his essay on the historical unity of the Russian and Ukrainian people.[101] It was his historical justification for the war. The Kremlin has framed the Ukraine conflict as a modern-day struggle against a new Nazism, a narrative that links directly back to the Second World War, known as the 'Great Patriotic War' in Russia. The war was not only the defining event in Soviet history but also, given the Soviet regime's many crimes – show trials, labour camps and genocidal mass starvations – a redeeming one.

Russia also has a long history of setting up political 'front' organisations, beginning in the 1920s in Europe with the German communist agitator Willi Müzenberg, head of the Communist Youth International.[102] After the Second World War, multiple groups were added to the list. By the 1960s, some fifty Soviet friendship organisations were engaging with people in 188 countries, including members of trade union groups, women's groups, youth groups and church and peace groups. These organisations, in Europe and the US, were cynically referred to inside the USSR as 'transmission belts', defined by John C. Clews as 'organisations not openly connected with the Communist Party, but which it uses as an indirect way of promoting its policies and action'.[103]

From the early 2000s to 2014, Russia's 'fifth column' in Ukraine had a growing number of front organisations through which to operate. These included pro-Russian political parties, public organisations, Cossack movements and the Russian Orthodox Church.

The first time I came across 'Cossacks' doing Moscow's bidding was during the Moldovan/Transnestria conflict in 1991. They wore old Cossack garb but were thoroughly Sovietised – the Cossacks were killed off as a cultural force by the 1930s. Despite their assault rifles, they struck me as being more Gilbert and Sullivan than special forces.

In recent years, the most influential GoNGO has been Rossotrudnichestvo, otherwise known as the Government Commission on Compatriots Living Abroad, which sits under the Russian Ministry of Foreign Affairs. Its leader specifically cites the USSR as an inspiration behind the current organisation.[104] Estonia's KAPO secret service, more vocal and critical than Ukraine's was at the time, reported that Rossotrudnichestvo's purpose was to organise and coordinate the Russian diaspora to support Russian foreign policy. It was tasked with nurturing fifth columns of agitating Russians in the former Soviet republics and to be at the service of the Russian state by helping to ferment ethnic and/or linguistic divisions. As KAPO reported, 'The compatriot policy aims to influence decisions taken in the host countries, by guiding the Russian-speaking population, and by using influence operations inherited from the KGB, and also by simply financing various activities.'[105]

In the first decade of this century, a number of spin-off organisations, such as Impressum, Format-A3, Skovoroda and Izborsk, were set up in locations such as Crimea, Kyiv, Moldova and the Baltic republics. These cultural and historical organisations were used to sell an aggressive narrative of new Russia's might. They portrayed former Soviet republics as failed states and attempted to unite Russians living outside Russia behind a common Kremlin-led agenda, ripe for manipulation. 'Moscow's goal is to keep a yearning for the

Soviet Union alive in the Russian-speaking communities of these countries, and to prevent their natural integration in the local society,' commented Estonia's KAPO.[106]

In Ukraine specifically, these groups questioned its 'artificial' separation from Russia and stirred division. In Poland, a Russian-funded NGO was set up to create friction between Ukrainian and Polish populations by manipulating perceptions of historical events.[107] Prior to 2022, there were acts of violent provocation aimed at Polish tourists in western Ukraine. Russian-backed NGOs have also been used in the EU to manipulate European target audiences.[108] At the same time, the Russian government has shut or limited foreign NGOs and cultural bodies in Russia, such as the British Council, seeing them as tools of foreign states. It has 'unmasked' diplomats working with Russian NGOs as spies.[109] Putin has described Russian politicians who take Western funds via NGOs as 'jackals'.[110]

Russia has also used cultural tools to unite the Russian diaspora in occupied territories. A music festival, organised by the Russian Ministry of Culture and featuring Russian artists, toured the cities of the occupied Donbas region in February 2016.[111] This is not the first time Russian cultural events have been used in the former USSR following paramilitary conflict. Following the annexation of Abkhazia and South Ossetia from Georgia in 2008, South Ossetia's capital, Tskhinvali, hosted the St Petersburg Mariinsky Orchestra, who played Shostakovich's 'Symphony No. 7', nicknamed the Leningrad symphony.[112] The Mariinsky Orchestra was also used in the Syrian conflict.[113] In the midst of the Syrian desert, in the middle of the civil war, Putin flew the Mariinsky Orchestra out for a concert at the Roman ruins at Palmyra. It was a show-stopping moment and a global media event, organised to celebrate the recapture of the Roman ruins from the ISIS terror group.

Finally, youth and sporting events have also been liberally used as tools of annexation and assimilation. The event 'I, a citizen of Russia' took place in June 2010, organised by South Ossetian youth groups. A Russian week was held shortly afterwards, with lectures and talks on the Russian Army and the future of Russia and South Ossetia. Putin has been clear about their role, stating that 'physical culture and sport are not entertainment but literally a matter of national and political interest'.[114]

MILITARY POWER

The tools of military power are well known; they need no introduction here. Where they are visibly changing – through meat assaults, the battlefield saturation of drones or electronic warfare – these are dealt with elsewhere in the book. What I will briefly look at here is first, how violent military force segues with sabotage and political warfare; second, the role of secret and special forces in the 'near abroad'; and third, how prisoners of war are used as tools of psychological warfare.

As the head of Britain's MI5 has said, the Kremlin is on a 'sustained mission to generate mayhem on British and European streets. We've seen arson, sabotage and more.'[115] This is not tabloid journalistic hyperbole or James Bond fiction but a serious statement from the head of the UK's domestic spy agency. Currently, Russia seems to be aiming to stretch and stress the resources of NATO states' security agencies, rather than sabotaging as a prelude to conventional war. Nevertheless, there is significant activity in this area.

The first known act of sabotage in a NATO state was in 2014, when a Czech arms dump was blown up, killing two people, although Russia's involvement was not confirmed for several years after.[116] There was a step change after 2022. The Czech foreign minister has reported that there have been up to 100 suspicious incidents in Europe in 2024 alone that might be attributable to Russia.[117] Up to sixty of Putin's enemies in Russia and Europe have suffered 'mysterious' deaths since the 2022 invasion.[118] Arson attacks have taken place in the UK, Poland, Germany, Lithuania and Latvia. Diplomatic expulsions and a tightening of security have weakened the Kremlin's ability to directly control operations, so some sabotage is conducted by criminals and those recruited by the dark web, meaning that the work may be of poorer quality and more easily disrupted. GPS jamming, endangering civilian aircraft, has happened regularly over the Baltic.[119] In North Africa, the EU's border force claims that Putin is establishing militias to control immigration flows into Europe, weaponising immigration with the intent of destabilising European societies and politics.[120]

The Russian Main Directorate of Deep Sea Research, known as GUGI, has been closely studying the vulnerability of the underwater cables that provide so much of our communications and internet access. The Royal Navy and others are concerned.[121] On 18 November 2024, the day after the US cleared US and UK missiles to be fired into Russia, two deep-sea cables connecting Sweden to Lithuania and Finland to Germany were cut.[122] On 26 December 2024, the Estlink 2 underwater electricity cable linking Finland and Estonia was damaged by the anchor of the Eagle S, a vessel suspected of being part of Russia's 'shadow fleet' carrying embargoed products.[123]

The unit behind much of the onshore sabotage, cyberattacks and assassinations is the GRU, Russia's military intelligence agency (its formal title is the Main Intelligence Directorate). The GRU's role is very different from that of US or UK military intelligence organisations. Whilst the GRU does collect foreign intelligence using human, cyber, satellite and signals intelligence, it also conducts clandestine physical operations and cyber warfare. It also has Russia's special forces soldiers under its command.

The GRU has played an important role in the development of Russia's integrated conflict plans. It traces its heritage back to 1918. In the 1920s and 1930s, then known as the Fourth Directorate, it had a reputation for 'aggressive and often careless operations' and for coming into conflict with other parts of the Soviet state, often the KGB.[124] During the Cold War, the GRU regularly falsified the rate of military production in NATO states to help justify the extraordinary levels of Soviet defence expenditure. When Anatoly Serdyukov became Minister of Defence in 2007 and introduced his 'New Look' reforms, he brought with him former KGB man Vitaly Shlykov to sit on the ministry's board. Shlykov was a renowned former spy, unmasked and imprisoned for two years in Switzerland in 1983. He later become a defence minister under President Yeltsin. Critically, he had also spent time as the head of economic intelligence in the GRU, where he became aware of the organisation's record of exaggeration.

Shlykov and Serdyukov set about doing two things. First, they made the GRU subordinate to the Ministry of Defence. Second, they turned it into an intelligence organisation rather than a special forces unit. The GRU shrank and its forces were due to be reassigned to the armed forces. It even lost its name at one point and its insignia, a black bat. It was, allegedly, Shlykov's revenge for the GRU's unreliable Cold War reporting.

'It became about intelligence, not killing,' says FSB expert Andrei Soldatov. 'But it was also about humiliation.'[125]

To the delight of many in the armed forces, Serdyukov was sacked in November 2012, ostensibly for having an affair. When the initially popular Sergei Shoigu took over, he immediately and successfully lobbied to restore the GRU's role. The GRU was repopulated with the old operators and its old mentality. It grew quickly. Its new boss, Igor Sergun, was both politically astute and a proponent of active operations. They were given charge of the Crimean operation, which was a triumph. By comparison, the FSB, the progeny of the old Soviet KGB with whom the GRU had often clashed, failed in its task to keep Yanukovych in power in Kyiv. Russia's Syrian operation, where GRU work included coordinating air strikes with the Syrian government and pro-Assad militias, reinforced the GRU's reputation for success.[126] Operations in Europe followed, including the attempted poisoning of former GRU agent Sergei Skripal in Britain. The GRU also oversaw relations with the Wagner Group, another organisation that attempted to shortcut military bureaucracy and deliver Putin the service he wanted.

Putin was sold on the GRU. It delivered – at least sometimes – and was loyal. 'Putin was fascinated. Finally, he found an agency which was very active, very aggressive, had lots of people ready to go and kill and bomb and whatever,' says Soldatov.

For the GRU, cyber warfare is a vast and growing area of conflict in its own right and one that can deliver global results whilst being run out of Moscow. In Ukraine, it's been used not only to harvest information and sabotage military action but also as a testing ground for malware and cyber tactics to be used against Western targets. The most well-known case is that of SolarWinds, whereby Russian hackers sabotaged lines of code in a 2019 software update. SolarWinds's Orion software is used by thousands of businesses globally to help run their systems.[127] By rewriting 4,032 lines of code on the routine update, the Russians opened a 'secret backdoor' to

18,000 infected networks – a tactic known as a 'supply-chain operation'.[128] That enabled them to rummage through the files of the US Department of Justice, State, Treasury, Energy and Commerce – a total of nine departments and agencies – for months until detected in late 2020. Microsoft president Brad Smith called it 'the largest and most sophisticated attack the world has ever seen'.[129] A similar tactic had been tested in Ukraine in a 2017 cyber operation called NotPetya, whereby the GRU infiltrated a widely used piece of software to break into Ukrainian networks.[130] NotPetya appeared to be designed to damage infrastructure software rather than spy but was nevertheless seen to be a dry run for SolarWinds in the methods used. At the end of that attack, the software self-destructed.

Prior to the re-emergence of the GRU, espionage and political warfare work in the 'near abroad' had been overseen by the FSB. In the late 1980s, this was put onto a formal footing when the Fifth Directorate of the FSB was charged with espionage work in former Soviet states. This directorate was initially quite small, launched in 1998 by Putin himself with the task of recruiting foreigners working on Russian soil. But a more promising and exciting role for the directorate soon became apparent. Russia's foreign intelligence agency, the SVR, had signed an agreement not to spy on the states of the former Soviet Union but no such promise had been made by the FSB.

Whilst the formal FSB work may have only begun in 2000, Russian agencies and military forces did engage in disruptive work in the former Soviet Union in the 1990s and appeared to do so to support Russia's 'managed' conflicts. These managed conflicts follow a template. Ethnic or other rivalries are fermented and local politicians and ethnic groups, supported by Russian actors, raise current or historic grievances. Political front groups are formed if not already in place. Acts of provocation take place. Violence breaks out, seemingly from nowhere. Force is escalated until such a time as the target capitulates and Moscow's demands are met, after which violence suddenly dies down.

This 'managed' conflict scenario was witnessed, in chaotic circumstances, in Moldova and Georgia in the early 1990s, when the governments of both states were trying to move out of Russia's orbit. Georgian leader and former Soviet Foreign Minister Eduard Shevardnadze was clear on the Russian role in manipulating an already complex relationship between ethnic Abkhaz and Georgians prior to the 1992–3 war, in which 9,000 Georgians and Abkhazians died and 250,000 Georgians, who made up nearly half the population of the Abkhaz region, were displaced. Shevardnadze said:

> These are the bastards, who did everything they could to raise Abkhaz separatism to the level of fascism. They were the ones who provided the financing, they were the ones who supplied all the modern armament … Training was carried out with their help, and they even took direct part in the fighting. That is what I call the policy of reactionary Russia … We have been the victim of these games, of this confrontation in Russia … They were huge forces, which Georgia had no chance of countering.[131]

The conflict was notable for the steady escalation of Russian military support for the Abkhaz, which represented only a small minority of people in that region. Two ceasefires were agreed with Georgia, during which time the Abkhaz rebels were rearmed and support to them was increased. The ceasefires were cynically broken by the Abkhaz and their Russian backers, prior to a successful advance on Sukhumi, the capital of Abkhazia, by which time Russian aircraft and artillery were being used in open support of the Abkhaz separatists. I was in Abkhazia in the late 1990s and well remember being cheerily told that 'of course the Russians helped us' by the political leaders of the region. As well as military advisers, Russian military forces supporting the Abkhaz against the Georgians amounted to twenty T-72 tanks, a landing force battalion, twenty armoured personnel carriers, Grad rockets, Uragan rockets and twelve artillery pieces staffed by Russian officers.

Finally, Russia has also illegally used prisoners of war (PoWs) for propaganda purposes and, through murder, torture and ill-treatment, to inflict psychological pain on the Ukrainian population. This has been ongoing since 2014 and has become significantly worse since 2022. A former Ukrainian PoW from the first invasion in 2014, Edward Kulinich, described to me back in 2017 the deliberate use of prisoners for propaganda purposes. On one occasion, Ukrainian prisoners were offered the chance to talk to their relatives on mobile phones, provided they explicitly explained that a prisoner exchange was being blocked by Ukraine.[132] The incident, Kulinich said, was filmed for propaganda purposes, with no such prisoner exchange planned. On another occasion, he said, he was driven to a fake prisoner exchange. 'The exchange didn't happen because it was not even planned. They planned to do a TV report for the Zvezda TV channel.' Zvezda is the channel of the Russian defence ministry. In August 2014, a story from Zvezda did indeed falsely report that Ukrainian authorities had reneged on prisoner swaps.[133]

Since the 2022 invasion, there has been 'systematic and widespread use of torture of Ukrainian PoWs' according to a United Nations report.[134] Since August 2024 alone, the United Nations has received credible evidence of the murder of dozens of Ukrainian PoWs.[135] Thousands more are being held incommunicado.

The experience of Ukrainian soldier 'Dima', thirty-nine, was typical of many. He was captured on 12 April 2022 and held for twenty-one months. After being captured, Dima was taken to a prison complex south of Donetsk called Olenivka. Later that year, Olenivka became the infamous scene of a massacre when an explosion destroyed a part of it, killing more than fifty and injuring at least seventy-five. The Russians claimed the prison was hit by a US missile, but the more likely explanation is that it was destroyed to hide evidence of the systematic murder and torture of men from Ukraine's elite Azov Brigade.[136]

It was already a brutal hellhole before the bomb. Dima said that after he arrived at Olenivka, PoWs were forced to run a gauntlet of seventy prison wardens, who would beat them with metal pipes and sticks. The unlucky ones suffered broken arms and legs, for which there was no medical treatment offered. From there, he was taken into Russia. Months of physical and mental pain followed. Hours were spent in stress positions. The PoWs were underfed so that a form of slow starvation took place. Some emaciated men, Dima said, lost 40 kilograms. Sleep deprivation was common and the cries of tortured men were audible in the cells during day and night. Skin infections were rife; clothes were neither changed nor washed for months. Showers were once a week. There were no doctors, no medical care and no treatment of injuries or broken bones. Some men cracked under the pressure, attempting suicide by slicing their veins on rocks or jagged metal or cracking their heads open. In such cases, a group punishment was imposed on the entire cell. There are countless such stories. It was, Dima said, 'horror from the beginning'.[137]

There were other experiences Ukrainian soldiers found even more difficult to talk about, such as male rape and sexual violence.

'They don't want to admit to it, not even to psychologists,' said Petro Yatsenko, a writer who helps to support PoWs to reintegrate.[138] Unsurprisingly, mental health problems are not uncommon, and the longer the prisoner has spent in captivity, the worse they are. Representative visits from the International Committee of the Red Cross (ICRC) are few and meetings with prisoners tend to be communal and witnessed by Russian captors. Yatsenko recounted one incident of a prisoner who complained about the lack of ICRC contact. 'When they had gone, this guy was tortured by the jail administration. The torture continued for two days. At the end of this, he killed himself.' It was, he said, a 'very painful story'.

DIPLOMATIC WARFARE

In the Soviet Union, there was no division between diplomatic and informational activity. In Western terms, message and narrative discipline was high due to the totalitarian nature of the state: journalists, diplomats, spies and party officials were vehicles for the projection of Soviet power. The evidence suggests that in eastern Europe, in the Balkans and Syria, Russian diplomacy has again mirrored Soviet diplomacy, which was, according to the United States Senate, 'not diplomacy in the usual sense of the term' but 'another and one of the principal spheres of Soviet propaganda'.[139] Russian ambassadors are again acting not only as spokesmen for the regime but as purveyors of destabilising and provocative narratives, which fit into Russian disinformation tactics and strategies.

Putin's conflict diplomacy aims to weaken and overthrow the West's dominance in the struggle for the 'new world order' in the coming years. One tactic has been to conduct a battle for narrative and influence in the developing world in a new anti-colonial campaign, aimed to undermine the standing of the US and its allies. I saw it for myself in November 2024, when a friend working for a European spy agency passed me a read-out to show how the Russians were working to weaken the UK. At the time, Britain's new Labour government was trying to negotiate a deal with Mauritius to hand over the Chagos Islands to them, on which the strategically valuable Diego Garcia air base was sited. Many in the UK thought the decision a foolish one, driven by a dogma within Britian's Foreign Office. Worse, Russian diplomats were trying to damage the UK's relations with Mauritius and use the issue of sovereignty over the Chagos archipelago as a 'conflict generator'.[140] Meetings and events were organised by the Russian Embassy, the outcome of which was a joint declaration demanding the 'decolonisation' of Mauritius and the end of the military occupations by the US and the UK.[141]

Turing to Ukraine and the former Soviet territories, one particularly valuable tool used by the Kremlin has been 'passportisation' – distributing Russian passports to those in occupied or disputed territories. Russia has given out passports in eastern Ukraine to create Russian citizens, as well as in the Georgian enclaves of South Ossetia and Abkhazia and the Moldovan enclave of Transnistria.[142] Passportisation is an important part of buttressing Russian control of a newly seized territory, as well as giving it a pretext for intervention. In occupied eastern Ukraine, a refusal to take a Russian passport means denial of basic services, loss of job if working in the state sector and questioning or worse by FSB forces.

Russia has used more creative forms of public outreach too. Perhaps the best example of unorthodox diplomacy has been through Putin's use of biker gangs in a semi-official capacity, most notably the Night Wolves. His association with the Night Wolves started in August 2011, when he joined them for a ride. Since then, the group has supported the Kremlin's annexation of Crimea and the war in eastern Ukraine. Gang leader Alexander Zaldostanov told a Russian TV channel that the Night Wolves had become a 'state-recognised instrument of public diplomacy'.[143] In spring 2015, the Night Wolves rode through eastern Europe following the route of the Red Army to Berlin. Their website is littered with references to the retaking of Crimea and they present themselves as the 'motorclub of the Russian spirit, motorclub of patriots!'[144] Alexei Navalny, who was later assassinated in prison at the hands of the Russian state, claimed that the Night Wolves received 56 million roubles ($1.1 million dollars) in government funds, a third of which was allotted for a motorbike show in Crimea.[145] In May 2015, the government allegedly allotted 227 hectares of land to the bikers for military-patriotic education in the Crimea at a peppercorn rent.[146]

As with all elements of Russia's new total war, diplomacy works to reinforce the joint effort. It is especially difficult to separate the interlinked tools of 'information warfare' from the tools of political warfare, espionage and diplomacy.

On 4 February 2014, when Ukraine was in chaos and without a government, pro-Russian media leaked an audio recording of a conversation between US Assistant Secretary of State for Europe Victoria Nuland and US ambassador to Ukraine Geoffrey Pyatt. Nuland and Pyatt were discussing the composition of the Ukrainian government and Russian interference. In the course of the conversation, they were dismissive of the role of the EU. 'F*ck the EU,' she said in an apparent reference to their differences over policy.[147]

The leak almost certainly came from an intercept of the conversation collected by the Russian FSB, and that's certainly what the US implied when it ascribed the leak to 'Russian tradecraft', calling it 'a new low'.[148] The story was leaked to Russia Today, which used it to goad the US over its involvement in forming a Ukrainian government. Putin's advisers called for Ukrainian forces to crush what he said was an American-backed coup. Russian diplomats went into overdrive in Europe and elsewhere, accusing the US of orchestrating events and effectively being behind the chaos. The incident ticked many informational boxes for Russia. It allowed the Kremlin to show that the US was meddling in Ukrainian affairs and that Ukrainian politicians were in hock to the US. It created friction between the US and the EU and it facilitated a near-hysterical response in Russia.[149]

• • •

In this chapter, I have attempted to do what has rarely, if ever, been done: to show the extraordinary range of tactics and tools involved in Putin's theory of war and to give an idea of their breadth and how they are integrated. In doing so, this shows how Russia's new total war is a reinvigorated form of conflict that combines traditional ideas of war and subversive war – indeed, all the tools of the state, from culture to energy and sport to bikers' clubs – to maximise power in service of the Kremlin's antagonistic agenda.

At its heart, Russian conflict is primarily a state of mind, from which flows actions across the virtual, psychological and physical domains. How military action is used to drive psychological pressure is the subject of the next chapter.

CHAPTER 9

STORIES FROM THE FRONT: THE SURGEONS OF KHARKIV AND THE SHAHED HUNTERS OF ODESA

'You need to be prepared that this is the last day of your life.'

– Dr Ivan Parkhomenko[1]

Dr Ivan Parkhomenko is showing me around Hospital No. 25 in Kharkiv, a city on the edge, physically and psychologically. 'I don't know what mental health is anymore,' he says. 'You need to be prepared that this is the last day of your life here.'

Kharkiv is Ukraine's second city and is a regular target for Russian missile and bomb strikes. Before the war, it was the country's tech and university hub, its economy boosted by thousands of foreign students from developing nations, drawn by its reputation for technical courses such as engineering. The students are long gone. Their dorms and studio flats are now occupied by Ukrainians driven from their homes in towns nearer the front line or from cities such as Bakhmut, which has been all but obliterated. Kharkiv is about 30 kilometres from the Russian border. Rumour has it that if the Russians had seized the city in 2022, it would have served as a capital for Russia's own Ukrainian republic, just as it did after the Russian Revolution in 1917.

This sprawling industrial city, Ukraine's answer to Birmingham, is hit nearly every day. Ukraine's Ministry of Defence reported in September 2024 that Russian forces launched attacks on Ukrainian cities every day of the month with 1,339 Shahed drones, 1,107 of which were downed by air defence, as well as KH-59 cruise missiles and Iskanders.[2] Shaheds are Iranian-designed drones that fly relatively slowly but can be produced and used in large numbers. Weaving across Ukraine, they sound like flying lawn mowers. KH-59s are more sophisticated Russian-made cruise missiles that fly low, at faster speeds than the Shahed drones. Iskanders are short-range (up to 300 miles) ballistic missiles. They fly high into the atmosphere before falling fast to earth.

The day Ivan shows us around, three strikes have been recorded, most probably by S-300s, he says. S-300s were originally built as air defence weapons to shoot down fast jets but are now being used against ground targets. I ask if the Russians have changed the warheads. Ivan shakes his head and explains why the S-300s have a particularly unpleasant reputation. 'It's the same warhead. It explodes ten meters above the ground. It's packed with *plomb*… [he searches for the word in English] *lead* and steel'. Ivan explained that the steel destroys strong material whilst the molten lead rips through much else. Both obliterate flesh and bone.

If the first element of the Kremlin's tripartite strategy is to hold frontline positions and then wear down Ukrainian forces through relentless 'meat assaults' backed by artillery and drone strikes, the second part is to wear down civilian morale by attacking electricity supplies. The Kremlin wants to make life hell for ordinary people and break their will so that the country's leaders will sue for peace on Russian terms, even if it means giving up land and a 'Western' future. According to Russian theories of warfare, a major target – arguably the primary target – is the adversary's mind. The Trump administration's partial withdrawal of support in February and March 2025 was not only a military blow but a psychological one as well.

Whilst Russian forces would have preferred a quick conquest of Kharkiv in 2022, the fall-back option is to make the city unliveable for its population. Thus, Kharkivans are always waiting for the next explosion. Ivan takes us to see a bomb shelter being refurbished into an underground operating theatre. 'If there are many patients and 24/7 shelling,' he explains, 'we can't operate intensive care on second or third floors – they are too dangerous. So we are preparing an underground operation room. There's water and canned food – we'll be able to survive down here.'

As we walk across the grounds, there's the noticeable 'clump' of a missile landing in the distance.

'You'll never hear your own. That's what soldiers say,' Ivan jokes.

Where are the air alarms, I ask? They had sounded regularly between 9 p.m. and midnight the previous night, with anti-aircraft guns opening up on targets at 3 a.m., waking me up. We had accidentally stayed in the north-eastern suburb of Saltivka, one of the noisier parts of town on account of Russian weapons falling short and hitting buildings there. Ivan explains that the air force doesn't have time to turn on the sirens, especially if missiles are launched from near the Russian city of Belgorod. 'Their flying time over Ukraine is thirty seconds, maybe forty – less than a minute that's for sure. They'll have landed by the time the air siren goes off.'

When the sirens do go off in Kharkiv, it's generally to warn that Russian planes are in the sky. We look at the air raid siren app as it starts to sound. This one tells us that jets – how many is unclear – have just taken off. That means that Kharkivans may have half an hour or so to get to shelters before the bombs the planes are carrying can be launched and landed on the city. Most people do not take the app's advice, despite a voice gently reminding them 'your overconfidence is your weakness'. It is only on severe days that people take to the metro for cover.

Kharkiv is within range of Russian air-launched glide bombs – KABs in Russian and Ukrainian, FABs in English – weapons which may yet change the course of the war. These highly destructive bombs are, to all intents and purposes, the poor man's cruise missile and an example of versatile, cheap adaptation. Glide bombs are freefall, unguided bombs, which have strap-on wings and a navigation device attached to them. 'KAB/FAB' stands for high explosive. It's followed by a number, which indicates its size in kilograms. The most common glide bomb is the FAB-500, a 500-kilo bomb carrying a high explosive charge. The explosive charge is less than half of the overall weight of the weapon, so a FAB-500 carries a charge of around 150 kilograms. The rarer FAB-3000 M-54 carries 1,400 kg – nearly a tonne and a half of explosives – but has a shorter range due to its heavier weight.[3] The FAB-3000 throws shrapnel out to a radius of nearly 1 mile, although the blast range on all of them is big enough to cause destruction regardless of whether they hit their targets precisely. FABs have no heat signatures – they have no motor – so they are difficult to identify and shoot down, although some are now being fitted with rocket boosters to extend their range. They are cheap compared to the cost of more sophisticated missiles such as Iskander and Kalibr cruise missiles, which cost the Russian Ministry of Defence perhaps $1 million per missile.[4] They are launched at height from Russian bomber jets from the safety of Russian air space, reducing the risk to pilot and plane. They can glide for up to 60 km. Whilst Kyiv is not (yet) within their range, Kharkiv is. Russia has many thousands of these bombs in storage.

Silent and deadly, they fly until they impact on a block of flats or a shopping centre or a road junction. To be in a city being hit by them, listening to the sound of their implosion, is to feel an acute sense of vulnerability, especially at night.

Like many industrial cities, Kharkiv has a strong sense of identity, which is, for the moment, helping to keep it functioning. At the start of the war, when Russian troops were at the gates of the city, perhaps half its population of 1.7 million fled. Whilst some have returned, the number of people is well down in comparison to the start of the war. At night, driving around the city is eerily quiet. Streetlights may be off to save electricity or because there is none.

However, Hospital No. 25's renowned director Dr Kyrylo Parkhomenko, Ivan's father, remains resolutely upbeat whilst acknowledging the danger. 'Like everyone here, I have constantly 99 per cent of stress. Even a simple walk can be your last, but it maybe will be surprising for you. I don't know any person that left Kharkiv last year. Kharkiv is a special city.'[5]

Whilst media coverage has, for good reason, mainly focused on the experience of soldiers, there are many quiet heroes in this war – train workers, emergency workers and doctors. Every doctor whose stories I have listened to in Kharkiv, Poltava and Kyiv spent the opening months of the war working without a break, sleeping in hospital corridors or basements. Many did not leave the confines of their hospitals for the first few months of the conflict at all.

As Ivan describes it, 'For more than a hundred days we just lived in there, slept on the floor, ate together, everything. We were 24/7 in the operating room or just sleeping. That was when Russia was two minutes from Kharkiv, with rockets landing in the grounds of the hospital.'

The day before I met Ivan, twelve rockets and missiles were

launched at the city and ten of them made it through Kharkiv's tired defences. 'They shot into a sports complex, some parks, some roads, some civilian buildings. So what was the purpose of this?' he asks in disbelief. I visit the bombed sports centre, used as a training site for some of Ukraine's Olympic athletes. Smoky dust rises from the remains and there is a smell of charred destruction in the air. Around me, emergency workers are repairing gas and other mains supplies. This is in the middle of a residential area with tall, Soviet-era blocks. A young mother from a neighbouring apartment block walks past in tears, clearly still suffering from shock.

The emergency workers' task has become more dangerous due to the illegal practice of double tapping: hitting a target and then waiting for rescue workers, medics and others to arrive and then striking it again with the specific aim of killing them. In Kharkiv alone, eight such individuals have been killed and fifty-seven injured, almost all in Russian double-tap attacks. 'It's hard to find words when you talk with relatives. The people who do this are terrorists,' Yevhen Vasylenko, a member of Kharkiv's emergency services, tells me. 'In this war, we are losing our best people.'[6]

What effect is the bombing having on civilians? The most common symptom of stress in the city is sleep disorders, according to local psychologist Vitali Khrystenko, but the wider problem is that 'nobody's planning for the future. They are just living for the day.'[7] He and his colleagues give limited help to civilians and soldiers alike, but they can't separate their patients from the source of their trauma – the rockets that are killing and injuring at random. Instead, they do the equivalent of psychological patchwork. 'We don't "cure" people here. We just provide them short-term, imperfect help and support.'

That immediate stress exists alongside other tensions between those who stayed in Kharkiv and those who left to return later and between the majority who have resisted and those suspected of 'spotting' (helping the Russians with targeting information). Vitali remembers one such case vividly. He was delivering food aid to a block of flats and in the darkened basement he found two groups: on one side, a young couple looking badly bruised and on the other, a large group of women, some of them quite elderly, who had accused them of spotting for the Russians and, despite their age, had severely beaten the young couple. The women had the couple trapped and were waiting for the police to arrive. Their fate was unclear. Some collaborators are put on trial and some, it is rumoured, are allowed to escape by those in the pay of the Russians.

Those with a role and purpose in defending the city or with relatives in the armed forces tend to have better mental health than those who are less psychologically committed. Others, including internal refugees who have come to Kharkiv with very little, live from day to day, hoping against hope that they might return home. The older ones struggle with money and finding work. Their stoicism hides lives of quiet despair. The war affects people in many different ways. Ivan, for example, has put off starting a family. Surely, I ask, that is giving Putin what he wants? Ivan disagrees. 'If I will just die in this hospital because of some rocket or shell, my children will be without me. So what is the point to try to bring in this world a life that will be abandoned by you?'

He's adapted to the sounds of the bombs and explosions. This has become the new normal, although he still finds the sound of the spin cycle on a washing in machine stressful, saying, 'It's 100 per cent the same sound as a low-flying Russia plane.' Father and son laugh at the incongruity. Ivan's father jokes about being in the 'quieter' city of Poltava ninety minutes away and jumping at the sound of doors slamming. 'People in Poltava look at us as if we are freaks.' However, even in Poltava the bombs are now falling more regularly. An attack that took place the day before we arrived in Kharkiv left over forty dead; it is very likely the target was identified by a fifth columnist working for the Russians.

Vitali reminds me that it is important to find hope in the small things in life. When the bombings were at their worst in Kharkiv, he and his wife slept in the hallway of his fourth-floor apartment in order to have two walls between them and any missile, as per the official advice. The artillery implosions in the district left the house rumbling like an ongoing earthquake. Yet in between the attacks, Kharkiv's municipal workers kept to their routine, cleaning up the streets and clearing away debris. 'I collected all the sweets in my apartment and ran down to give them to them. The smiles showed their appreciation. It was a happy moment.'

• • •

Whilst the Kremlin strikes fear into Ukrainian hearts by directly hitting urban targets, it is also methodically degrading the country's energy generation and supply. A freezing population, in Putin's mind, will be more pliable to Russian demands.

I am in a power plant in the west of Ukraine – I've been asked not to reveal the location. Director Serhii, a stocky and easy-going man in his late fifties, is showing me around the plant – or what is left of it. We are in the vast turbine hall, built decades ago when the Soviet Union was developing the Ukrainian electricity grid. It's been struck more than half a dozen times by missiles, bombs and Shahed drones. Every time it gets hit, its employees clean up – it's good for morale, if nothing else – but there is no electricity flowing. The boilers and turbines that make up the power-generating units have been bent out of shape, whilst the thick, rolled-metal wires that carry the electricity on the stubby-armed red and white pylons that sit in rows alongside the plant hang limp in the air, ripped from their moorings by the power of the blasts. Above them, plastic sheets originally put in place to cover the many shattered windows have themselves been shredded by subsequent strikes. They flutter like tattered and torn dirty grey plastic flags. Inside the cavernous hall, mounds of dark grey dust sit on pipes bent out of shape and on top of 1960s control panels, giving the place a post-apocalyptic feel.

The first time a Russian X-101 long-range cruise missile slammed into the plant was on a winter evening in 2022. Serhii heard the explosion as he was driving in to work.

'I knew it was the plant. There isn't another target around here. I prayed to God that no one [was] injured.'[8] He arrived to join his workers in the communal bomb shelter, where some of his staff were kneeling in prayer. They worked day and night to give the plant some security, filling and placing sandbags and negotiating air defence. Russian warfare, for Serhii, 'is impossible to explain'. Looking around his shattered domain, he says, 'It's not a human way of behaviour. They want to just destroy everything.'

However, for better or worse, there *is* a logic to this part of the attritional struggle. Whilst the battle that gets the most media attention is on the front line, the battle that will decide Ukraine's fate takes place at the power plants – encompassing 100 or so main sub-stations – and along the pylon lines across the country. Without electricity and energy, Ukraine will not be able to heat homes or drive what remains of its industry. Small generators can keep some homes and small businesses going, but a nation without enough electricity and heating in winter will struggle to survive. Ukraine needs to keep its civilians warm, as well as its troops supplied.

If it fails, electricity shortages – combined with daily missile strikes causing actual and psychological damage – may push another 1 million refugees into eastern and central Europe, just as western Europeans tire of the Ukraine crisis. So, whilst Russia's war on the physical front line is designed primarily to attack Ukraine's *means* to defend itself, Russia's war on the psychological and industrial fronts is designed primarily to destroy Ukraine's *will* to fight. It's a war 'for the economy, for production capability and for the spirt of our people,' Serhii explains.

During the Cold War, Ukraine was an over-producer of energy. Its 750-gigawatt power lines, linked to nuclear and coal-fired power, were designed to produce large amounts of energy with minimal transmission loss into eastern Europe. The aim was to encourage economic and political dependency on the Soviet Union. After the collapse of the USSR, Ukraine started to run down its energy production and rely on cheaper Russian imports, especially from coal-fired power stations. It did so to keep prices down and to keep its industrial regions, with a higher Russian-speaking population, happy. In the short term, this policy made the energy that drove Ukraine's inefficient large industries cheaper, but in the long term, it increased dependency on Russia.

Dmytro Sakharuk, executive officer of one of Ukraine's largest power-generating firms, DTEK, which has now seen much of its productive capacity destroyed, explains: 'They wanted to connect Ukraine [to Russia] using as many links as possible. Energy was one of them.'[9]

Immediately before the war, Ukraine was producing 30 gigawatts of power. By early 2024, this had been reduced to 13 and by the end of 2024, it had been reduced to around 10 gigawatts. The country has a third of its pre-war capacity left, and whilst demand is down thanks to the destruction of its industrial base, it is now higher than supply. As of winter 2024, there is an import supply capacity of only 1.7 gigawatts from European states.

So critical is the issue of the energy grid that its disconnection was almost certainly tied to the Russian invasion date. Prior to the war, Ukraine had been planning to change from the Russian grid to the European one. Such a switch would have entailed closing off from both systems for a period of approximately seventy-two hours. If the Ukrainian grid had remained attached to Russia, any war damage could have impacted the Russian grid. As Sakharuk explained, the grid is like an organism, with problems in one country feeding into another. Ukrainian requests to turn off the system were repeatedly refused, with the Russians citing issues with a nuclear power plant as their excuse. Both sides finally agreed a switch-off time in the early hours of 24 February 2022. Three hours later, Russian forces crossed into Ukraine.

'I think that was an intentional coincidence, let's say,' comments Sakharuk.

From October 2022 until March 2024, Russian missiles primarily targeted the transmission and distribution infrastructure, aiming to prevent electricity being transferred around the country. Attacks on power plants were relatively rare. The thinking behind this may have been that if Russia had succeeded in conquering Ukraine, the system could be put back together relatively quickly. Repairing a sub-station is much quicker than repairing a power-generating unit of boiler and turbine; the first takes days or weeks, the second takes many weeks or months. 'The initial tactic was to disconnect the country,' said energy expert Aura Sabadus.[10]

In March 2024, the tactics changed. Russian attacks systematically destroyed the entire infrastructure, from power plants to substations to transmission lines. Nine waves of missile and drone strikes destroyed coal-fired power plants producing over five gigawatts of energy between March and August, with 200 missiles in each attack. Two further mass attacks took place on 17 and 28 November 2024.[11] Some targets, such as the massive Kakhovka dam on the Dnipro River, had already been destroyed. Indeed, destruction of the dam was an example of creative targeting for multiple effects, despite its wanton illegality. First, it flooded Ukrainian military positions; second, it caused civilian chaos and pressured the emergency-services infrastructure; and third, it reduced potential electricity capacity.

As quickly as they were bombed, Ukrainians tried to repair the plants. The UK, the US and other states sent generators and sub-station equipment. Further air defence was allocated and substations had surrounding concrete walls built. But just as on the battlefield, Putin sought to destroy will by attrition. 'There was a cycle of destruction and repair,' said Sabadus. 'The Russians were destroying and the Ukrainians were sending the engineers on the ground to repair, and within a couple of hours or a couple of days, they were destroyed again.'

These attacks took advantage of a window of opportunity caused by the reduction in military supplies from the US, beginning in early 2024. They overwhelmed the dwindling stock of air defence missiles.

'They not only knew it, they did everything they could to exhaust our air defence,' says Sakharuk. 'In January and February [2024], they sent drones every night to Ukraine in order to force us to spend air-defence munition against those drones.' Russia launched large-scale attacks on energy supplies on 22 and 29 March and then again in April, May, June and July. Air defence units that had run out of ammunition were reduced to watching their radars as the missiles came in. The only defence that worked were heavy machine guns, but even then, they are only effective against slow-moving drones.

As of late summer 2024, Russian bombing switched from the power plants to refocus on the transmission system, specifically the 100 or so major sub-stations that are the links between the power stations and the smaller sub-stations. Sakharuk gave an example of one day's worth of attacks the week we met in September 2024: 'On Monday they sent how many? One hundred and twenty-six missiles and almost one hundred drones. So, the total is almost two hundred items. In order to intercept them, you need a very big stock of munitions.'

• • •

The task of defending cities and their energy supplies falls to Ukraine's air defence system. At the top end are the limited number of US-made Patriot systems, then the medium-range systems donated by NATO states, as well as sophisticated Soviet-era equipment such as BUKs – it was a Russian-supplied BUK that shot down Malaysian Airlines Flight 17 over eastern Ukraine in the summer of 2022, killing 298 passengers and crew. Below the BUKs are large but old Soviet systems such as ZSU self-propelled weapons – twin anti-aircraft guns mounted on an amphibious tank base – and shorter-range shoulder-launched systems known as MANPADS.

Due to a variety of factors – Ukrainian sale of military equipment to Russia in the decades prior to the war, the lack of investment in defence and a lack of Western support – this layered defence has many holes in it.

At the tactical end of that patchwork of defence, volunteers and territorial defence units are tasked with shooting down slow-moving drones. Despite being at the less sophisticated end of the scale, their work is some of the most important, due to Russian reliance on the slow Shaheds and the amount of them being sent to Ukraine.

Tonight, I am in a dark winter field a few miles north of the Black Sea coast to meet the Shahed hunters of Odesa. They may sound like characters out of an ancient Black Sea tale, but every night these modern volunteers go out with heavy machine guns – in this case, a Browning welded onto the back of a pick-up truck – to shoot down the Iranian-designed drones, which snake across land and sea to their city. The Browning is decades old, but it is not the oldest air-defence weapon. The volunteers of Kyiv's DFTH 31 unit (DFTH translates as Community Territorial Voluntary Formation) were, until the summer of 2024, equipped with two Maxim guns linked together – the same Maxim gun in the service of the Imperial Russian Army in 1910 and based on the British machine gun of the same name designed in 1884.

Odesa experiences few glide bombs. The risk to Russian pilots flying out to the Black Sea to drop them is too great. Instead, the city and the military and civilian sites in and around it are targets for drones and sometimes missiles, which come in at relatively close range from Crimea.

There are plenty of targets in this port and military city. Almost every time I visit a unit, we end up in a bomb shelter waiting out attacks. These occasions sometimes make for the best conversation. In April 2022, weeks after the invasion, I met the head of the southern front, Major General Andrii Kovalchuk, at his headquarters. Just as our meeting was coming to an end, the air raid siren started. 'We can't let you out on to the streets,' he told me and invited me to his bomb shelter. As we waited for the danger to pass, we made small talk. I asked about rumours of the Russian cruiser *Moskva* being sunk. He smiled and took out his mobile phone to show me footage from a drone hovering over the ship. We watched the *Moskva* burning as he smoked a cigarette.

Tonight, I am with call signs Starshina (Sergeant Major), Rozmaryn (rosemary) and Chornyy (black), who are explaining to me how they shoot down Shaheds. I jump into the back of the white pick-up truck. Chornyy puts wrap-around thermal googles on me and I see pitch-black night lighten up into shades of bright grey. I take hold of the Browning machine gun.

'Lean back on the balls of your feet, on your heels,' Chornyy explains. I look round to make sure I am not falling off the back of the truck, but I do as he says, and it's surprisingly comfortable. Rozmaryn tells me that you need to feel yourself as an extension of the weapon: 'Rock backwards and forwards as it fires and use your biceps to absorb the recoil of the weapon,' he says. In Ukrainian tradition, they have tinkered and innovated with the best way of firing and have added two gold-coloured bicycle shock absorbers to help soak up the kick of the heavy calibre weapon on the truck. Rozmaryn has shot down twelve drones and spends some of his time training others how to use an old Browning and the software package for the goggles.

Starshina adds, 'You need to understand that 12.7 calibre is quite heavy, quite a big hit, so you need to have your legs positioned steady.'

He gestures to his legs, a shoulder's width apart and slightly bent. 'And the weight on the biceps, so you use your bicep, almost like a suspension.'

The trio are part of the 43rd Air Force Regiment, which is equipped with a variety of weapons, including Stingers and Iglas (hand-held MANPADS) and ZSUs. They have more sophisticated weapons too.

I wanted to visit the unit not only because volunteers are such an important part of Ukraine's war story but also because they remind me of my favourite piece of writing, a script from a Second World War-era radio programme named *Postscripts*. The show was hosted by J. B. Priestley. Only a small number of Priestley's works remain in print now, but his plays *An Inspector Calls* and *Time and the Conways* are still performed. He was one of our great twentieth-century writers and in that desperate summer of 1940, Priestley's radio broadcasts were the most listened to after Churchill's. The second *Postscripts* broadcast came out just after the fall of Paris in June. Dunkirk had been taken. Poland was lost. Nazi Germany seemed all-conquering. We were facing the destruction of our nation, our empire and our values. Priestley had joined the Home Guard on the Isle of Wight, my old constituency, and one of their tasks, like Ukraine's volunteers today, was to help man the air defences. The high downs on the island, especially in Chillerton and Mottistone, were the perfect place to site machine guns to defend the approaches to the naval and port cities of Portsmouth and Southampton.

With a gentle but passionate patriotism, Priestley talked of his time with the volunteers on the island. The Isle of Wight had an old-school rural economy and his comrades were representative of these rural trades: shepherds, farmers and farm labourers. Priestley felt that he'd 'wandered into one of those rich chapters of Thomas

Hardy's fiction in which his rustics meet in the gathering darkness on some Wessex hillside'.[12]

The cast of people I met in Ukraine's volunteer units had the same eclectic mix, though updated for our era: businessmen, teachers, students, local councillors, AI and tech geeks, as well as marketing and PR types. Rozmaryn was a 23-year-old chef who returned from Poland a month before the war to serve his nation. His favourite recipe is steak in rosemary butter, hence the name. Starshina is a former paratrooper turned maths teacher turned businessman.

Back then, Britain faced the new generation of city-destroying German bombers and their fighter escorts. On the island, we tried to shoot them down to protect ports on the Solent. Now, Odesa's Shahed hunters similarly protect Odesa's people and its port, vital for exporting grain and other agricultural staples. They are facing an expanding 'family' of drones. Shahed payloads range from 20 to 60 kilos and their speed is increasing up to 200 km per hour, with some experimental ones even faster. Most evenings, the teams, who may be resting at home or in the base, get the call to fan out to different positions. Along with the drivers, they work in teams. One works as a 'spotter', armed with a powerful green laser that bounces off the underside of the clouds, and the other mans the Browning, ready to shoot down the drone.

How long they have to shoot depends on the drone's trajectory. 'Sometimes they can fly behind you, sometimes laterally, sometimes across.' Starshina gesticulates in different directions to make his point. As we talk, we look at his tracking screen to see what Russian reconnaissance drones are in the air. He points to the small red moving icons on the tablet screen and we watch the drones flying along the Dnipro River, marking the front line in the south of Ukraine.

Starshina explains that the green ammunition box containing 100 rounds lasts sixteen seconds, whilst the time for a Shahed to come in and out of a unit's line of sight is generally around six seconds. The teams need to be sharp and quick, especially if the drone is coming towards them. 'The spotter on the ground, they will know more or less when it's coming and the field of vision, the direction,' Starshina continues. As soon as the spotter sees the drone, he will shout, 'I have a target!' The gunner follows the laser and has a few seconds to hit the Shahed before it is out of range and heading to destroy another building in Odesa.

CHAPTER 10

REINVENTING UNITY: MERGING TWO WAYS OF WAR INTO ONE

'The Soviet system was a lawless system, and the KGB was a tool of lawlessness.'

– Oleg Kalugin[1]

'Subversive warfare' is an unhelpfully vague term, especially for students of war and conflict. The term often used by the Soviets to describe the panoply of subversive conflict – also known as political warfare – tools was 'active measures'. Broadly, this was the name given to the way of war waged by the KGB and the Communist Party in its ideological struggle against capitalist democracies during the Cold War, a ubiquitous but invisible form of conflict fought until the late 1980s. Few Westerners, and fewer Russians, have heard this term and yet, through the information campaigns that were aimed at us, the manipulation of Western organisations – from 'peace' campaigners to co-opted left-wing politicians – and the violent terror groups and paramilitary anti-colonial 'liberation' movements formed in the developing world, there was a form of permanent struggle being waged against our societies across the globe.

Whatever name it has gone by – political warfare, subversive conflict, active measures – this form of conflict is characterised by the use of propaganda and disinformation, blackmail (*kompromat*), forgeries, covert or overt propaganda, 'front' groups and NGOs, as well as unconventional forms of violence such as assassination and the funding of terrorist and paramilitary groups. Its purpose was to demoralise, destabilise, divide and generally weaken opponents, either as a long-term aim or as a stage of the political or physical destruction of targets.

Western understanding of active measures was hindered during the Cold War era due to a dearth of research. There was a lack of material – the KGB has rarely shared its secrets – there was confusion over what was being studied – no agreed definition means no precise area of study – and there was perplexity in the West over the idea of non-military conflict. As discussed, the Western mind has often understood 'war' and 'peace' to be terms distinct from each other, whilst Russia, then and now, has seen itself in a permanent struggle against the West. Subversive forms of conflict operate in a 'grey' space of neither war nor peace.[2]

The concept of active measures is also little known in the former republics of the Soviet Union; only a handful of Ukrainians out of over 150 interviewed for this book were aware of the term.* The 1976 edition of the *Soviet Military Encyclopaedia* made no mention of active measures, nor did the 1983 edition of the *Russian Military Dictionary*. I've found only one definition of active measures in Russian, in *The Counter-Intelligence Dictionary from the Higher Red Banner School of the Committee of State Security [KGB] of the Soviet of Ministers of the USSR*, 1972 edition.[3] Active measures is

* And one of those only because the interviewee (Zalishchuk) had read of it recently in a Western newspaper article.

described as a form of 'counter-intelligence', enabling penetration of the enemy, misleading him, seizing the initiative and 'undermining his subversive actions'. The definition is itself an example of disinformation in that it presents active measures as a defensive device, rather than an active tool in the ideological struggle.* The KGB kept this form of conflict hidden even from its own people. It helps to explain Russian ignorance about this form of warfare, even within some military circles.

THE FIRST ERA OF ACTIVE MEASURES

Whilst it's arguable that some active measures-style provocations occurred during the pre-Soviet era – the Tsarist secret police, the Cheka, engineered 'special actions' such as blowing up printing works or setting up illicit bomb-making factories to entice and then expose Russian revolutionaries – subversive warfare started in earnest with the revolutionary Soviet state, dedicated to the global overthrow of capitalism.[4]

Operations were initially coordinated either in Stalin's personal secretariat or in the unsubtly named Secret Department (*Sekretny Otdel'*).[5] Whilst some early Soviet campaigns were amateurishly designed, there is evidence that relatively complex subversive operations were undertaken even in the early years of the USSR. By 1925, the Politburo – the powerful governing body of the USSR – was referencing its tactics of 'active intelligence', a mix of sabotage work, partisan action and 'military-subversive groups' similar to the paramilitary elements of active measures.[6] At the same time, the People's Commissariat of Foreign Affairs was circulating forged documents

* This appears to be a Soviet/Russian trope, identified in previous chapters.

as part of disinformation campaigns.[7] Soviet-instigated uprisings took place in Hamburg in 1923 and in Estonia and Romania in 1924.

Most notoriously, between 1921 and 1927 the Soviets launched complex operations to infiltrate anti-Bolshevik organisations in the West, most notably Operation Trest. Trest set up a fictitious underground movement in western Europe, the Monarchist Association of Central Russia, to infiltrate anti-Bolshevik organisations and tempt their members to return to the Soviet Union, ostensibly to take part in operations against the Soviet government.[8] On return, these counter-revolutionaries were arrested and executed. The British spy Sidney Reilly was the most famous victim of this operation.[9] Lured back to Soviet territory, he was captured and tortured before finally being killed on Stalin's direct orders, shot at close range whilst walking in a wood in Moscow after his interrogation.[10]

Trest combined front organisations, (dis)information operations and espionage, both passive and active, as well as imprisonment and torture, assassination and murder.[11] It has been described as the USSR's first large-scale offensive campaign against its enemies.[12] The success of Trest was not just in exposing 'traitors' in the ranks but also in demoralising Russian emigres, undermining their ability to trust each other, destroying the coherence of anti-Bolshevik groups and discrediting them in the eyes of nascent Western intelligence. It was complex and sophisticated, ahead of its time and successful. It mixed an efficient use of resources with infiltration, demoralisation and destruction of its enemies. Senior KGB man turned British agent Oleg Gordievsky described Trest, with its mix of physical and psychological outcomes, as 'one of the classic peacetime deception operations'.[13]

Similar operations took place after the Second World War to infiltrate eastern European resistance groups, with the same demoralising results. A small number of diplomats and politicians could see this new Soviet style of conflict – in 1927, Britain's ambassador to Berlin Sir Ronald Lindsay described Soviet subversion as a 'new kind of war' and called for a spectrum of actions to counter it.[14] But too many in the West remained naive or culpable, especially on the political left, which was either co-opted by propaganda, wilfully naive or downright treacherous.[15] From its early days, the concept of integrated, espionage-led, subversive operations, including deception and disinformation, was rooted in the Soviet Union's founding culture.[16]

THE SECOND ERA OF ACTIVE MEASURES

Following the Second World War, Western governments became aware of active measures as an increasingly coherent and sophisticated body of ideas due to the testimonies of Cold War defectors. Amongst the first were eastern European secret service operatives Ladislav Bittman from Czechoslovakia and Laszlo Szabo from Hungary. They defected in the mid-1960s, bringing the secrets of active measures to Western spy agencies.[17] Others who have contributed since then include KGB agents Stanislav Levchenko, Oleg Gordievsky and Vasili Mitrokhin, GRU agent Stanislav Lunev, Soviet diplomat Aleksandr Kaznacheev and Ion Pacepa from Romania's secret services. In the early 1990s, during the post-Soviet thaw, senior Soviet official Pavel Sudoplatov also wrote of his experiences.

In his testimony to the US Congress, Bittman explained that the term 'active measures' had evolved in the late 1950s to distinguish it from passive measures such as spying and other forms of information gathering. Bittman's equating of 'covert action' with 'active measures' is noteworthy:

> Until the 1950s Soviet bloc covert action was designed and conducted by individual territorial, operational departments without a well-orchestrated effort and clearly designed long-term strategy. The situation changed when the KGB established the special department for active measures around 1959.[18]

Most Soviet allies followed suit between 1961 and 1964, establishing their own active measures departments.[19] As a result, operations throughout the 1960s became systemic and more sophisticated. By the end of the decade, active measures had become the responsibility of KGB Service A, based at KGB headquarters in Yasenevo, with more staff based at the Novosti news agency and further agents attached to embassies throughout the world.[20] Two types of active measures operations were conducted: KGB-only operations, of which there were hundreds each year, and fewer but more significant operations that were co-sponsored by the Communist Party.[21]

Many of these examples were disinformation stories, planted to damage the West and its allies. According to Mitrokhin, in his book co-written with British historian Christopher Andrew, the KGB planted 5,510 stories in 1975 alone.[22] Some of those started in India, where agencies of the USSR controlled ten newspapers and one news agency.[23] The intention may not have been to focus on India per se but to use connections in the free media to encourage the distribution of fake stories that the KGB and the Communist Party were planting, which would then be recirculated by the KGB as examples of genuine journalism. In some senses, India played the role of the internet today – as the starting point of fakes, forgeries and conspiracy theories planted deliberately by the Soviet Union.

The most famous disinformation exercise, known either as Operation Infektion or Operation Denver, was the global disinformation

A Sarmat soldier grabs a moment of contemplation, leaning on a piece of 'trophy' kit. © Annabel Moeller

At least twice a week, Panoushka and her small team are dropped off deep in the 'drone zone'. They walk for at least an hour and then hide at the edge of a tree line or in a building, meticulously camouflaging themselves. For several hours at a stretch, she will watch the scene in front of her, waiting for her targets to wander into her sights. Panoushka is a sniper and one of the best in the business. But for her, the most difficult thing she has done in the past year was to bury her partner. 'For that moment, I had to be a warrior – not just a woman who had lost the love of her life but also a soldier who had lost my brother in arms,' she told me. © Annabel Moeller

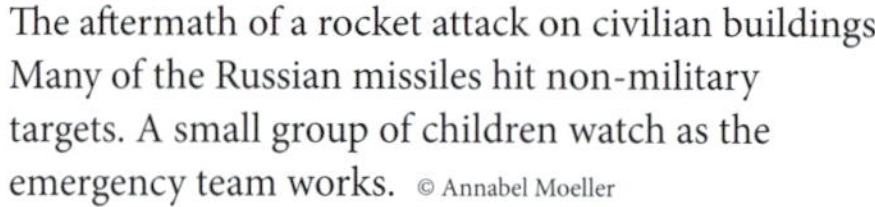

The aftermath of a rocket attack on civilian buildings. Many of the Russian missiles hit non-military targets. A small group of children watch as the emergency team works. © Annabel Moeller

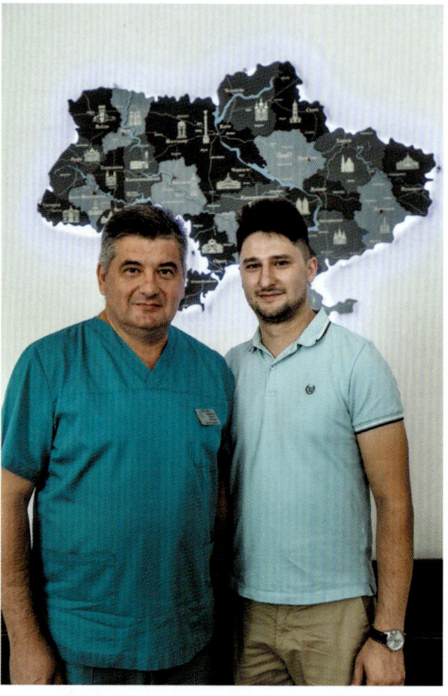

Dr Kyrylo Parkhomenko, director of Kharkiv's Hospital No. 25, with son Ivan, who is also a doctor in the hospital. Medical teams spent the opening months of the war working without a break, sleeping in hospital corridors or basements. Many did not leave the confines of their hospitals. © Annabel Moeller

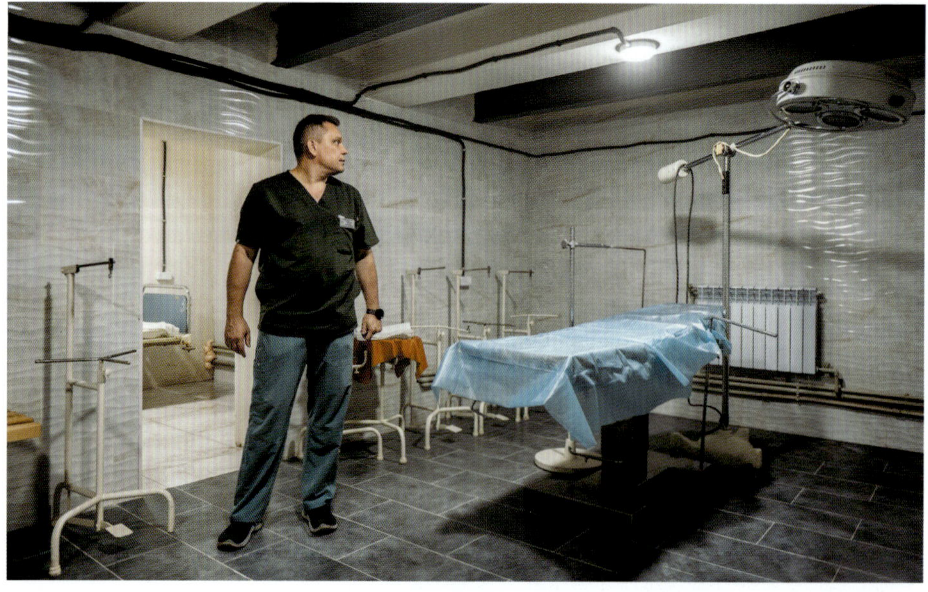

Chief surgeon Maxim Suplichenko looks at the new underground operating theatre. Ivan Parkhomenko explains: 'If there are many patients and 24/7 shelling, we can't operate intensive care on the second or third floors – they are too dangerous. So we are preparing an underground operation room. There's water and canned food – we'll be able to survive down here.' © Annabel Moeller

What effect is the bombing having on civilians? The most common symptom of stress in the city is sleep disorders, according to Kharkiv psychologist Vitali Khrystenko, but the wider problem, he says, is that 'nobody's planning for the future. They are just living for the day.' Here, a woman takes some of her possessions from an apartment block struck by a Russian missile. © Annabel Moeller

Kharkiv has lost many buildings, both old and new. © Annabel Moeller

The day before I visited, twelve rockets and missiles were launched at the city and ten of them made it through Kharkiv's defences. Around me, emergency workers are repairing gas and other mains supplies in the middle of a residential area with tall, Soviet-era blocks. A young mother walks past in tears, clearly suffering from shock.

© Annabel Moeller

The Kremlin has been specifically targeting electricity and energy supply in order to destroy Ukrainians' will to resist. Vladimir Putin believes a freezing population will be more pliable and more willing to seek peace on his terms. This power plant in the west of Ukraine has been struck more than half a dozen times by missiles, bombs and drones. This is its destroyed control panel.
© Annabel Moeller

The boilers and turbines that make up the power-generating units in this power station have been bent out of shape by repeated attacks. © Annabel Moeller

Bombing cities is part of the Kremlin's plans to break Ukrainians' will to resist. I talk with call signs Starshina (Sergeant Major), Rozmaryn (rosemary) and Chornyy (black), who explain how they shoot down Iranian-designed Shahed drones aimed at Odesa. Starshina and I watch live footage of Russian drones over the Dnipro River, whilst Rozmaryn and Chornyy prepare their equipment. © Annabel Moeller

Rozmaryn has shot down twelve drones and now spends some of his time training others how to use the old Browning machine gun and thermal goggles to shoot down Shaheds. © Annabel Moeller

Soldiers from Kyiv's DFTH 31 volunteer unit share some good-humoured banter. DFTH translates as Community Territorial Voluntary Formation. They are Ukraine's equivalent of the UK's Home Guard, aka Dad's Army, during the Second World War. © Annabel Moeller

Call sign Gagauz, from the Gagauz ethnic group, originally from south of Odesa, waits for Russian drones. The night we visited, there were none. Putin instead dropped a ballistic missile minus its nuclear warhead on Dnipro, as if to say: I can be the destroyer of cities. © Annabel Moeller

Call sign Arty saw some of the worst of the initial fighting. His men died around him as they took shelter in a building being pummelled by Russian mortars. Then, 140 litres of fuel stored in the building went up in flames, creating a fireball that incinerated his men. 'They thought everyone was dead; I got lucky.'

© Annabel Moeller

Russian security services experts Andrei Soldatov and Irina Borogan. Ahead of the 2022 Ukraine invasion, 'the FSB was gathering information, which they did badly, to please Putin, not to inform him,' says Soldatov. 'The main assessment was that the Ukrainian state was a failed state … so, in a time of a crisis, it would just collapse.'

© Annabel Moeller

Of all the abuses in this war, one of the most shocking is the stealing of children. This is a deliberate tactic of the Russian state. Children are used as weapons by a regime that wishes to reprogramme them to hate their birth country. Children in the occupied territories are being indoctrinated to see Ukraine as a 'neo-Nazi' state and trained to fight against it. Ksenia (*left*) battled to find her younger brother and flee Russia with him. Rostyslav (*right*) attended a Russian military academy before he escaped. Their stories, Ksenia says, were different but united by one common theme: 'We were kidnapped by Russia.' © Annabel Moeller

Kostya Nemichev, call sign Brather, set up the Kraken Regiment with his closest friends, backed by Ukraine's military intelligence (HUR), to support the defence of Kharkiv in 2022. There is a bounty on Nemichev's head and his picture is displayed in every Russian police department in the border territories. © Annabel Moeller

One example of Ukrainian military intelligence's otherwise secret work is the sabotage of a Russian warship by Hoha, a Russian serviceman from a Ukrainian background. He destroyed his vessel's control room and fled to Ukraine. © Annabel Moeller

Marina Litvinenko, whose husband, former KGB man Alexander (Sasha) Litvinenko, was an early victim of Putin's willingness to assassinate his enemies. © Annabel Moeller

project to convince the world that HIV had been developed by American military scientists.[24] The KGB's campaign was launched via Indian newspaper *The Patriot* in an article published on 17 July 1983 entitled 'AIDS May Invade India: Mystery Disease Caused by US Experiment'.[25] After a couple of false starts, the story took off in the West and was covered by many reputable newspapers and broadcasters.

Western nations have been and often still are confused by Russian ways of war because their default view is often to see conflict as something limited to conventional ideas of military force, albeit with an information or 'influence' component. Even when a broader definition of conflict is used, it still doesn't necessarily cover the extraordinary range of tactics used by Russia or an understanding of how complex their subversive warfare operations, sometimes running alongside conventional military force, are. In the West, there is still no broadly accepted definition of active measures and, of course, during the Cold War the Soviet Union did not provide an accurate one. This was highly beneficial to Moscow, as without a definition it was more difficult for the West to counter.

Cold War working definitions of active measures fell into three categories. The first was a narrow interpretation to describe a form of information manipulation aimed to subvert, demoralise and divide. The second included information and disinformation operations but also political tools. The third was a broad definition, including not only information operations but also violent, physical operations, ranging from assassination to support for terrorism and insurgency. This third definition encapsulated all the active, as opposed to passive, work of the KGB, hence the euphemism active measures.

US institutions also tried to define active measures during the

Cold War. The State Department described it as covert or deception operations in support of Soviet foreign policy, saying that their goal was to 'influence opinions and/or actions of individuals, governments and/or publics'.[26] The tools of active measures were outlined as disinformation, forgeries, use of front groups and 'friendship' societies, pressure groups and peace groups, communist and leftist political parties and use of agents of influence. The State Department also questioned whether propaganda was included, saying that it, as well as 'other efforts employed by the Soviets to influence public perceptions – such as cultural programmes, radio broadcasting, and publications – may not be active measures in themselves but may be the vehicles used to promote and sustain active measures'.[27] Their report also said that active measures was distinct from 'espionage and counterintelligence, and from traditional diplomatic and information activities'.[28]

By contrast, the US House Committee on Intelligence provided a much broader definition that encompassed the full range of subversive activities, violent as well as non-violent. It defined active measures as:

> Manipulation and media control, written and oral disinformation, use of foreign communist parties and front organizations, clandestine radio broadcasting, manipulation of the economy, kidnappings, paramilitary operations, and support of guerrilla groups and terrorist organizations. Under Joseph Stalin, active measures also included political assassinations.[29]

In 1980, John McMahon, CIA deputy director for operations, gave a similarly broad definition in written testimony to Congress. He defined active measures as the combination of written and oral disinformation, including forgeries, false rumours and falsely attributed propaganda; manipulation and control of foreign media; manipulative political action, including blackmail and kidnap; use of agents of influence; use of foreign communist parties and international front groups; and support for international terrorist organisations and national liberation movements.[30] Other experts also saw in active measures a broad category of tools. A few even included conventional 'military manoeuvres', foreshadowing the total war, integrated approach that defines our modern understanding of Russian conflict.

Soviet defectors also gave differing interpretations of active measures, though overall they tended to offer broader definitions and noted that definition was secondary to outcome. In *Inside a Soviet Embassy*, defector Aleksandr Kaznacheyev described how, whilst working in Rangoon, he would receive propaganda articles from the KGB in Moscow and then translate and place them in Burmese newspapers. The Soviet news agency TASS would reprint articles and circulate them to other publications in the region as 'genuine' material. Kaznacheyev referred to this process as 'psychological warfare' rather than active measures.[31] However, it is clear what he was talking about. He commented that this 'gigantic mechanism' was part of the

> worldwide propaganda network of the KGB which receives its orders directly from the Central Committee of the Communist Party of the Soviet Union. In order to divide and destroy those who have the courage to oppose the aims of Soviet rulers it employs intimidation, lies, defamation, and slander. Its tools are a subverted press, corrupt and traitorous editors, opportunistic politicians, bribery and forgery.[32]

Former Tokyo-based KGB agent and defector Stanislav Levchenko explained that his tasks had been to divide Japan from the US, prevent closer relations between Japan and China and build the Japanese socialist movement. He defined active measures as 'a catch-all phrase that describes both overt and covert techniques for influencing the actions, events, and – sometimes – the behaviour of foreign countries'.[33] Examples were undermining the confidence of citizens in their leaders and destroying the credibility of a nation or of its leader or disrupting relations between nations. 'Frequently,' he said, 'active measures will attempt to skew public perceptions of events or of the meanings of those events.'[34]

Andrew and Mitrokhin reported that in the 1960s and 1970s, Soviet active measures operations included fabricating a conspiracy linking President Kennedy's assassin, Lee Harvey Oswald, to the extreme right and attempting to manipulate ethnic violence – including acts of terrorism – in the US to undermine its internal cohesion.[35] In these cases, information 'warfare' was designed to have a real, violent outcome. Modern examples of this include Russia's attempts to 'sow discord in the US political system' before and during the 2016 elections, as documented in detail by the US Justice Department.[36]

KGB defector Yuri Bezmenov, the child of a Soviet general, was a KGB agent stationed in India in the 1960s. His defection was one of the more colourful of the Cold War. He escaped by travelling through India on the hippie trail for months, before making his way to Greece and then Canada. Whilst his Soviet 'cover' was as a journalist, in reality Bezmenov worked in the KGB's research and counter-propaganda department. The department collected information on opinion-forming individuals. Those sympathetic to the USSR were promoted in the media, whilst those opposed were 'blackwashed' (smeared), blackmailed and destroyed, morally and sometimes physically.[37] Bezmenov stressed the long-term nature of active measures as an attritional, generational process, carried out to subvert a nation's values. This, he said, was the true task of the KGB: 'Only about 15 per cent of time, money and manpower is spent on espionage as such. The other 85 per cent is a slow process, which we call either ideological subversion or active measures.'[38]

Through this, we again see the stress on long-term outcomes, creating divisions and damaging alliances. However, Bezmenov adds an additional point: the claim that much of the Soviet secret service's time was taken up not with traditional ideas of spying but with the active spread of subversion. If true, the dominant Cold War task of the KGB was in the *active* business of active measures, not in the *passive* business of information gathering or intelligence assessments. This view was supported by former KGB General Oleg Kalugin, who described subversion as 'the heart and soul of Soviet intelligence'.[39] Kalugin stressed the political and campaigning side of its work:

> The [KGB] programs – which would run all sorts of congresses, peace congresses, youth congresses, festivals, women's movements, trade union movements, campaigns against US missiles in Europe, campaigns against neutron weapons, allegations that AIDS … was invented by the CIA … all sorts of forgeries and faked material targeted at politicians, the academic community, at [the] public at large.

All this aimed to drive a wedge between Western nations and 'weaken [the] military, economic and psychological climate in the West'. In particular, the Soviets wanted 'to make America more vulnerable to the anger and distrust of other peoples,' he said.

Senior Romanian spy-turned-defector Ion Pacepa explained that active measures didn't just incite violence through manipulated information but also included actual acts of terrorist violence. As an example, he said that from the 1960s onwards, Warsaw Pact spy agencies such as Romania's encouraged the rebirth of modern antisemitism by the publication and mass distribution throughout the Middle East of *The Protocols of the Elders of Zion*, a fake, Tsarist-era antisemitic conspiracy tract.[40] He went on to say that international terrorism was 'conceived at the Lubyanka, the headquarters of the KGB, in the aftermath of the 1967 Six-Day War in the Middle East. I witnessed its birth.'[41] He claimed that aeroplane hijackings carried out in the twentieth century by the Palestine Liberation Organization were the brainchild of the KGB. 'Airplane hijacking is my own invention,' Soviet KGB General Aleksandr Sakharovsky allegedly boasted to Pacepa.[42] Sakharovsky has also been credited with perfecting assassinations to look like car accidents, another tool of covert war.[43]

Bittman, the original Warsaw Pact whistle-blower, said active measures was 'an elegant expression for activities called in plain English "dirty tricks".'[44] The Soviets, he said, perceived 'no sharp distinction between propaganda and action, political operations and military actions, or overt and covert actions'.[45] That is still true today. What Putin has done is to put all these tools into a single way of war and a single understanding of conflict. He has merged active measures with the other tools of state power, ranging from religion to economics, and military actions. This form of conflict is integrated across the full spectrum of Russian state power.

In the words of two Western experts, 'Soviet leaders do not regard war and politics as distinct conditions; rather, from their perspective, politics is a continual state of war carried on by a wide variety of means.'[46] As General Kalugin said, 'The Soviet system was a lawless system, and the KGB was a tool of lawlessness.'[47]

There are several critical points that it is worth just briefly re-emphasising here. First, the Soviet Union developed, as part of its founding culture, subversive operations that evolved quickly into relatively complex campaigns, using disinformation and deception, espionage and paramilitary and proxy violence to demoralise, divide and defeat its enemies. This was the first era of subversive active measures operations.

Second, these subversive operations continued to evolve after the Second World War so that by the 1960s, the Soviet Union and its partner nations had their own standalone active measures departments for mass-scale disinformation campaigns and complex, covert-action operations. This became the second era of subversive active measures operations and it lasted thirty years.

Third, whilst definitions differ, some of those who knew active measures best defined it as the entire suite of 'active' operations conducted by the KGB, sometimes with the Communist Party's input. There are convincing grounds, therefore, to see active measures as the body of theory and practice of the Soviet Union's twentieth-century way of subversive, political warfare. Whilst psychologically based, manipulative information operations were a critical element of active measures, the 'active' elements, such as support for terror groups, political and paramilitary violence, were also integral. Finally, KGB defectors have said that active measures became the dominant overseas task for the KGB in the latter half of the Cold War, eclipsing espionage.

Therefore, I believe that the subversive struggle (*bor'ba*) of active measures should rightly be seen as a way of war in its own right, alongside ideas of conventional war (*voina*). This is especially important today given Putin's struggle against Ukraine and the West and his use of agents of influence within the West to undermine and divide Russia's enemies.

Thus, for the purposes of this book, active measures is defined as the *active*, as opposed to *passive*, tools of subversive warfare, including violence and military operations in support of them. This is the definition most often used by Russian and Soviet sources and reflects the flexibility in thinking and action of the current Russian state, which itself is rooted in historic approaches to conflict practised by the USSR and even the Russian Empire.

SIMILARITIES BETWEEN ACTIVE MEASURES AND RUSSIA'S NEW WAY OF WAR

Not only is active measures the framework for the theory and practice behind covert conflict but it also provides a fundamental underpinning of Russian ideas about conflict today. I believe that there is a clear link between operational phasing in Soviet-era active measures and operational phasing in current Russian military thinking. This shows the influence of subversive warfare on contemporary current military planning and thinking and the extent to which Russia's new way of war is a new form of total war, involving all the tools of the state.

So what is operational phasing and why is it relevant here? Operational phasing is essentially the sequencing and order in which a nation or organisation teaches its armed forces – and, in some countries, its security agencies – to conduct conflict. It is the chronological roadmap for a way of war – what to do and when to do it.

To compare these two models of operational phasing, I am going to return to the India-based KGB defector Yuri Bezmenov. Once

Bezmenov had successfully fled the country via the hippie trail, he made his way to the West. Once there, he gave a series of interviews outlining, amongst other things, active measures operational phasing,* describing it as a four-stage process: demoralisation, destabilisation, bringing to crisis and normalisation.† His claims fit with all that we know about the purpose and tactics of active measures.

In the first stage, demoralisation, Bezmenov described a multi-year process whereby ideas were introduced and implanted into a society to help to break down societal consensus. In this process, opinion-formers were identified and recruited from various areas of national life – religious, educational, social – and from government administration, law enforcement and unions. In the West, these people were either witting or unwitting agents of Soviet influence. The former were out-and-out traitors, such as the Cambridge spy circle; the latter might be union leaders, 'peace campaigners' or left-wing pressure groups, who may or may not have known the role they were playing in wider Soviet plans. This latter group were apocryphally referred to by Lenin as 'useful idiots'. There remain not only traitors but also useful idiots in the West today.

In the second phase, destabilisation, society was, in Bezmenov's words, 'heated up'. What the Soviets described as 'contradictions in society', such as race and class divisions, would be manipulated to erode cohesion and trust. Faith in government and its institutions would be aggressively undermined. So-called sleepers – long-term agents of influence – would be 'awakened'. Bezmenov explained: 'As long as these groups come into antagonistic clash, sometimes militantly, sometimes with firearms, that is "destabilisation" … the

* Whilst Bezmenov is a single source, evidence from General Kalugin and other Soviet/Russian authors supports Bezmenov's claims about active measures phasing.

† This book will in part use Bezmenov's sequencing.

sleepers, many of whom are simply KGB agents, become leaders of the process of destabilisation.'[48] During this period of crisis, state bodies would be weakened and alternative power structures, designed to seize power at the allotted time, would be formed. It is important to note here that whilst the West was often a target, societies in the developing world, with weaker institutions and coherence, especially Africa, were much more vulnerable to this form of systemic deconstruction, especially if violence was used.

Destabilisation evolved to phase three, bringing to crisis. State bodies either collapsed or their leaderships were overthrown in what was, effectively, a managed coup. Once power had been transferred to new structures or new people or both, the process of normalisation, phase four, took place. 'Normalisation is a very ironic word, of course,' Bezmenov commented.[49] During the 'normalisation' period, Soviet control would be brutally enforced. Many of those who helped bring about the crisis – campaigners, free thinkers, the ideologically committed – would be eliminated. As soon as you had fulfilled your task, Bezmenov said, it was 'goodbye comrade'.

This four-stage KGB process is similar to the six-stage current operational-phasing model presented by Russian armed forces Chief of Staff Valeri Gerasimov as a conflict template. In fact, it is arguably identical in aim, if not in exact wording. Gerasimov's sequencing is contained in a 2013 article written by him, in a table entitled 'The Role of Non-Military Methods in the Settlement of International Conflicts'.[50] The chart identifies six distinct phasing periods. These are: hidden genesis, escalation, beginning of conflict action, crisis, resolution and, finally, restoration.

Whilst this phasing is clearly not designed for *all* operations the Russian Army might face – nuclear war or conventional naval war, for example – the table and the article do indicate the centrality of the integration of different forms of war. First, because the operational phasing is for 'international conflict', we can assume it has a wide use. Second, it is a style of warfare regularly practised by the Russian state. Multiple military and non-military tools have been used not only in Ukraine but also in the 1990s in more basic guises in Georgia and Moldova, albeit in a much less sophisticated way. Third, even when this type of 'curated' conflict won't be conducted precisely as laid out in the template, its existence shows the significance given to integrated warfare by Russia. Short of, for example, defending itself from a conventional invasion or supporting China in a naval war in the Pacific, the operational phasing described by Gerasimov is the phasing for many military operations and especially the curated, managed conflicts conducted in the former Russian Empire and Soviet territory. His article should therefore be interpreted as a broad guide for integrated, complex operations. Additionally, the similarity between the current Russian conflict model and the previous KGB active measures template suggests that Gerasimov's phasing has been influenced or inspired by the KGB's long-term, four-stage process.

Gerasimov's phasing provides more evidence, on top of the wealth of evidence already presented, that conceptually, modern Russian thinking around conflict is significantly influenced by the subversive warfare tradition – effectively Russia's second way of war. Indeed, the similarity of phasing demonstrates that subversive warfare, by whatever name it is known – active measures, subversive warfare, political warfare etc. – sits at the heart of Russia's new way of war. This doesn't, of course, mean that the Kremlin has done away with traditional, conventional military practice or that warfare no longer includes regular violence. After the 2022 invasion, that argument can't be treated seriously, if it ever could be. But it does show

how military and non-military action in conflict are mutually reinforcing and how military and non-military practices are designed to work together efficiently so that they become more than the sum of their parts – even in times of traditional, conventional war.

Despite the glaring failings in Russia's military operations in Ukraine, it has often succeeded in integrating its military and non-military tools. Indeed, the integration of phasing and doctrine, and the breadth of tools used, shows that Russian conflict strategies, whilst subversive and aggressive, are not just military – or certainly not in the traditional, conventional sense of military operations. Military action will be run by the armed forces, but war and conflicts won't be. Whilst this may be said of the theory behind all major military force doctrine, it is arguably truer in Russia than elsewhere.

The influence of KGB thinking on modern Russian warfare raises an important question. How important was President Putin's role in this process and could the development of the Russia's new total war have happened without him? Could the role of the 'Chekists' – the nickname given to Russian secret agents – explain Russia's hostile turn? Russian author Igor Panarin argued that the Crimean operation in 2014 worked because it was carried out 'to a single plan under the personal control of V. Putin'.[51] Is this blind praise of a dictator or an indication of Putin's close oversight of Russia's new way of war?

Academic Mette Skak argues that the role of the 'Chekists' has been overlooked in the reshaping of Russia following the collapse of the Soviet Union.[52] The KGB was a vast organisation, with nearly 500,000 staff and 11 million informers.[53] It boasted a human network that 'penetrated every Russian institution', with tens of thousands more in reserve.[54] The KGB was an institution above the law and the last line of defence of the state *and* the regime, which were seen as one and the same. Therefore, the KGB/FSB was not/is not merely an institution but a pervasive, controlling influence on Russian society.

KGB historian Yevgenia Albats argued in 2004:

> By training, Putin is a man of control. He spent a major part of his life in the KGB, whose leaderships and agents were entrusted by the Communist Party with safeguarding the regime. The KGB taught its soldiers well; its institutional culture has not been easily thrown off and its imperatives have proved stronger than Putin's leanings toward democracy.[55]

First and foremost, Putin is a man shaped by the belief that the USSR was undermined by indirect warfare. According to Ukrainian popular philosopher Volodymyr Yermolenko, he is consumed by 'a paranoia that the Western conspiracy … destroyed the Soviet Union.'[56] This continues, Yermolenko says, to be reflected in the very deep antagonism felt by his leadership towards pro-democracy 'colour' revolutions: 'OK, you destroyed Soviet Union, I will destroy European Union, and you made all these rebel colour revolutions, so I will use your rebel forces to disrupt you.'

Others I have interviewed also see Putin as indispensable to Russia's form of warfare. 'I think that Putin's personal role is very great. He brought up this system. He is its father,' says Vasiliy Kravets, a lecturer in a technical college in occupied Ukraine.[57] 'His role as a leader in Russia is very great, because Russia is an authoritarian country,' says academic Ihor Rushchenko.[58] A senior Ukrainian HUR source also told me, 'He is an old KGBist. He knew the tactics and procedures that have been used, and he simply increased them.'

Other interviewees were more circumspect, however, believing that whilst Putin may have been influential, the secret state 'system' would have produced a similar outcome, given the roots of this form of war are embedded deep in historic Russian behaviours. 'I am not inclined to believe that only Putin is to blame,' says interviewee Roman Burko. 'He is just a pawn in all these games. He is just the face of all these processes.'[59] Kharkiv academic Nataliya Zubar agrees. A man such as Putin, she said, would have come to power anyway, 'and if not Putin, there could be some other'.[60] Other interviewees saw Putin as the outcome of a counter-revolutionary process whereby the intelligence agencies, once all-powerful, put forward one of their own representatives to lead Russia. Volodymyr Chystylin calls this 'a person of the system who would personify those hopes of the political elites of Russia'.[61]

So, either Putin was the instigator or he was a vital cog in an autocratic system that was reverting to type after a half-hearted, failed attempt at reform. Either way, most agree that the processes that he may have encouraged or ordered were happening anyway. Therefore, rather than being the sole founder of a new way of political war, he could more accurately be seen as one of those influential figures who ensured the reconstruction of the KGB system of control, whose practices were already, in an ad hoc way, being rebuilt. By merging those tools with military power, he was, if not the architect, then certainly the midwife of Russia's new way of war.

THE INFLUENCE OF MILITARY TRADITION ON RUSSIA'S NEW WAY OF WAR

Given the influence of the subversive military tradition on Russian thinking, has there been any role for traditional military thinking in doctrine?

The answer is yes. There are ways in which military theory can, albeit at times tentatively, be said to have influenced Russia's new way of war at the conceptual, strategic and operational levels. These influences are rooted in Soviet military theory, born in the Russian civil war and developed in the 1920s and early '30s, when the Soviet Union underwent a period of profound change in thinking about war.[62] The influences are rooted in the Soviet tradition of unity, flexibility and coherence, as well as the desire to create a revolutionary method of warfare. The evidence for this is suggested not only by current military leaders and thinkers but is also reflected in doctrine and the tradition of Russian creative thinking.

Chief of Staff Gerasimov, in several articles and speeches, attempted to find connections between the new way of war and Russia's traditional military thinking. He paid homage to the military intellectual pioneers of the USSR, describing that generation, many of whom were murdered in the Stalin-era purges, as 'extraordinary personalities with bright ideas. I would call them science fanatics in a good sense of the word.'[63] He also makes an unflattering comparison with the current state of military thinking. Comparing contemporary military thinkers and leaders with the 'fanatics' of the 1920s and 1930s, he lamented 'maybe we're just missing such people today'.[64] I interpret Gerasimov's slight as an expression of regret over the limited input of the armed forces into Russia's new way of war. Therefore, Western experts who describe Russia's new war as the 'Gerasimov doctrine' are mistaken. It is very much *not* his doctrine.

Gerasimov sought to find comparisons with the past. He outlined the need for 'special operations forces and internal opposition to create a permanent front throughout the territory of the opposing state' – namely, carrying out physical, political or psychological operations in the enemy's rear, complicating or undermining an adversary's efforts.[65] Special forces theorist Vladimir Kvachkov made a similar argument a decade before, asserting that the essence of special operations lay in developing a theory of deep operations, creating an 'active front in the enemy's rear'.[66] In that rear, he said, one should seek to find and exploit vulnerabilities, both physical and psychological, to prevent the enemy from mobilising.[67]

These remarks take inspiration from the USSR's interwar development of the concepts of 'deep operations' and 'deep battles' – the idea of breaking through enemy lines but then also continuing offensive operations deep behind them – pioneered by Aleksandr Svechin, Vladimir Triandafillov and others.[68] In his 1929 work *The Nature of the Operations of Modern Armies*, Triandafillov developed a calculus for determining how to conduct such operations.[69] The contemporary Russian academic and politician Andrei Kokoshin also credits Soviet theoretician N. E. Varfolomeyev with the development of deep battle concepts, defined as an entire series of operations – uninterrupted offensives, continuous and consecutively developed, logically linked, united in aim and leading to final victory.[70] These ideas, still relevant and influential today, were developed after the repeated failure of Russian armies to take advantage of breakthroughs in Austrian lines during the First World War.

Clearly, these theories do not work as exact comparisons today. But taking Gerasimov's and Kvachkov's concepts of a wide or permanent front in the enemy's rear – a 'deep operation' of sorts – one can see how fundamental concepts of military theory can be reinterpreted for Russia's new way of war. The active front in the enemy's rear today is the informational, political and economic battle, the political assassination, the disinformation campaign, the alliance with business lobbies over energy or pipelines, the politician manipulated by the Kremlin, the billionaire's support for a cause or campaign or a Putin proxy's use of the legal system to financially intimidate journalists. As Gerasimov reminds us, the result of these tools can be more destructive than 'real war'.[71] For example, NATO is, as of spring 2025, being deconstructed without a shot being fired against it, thanks to internal political divisions.

Additionally, if one sees in deep operations a theory of warfare that does not necessarily seek to physically destroy the enemy but instead 'to disrupt the enemy's ability or will to continue their operations', then the conceptual link is obvious.[72] Whilst there is a clear role for the physical destruction of the enemy, seen in both the 2014 and 2022 invasions of Ukraine, Russia's new way of war also allows scope for psychological defeat before battle, or for division and demoralisation prior to battle, or for non-military operations during the 'crisis' phases, so that victory and post-conflict restoration become more achievable at less cost.

The concept of 'operational art' also reinforces the link between today and the golden age of Russian military thinking. Operational art was a term used first by Soviet soldier and military theorist Aleksandr Svechin in 1923 and developed further in his 1926 work, *Strategy*.[73] It is the idea of unifying individual actions across a series of battles to achieve seamless effect and victory, combining the different elements of armed force and thus providing strategic coherence, which leads to victory. What has been developed today is arguably a new form of operational art, where military and non-military tools are integrated in this new, invigorated theory of conflict.

To summarise, I believe that Gerasimov's ideas about non-military forms of force, as well as the integration of military and non-military tools of conflict, are rooted in ideas of deep battle, updated for our age. By overtly integrating the tools of state power into the heart of military doctrine, Russia's new way of war can be seen to update these concepts of deep battle, arguably placing a greater emphasis on them than military action alone. Additionally, this new way of war represents a new operational art, not for the military alone but for the whole state. It uses all the tools of the state in a single, coherent, integrated way, maximising power in a world filled with Russia's enemies.

• • •

Before we leave this discussion of the roots of Russian thinking about conflict, there are two other disputes from the chaotic but inspirational revolutionary milieu of the 1920s and 1930s that add important twists to this argument today – echoes from history that continue to shape the present.

First is the intellectual battle between the champions of *attritional* versus *destructive* wars and which was best suited to the Soviet Union. Did the Soviet Union destroy its enemy with bold and decisive strikes or did it seek to defeat its enemies by wearing them down? Second, was there and should there be a revolutionary way of war to reflect the revolutionary communist state – and if so, what did this new war consist of?

As to the first, Svechin favoured the strategy of attrition. His viewpoint was shaped by German military historian Hans Delbrück's idea that war was either attritional or destructional.[74] In other words, the enemy is defeated by either being worn down over time or quickly and decisively defeated in battle – what he called a 'dualistic strategic paradigm'.[75] Svechin argued that in the case of invasion by an almost certainly technologically superior enemy, the Soviet Army should use the vast Russian hinterlands to regroup and counter-attack. Trotsky made similar points in 1922 when he said Russian troops should use the country's depth when faced by technologically superior enemies.[76]

The case for offensive strategy was led by, amongst others, Mikhail Tukhachevsky, commander of the Soviet western front in the Russo-Polish War 1920–21 and Red Army Chief of Staff 1925–8. Tukhachevsky criticised Delbrück and worked to discredit the Svechin school of thought in a debate that became increasingly bitter.[77] Tukhachevsky's belief in offensive warfare, rightly or wrongly, captured the spirit of the age and the revolutionary fervour of new and ideologically committed military commanders. 'Revolutionary' manoeuvre operations – swift, decisive and energetic – were favourably compared to the old, imperialist principle of positional, attritional warfare.[78] It was these ideas that won out – until the shattering blow of the Second World War.

This obsession with the 'offensive' fed the second question of whether the Soviet Union should have a uniquely proletarian military doctrine, reflecting the revolutionary nature of the state. Some assumed that revolution would bring about fundamental change in war as well as society. As far back as 1852, Friedrich Engels, joint author with Karl Marx of the *Communist Manifesto*, had predicted that the emancipation of the proletariat 'will have its particular military expression, it will give rise to a specific, new method of warfare'.[79] In his comment on the French Revolution, Lenin agreed, saying it had 'created, in place of the old war, a new revolutionary people's army, and created a new way of warfare.'[80] Soviet military theorist Giorgi Isserson argued that future war was to be a 'revolutionary class war' of great historical significance as communism and capitalism faced each other, with the Red Army not only defending the Soviet Union but also functioning as the first-class army of the proletariat.[81]

Mikhail Frunze, a Bolshevik military leader who in 1925 became chairman of the Revolutionary Military Council, argued for a doctrine reflecting the new communist society – a 'proletarian method of war'. However, his demands were rejected by Trotsky and Lenin as premature. Trotsky, who led the Red Army from 1918 to 1925, said that the Red Army was itself 'the military expression of the proletarian dictatorship' and did not need a 'contrived' military theory to accompany it. Lenin also rebuffed Frunze, saying a premature development of military theory risked 'communist swaggering'. After Lenin and Frunze's deaths – the latter possibly at the hands of Stalin – and the increasingly brutal purges of the 1930s, the debate over doctrine receded.

Whilst the Red Army was rejecting attritional strategies and embracing dynamic, decisive and destructive warfare, other parts of the revolutionary Soviet state were developing subversive warfare – the *bor'ba* tradition that would become known as active measures. I believe that this growing body of practice, involving espionage, disinformation, propaganda and deception operations, amongst others, amounted to the development of an *attritional* way of war, wearing down adversary societies over years, if not generations. And whilst the *bor'ba* tradition evolved over the life of the USSR, its roots too can be identified in the creative fervour of the 1920s. So, whilst *destructive* war became the dominant idea in the Red Army, *attritional* conflict became the dominant idea in what was to become the KGB and the Soviet Union's Communist Party masters.

These two themes of conflict became broadly complementary:

- War was overt; struggle was covert.
- War, in Soviet theory, was swift, decisive action. Struggle was

designed to wear down an enemy over time. So, war was annihilational and struggle was attritional.

- War was linked to destroying an enemy from without; struggle was linked to destroying an adversary from within.
- War was physical; struggle was psychological.

Finally, and critically, if one is looking for a Soviet way of war – the expression of revolutionary fervour so desired by Red Army commanders – it was finally achieved not in the evolution of military doctrine, as advanced and influential as it was, but in the development of a true revolutionary form of war: the subversive war of the secret agencies and the Communist Party. Its culture of revolutionary subversion, disinformation and fakery, of outsmarting adversaries through complex deception operations, of demoralisation and destabilisation, became the essence of revolutionary conflict and the ideological struggle.

So, the Soviet Union *did*, after all, evolve a remarkable new form of warfare representing the revolutionary essence of the Soviet Union. That new form of warfare was the political, subversive warfare of active measures. A century after its birth, Putin reunited it with military force in a new form of total war.

CHAPTER 11

STORIES FROM THE FRONT: THE CHILD STEALERS OF BELGOROD

'We were kidnapped by Russia.'

– Ksenia[1]

As seventeen-year-old Ksenia went to bed on 23 February 2022 in the home of her foster parents in the small Ukrainian border town of Vovchansk, north of Kharkiv, a framed picture of her and her brother, who lived there with her, fell to the floor. 'It was a bad omen,' she said. Four hours later, she sensed, half asleep, heavy rumbling in the attic of the house 'as if something heavy was being moved, like furniture'. After another three hours of disturbed sleep, she awoke and, bleary-eyed, went into the kitchen to make breakfast.

'The war has started,' her foster mother told her. 'I can't believe it.'

This was only the beginning of what would ultimately culminate in Ksenia's nine-month odyssey to get herself back to Ukraine, travelling deep into southern Russia to rescue her thirteen-year-old brother, at every step fighting adults who tried to keep them both in Russia.

'In my case, I was just very lucky that I could get my brother back and get back to Ukraine. Others were not so lucky,' she told me when we met in Kyiv.

At the other end of the country, in a village near Kherson, Rostyslav's world had fallen apart. The sixteen-year-old's mother, who was suffering from mental illness, had been taken into hospital. His granny, who had helped look after them, died. Then Russia invaded. For two weeks, he survived on canned food and money that had been left in the house and then by doing odd jobs for neighbours. He was eventually bundled into a military vehicle by Russian soldiers, who told him, 'You'll die here and no one will find you.' Taken to Russia, he found himself at a technical college learning Russian and being pressurised to accept a Russian passport. Within a fortnight, he had been evacuated to a summer camp in Crimea, after which he was to attend a military college where he would be trained to be a soldier. 'I was on my own, and when I turned eighteen, I'd be conscripted to fight against Ukrainians. I was in despair.'[2]

These are just two voices who experienced Russia's policy of child abduction, conducted against all the rules of war. The Russians have two targets. The first includes children transferred en masse from Ukrainian to Russian orphanages. It also includes children of foster parents who were persuaded or encouraged to decamp to Russia and children who may have lost contact with their parents due to the war or whose parents or carers may have been killed or died, such as Rostyslav's. On a crude numerical level, these children replace Russia's dead from the battlefield with new, younger citizens. Others will be used to populate sparse areas in Siberia and the far east of the country.

Russia's second target group is *all* the children in the territories occupied by Russia. This group numbers around 1.5 million, including in Crimea, almost all of whom will be subjected to indoctrination and militarisation. These children not only have a new Russian curriculum at school but face near-mandatory attendance at military-patriotic camps. They will be the new citizens of Putin's Greater Russia. The Kremlin's plan is for 15 per cent of all of Russia's mobilisable reserve to eventually come from its occupied territories. The aim is to raise hyper-patriotic citizens immersed in the *Russki mir* (Russian world) to join active and reserve forces and become the front line against Ukraine in any future war – the borderland troops of the future. The Kremlin is not only asset-stripping raw materials from Ukraine but also young humans.

As British expert Megan Gittoes, who has produced one of the few in-depth Western studies on Ukraine's stolen children says, 'These children are being absorbed by their aggressors, gradually indoctrinated and radicalised against their homeland. As they do so, their identity is being erased.'[3]

Russia occupies territory by means of physical control and occupies minds by means of psychological control. The front line is thus both *material* and *mental*. By fighting on both 'terrains', the regime plans to make liberation by Ukraine of its territory and people all but impossible in both the short and long term.

The numbers of children taken as of winter 2024 are unclear, but Kyiv believes that soldiers and agents of the Russian Federation have transferred or deported to Russia 19,546 Ukrainian children and young people, including infants.[4] Amongst them are 3,855 orphans and children deprived of parental care. Perhaps 400 have been returned, mainly from the Kharkiv area following the Ukrainian liberation of that territory. Ksenia and her brother are two of that number. However, actual numbers of the abducted are likely to be higher. Russian sources have presented widely differing figures, ranging from upwards of 200,000 children.[5] Ukrainians also say the number may be between 200,000 and 300,000.[6]

The first transport of children took place in Crimea after the 2014 annexation, with little opposition in the West. It restarted two days before the 2022 invasion, when children began to be moved from already occupied territory in Luhansk to Russia. Removing these children was a violation of Article 49 of the Fourth Geneva Convention, which states that, regardless of motives, individual or group forcible transfers 'as well as deportations of protected persons from occupied territory to the territory of the Occupying Power or to that of any other country, occupied or not, are prohibited'.[7]

Back in the border town of Vovchansk, Ksenia told the adults around her that she wanted to go to Kharkiv, where some of the town's population had already gone, or to Poland, where she had an aunt. Instead, she and her brother found themselves under immediate pressure to move to Russia and take Russian citizenship. Her foster parents didn't want to fund her journey to either Kharkiv or Poland, saying, not untruthfully but likely with other motives too, that it was dangerous. Vovchansk itself was becoming unsafe, given that Russian forces had made their headquarters in the fire station 500 meters away from Ksenia's house. She continued to attend school, despite the dwindling number of students, until one morning it was just her, her brother and the teacher. 'Go to Russia,' she was told. Without money, phone signal or options, they took the path of least resistance. Ksenia was driven to a dormitory in Shebekino, a Russian town just over the border. At the time, the front line was 25 kilometres south, on the outskirts of Kharkiv.

'They wrapped me up like a candy bar and sent me to Russia,' she said mournfully.

Ksenia stayed in Russia from September 2022 until May 2023. Over the spring, her hopes of getting to Kharkiv waned and her options seemed increasingly limited. Crossing the front lines became all but impossible. Shebekino itself was becoming dangerous as Ukrainians and Russians were exchanging fire nearby. She didn't know what would happen to her or what was happening to her brother. Pressure grew for her to go deeper into Russia. 'The adults around me were trying to brainwash me. I was promised refugee status, 100,000 roubles and a passport for Russian citizenship.' She refused. Eventually, the dormitory administrator called her in, swore and shouted at her, and told her that the dorm was closing and she was to leave. 'I was lost,' she said.

Ksenia's brother, meanwhile, had been taken deep into Russia. He had no mobile phone and she could only communicate with him through others. It turned out that their old foster parents' neighbours had fostered her brother and, she believed, eight other children – as many as they could – and had swapped life in Ukraine for Russian passports and a large house near Sochi, a coastal city on the far side of the Black Sea, near where Putin has one of his vast summer palaces.

Ukrainians are running out of options to find children taken to Russia before it becomes too late. 'Time is playing against us,' says Kateryna Rashevska, a Ukrainian lawyer collecting evidence on the abductions for the Ukraine-based Centre for Human Rights. 'There are teenagers in Russian families deported after the full-scale invasion and they would like to be returned,' she said. 'But there are also young children and they maybe even don't know that they were adopted.'[8]

The task has become more difficult because in some cases the names and personal details of the children are deliberately changed.

Ukrainians are disappearing into the Russian system, making these lost children all but untraceable, especially given the confidential nature of the Russian courts. Ukrainian researchers are reduced to going through individual websites. 'We are looking on the websites of different orphanages in Russia, for example. It's how we are finding them,' says Solomiya Khoma from the Ukrainian Security and Cooperation Center.[9] Their searching includes the use of software to show how a child may look as they grow older.

Child abduction researcher Onysia Siniuk explained to me that soon after the start of the invasion in 2022, Russian soldiers went to orphanages and children's institutions and started taking the children 'in bulk'.[10] Once inside the Russian Federation, the children 'were basically distributed among Russian institutions' and the process of custody began. Older children and young people were scattered throughout Russia. The Russian state, she said, 'started making programmes in universities, in technical colleges, for these children, for them to very quickly enrol in these classes, to incentivise them to join education in faraway places in Russia'.

I tell her I struggle to believe that in this day and age a permanent member of the United Nations Security Council could be engaged in a policy of stealing children from a nation it has invaded. Can this actually be true? 'Absolutely,' she stressed. Proof that the policy was premeditated can be seen in 'the fact that it started before the full-scale invasion, the fact that all of the system was already ready and they were talking about adjusting the legislation to make it possible for the Russians to take custody'.

As evidence, Siniuk referred to a series of Russian legal changes. Immediately after the invasion, the Ministry of Education passed Decree No. AB-631/05, aimed at identifying and re-educating deported children with poor Russian-language skills. Resolution

No. 348 enabled the integration of Ukrainian children from the Russian-named 'Donetsk People's Republic' and 'Luhansk People's Republic' into Russian society. Then, in May 2022, Putin signed Presidential Decrees 183 and 187, simplifying the process of Russian citizenship for Ukrainian children and removing the need for parental consent. This also allowed applications by the heads of institutions, enabling entire children's homes to be decamped to Russia and the children to be collectively 'passportised' as Russian citizens, supported by 'integration programmes' teaching Russian language and patriotic norms. Commenting on the move, Ukraine's Foreign Ministry said Putin had 'legalised the abduction of children from Ukraine'.[11]

Shortly before the authorities in Shebekino told Ksenia to leave the dormitory, she had made contact with a friend of her family's, who agreed to house her. She then made contact with her brother. Additionally, and critically, she was able to contact Ukrainian social services, who put her in contact with Save Ukraine, a charity that specialises in rescuing Ukrainian children stuck or trapped in Russia. She doesn't want to explain the legal and other techniques because others are using them now, but armed with letters, a 'friend' to drive her to Sochi and an understanding of the processes, she demanded Russian social services arrange a meeting between her, her brother and his new foster family. They refused at first, but she insisted and they relented. Even as she made the 800-mile trip, her brother's friend texted to ask her, 'Why are you coming? He doesn't want to see you.'

Three Russian professionals, including the head of social services, a psychologist and a social worker, met Ksenia. They were formal but unhelpful. The psychologist began to wear her down with questioning. Then the foster family and her brother arrived. 'I tried to hug him, but he turned his head away,' she said. He sat there, nervous and distant, fiddling with his zipper.

To their credit, the Russian social workers let Ksenia talk to her brother in private. 'He was intimidated by the stories he had heard,' Ksenia said. 'He was told, "There's a war there. You will be killed, don't go."' He burst into tears twice. He was disorientated and his foster family had clearly tried to influence him to stay. After two hours, she finally persuaded him by making a deal: 'Come for a month, and if you don't like it, you can go back.' The foster family were flabbergasted but had no choice but to let her brother go, as Ksenia had all the correct paperwork. They did, however, make a final attempt to keep both children. They told Ksenia, 'He's just started to study well; why can't you join us too?' The other Ukrainian children they had taken with them teased her, saying she wouldn't be able to afford to buy as many sweets as their foster parents.

That afternoon Ksenia left for home with her brother, travelling via a third country. Just before they left, one of the social workers, who had relatives in Ukraine, told her, 'Please don't be angry with us.' She struggled to make eye contact.

Of the experience, Ksenia said, 'They target people like me, children who have nothing and who are in a vulnerable state, who don't have parents or whose parents were killed, and they take those children and they change their names and they take them somewhere deep into Russia and sometimes there is no one left to find them and bring them back.'

Child abduction is not an isolated policy but part of a systematic and at times violent structure of control in the occupied territories. It is led by the FSB. At its core is the idea of 'passportisation' – the swapping of Ukrainian citizenship, passports and identity for Russian. In Russia, the regime presents the take-up rate of Russian passports as an indication of the policy's popularity. The reality is very different. The 'offer' is a blunt one and comes with a high price for adults now and for children in the future: accept Russian citizenship and passports if you want access to basic services such as healthcare and education, pensions and any form of public employment. Citizenship may also mean conscription.

'Without Russian passports, it's just impossible to survive in the occupied territories,' says Rashevska. 'We should understand this is the first aspect. And the second aspect is that life can't stop in occupied territories.' A brave few try to take their children out of the education system, she explained. 'I know the story of one family. Their mother just hid her son in order to prevent his journey into some *yunarmiya* [youth army] movement and not to send him to the Russian school.' With the help of the Ukrainian authorities, they got him out. 'It's a modern story of Anna Frank,' she said, referring to the young Dutch Jew who went into hiding during the Second World War. 'But of course you must be very brave in order to do it, because if Russians find you, it is a catastrophe for the whole family.'

There is intense pressure on people to collaborate with the Russian regime in the occupied territories and children can be used as leverage. Rashevska gave me one example of a Ukrainian policewoman who refused to collaborate. She was abducted and blackmailed. Her interrogators gave her documents showing that her son was being prepared for adoption by a Russian family and would be taken unless she co-operated. 'Of course, this woman accepted collaboration, because what can you do? I can't imagine how these people are surviving,' says Rashevska. In other cases, teachers, medical staff and others in official roles are subtly intimidated to send their children to military-patriotic camps as an example to other parents, who will then be more likely to follow suit. 'Russians unfortunately use these people because they are under their control,' Rashevska explains. Passportisation comes with other control methods too. These include the blocking of Ukrainian media and the imposition of aggressive and propagandistic Russian alternatives, the construction of a secret police network and the widespread use of torture and violence against Ukrainian citizens.

Medical care is also used as a form of control. When Kharkiv was liberated in the autumn of 2022, doctors Kyrylo and Ivan Parkhomenko, whom we met in a previous chapter, were told by friends who had lived under Russian control that patients were only able to seek medical treatment by taking Russian passports. This ties in with similar testimonies from others I spoke to. Even then, the quality of care appears to have declined rapidly. Kyrylo Parkhomenko was scathing. 'They didn't manage any kind of organised medical treatment; we are still fighting with the consequences of it right now,' he says. After the liberation, Kyrylo saw cancer patients whose illnesses had progressed from treatable to terminal. 'The occupying power did not help oncology patients at all. You can see the difference of patients that were being treated compared with those that came half a year ago in terminal stages that can't be cured.' The Russian occupying administration, he said, 'didn't care'.

Moreover, doctors who treated patients who refused Russian passports were themselves at risk of violence. 'I personally know people that were captured and even tortured because of their actions,' Ivan says. 'We're talking about our medical colleagues delivering help for Ukrainian citizens under occupation because they were not allowed to give any medical treatment without Russian government agreement.'

Without liberation, the future of the occupied territories is bleak. These 'Russian citizens' now fall under Russian laws and Russian mobilisation laws in particular. The 1.5 million young people in territory controlled by Russia are now being actively indoctrinated from their first year of schooling. When they are old enough, they are encouraged to join Russian military-patriotic organisations, with near-mandatory camps. The militarisation of young people is happening across Russia, not only in the occupied Ukrainian territories. But in the occupied lands, the risks are greater in rejecting a camp for your child. 'In the occupied territories, this is just dangerous to refuse because you'll be perceived as disloyal, and if you are disloyal, you may be deprived of parental care rights, you may be sent somewhere to a torture chamber,' says Rashevska.

The military-patriotic camps allow a child to be separated from their family and therefore a deeper level of indoctrination. 'When they go far away to Russia, they're separated from the family, they're separated from the usual circumstances and they are much more susceptible to what they're told,' says researcher Siniuk. The camps, across Russia, in Belarus and also in the occupied territories, mix harmless outdoor pursuits with propaganda. 'Russia is so great. Look how fun it is here compared to the occupied territories. Look how good it is here compared to the occupied territories – that's because the Ukrainian regime did that,' says Siniuk, referring to the destruction and damage caused by the Russian invasion. Russian children who have already been told these stories reinforce this messaging.

These actions reflect stories and behaviours going back to the Second World War. Modern messaging is rooted in the 'cult' of the Great Patriotic War and maintains a link between fighting Nazis then and now. 'When they're talking about "Nazism", they always link it to the current "Nazism" in Ukraine to justify the current aggression, and with it other themes, such as the fight against collaborators,' says

Siniuk – 'collaborators' being active pro-Ukrainian citizens. It also has echoes in past deportations, where populations were moved around the Soviet Union to punish some groups and replace them with more 'reliable' people. Over 600,000 'colonisers' have moved to Crimea, with generous bonuses being offered to teachers of physical and patriotic education in the occupied territories. 'Russian policies at the moment stem from and build on Soviet experiences,' Siniuk comments.

Back in Kherson, Rostyslav was told he was going to be taken to a camp near Yevpatoriia in Crimea. The first two weeks, he said, were enjoyable. Although he was not able to swim, the camp was by the sea. However, things began to change, slowly at first. One morning, the boys were called together by the camp commander and told, 'Kherson is not ours anymore and now you are our children. You will stay here indefinitely. In a month Ukraine will be no more. It is going to burn, and you will stay here.' Rostyslav said that the majority (70 per cent) wanted to go back to Ukraine, whilst the rest accepted or welcomed the change. More militarisation and indoctrination began to seep into the camp. The Russian national anthem was sung every morning. Children who refused to sing it got into trouble. If they refused once, Rostyslav said, they had to write an explanatory letter. The second time they had to report to the camp commander, a former member of Ukraine's former Berkut riot police, a unit with a thuggish and violent reputation. The third time they were put in solitary confinement. Rostyslav refused to sing the Russian national anthem and was put in solitary confinement on three occasions. In addition, there were occasional (but not systemic) acts of violence towards the children. Their treatment started to deteriorate.

Rostyslav was then enrolled in a military school in Kerch – he had no choice in the matter – and in the holidays he was kept in a camp for local troubled children, behind barbed-wire fencing. 'It was like summer camp but many times worse, with barbed wire and cameras,' he says. He was able to walk outside for two hours a day, one hour in the morning and one in the evening. The Crimean authorities issued him a Russian birth certificate. He tore it up. They issued a second one but refused to give it to him. They took his Ukrainian birth certificate and continued to press him to take citizenship. 'They told me, just sign. You'll get 100,000 roubles, you'll get an apartment, you'll live good. If you go back to Ukraine, you'll be homeless. You're going to live by the trash bin.' He refused.

A first attempt to get Rostyslav back to Ukraine failed. The mother of one of his friends came to collect her son. Working with Save Ukraine, she had been given documents to take not only her son but also his two friends, one of which was Rostyslav. The academy's director reluctantly allowed her to take her child and one other but refused Rostyslav permission to leave. Unknown to him, his mother had been made a Russian citizen, which meant that he would be one too. They would keep him against his will and aged eighteen, he would be issued with a passport, regardless of his wishes.

However, he was still in touch with Save Ukraine. A second rescue was organised for the day he was due to return to military college from the camp for his final year before potential mobilisation. He was told, 'You need to find a day when they will not start searching until late.'

There was a roll call at the beginning and end of every day, so Rostyslav would not be expected at the military college until 9 p.m. and would have the day to travel. They would not check on him until nightfall and then, perhaps unsure about his whereabouts, the college might not list him as missing immediately, thus buying him a few extra hours. Once the 6 a.m. roll call had ended, he walked a short distance and ordered a taxi. He was dropped off and walked fifteen minutes to a rendezvous point, where he was met by a person working with Ukrainian child-abduction teams. He was given a change of clothes and new papers. He ripped off his cadet epilates and tore up his old documents.

The pair cautiously made their way across the Kerch Strait Bridge, which links eastern Crimea to Russia territory, and drove into Russia. At the internal checkpoints, Rostyslav kept a check on his nerves. He was worried he might have been listed as missing or that he would get his story wrong or that his new papers would not be accepted. But the plan worked. He says that when he finally walked across the Ukrainian border, after a near 1,000-mile journey home, he 'felt the stress wash away'.

Both teenagers are now safely back in Ukraine after their remarkable journeys, testament to their willpower and strength of character. Both are studying in college. Ksenia plans to write a book collating the stories of stolen children who overcame psychological or physical abuse to make their way home.

The stories, she said, are all different, but united by one common theme: 'We were kidnapped by Russia.'

CHAPTER 12

THE UKRAINE CONFLICT STAGES ONE AND TWO: 2005 TO 2014, THE LONG CONFLICT AND THE FIRST INVASION

'Russia has found a recipe to counteract the colour revolutions.'

– Igor Panarin[1]

The three stages of the Ukraine War to date have been, briefly, the following.

Stage One: 2005 to early 2014. Conflict using non-military tools
Following the 2004–5 Orange Revolution, the Kremlin acts to stem Ukraine's drift towards the West by instigating a campaign using informational, political, economic, criminal and espionage tactics to return Kyiv to Russia's sphere of influence. The culmination of this campaign occurs in late 2013, when President Yanukovych, under intense pressure from the Kremlin, abandons a co-operation deal negotiated with the European Union in favour of one with Russia. Globally, Russia's relationship with the West steadily worsens.

Stage Two: 2014 to 2022. Conflict using military and non-military tools, with limited military force

Mass protests break out in Kyiv as a result of Yanukovych's volte-face. Having come close to 'flipping' Ukraine, the Kremlin loses control. The Yanukovych regime falls. Putin escalates by carrying out a long-planned annexation of the Crimean Peninsula and instigating a series of controlled uprisings in the south and east of Ukraine, 'curated' by Russian special forces with support from locally recruited paramilitary groups and organised crime.

Most of the uprisings fail, but two, in Donetsk and Luhansk, partially succeed thanks to a limited Russian invasion of approximately 10,000 soldiers. Putin denies his troops are in Ukraine. These modest victories give Russia a foothold. The Kremlin spends the following years pressuring Kyiv for political concessions as the price for long-term peace. It begins political-warfare operations against the US and in Europe, most notably in the 2016 US presidential elections.

Stage Three: 2022 to present. Conflict using all the tools of Russian warfare, short of nuclear weapons

The frozen conflict and subsequent negotiations fail to deliver the political outcome that President Putin wants – namely, control over Ukraine. The FSB and GRU build up their networks in Ukraine again. In 2022, President Putin orders a major ground invasion of Ukraine, although the main thrust of the invasion is aimed at population suppression rather than war fighting. Assumptions that Ukraine would quickly fold prove false. In ordering the invasion when he does, he fails to allow the Russian armed forces to properly prepare.

The Russian Army fails to capture Kyiv. As a result, the assault is recalibrated, first in the late spring of 2022 to wheel around to the east of the country and second, from the winter of 2022–3, to focus on its three-pronged strategy. The strategy is to first, hold the line and grind down the Ukrainian Army through relentless attacks; second, destroy Ukrainian will to resist by bombing cities and striking at energy supplies; and third, damage the link between Ukraine and its Western supporters. The Kremlin ramps up its information, sabotage, cyber and other operations in the West.

Let's have a look at these in a little more detail to gain an understanding of the various tools of war used at different periods. In this chapter, we'll look at stages one and two, before going on to examine stage three in the following chapter.

STAGE ONE

The 2004 Ukrainian presidential race pits pro-Russian Viktor Yanukovych against pro-Western Viktor Yushchenko. Yushchenko is poisoned with dioxin in September of that year but survives. The election is initially fixed in favour of the pro-Russian Yanukovych. Protesters, wearing the colour of Yushchenko's campaign, take to Kyiv's streets in protest – hence the moniker of the Orange Revolution. They succeed in having the vote annulled. In the run-off a month later, Yushchenko wins.

The Orange Revolution represents a watershed, as Ukrainians vote for a pro-Western candidate rather than a former Communist apparatchik or Soviet-era factory director. Soon after, Russian paramilitary preparations begin. In the Donbas, photographs are circulated showing special training camps, complete with Donetsk People's Republic flags.[2] In Kharkiv, an 'activisation of Russian organisations' takes place, funded by the Russian consulate and run from the nearby Russian city of Belgorod.[3] One Kharkiv activist told me that from 2005 onwards, local elites had been infiltrated and recruited by Russian agents. These processes happen elsewhere in Ukraine too. Several former senior military officers and secret agency generals tell me of a step change in Russian operations after 2005.

Russian media and culture become more pronounced tools of aggression. An increasingly strident news culture emanates from pro-Russian TV, where divisive and condescending narratives are peddled.[4] References to Ukrainian nationalist leaders are removed from history books. The Orthodox Church and cultural and historical clubs sell a sanitised view of Russian history and belittle the artificial separation of Russians and Russian speakers.

Ukrainian and Russian oligarchs establish powerful positions in industries and use those profits to channel money to pro-Russian political groupings, primarily the Party of the Regions.[5] Russian operations at this time were superficially inseparable from the tactics used by major organised crime. One senior member of a Ukrainian secret agency told me that a favoured tactic by the FSB, working through a convenient oligarch, was to create an artificial liquidity crisis in a bank or firm, forcing its sale to new owners that were controlled by the FSB. A Ukrainian bank overwhelmingly used by the country's defence firms was the target of one such Russian special operation. Should victims try to fight back, they would be hit with fabricated criminal cases launched by corrupt police or tax inspectors.

Energy is a particular target. Three major disputes over pricing take place in 2005–6, 2007–8 and 2013–14, whereby the Russian state seeks political concessions in exchange for cheap gas. Gas and the profits from it are also used to corrupt nominally 'pro-Western' politicians and fund overtly pro-Russian politicians. Nuclear power is used as another tool of influence. In 2006, Andrei Derkach, son of former SBU boss Leonid Derkach – also allegedly linked to major crime figures – was named as head of Energoatom, the Ukrainian nuclear power state company. He signed a series of deals that 'created a dependence on the Russian nuclear industry'.[6] Despite concerns reported in the Ukrainian media, the deals went ahead. Derkach has since been arrested and charged with spying for Russia.[7]

Outside Ukraine, Putin makes public his hostility towards the current world order in his now infamous Munich Security Conference speech in 2007. Western analysts ignore it, deriding those who raise fears of a new Cold War. Ukraine is not Russia's only target this time. The tools and tactics of Russian warfare become visible elsewhere.

Assassinations take place outside Russia. On 1 November 2006, former KGB agent Alexander 'Sasha' Litvinenko sits down to supper with his wife Marina in London. The date was a special one – it was the anniversary of their arrival in the UK to seek political asylum. 'This 1 November was even more special, as we celebrated it as British citizens for the first time,' Marina told me.[8] She had prepared a recipe from her mother that Sasha loved, chopped chicken with garlic and sour cream. As they go to bed that evening, he starts to feel unwell. He worsens during the following day. Initial ambulance team assessments give way to more serious fears. 'Sasha couldn't eat, couldn't drink. He vomited,' says Marina. It takes ten days for doctors to realise the cause wasn't just E. coli, but even after that they refuse to believe it could be something more serious. In the meantime, Sasha's hair falls out and his skin turns yellow. In her desperation, Marina contacts experts who had treated poisoned Ukrainian presidential candidate Viktor Yushchenko.

'Every time when we ask to check him for poisoning, they just very much suspected we may be not stable mentally,' Marina says. Whilst she hoped there was an innocent explanation, Sasha immediately feared what was happening. 'He knew this from the beginning. Sasha said this from the first day.' When Marina said it might be bacteria, her husband answered sarcastically, 'Yes, I know this bacteria, it has *pagon* [military rank].' He dies on 23 November of acute radiation syndrome caused by polonium-210 poisoning.

Elsewhere, Estonia is subjected to one of the first state-sponsored cyberattacks in 2007. In 2008, Russia and Georgia go to war following a provocative outbreak of violence by Russian-controlled separatists in the territory of South Ossetia, nominally within Georgia. On 1 August of that year, South Ossetians shell Georgian villages. Georgia responds by engaging the South Ossetians. Russian forces, in place already following military exercises, launch a significant, pre-planned operation on 8 August, citing the defence of civilians and accusing Georgia of genocide, taking both the military and informational offensive. Students of Russian strategy note Russia's use of reflexive control techniques in two ways: first, by staging provocations that they know the Georgians would react to, especially given their understanding of the country's leader, and second, by manipulating French president Nicolas Sarkozy to drive through a peace plan 'drafted in Moscow' due to 'a false perception that Georgia could be lost altogether'.[9]

Back in Ukraine, disillusioned voters oust Yushchenko in 2010. Whilst some reforms take place, his time in power is marked by infighting and corrupt deals over energy supply, manipulated by Russia. Yanukovych takes power. He oversees an intensification of corruption. I asked a former Ukrainian SBU general how many Russian agents were in their ranks at this time. He told me there were 'not hundreds, but dozens' of individuals whose loyalties lay with Moscow and not Kyiv.[10] Was enough done to counter Russian subversion? 'The answer is definitely "no",' he replied. The military is hollowed out and weaponry is removed from Crimea.

The shake-down of businesses becomes even more systemic under Yanukovych. One former activist, 'Sasha', said that organised crime operated at three levels. At the two lowest levels were those controlling open markets or those who intimidated small shop keepers. The third layer, he said, became 'very intertwined with the government' and would see a senior police or intelligence officer visit the business and openly demand shares in it. Mimicking the language of the official, he explained:

> Hmm, you're producing furniture, you are exporting it to Moldova, to Belarus. It's quite a nice business, you're a good guy, we believe you can share 50 per cent of your business for free – if you still want to do business. Here are the documents. This is a specific entity registered in Netherlands, which was created by a specific entity registered in Cyprus, which was created by the specific entity registered to Bahamas.[11]

The business would then be shared with Yanukovych or his people, or sometimes with a regional police chief. 'And that was one of the reasons why Maidan [the 2013–14 protests] was so supported by the businessmen,' Sasha explains.

Yanukovych arrests and puts on trial his main opponent, which in turn stalls negotiations with the EU over closer trade and political links. Eventually, the talks, which begun in 2007, continue. Diplomats told me that the Russians were so convinced that no deal would be done, they paid little attention. Yanukovych himself seeks advice as to whether the deal might damage him personally. He is told it will not. He engages in negotiations because, despite his dependence on Moscow, he needs to demonstrate a pro-European outlook to much of his Ukrainian electorate, especially in the centre and west of the country. The Kremlin is shocked to find out, in the late summer of 2013, that Ukraine is actually close to an agreement with the EU. Putin summons Yanukovych to Sochi and puts him under intense pressure, professionally and personally. He abandons the Deep and Comprehensive Free Trade Area being negotiated between Ukraine and the EU and announces instead talks to join the rival Russian-led Eurasian Customs Union and a Russo-Ukrainian action plan.

Mass protests break out in Kyiv in 2013. They become violent. Threatening texts are sent to protesters warning them to leave Independence Square, the heart of the protests. Snipers fire into the crowds. In Kharkiv, protesters are poisoned. The national crisis drags on for weeks. Over 100 people are killed. On 21 February, Yanukovych agrees plans for new elections but flees soon afterwards. A brief attempt to set up a rival pro-Russian capital in Kharkiv is thwarted by thousands of protesters. Having come very close to 'flipping' Ukraine, the Kremlin, despite the small army of FSB fifth directorate agents around Yanukovych, loses control.

STAGE TWO

The fall of Yanukovych damages the Kremlin's political influence over Ukraine. Russia wanted a calm, quiet but irreversible return of Ukraine to Russia's sphere of influence. Instead, it found itself in a crisis, brought to the boil not by its own agents working to its own phasing plans but by Ukrainian activists desperate to prevent state capture by the Kremlin. The quick dash through the phases of conflict (escalation, beginning of action and crisis) was not of Russia's making but was driven by anti-Russian, pro-democracy and nationalist forces in Kyiv.

Putin responds by putting in place his own escalation to regain the initiative. He orders an operation to annex Crimea on 22 February.[12] 'Managed conflicts' are also created across the south and east of Ukraine. A string of local *coup d'états* are launched, designed to replace Ukrainian with Russian-controlled authority and force Kyiv into a humiliating peace.

Preparatory work had taken place for years in Crimea. For Christo Grozev, one of the brains behind the online investigative agency Bellingcat, Crimea remains the best example of Russian integrated planning. 'The Crimea annexation … had everything,' he says. 'It had political technology, it had media strategy, it had protest groups, all curated from Moscow by the secret services. And then it had the army at the same time, and it had also a corruption of the enemy army as part of the strategy of bloodless takeover.'[13] It even had religious pilgrims, with a senior member of the GRU travelling to Crimea to set up local cells under the guise of accompanying a religious artefact. The Crimea operation is sometimes seen as an easy one for the Russians, but Russian assessments produced in the years before the annexation showed otherwise. 'They did have pollsters deployed there in the end of 2013. We actually got access to some of the hacked leak materials,' Grozev says, 'and you could clearly see that they themselves did not consider it friendly territory. They needed to do a lot of brainwashing and false flag scare tactics in order for the population to begin fearing Kyiv as a centre of power.'

On 26 and 27 February 2014, Putin announces major exercises in eastern Ukraine involving 50,000 men and a smaller, secondary exercise in the Black Sea involving 7,000 men and thirty-six ships. The exercises mask Russia's true plans. Attention is focused on the east whilst the Crimean operation begins. Russian special forces secure Crimean government buildings and other strategic locations.[14] On 27 February, Russian units take Belbek airfield in Sevastopol and later Simferopol airfield, where they land 2,000 soldiers.[15] The coup is actively supported by organised crime.[16]

Whilst Western governments remained fearful but confused, local journalists were beginning to report the true picture. On 2 March 2014, Roman Burko was near the Russian military base at Sevastopol when he saw Russian troops deploying. He grabbed his camera and recorded the footage. 'They didn't have insignia, but they had ammunition, they had weapons – it was clear that they were Russians,' he said. One of them pointed his weapon at Burko and told him, 'If you don't stop filming, we'll sew you [slang for killing him].'[17] Burko said several soldiers came for him, but he managed to escape. 'I ran back, took off all this data, posted it on the network, and in the very first days it gained more than two million views on the YouTube channel.' Burko quickly found himself to be in demand. He was also being hunted by the Russian authorities and a group of Kuban Cossacks working with them. One afternoon, Burko received an urgent message from friends monitoring Russian comms; they were coming for him. 'We had only a few hours before the FSB might "pack us up"', said Burko. He threw a couple of T-shirts and laptops into backpacks, turned off his mobile phones and removed the SIM cards so that they could not be tracked and fled north.

Russian soldiers appear on the streets of Crimea. Photographed smiling, helping civilians and chatting with locals, they quickly acquired the nickname 'little green men' (*zelyonye chelovechki*) or 'polite people' (*vezhliviye ludi*).[18] The Crimean Parliament, riddled with organised crime representatives, passes its allegiance from Ukraine to Russia. Defections to the new Russian-controlled authorities rock Ukrainian morale. Who could be trusted?

Whilst this was happening, a remarkably sophisticated information operation was being run, with multiple campaigns hitting different targets. False reassurances were given to the German and other governments.[19] The FSB hacked and leaked US diplomatic conversations to damage US credibility and drive a wedge between the US and EU states. Whilst the Russian military and GRU, with their local political and organised crime allies, were actively curating the Crimean uprising, its diplomats were persuading its critical EU partners that it was doing no such thing. At the same time, its media outlets were attempting to persuade the rest of the world that the crisis was the result of US actions – the creation of an alternative reality.

The Russian state supports the operation by means of intense barrages of virulent state propaganda built around the themes of Ukrainian moral, legal and political illegitimacy. Ukraine's regime is portrayed as a proto-Nazi puppet of the US and as the result of an illegal coup. Where possible, pro-Ukrainian voices are silenced. Burko's InformNapalm – Ukraine's answer to Bellingcat – is repeatedly hit with denial of service attacks, as well as attempted hacks.

In Crimea, the successful subversion of Ukraine's authority signals the end of operational phases. Crimea's March 2014 accession into the Russian Federation marks phases five and six, 'resolution' and the 'return of peace and post-conflict management'. Pockets of political resistance are stifled, opposition by the Crimean Tartars is suppressed and journalists are arrested.[20] Russian passports are handed out. New economic and transport agreements are signed.

Russians are steadily brought into the peninsula in the years that follow.

The annexation of Crimea was a near-perfect coup. The Kremlin regained control. It spread confusion amongst Western and Ukrainian leaders using disinformation, deception, concealment and other measures designed to confuse and affect decision-making. Professor Igor Panarin, one of the architects of Russia's information warfare policy, was at the Kremlin for the celebration of Crimea's incorporation into Russia on 18 March 2014. The same day, he wrote approvingly on social media that Russia's actions had been personally coordinated by Vladimir Putin. 'Russia,' he said, 'has found a recipe to counteract the colour revolutions.'[21]

OPERATIONS IN SOUTHERN AND EASTERN UKRAINE

If the Crimean annexation was a textbook example of a managed *coup d'état* going through Russian operational phasing, Russia's eastern and southern Ukrainian operations were less successful, despite initially following a similar pattern. There were three main actors: the FSB, the GRU and the presidential office. The FSB led in Luhansk and the GRU in Donetsk.

The 'start of conflict' and 'bringing to crisis' phases witness the emergence of aggressive and intimidating organised pro-Russian protesters on the streets, often involving the use of paid thugs, known locally as *titushki*. These protests, sometimes referred to as the Russian Spring in the pro-Moscow media, take place with a mix of bused-in and local pro-Russian groups.

In Ukraine's second city of Kharkiv, following increased levels of disorder from mid-February 2014, self-proclaimed separatists attack pro-Kyiv protesters with clubs and wooden bars and drive vehicles into them. In desperation, pro-Kyiv civilians barricade themselves into government buildings. Skirmishes continue in the days that follow. Protester Konstantin Oleynik had his teeth kicked out by members of the Berkut security forces, whilst his friend, a university teacher, had their head crushed after a particularly savage beating.[22]

Kharkiv academic Nataliya Zubar says she was poisoned during the Kharkiv protests: 'We had our EuroMaidan [pro-democracy] Kharkiv assemblies near the Shevchenko monument and we always had the table with hot drinks, because it was a very cold winter. And there were special people attending to these drinks as we were aware of the danger of being poisoned. And I usually came to get my cup of hot tea myself.' However, that day she was handed a mug of tea by a fellow protester. On the verge of collapsing when she arrived home, she spent two weeks fighting a lung infection. 'I wanted to have some biochemical tests,' Zubar continued, 'but my family doctor said, "Don't do it, because we have a very uneven political situation here in Kharkiv. We don't know what could come from your tests…"' She feared arrest or interrogation or violence at the hands of pro-Russian forces. Instead, she went to Kyiv for tests. The tests were inconclusive, but she found others suffering with similar symptoms.

Pro-Russian protesters quickly morph into organised, armed separatists – in reality, GRU- or FSB-led groups with a local veneer of thugs and criminals. The GRU moves its operations from Belgorod to Kharkiv in early March.[23] In April, its fighters move into towns in Kharkiv and the Donbas in order to cause havoc. In Sloviansk, local official Denys Bihunov watched as Russian paramilitary arrived on 12 April 2014, under the banner of the Donetsk People's Republic. They were led by the infamous 'Strelkov', otherwise known as the FSB/GRU veteran Igor Girkin. Rumour has it he paid $15,000 in bribes to buy his way through checkpoints.

The fighters brought with them, Bihunov says, an atmosphere both oppressive and confusing, accompanied by the 'propaganda of total disinformation'.[24] Strelkov's men justified their presence by citing rumours that Ukrainian 'fascists' from the Right Sector group were descending on the town. The separatists, Bihunov added, carried out a small number of assassinations to instil compliance. He cited the killing of Volodymyr Rybak, a local councillor from the nearby town of Horlivka, who was murdered trying to prevent the Ukrainian flag from being taken down. Bihunov says that Rybak was kidnapped from Horlivka and taken to Sloviansk, where he was tortured and killed.

'I would say that he was executed with a special sadism,' Bihunov observes. 'On the body they found traces of burns, torture … they ripped open his stomach.' He was thrown into a river, weighed down with a sandbag and his body was widely shown in the media. 'We saw a man who was unarmed, who was just trying to protect the Ukrainian state flag on the building. He was not just killed but demonstratively destroyed, as they crush an insect.' Bihunov said that fear took hold in the local population. 'I remember this moment when I thought … it is necessary to somehow go to the SBU [Ukrainian secret service], to the army, to somehow convey information to someone – but fear enveloped me. I understood that we were in complete chaos.'

Fear and uncertainty generates compliance. Vasiliy Kravets, a lecturer in a technical college in occupied Ukraine, told me how 'violence and fear' were used by separatist 'counter-intelligence' representatives who visited the college to ascertain the loyalty of staff. 'There were threats to everyone … an order was issued at the academy by the rector that everyone who collaborates … who co-operates with Ukraine, will deal with counterintelligence,' Kravets says.[25] Whilst this was going on, 'many of my colleagues from other universities were arrested, thrown into cellars, kept there, beaten, not fed'.

Whilst these acts of violence and intimidation are being conducted, Strelkov and his team portray themselves as glamorous heroes. Their newspaper, entitled *NovoRossiya* (New Russia), made stylistic reference to the Hollywood film *300*, a fictionalised retelling of the end of the Battle of Thermopylae where a small number of Spartan warriors stood up to a larger foe.

Despite its unpleasant absurdity to Western eyes, Russian propaganda was successful in eastern Ukraine, in part because it was the culmination of a decade of repetitive work, which built on narrative tropes familiar to Russians. However, in key cities like Odesa, Dnipro and Kharkiv, the uprisings fail to overthrow local police and political authorities. In Odesa in southern Ukraine, pro-Russian protesters are met by organised opposition. Weeks of low-level violence culminate in forty-six pro-Russian protesters being killed on 2 May, burnt to death in a trade union building where they were trapped. The fire has been exploited since by Russian propagandists.[26]

So, the operational phases designed to lead to a collapse of Ukrainian authority failed. Ukrainian state power bent, but it did not break. Why is a matter for conjecture, although again many interviewees spoke of the role of civic society groups who confronted pro-Russian protesters, even when they faced physical intimidation and violence.[27] 'Kharkiv is considered the capital of the volunteer movement, and according to some statistics, there 80 per cent of Kharkiv people helped or volunteered ... or gave things or money,' Kharkiv resident Volodymyr Chystylin told me.[28] Chystylin gave some examples of how citizens helped: camouflage-net weaving, preparing rations, giving psychological support to volunteers returning from the front line and opening a military hospital.

That summer, as Ukrainian forces begin to overwhelm separatist groups and the Russians do not generate popular support in most areas, Putin reacts by escalating again. Artillery begins firing from Russian territory onto Ukrainian positions. Russian reconnaissance and special-operations units begin procedures in Ukraine from mid-July and large-scale movements into Ukraine begin from mid-August. Whilst much of the Western media continues to report the conflict in terms of civil discord within Ukraine, online detectives at InformNapalm as well as the Ukrainian Cyber Alliance track the flow of Russian units into eastern Ukraine by monitoring social media, especially Russia's version of Facebook, Vkontakte. An estimated 90,000 troops from twenty-eight military units had been stationed in Crimea or along the eastern Ukraine border. By the end of August 2014, up to 6,000 Russian soldiers – minus their insignia to create the barest fig leaf of deniability – are in Ukraine, increasing to 10,000 by the end of the year.[29]

Over a summer and autumn of chaotic fighting, the GRU-led 'separatist' groups are largely replaced by Russian brigades and Ukraine's armed forces find themselves in direct confrontation with Russian soldiers, minus their identifying insignia.

Russia begins hollowing out the Ukrainian armed forces, working to compromise it through the Ministry of Defence itself but also carrying out procedures at the operational and tactical levels. The 2014 invasion sees the first example of so-called app-jacking, a sophisticated and inventive operation very likely planned by the GRU. It had placed malware on a popular Android app developed by a Ukrainian artillery officer for use with the Soviet-era D-30 howitzer, a large artillery gun that fires shells with a range of 13 miles. The

Russian-infected version of the app was seeded onto Ukrainian military forums, where it was downloaded by some artillery officers. Once installed, the app fed the location of the Ukrainian artillery positions back to their Russian adversary, making targets of the artillery crews themselves.[30] The Ukrainians are thought to have lost between 15 and 20 per cent of their D-30 howitzers in combat operations. This was one of the reasons why.

Some of the better commanders were acutely aware of the need to protect their units from Russian espionage and poor Ukrainian security. 'On all the levels ... there were Russians or recruited agents,' one commander told me.[31] As a result, he never followed precise orders. 'I have never placed my positions where the headquarters told me. I have never gone for the attack along the route that the headquarters told me.' As a result, he said, he lost far fewer men than other commanders.

Russian disinformation and psychological operations spread chaos, making Ukrainian resistance less effective. Ukrainian Ministry of Defence adviser Liubov Tsybulska told me how Russian special services worked 'very skilfully' on different target audiences. 'There were messages for soldiers. There were messages for their families,' she says. 'There were messages for the western and eastern regions. This is a complex matrix, but in an acute crisis, each message finds its recipient.'[32] Whilst some Ukrainian units still continued to fight, others, through lack of kit, low morale and poor leadership following years of Russia's hollowing out of Ukrainian armed forces, were 'literally paralysed' with indecision and fear. 'They lacked the confidence to attack and even to repel the attack. Because they had been "prepared" by the Russian traditional media and social media that it made no sense to resist, that Ukraine would lose anyway,' Tsybulska explains.

Despite these intense pressures, Ukrainians fight desperately to slow and then reverse their territorial losses but fail to retake the territory originally lost in the Donetsk and Luhansk oblasts. They suffer two significant defeats at Ilovais'k in August 2014 and Debal'tseve in January 2015. Two rounds of peace deals are eventually signed, Minsk I and II, both products of Russian battlefield pressure combined with the Kremlin's diplomatic offensive and manipulation of Western politicians.

SUBVERSIVE WARFARE PRIOR TO 2005

Before we move on to the 2022 invasion, there is a question to be asked. Did Russian subversive warfare against Ukraine begin in 2005 or before? Some argue that systemic attempts to undermine Ukraine begun as early as 1991. One interviewee noted the interconnected pattern of conflicts in the USSR, suggesting wars took place where nations were trying to move out of the Kremlin's sphere of influence. 'Everything that happened in the Caucasus, everything that happened in Transnistria [Moldova], everything that happened in our country afterwards is one chain,' one told me. Additionally, one can look at the evidence from Sweden's Defence Agency, which recorded fifty attempts by the Kremlin to use energy supply as a weapon in Russia's relations with Ukraine and other former Soviet republics between 1991 and 2006.[33]

'I would say that the war started in 1991, because in Russia even democratic opposition leaders like Yeltsin said that [if] Ukraine declares independence, Russia would start questioning Ukraine's borders,' Kyiv pollster Anton Grushetsky told me.[34] 'But Russia was too weak [to act] then.' So the intent was there, even if the capability was lacking. Others, Grushetsky jokes, would say that Ukraine has always been at war with Russia, a reference to the battle to retain Ukrainian identity after the Zaporizhzhian Cossack republic was subsumed into Russia in the mid- to late eighteenth century.

Before 2005, Russian political consultants worked with the pro-Russian Yanukovych to manipulate fault lines in Ukrainian society, targeting the eastern Ukrainian population, which either spoke Russian or a mixed dialect of Russian and Ukrainian, known colloquially as *surzhyk*, after a bread that contains a higgledy-piggledy mix of ingredients. Although polling suggested people's priorities were rule of law, the economy and justice, Russian political technologists worked to create divisions over language and loyalty, arguing that those in the east were being treated as second-class citizens. The Russians had an easy and fertile territory, given the corruption in Ukrainian politics at the time. Former activist Sasha, now a government adviser, told me of the type of intimidation typical in the early 2000s, citing an election in the town of Mukachevo in western Ukraine in early 2004. 'The fraud there was spectacular,' he said, describing how the authorities brought in gangsters to beat members of Parliament trying to protect the ballot boxes where votes were cast. 'It was not only organised crime, it was organised crime and police, when organised crime and police were working together and police were executing orders given by the organised crime.'

Other experts take an even longer view, looking back at the long tradition of Soviet subversive war. Ukrainian think tank head Mykhailo Honchar saw in Russia's hybrid war some old techniques, which had been updated. 'From our point of view, many say … these are like old techniques … The Soviet Union also used the methods of hybrid warfare.'[35] StopFake boss Yevhen Fedchenko, when asked about the historical provenance of Russian subversive conflict, answered, 'It's connected, of course, because I mean nothing is happening out of the blue. This system is … based on heritage and traditions and it's refurbished according to the current moment.'[36] Fedchenko also linked active measures to the present day: 'The current disinformation campaign is simply a continuation of the policies that began during the Soviet era … in short, Soviet active measures never actually went away.'[37] This is despite assurances given to the US in the 1990s that the Russian Federation had ceased such operations.[38]

Continuity was seen not only in the tools used but also in the Russian tradition of creative thought, devising new concepts of conflict as well as new weapons. Zubar identified a similar continuity, using as an example non-military psychological, acoustic, biological and environmental weapons programmes. She described work in the 1970s and 1980s by Kharkiv's Academy of Missile Forces that focused on 'acoustic and visual influence on perception'. Whilst experiments on visual influence failed, acoustic experiments proved more successful. She explained the experiments to me: 'What worked at that time was acoustic influence. When they inserted different types of sounds, noises, pitches into the soundtrack of a radio or TV transmission … that actually affected people … The head of this department … was very unhappy that he was forbidden by the KGB to carry his research outside of Kharkiv. He used to say, "We have a powerful technology! We can control people's minds! Why am I not allowed to use it?"'

This testimony, and the evidence provided by Russian authors in *Voyennaya Mysl'* and other publications, provides evidence of Soviet research into experimental theories and tools of conflict.[39] This continues to be relevant, given the development of new and updated tools, ranging from use of the internet to poisons such as Novichok and, potentially, microwave weapons.[40]

Conceptually, Zubar says, Russia's new way of war was the summation of its 'eternal state of ordering and chaos'. She also uses as an example the idea, popular in both nationalist and communist circles, of a perpetual war of values against the West, quoting the fascist philosopher Aleksandr Dugin and the Russian politician and author Vladimir Lisichkin: 'Ukraine now is actually a battlefield of values, not only for territory.'

In 2022, that battlefield was to grow exponentially.

CHAPTER 13

THE UKRAINE CONFLICT STAGE THREE: 2014 TO 2022, THE SECOND INVASION

'I need ammo, not a ride.'

– President Volodymyr Zelensky

Vladimir Putin's invasion of Ukraine, launched in the early hours of 24 February 2022, was large-scale – involving over 100,000 troops – but it was not a traditional military invasion. For the most part, Russian units did not enter Ukraine prepared for battle; instead, they advanced in unwieldy and meandering columns, vulnerable to Ukrainian air power and artillery. The invasion was, much like Russian warfare, hybrid. It was part military action, part show of force to subdue the population and part military support for an FSB-organised *coup d'état* in Kyiv, aimed at eliminating Ukraine's political and military leadership. Only after the initial plans failed did it transform into a war-fighting operation.

Plans had been in development for at least six months. There is ongoing debate regarding which Russian institution led these efforts. Britain's Royal United Services Institute reported that the FSB was selected to lead the initiative.[1] However, Ukrainian intelligence sources indicate that it originated within the Russian Security

Council. The refusal to call it a conflict, invasion or war and instead apply the euphemism 'special military operation' was not just a presentational description but had a significant, real-world impact on military preparations for the invasion, with disastrous results for the Russians.[2]

Russian forces were, in the words of one British military observer, 'devastatingly inept' in their original mission to take Kyiv.[3] By September 2022, Russian positions had collapsed around Kharkiv, allowing Ukraine to regain territory along its north-eastern border. I was in Ukraine that weekend and the sense of optimism that Ukrainians would win was profound. Sadly, overconfidence and slow arms supplies from the West enabled Russian forces to regroup and prepare their defence. By the end of 2022, the conflict had evolved to static and attritional trench warfare. Sieges, including that of Mariupol and Bakhmut, and two major offensives by Ukraine in 2023 and Russia in 2024 yielded only modest ground but at the cost of thousands of lives – tens of thousands in Russia's case.

Since the winter of 2022, Russia has arguably returned to an integrated military, economic and political strategy under a plan initially overseen by the brutal but effective Russian commander Sergey Surovikin, then in command of the Russian forces. As a reminder, the plan was comprised of three main elements:

1. Hold the line by developing deep defensive positions and once secured, slowly grind down the Ukrainian Army through attritional war.
2. Destroy Ukraine's will to resist through the destruction of its electricity infrastructure and the bombing of its cities. If a city like Kharkiv couldn't be physically taken, it should be made uninhabitable. Ukrainians must be made to freeze to break their morale.

3. Damage the financial, military and psychological linking to the West, without which Ukraine cannot fight the war.

So, hold the line, make life hell, break the link. Even now, amidst an intense, globalised military conflict, Russia's tactics are arguably focused on the mind and will of the enemy and its supporters. The first is clearly a military aim, the second is military targeting to affect civilian will and the third is the use of non-military tools to target decision-makers and populations in countries supporting Ukraine, in order to reduce Ukraine's military capability over time. President Trump's re-election has produced little short of euphoria in Moscow. How justified this reaction is remains unclear.

The 2022 invasion began when it did thanks to a series of misjudgements by Putin, Ukraine and Western nations. Ukrainian intelligence agencies are confident that Putin ultimately decided on the invasion only days before it occurred. In making this decision, he neither adhered to Russian operational phasing nor to a plan that was being prepared to create chaos in the Ukrainian political landscape.

At the same time, Ukraine did not believe Russia would launch an invasion until shortly before it began. UK and US assessments were initially viewed with suspicion. Ukraine's generals examined Russia's own doctrine and found, accurately, that many of the elements necessary for the invasion were lacking. For instance, logistical supply was not in place. According to Russian doctrine, a soldier requires over 100 kg of supplies daily, including ammunition, food and fuel, so according to their own doctrine, the Russian armed forces were not ready for a war-fighting invasion. Ukraine's leaders suspected Putin would reignite the conflict in eastern Ukraine during the summer of 2022. If successful, this would compel

Zelensky to negotiate under terms highly favourable to Russia, potentially making concessions that would destabilise his country.

Ukraine's assessment was shared by many NATO allies, whose military hierarchies interpreted Putin's actions through the lens of professional soldiers applying doctrinally based evaluations, rather than through the political perspective of the FSB and Putin himself. Some Western governments convinced themselves that Putin was 'sabre-rattling'.

Russia's posture throughout the latter half of 2021 instilled fear amongst Western nations. It acted as a deterrent to them supplying Ukraine with arms – national governments feared that any military support to Kyiv might serve as a pretext for invasion by the Kremlin. Consequently, European leaders spent 2021 and early 2022 beating a path to Putin's door. The lesson he probably learned was that the West, fearful, indecisive and unwilling to back their ally, would be unlikely to take meaningful action. They would be reduced to powerless condemnation. Western assessments of the Russian Army and Ukraine's resolve were wrong. Yet again in the modern history of Europe, deterrence did not deter.

However, at the heart of the invasion was a miscalculation by Putin. A member of the Ukrainian intelligence community told me, 'Putin personally believed that Joe Biden and the West would be so scared of the fact of the invasion that they would start negotiating and he could actually achieve his preconditions through that additional pressure.'[4] As the military convoys slowly snaked down Ukrainian roads, Putin seems to have calculated that overwhelming force would panic both Ukrainian and Western leaders into making the concessions he wanted. Talks would need only pressure from the Biden administration and confusion at the top of Ukraine's government before the situation concluded or unravelled in the

Kremlin's favour.[5] And indeed, by the end of March 2022, Ukrainian negotiators had made some sizeable concessions, offering military neutrality (whilst still applying for EU membership) and talks on the status of Crimea.[6] Despite this, Moscow insisted on its maximum war aims, including the replacement of the Kyiv government. By the time Russian soldiers got to Kyiv to dust off their parade uniforms, Putin had initially hoped the new Ukrainian government prepared by the FSB would be ready to be installed. But Putin, like the West, failed to anticipate the mobilising of Ukrainian society and its soldiers' decision to fight and fight hard. By May, peace talks had become deadlocked, with Zelensky more confident in his military options, boosted by Western support, intense national anger after the exposure of Russian mass killings in towns such as Irpin and Bucha and growing Ukrainian success on the battlefield.

Why would Putin have been so delusional as to think that Ukraine would collapse into his lap? To understand the answer, we need to go back a few years.

The events of 2014–15 left Russia with territorial footholds in eastern Ukraine. The Luhansk and Donetsk People's Republics were Moscow 'fronts' controlled by the FSB, the GRU and the presidential office between them, as the 'Surkov Leaks' report revealed.[7] However, that did not result in the collapse of the Ukrainian state, nor, in the intervening years, did the Minsk peace process enable Russia to 'fold' its seized territory back into the Ukrainian state in exchange for a veto over Ukraine's future direction, under the threat of further violence.

Russia therefore returned to the early stages of its operational phasing to rebuild its influence after 2014. There were some acts of physical violence, such as regular ceasefire violations, along the front line, as well as suspected Russian sabotage attacks on half a dozen Ukrainian arms dumps between 2014 and 2018, destroying more than 210,000 tonnes of ammunition. Deep penetration of the SBU and the political establishment continued, although with more difficulty than before 2014 due to Ukrainian countermeasures. For example, some Ukrainian HUR units were formed from scratch with a younger generation. 'That's where the Budanov generation comes from,' says commentator Harry Halem, referring to the current head of the HUR, Kyrylo Budanov, and comparing the HUR favourably to Russia's FSB, with its 'nepo babies and organised crime'.[8] Halem explains: 'It's responsible for special operations, black ops in Russian territory and Crimea, and it was trained by the CIA and entirely comprised of Ukrainians who did not grow up in the USSR. Everyone in the unit was in their twenties – the point is they would get guys who did not remember the Soviet Ukraine.'

However, despite countermeasures, Russia's networks remained. Recent arrests of alleged Russian spies have enhanced our understanding of the Kremlin's plans in Ukraine. Senior SBU officer Major General Oleg Kulinich – his Russian codename was Kotyhoroshko, a mythical Ukrainian folk hero born from a pea pod – was charged with high treason in July 2023.[9] Ukrainian investigators accused Kulinich, who ran the SBU's Crimea department, of deliberately obscuring Russia's military build-up in the peninsula.[10] SBU counter-intelligence was simultaneously infiltrated, meaning that the chance of Kotyhoroshko and other agents being unmasked prior to the war was slim. Kotyhoroshko was a valuable asset for the Russians, but perhaps more valuable still was the role that officials around Zelensky loyal to Russia might have played to trigger Ukraine's internal destabilisation.

The new Russian plan, at least on paper, appears to have been as

The aftermath of an air-launched freefall bomb. This building in Izium, eastern Ukraine, was blown into two, killing the people in and around it. © Annabel Moeller

Natalia and Olena with Matilda, a beautiful grey cat with striking orange eyes, whose sixth sense of when artillery shells would strike helped save their lives. When their village in eastern Ukraine was invaded by the Russians, men were taken away and bodies were left lying where they fell. In villages around Kyiv, the situation was even worse. Thousands, in towns such as Irpin and Bucha, were killed in cold blood. © Annabel Moeller

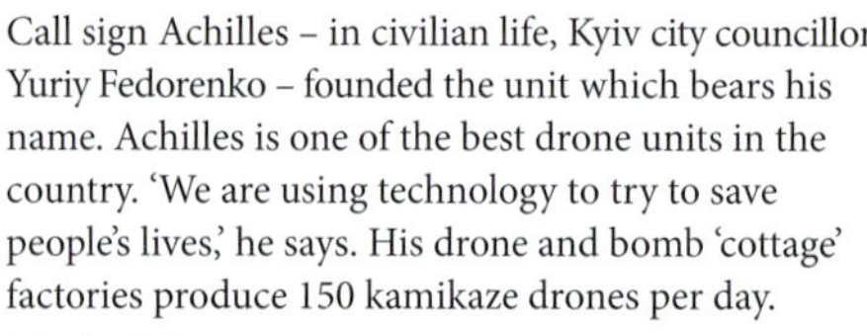

Call sign Achilles – in civilian life, Kyiv city councillor Yuriy Fedorenko – founded the unit which bears his name. Achilles is one of the best drone units in the country. 'We are using technology to try to save people's lives,' he says. His drone and bomb 'cottage' factories produce 150 kamikaze drones per day. © Annabel Moeller

Call sign Yangrr (young and angry) is the officer in charge of Achilles's bomb factory. It's effectively a military recycling centre. They take old explosives from wherever they can and refashion them to be attached to the underside of drones. 'There is nothing that we can't recycle or don't know about. We have no other choice,' says Yangrr. © Annabel Moeller

Call sign Dev, short for Developer, goes backwards and forwards between the battlefields of eastern Ukraine and his unit's tech hub, situated in what looks like a detached, run-down house in the suburbs of a frontline town. He is the chief technical officer for Achilles. The drones are assembled and made ready for war by perhaps two dozen men. Everyone here is an Achilles soldier, most of whom have already served as drone pilots. © Annabel Moeller

Achilles's bomb factory. Everywhere I look, there are warheads, circular anti-tank mines or 'bricks' of black explosives. Everything seems detonatable. The factory is deep in a nuclear bunker, beneath a dark industrial landscape dominated by bomb-damaged factories. © Annabel Moeller

A soldier wraps ball bearings around a charge to increase the weapon's lethality.

© Annabel Moeller

The unit's staple weapon is a rocket-propelled grenade warhead, which they disassemble and rebuild. A soldier with steady hands saws through the metal casing around the explosive. It's done by hand to control the temperature and ensure no catastrophic reaction takes place.

© Annabel Moeller

НОВОРОССИЯ

ОБЩЕСТВЕННО-ПОЛИТИЧЕСКОЕ ДВИЖЕНИЕ "ПАРТИЯ НОВОРОССИЯ" №3 11 ИЮНЯ 2014

Народное ополчение Донбасса и ОПД "Партия НОВОРОССИЯ" в интернете:

vk.com/p.novorossia
facebook.com/groups/p.novorossia
vk.com/polkdonbassa
facebook.com/polkdonbassa

ВСТУПАЙТЕ В РЯДЫ НАРОДНОГО ОПОЛЧЕНИЯ ДОНБАССА!
ЗАЩИТИМ СЛАВЯНСК!

Игорь Стрелков

Russian paramilitary forces invaded Sloviansk on 12 April 2014, under the banner of the Donetsk People's Republic. They were led by the infamous 'Strelkov', otherwise known as the former FSB/GRU veteran Igor Girkin. Whilst murdering locals, Strelkov's men portrayed themselves as glamorous heroes. Their *NovoRossiya* (new Russia) newspaper referenced the film *300*. The headline proclaims, 'Steel Russians, 300 Strelkovites.'

Pocket-sized leaflets issued to some Russian soldiers tell them why they are being sent to Ukraine. 'Ukraine is a terrorist state,' it exclaims in capital letters. 'Today, weapons speak for us. The time for peaceful decisions is no more.' © Annabel Moeller

Ukrainians combine a sense of humour with deception. The signpost on the main road to Odesa reads 'F*ck off', 'F*ck off again' and 'F*ck off back to Russia'.

Author's collection

Two revolutions sparked the first two phases of Putin's war in Ukraine. The Orange Revolution 2004–5 was a series of protests against a fraudulent presidential election. The results were annulled and a pro-Western candidate was voted in during a second run-off, triggering the first phase of the Kremlin's actions in Ukraine.

© Alexandr Zadiraka / Shutterstock

The 2013–14 Revolution of Dignity, also known as EuroMaidan, was sparked by President Viktor Yanukovych's attempts, under intense Russian pressure, to reject an EU deal and effectively move the country back into the Kremlin's sphere of influence. The protests sparked the overthrow of Yanukovych and Putin's decision to annex Crimea, launching the first invasion of eastern Ukraine under the guise of separatist uprisings.

© Sergii Figurnyi / Shutterstock

Trenches have played an important part in this war. Russia's vast and deep trench system blunted Ukraine's failed counter-offensive in 2023. Soldiers live in them for months at a time. (*Above*) A trench on the Kharkiv lines in daytime; (*left*) conditions inside them, with plywood and sheeting to keep some warmth in and an icon over them for protection; (*below*) a trench belonging to the DFTH 31 volunteer unit at night. © Annabel Moeller

Russian forces reached the gates of Kyiv in 2022 before being repelled, in what is likely to be seen by historians as one of the most consequential battles of the twenty-first century. © Pictorial Press Ltd / Alamy Stock Photo

Russian forces in eastern Ukraine have generally advanced not through tactical supremacy but by attritional obliteration of what is front of them, generally a combination of relentless meat assaults and massive artillery attacks. This is the remains of Bakhmut, a city in eastern Ukraine. © Anadolu / Getty Images

Destroyed Russian equipment on display in front of the Baroque splendour of St Michael's Golden-Domed Monastery, Kyiv. © Annabel Moeller

Kharkiv military cemetery. Over 45,000 Ukrainian soldiers have been killed, with more than 300,000 injured in some form, in addition to the tens of thousands of civilians dead. © Annabel Moeller

Some of the gravestones feature images of the soldiers lasered into the stone, so animated that it looks as if the dead are still with us. On the right, Smirnov on his mobile phone; in the centre, Sergii Mikolaiovich Gerasimenko; and on the left with his picture and name on a wooden cross, Maksim Oleksandrovich Kurochka.

© Annabel Moeller

follows. Russia's agents around President Zelensky would persuade the Ukrainian leadership to reject the bid for membership of NATO and the EU and instead opt for a neutral status more friendly to Russia.[11] The primary purpose may not have been to force Ukraine to a more neutral position, useful as that might be, but to spark an internal political crisis. The FSB appears to have been planning a series of events where, under advice from Russian agents of influence, Zelensky would abandon Ukraine's NATO and EU membership hopes. Pro and anti-Russian groups, some of which would be controlled by the FSB, would then take to the streets in protest. Within them would be paid criminals and agents provocateur, who would spark confrontation and bloody violence. Hoping for a resolution, some Western political leaders might have supported this plan without realising its true purpose.

The Ukrainian intelligence source told me, 'I think it was pretty sound. It was the idea that under that pressure, both from Russia and the West, Zelensky would give some concessions to Russia.' Those concessions, he said, would be considered by Ukrainian society as a national betrayal, triggering mass protest. 'The Russians would weaponise that destabilisation. They would organise a false-flag *coup d'état* inside the country. The nation's leadership would be 'decapitated and destabilised'. Outside the country, Russian information operations would paint Ukraine as a failing state in thrall to extremism and label the protests a 'Nazi' coup. The danger posed by pro-Russian political groups, along with their associated martial arts clubs, had already been highlighted in the Ukrainian media. Their activities continued unimpeded by the police. Russia had also been investing in the establishment of security firms to support its planned coup. Russian military intelligence had been transferring approximately $3–4 million every few months to alleged long-time Russian agent Andrii Derkach, for him to start and fund such firms.

For whatever reason, this plan – to escalate things and bring Ukraine to crisis – didn't happen. There was no opportunity for the FSB, the GRU and their agents to build street protests and gradually engineer a coup. Putin short-circuited his own subversive operations. The invasion occurred without the necessary 'shaping' operations or 'initial period of war' planning.

It is doubtful whether this operation would have been successful anyway. It might have worked in the chaotic conditions of 2014, but by 2022, a new political generation had come of age. War against Russia was not an abstract concern of Ukrainian nationalists but had actually happened. It was more difficult for Russia to conduct information operations in Ukraine both for physical and psychological reasons. Physical because Kyiv had blocked Russian TV channels and psychological because by 2022, Ukrainian society had become less naive about Putin's intentions, even if they were still too trusting of Russia overall.

Russian assessments of Ukrainian society appeared to be fundamentally no different than they had been in 2014. The FSB continued to show a condescending arrogance towards their adversary, whose societal strengths they ignored. Ukraine's vigour was not in its political or security elites – which were still partially compromised, although to a lesser extent than in 2014 – but in its civil society. 'The FSB was gathering information, which they did badly, to please Putin, not to inform him,' says Russian security services expert Soldatov. 'The main assessment was that the Ukrainian state was a failed state … so, in a time of a crisis, it would just collapse.'

In his invasion address, a snarling Putin cited a list of historic

Russian grievances against the West. Putin claimed a genocide was taking place in the east of Ukraine. The US and its underlings represented an 'empire of lies', which had deceived Russia and was now trying to 'finish off' and 'destroy' it.[12] Zelensky responded to Putin by declaring martial law and a general mobilisation of all Ukrainian males between eighteen and sixty.

With the Russian ground invasion came a series of supporting measures to help make Ukraine more vulnerable. The Russian air force launched air and missile attacks on Ukraine's air defence. Ukraine suffered significant and repeated cyberattacks. Hackers from the Russian space agency struck the energy system whilst a unit known as Sandworm struck other government targets.[13] Further attacks crashed Ukraine's military communications in the initial hours of the invasion. A back-up system, put in place just two months before, kicked in.[14] Ukraine's energy system was isolated a few hours prior to the invasion. Senior Russian military officers phoned up their opposite numbers and urged passivity. So did Putin in his address. As the invasion progressed, Russia's agents and those accidentally or purposefully doing its bidding continued to press Zelensky.

Zelensky, to his credit, didn't budge. Indeed, in the months before the war and at its start, President Volodymyr Zelensky did two things that saved his country – or, rather, he didn't do two things. First, he refused to relent to pressure to give concessions to Russia, which would have risked mass protests and chaos. Second, when the invasion started, he did not flee. Famously, he asked for ammo, not a ride. On the evening after the invasion, he recorded himself outside the presidential buildings in Bankova Street with other members of the administration. Holding the camera, he panned slightly to show his immediate team around him, saying, 'We are all here, our soldiers are here, the citizens of our country are here. We are all here, protecting our independence, our country, and it will continue to be this way. Glory to our defenders. Glory to our heroes. Glory to Ukraine.'[15]

The video he recorded is probably the most influential 'selfie' in history. It was the selfie that saved Ukraine.

Despite elements of preparation having taken place, the Russian military appears not to have undertaken what they call initial period of war (IPW) planning, roughly equivalent to what in US military phasing would be known as phase 0 and phase 1. 'There is a whole school of thought of things you do before you start a war and they didn't do that stuff, it got thrown out of the window,' said Colonel Charles Bartles, an analyst at the Foreign Military Studies Office, Fort Leavenworth, Kansas.[16] 'IPW was not followed. It's a baffling thing, the Russians put so much effort and thinking into what they would do in the initial period of war, and then they don't do it.' The assumption of a permissive environment meant, presumably, that thorough IPW plans were either partially or largely forgone. From this perspective, the failing of the operation was not at the military level but at the strategic level. The Russian Army was set up for failure.

The main Russian effort during the invasion came from Belarus in the north, down both sides of the wide Dnipro River. This was potentially disastrous for Ukraine; its leaders had not expected an attack on Kyiv from the northern route. Ukraine's best brigades with the most fighting experience were all in the east of the country and were to be successfully pinned down by the Russian eastern axis. Deception as to the true intent of the operation was successful, if only because the Russian Army didn't know it was going to invade until twenty-four hours before. Kherson was easily taken and by early March the Russians achieved a land corridor linking Crimea to the Donbas, which they steadily expanded and finalised after the brutal siege of Mariupol that ended in late May. Mariupol set a pattern for Russian tactics which saw besieged towns and cities slowly reduced to rubble by artillery and, later in the war, glide bomb strikes. At least 10,000 civilians are thought to have been killed in Mariupol alone. The Azov Brigade's last stand in the steelworks cemented its role as Ukraine's most admired military unit.*

By mid-March, the Russian encirclement of Kyiv was failing. Ukraine's regulars, reserves and special forces had conducted a running battle against the invading forces. US Javelin and UK NLAW anti-tank weapons and Turkish Bayraktar drones caused chaos in the extended convoys, although one should not underestimate Ukraine's traditional artillery. In Kyiv itself, Russian special forces soldiers had been killed or captured and assassination attempts against Zelensky thwarted. Critically, Ukraine's success in repelling the Hostomel Airport attack, six miles from the heart of Kyiv, prevented Russian forces from gaining a bridgehead close to the city centre. Other attempts to enter the city via the suburb of Obolon and towns to the north, such as Irpin and Bucha, failed. The last two became a byword for civilian murder and Russian brutality. By the end of March, Russian troops had retreated from around Kyiv and had been redeployed in the east in a series of battles in cities and towns previously little-known outside Ukraine, such as Severodonetsk and Lysychansk. The Russian retreat from Kyiv and later around Kharkiv revealed the extent of civilian suffering and the cruelty of Russia's soldiers.

* Polling supports this assessment.

OCCUPATION

Occupation has been a brutal experience for Ukrainians. It still is for those living under Russian rule. I first visited the towns of Bucha and Irpin in mid-April 2022, the same day as the head of the International Criminal Court. The Russians had left a fortnight before. Ukrainian soldiers and emergency workers had removed bodies from the streets, where dozens of the 400 civilians killed in the town had lain for weeks. Elsewhere, they were still finding decaying corpses in gardens or hidden in basements. As I walked down one side of a street in the town, corpses were being exhumed on the other side. Men and women in dark-blue overalls with the words 'War Crimes Prosecutor' printed in white on their backs recorded the sad process. Over 100 of the souls killed by Russian soldiers were buried in a rough, linear mass grave around Bucha's newly built St Andrew's Church.[17]

Whilst Bucha became a household name, there are many towns and villages unknown outside Ukraine where Russian soldiers behaved brutally. In the nearby village of Motyzhyn, a dozen villagers died, as did many of those fleeing Kyiv towards Zhytomyr, a small city 60 miles to the west. Villagers met me to talk of their experiences.

'They were executing people no matter what,' said resident Fedor, a sprightly pensioner.[18] The Russians, he said, 'behaved terribly, everywhere around here', listing nearby villages and gesturing with his hand. The head of their village council, Olga Sukhenko, fifty, was beaten and shot. 'They took her, interrogated her and after that they executed her.' For good measure, he said, the troops executed her husband and her son too. 'They were a lovely family,' he lamented. 'She would do anything to help you.' One of the horrible ironies of villages like Motyzhyn is that people were fleeing to it, or through it, because they believed it was safer than staying in Kyiv. The opposite was the case. 'People were cutting through the village trying to escape. Many died.' His friend, trying to get away from Kyiv, was shot at. He survived, but his wife and child were shot dead. 'Everywhere, it was the same story,' Fedor sighed.

I wanted to know more about the occupation, so I visited a village near Izium in the far east of the country named Kamianka. We drove through small towns and past buildings ripped in half to meet Natalia and Olena and their collection of animals, who helped them get through the war unscathed. One cat called Matilda, a rather beautiful if dusty grey feline with striking orange eyes, helped to save Natalia and Olena's lives. She had a sixth sense of when artillery shells would hit the small village of Kamianka (Little Stone is perhaps the best translation). A few seconds before Natalia and Olena would hear the shells, Matilda would scamper into the house. They would climb down into the relative safety of their little basement, where they would sit out the bombardment that killed many of their neighbours with Matilda. They were joined not only by Matilda but by a growing collection of cats in the village that would congregate with the family, their owners either having died or fled.

When I visited in the summer of 2024, Kamianka was still largely deserted. There is little of the village to return to. Many of the houses are bombed-out wrecks, sitting in overgrown gardens. Land mines have been seeded around the village. On the left-hand side of the dusty track that snakes through the village are the upside-down red triangles linked by red wire with the words 'Warning, Mines!' The sound of shelling is still audible in the far distance. The village is typical for eastern Ukraine. It is dotted with bungalows, though very different bungalows from those you might see in the UK, US or Western Europe. Often built before the First World War, these one-storey buildings are stout, red-brick houses, sometimes painted white. They sit in a modest but useful plot of land, cultivated for food or raising animals. The loos were a wooden-framed hole in the ground at the back of the garden. Some still are.

Ukraine was a society urbanised quite late by European standards and the links with a peasant past and the rural economy are strong in almost every family. The disaster of the Holodomor, the forced famine that killed several million Ukrainians in the 1930s, and the need to produce one's own food due to the failure of Soviet agriculture are fixed in the collective psyche. A few old folks still remember those horrendous days. More recently, Ukrainians survived the collapse of the Soviet Union by going back to the land, relying on parents and grandparents to grow vegetables, potatoes and garlic, make jam from the ubiquitous apple trees growing in seemingly every plot, pickle vegetables for winter and raise chickens and pigs. What they couldn't grow, they bartered for: petrol, vegetable oil or other items.

Fast forward to the war and one day in February 2022, Russian soldiers arrived. Natalia remembered that they were surprised to see villagers still in their houses. Two entered her compound. 'The first thing they said was, "What are you doing here?" One turned to the other and asked, "Well, should we just shoot them?" The second replied, "No, we'll take them to the commander, let him decide."' Their lives were spared, but they were ordered not to leave their little compound on threat of death. 'Do you want to survive?' the soldiers asked. 'This is your territory, your yard. Don't go anywhere and don't get involved in anything.'

Through their wooden fencing, they saw that Kamianka's men were being rounded up. 'Our boys were tied up, had bags put over their heads and [were] led away. And we women were left just like that.' Villagers that were killed, either by Russian troops or Ukrainian shelling, were left where they fell. Their village street 'was covered in blood, many bodies lying there, both Russian and Ukrainian,' Olena says.

The family kept as low a profile as they could and spent their days tending to their small collection of livestock. 'We had livestock, geese, piglets and the like. We were all busy; there was no time to be bored,' Olena tells me.

She had heard of civilians being killed and did her best to find common ground with the soldiers. 'Here, it was a situation where everyone wants to live. We had a child with us and I didn't want to be raped in front of the child,' she said bluntly. The situation 'needed to be handled a bit more gently … to speak normally. When we spoke normally, the anger and irritation [from the Russian soldiers] faded and then a normal person would come.' In doing so, she opened a window into the soldiers' thinking. At times, she felt almost sorry for them. Some of the soldiers told her that they knew they would not see their homes again. One Russian soldier told her, 'I know that my path is one way.' Another understood that the invasion would create generations of hatred between Russians and Ukrainians. 'We know we will never be forgiven, not us, not our grandchildren or great-grandchildren,' he told her.

One or two believed in their mission. 'We came to free you from the Nazis,' one said. Natalia gently replied to him, 'We don't have Nazis, but we have different nationalities. Our school principal was Russian. The head of the garage was Tajik in the *kolhoz* [collective farm] and the director of the supermarket was Dagestani. We have Belarusians and Armenians living here too.

'I explained this to them and they said they were told something completely different. They were told things that made our hair stand on end,' Natalia said with concern.

Within days of arriving, the Russian soldiers told them that they were already filling out death certificates for teenage conscripts. 'They were sent there just to die,' said Olena. 'The eighteen-year-old kids were in shock, with scared eyes, crying, saying, "We don't want to kill."' Some conscripts had had their documentation changed unknowingly, so they were registered as contract soldiers or *kontrakniki*. This bureaucratic sleight of hand allowed them to be sent to Ukraine. Other soldiers complained to her that they had been promised 'insane' amounts of money. They were deceived about the money, she said, and they were angry. 'They were starting to say things against Putin: "We were against him, we were fooled."' Some were drafted, some knew they were going, some intentionally, and some were tricked, lured by money.'

Then, one day in September 2022, this unhappy army pulled out overnight and without warning. 'For two days, it was silent – nothing was happening and we couldn't understand what was happening,' said Natalia. Then soldiers appeared. 'We looked and I asked, "Who are you?" and they said, "We are Ukrainians."' At this point, Natalia, otherwise stoical and conversational, was lost for words and her eyes welled. 'You have to live through it to understand; it's hard to convey. Throughout the occupation, everything happened – I don't want to remember it. I never cried, no matter what. I was like a wound-up spring and when our troops arrived, then the tears came.'

RUSSIAN WEAKNESSES AND STRENGTHS

Since the disaster of 2022, Russia has adapted. Western moral disapproval or military condescension does not equate to Russian defeat any more than stories of plucky underdogs prove a Ukrainian victory. There has been too much 'toxic optimism' in the Western media.

Russian forces are learning, despite a brutally wasteful military culture. Politically and economically, the Kremlin retains a creative and flexible approach to conflict, even if militarily they use tactics scarcely believable in the modern era. As of early 2025, they are slowly gaining ground, albeit at a high cost. They are arguably now beginning to set conditions for Ukraine's slow defeat via negotiations or relentless attritional warfare. Despite the remarkable achievements of the Ukrainians in seeing off Russian forces, it is Ukraine's economy that has declined sharply, not Russia's, and it is Russia that is in possession of 20 per cent of Ukraine's territory, despite Ukraine's incursion into the Russian region of Kursk in the summer of 2024.

A critical strategic question remains. Why did the Russian leadership, and Western analysts, overestimate the power of the Russian Army at the start of the war? Second, what did the Russian armed forces do wrong? Third, how are they improving now?

RUSSIAN OVERCONFIDENCE AFTER SYRIA

I believe that Russia's military leaders were overconfident about the abilities of their forces in part due to their performance in the Syrian civil war. Relative success in Syria may have convinced the Kremlin and the West that Russian military reforms had been more fruitful than they were in reality (the 2024 collapse of the Bashar

Assad regime is a setback for the Kremlin but does not affect the argument presented here). Those internal military reforms started in earnest after the 2008 Russo-Georgian War, which 'uncovered glaring gaps in capability, problems with command and control and poor intelligence.'[19] These discoveries were used to help drive reform.

Russia's operation in Syria bore a superficial resemblance to the Western intervention against ISIS but proved more effective. Both were light-touch operations, where ground combat was intended to be conducted by local, indigenous forces – the Iraqi and Syrian Kurds in the West's case and in Russia's case, the Syrian regime army, Alawite militias loyal to the Assads and militias supported by Iranian forces.

Russian forces entered Syria in September 2015 in order to support the crumbling regime. They provided air power (in an easy, uncontested space dominated by Russian air defence), command and control functions, logistics, military advisers and special forces with forward air controllers to help confirm and destroy targets. They also provided information warfare support – most notably when Putin brought St Petersburg's Mariinsky Orchestra to the ancient Roman ruins of Palmyra. They additionally offered espionage advice and political cover at the UN Security Council. In Syria, Russia utilised the non-conscript, professional components of its military forces: trained specialists, ambitious military officers, pilots and crews. Wagner mercenaries were also employed. This was done on a manageable scale, with its Syrian and Iranian allies bearing nearly all of the fighting casualties.

Putin also played his diplomatic and political hand with skill and determination in Syria. His surprise deployment of troops left Western nations confused as to how to react, as did his negotiations to prevent the US and its allies bombing Syria after the Assad regime's repeated use of chemical weapons, beginning with the attack in the Damascus suburb of Ghouta in 2013. The Russians and the Syrians ruthlessly targeted what moderate Western opposition there was until the conflict became a choice between the brutality of the Assad regime and the brutality of jihadi extremism. Confused by the complexity and moral ambiguity, the West lost interest, despite the mass killing of civilians and the repeated use of chemical weapons – over 300 times – only temporarily halted in 2017 by a series of attacks by the US, the UK and France, which were as ineffective as they were well signalled.[20] Thus, the Assad regime was saved – for several years at any rate – by a limited but effective military campaign from Russia (and Iran), mixed with a ruthless policy of destroying Assad's moderate enemies and Putin's decisive political and diplomatic manoeuvring.

The Syrian conflict allowed the Kremlin to try out new kit and tactics. They learned. They deepened their relationship with Iran and invested in their air defence capabilities in the eastern Mediterranean. They learned that whilst reducing cities to rubble did not necessarily defeat a civilian population, bombing of hospitals *did* have a significant effect on civilian morale. They 'double tapped' the White Helmets emergency teams – bombing a site, then bombing it again once emergency workers arrived – a tactic they now use in Ukrainian cities. They ran a relentless psychological warfare campaign against Western targets. They bombed and killed Western journalists whose profiles aided coverage of the war. Putin saw too how Western insularity and weakness and short-term news cycles enabled him to acclimatise the world to the use of chemical weapons by his client-ally Assad. He saw how panicked civilians created vast refugee flows that overwhelmed the enemy, and indeed parts of Europe, a useful side-effect that drove internal frictions in EU countries. Since then, Russia and its ally Belarus have pushed refugees towards borders in Norway and Poland as an irritant to governments and to add to Europe's fractious debate over immigration. On the Ukraine front, chemical weapons – banned choking and tear-gas agents – have occasionally been used to flush Ukrainian soldiers from frontline positions.

As in the Spanish Civil War in the 1930s, in which the Nazis and Soviets 'blooded' their armies, Syria was the brutal reawakening of Russian power. By contrast, it was a diplomatic failure for an indecisive West and, for good or ill, the end of 'something must be done' diplomacy. The Russian media revelled in Putin's 'humiliation' of President Barack Obama, a particular figure of hate. Putin and his generals believed the Russian Army had been rebuilt, certainly enough to be a global force again. This, combined with Russia's integrated doctrine that maximised Russian power and influence and Putin's diplomatic ruthlessness and nimbleness, persuaded Putin that he could outsmart, outmanoeuvre and outlast his adversaries. When British officers visited Moscow on the eve of the 2022 invasion, Chief of Staff Gerasimov boasted that he commanded the second-most-powerful army on earth.[21]

So why was this not reflected in Ukraine? I have a series of observations, some indicative of the Russian military machine and some specific to the Ukraine operation. Broadly, the reform of Russia's armed forces was not yet complete. The move from a mass army had started, but a Western-style force was still some way off. As US expert Michael Kofman argued a decade after the Georgian War, 'Russia effectively walked away from the Soviet mass mobilisation army, but a more modern force, able to conduct combined arms warfare, and work jointly between the services, remains a work in progress.'[22] Although parts of the Russian armed forces had moved to employ professional contract soldiers (*kontratniki*), conscript soldiers were still needed. Conscripts' training is limited and they are, by all accounts, difficult to lead in battle. Their use by Russia in the Ukraine War added to numbers but not to effectiveness. Some were there, as discussed, because they had been deceived.

Russia also still lacks an effective non-commissioned officer (NCO) cadre – junior leaders, such as corporals and sergeants, who are the fighting backbone of armies. This was not an issue in the Syrian deployment but was exposed in Ukraine. Corruption also remained a significant problem, not only in the Russian military but in relation to Ukraine too. FSB budgets for espionage work – building up agent networks, bribing agents, soldiers and politicians – were regularly siphoned off. For example, Ukrainian prosecutors reported that alleged Russian spy Andrii Derkach creamed off much of his funding so that it 'ended up in [his] pockets' rather than being spent on developing private security firms to support Russian intervention.[23] Ironically, Russian corruption undermined Russian efforts to corrupt Ukraine. There have also been rumours of caches of arms and gold buried in locations in Ukraine. 'Some of this [FSB] money was literally buried in the ground. For instance, there was a big programme, I was told, about making caches of weapons and gold on the soil of Ukraine,' says FSB expert Soldatov. 'The idea was to use this gold in the time of war. So literally, they just buried the gold, at least officially, in Ukraine for the war. How much gold is there? Nobody knows.'

As previously mentioned, Russian forces were not given time for thorough preparations. They assumed, thanks to flawed FSB assessments, patchy opposition at best. Political arrogance prevented a clear idea of the scale of the task. Russia did not deploy a war-fighting invasion. At the start, troops had barely been briefed and had little pre-deployment training.[24] They were told what the operation was twenty-four hours prior to its start. According to the Royal United Service Institute's experts, 'Russian troops lacked ammunition, fuel, food, maps, properly established communications and, most critically, a clear understanding at the tactical level of how their actions fitted into the overall plan.'[25] It was a military horror show. The static columns may have looked impressive from a distance, but they represented not an overwhelming show of power but a series of poorly defended targets. Yet despite this, the 'yes' culture of the Russian military continued to paint a false picture of preparation and competence. One Ukrainian special forces soldier joked about Russian tank and APC kit lists from captured documents: 'I have never seen so much 100 per cent readiness in my life.'[26]

Instead of overwhelming the Ukrainians, Russian troops entered the country ill-prepared and under-resourced and found around Kyiv an initially chaotic but determined resistance, which became stronger as Ukraine was able to mobilise its reserve forces. In 2014, the Ukrainians appeared dazed and confused by Russian actions as if they did not believe that they were at war with their 'brother' nation. In 2022, it was the Russians who appeared confused, especially when soldiers started dying.

There was also a lack of 'mission command' – whereby officers through the ranks take the initiative to deliver on their commanders' intent. This may have been because there was very little by way of intent revealed to them and a lack of alternative courses of action when troops failed to reach assigned locations. Russian commanders, it is said, prefer simplicity over flexibility.[27] When initial plans failed, their lack of flexibility and lack of initiative made their units sitting ducks. As the Royal United Services Institute reports,

'The Russian plan's greatest deficiency was the lack of reversionary courses of action.'[28] Commanders had no new orders to follow. Russian units did not know who was around them or in neighbouring areas of responsibility as they moved to war fighting rather than population pacification. The most damning fact of the initial period of the invasion was that 'for the period of March, most of the radio exchanges of Russian troops at the brigade-BTG [battalion-tactical group] level consisted of information about the locations of units and individual elements, and only 10–20% related to combat management.'[29] In this way, in the opening stages of the war, almost all Russian military conversations, generally on insecure comms, involved finding out who was where rather than fighting the war.

Not only did Russian soldiers not know who was around them but they may also have been unaware who was in their formations. The main fighting units of the Russian Army were the battalion tactical groups (BTGs), formed of disparate groups where many of the personnel and commanders only came together when the BTG was being formed. BTGs came out of the reform of the Russian armed forces following the Georgian invasion, driven by shrinking manpower but also the need to create more flexible units on the battlefield. These tactical formations, part of Russian military thinking for a decade, had, or were meant to have, three infantry companies, plus tank, anti-tank, artillery, missiles and air defence attachments for a unit strength of upwards of 800 soldiers, perhaps 300 of which were infantry.[30]

The BTGs performed competently against Ukraine in 2014, despite some observed weaknesses, but they lacked sufficient supporting equipment to be able to observe, target and attack at the same time.[31] In the first year following the 2022 invasion, these structures came under intense pressure. The UK's Ministry of Defence said that the BTGs lacked enough professional infantry soldiers and junior officers to operate effectively, whilst artillery given to BTGs prevented a coordinated mass weight of firepower – in other words, artillery became too disjointed and was not used at scale. The result was that commanders were not able to use the BTG model.[32] All this and more contributed to the disaster of 2022 for the Russian military, reported in great detail in the West and occasionally on Telegram channels to Russian audiences, although not reflected in Russian mainstream coverage. However, since then, the state and the armed forces, despite setbacks such as Yevgeny Prigozhin's short-lived mutiny in June 2023, have been rebuilt.

UKRAINE WEAKNESS

Ukrainian military competence and morale is almost always superior to that of Russia in tactics, strategy, ethics and values. They are acting in line with international law in defending their territory, and unlike Russian soldiers, whose behaviour is often shocking, they endeavour to obey the rules of war. Ukrainian medical chains are comparable with the West; Russia's appear sometimes medieval. Overall, there is little comparison. However, that does not mean that Ukraine is not immune to problems. Some of its problems are hidden both in Ukraine and internationally due to what is best described as a form of 'toxic optimism', evident especially in Western reporting, which often overstates Russian weaknesses and Ukrainian strengths. This has resulted in a failure to address problems.

First, it is important to note that the Ukrainian Army is tired. The reservists who bolstered the regular army and special forces to save Ukraine in 2022 went through a baptism of fire, one they were willing to endure to save their nation. 'You go through several stages in terms of psychology: shock, fear, then acceptance,' one special forces volunteer explained to me, adding that this was especially true after he saw comrades die.[33] 'It happens to everyone because more than 90 per cent of Ukrainian servicemen, they never served in the army. They're from civilian life.' These soldiers have been discovering the reality of modern war, which is still very different from that imagined in the movies. 'The majority of our units which we were serving with, they didn't even see the Russians. They were spending all the time in shelters or in trenches under heavy Russian fire,' he continued. Much of Ukraine's army has served since the start of the war. There have been four ways out: transferring to a non-frontline role, going AWOL, death or severe injury. There is a joke amongst soldiers: 'In 2022, there were a lot of motivated guys, but they gave us minimal equipment. Now there are fewer motivated guys, but a bit more equipment.'[34] That tiredness seems more exacerbated amongst female soldiers, who have either put off having families or whose absence from their families has been painful.

Officers and experts I have talked with highlight the following selection of issues. I will start with tactical and operational issues – that is, things that are happening on the ground – and then go up to the more strategic level.

There appear to be weaknesses in two specific operational areas: in the rotation of troops and in reporting. Russian forces have sometimes made territorial gains when Ukraine has rotated troops badly. This process of rotating troops out of an area and bringing in others is known in military circles as a relief in place, shortened to RiP. 'When Russia has made advances or breakthroughs, it's often because Ukraine makes certain mistakes and one is during relief in place, which as militaries well know, is a really dangerous operation to do,' one Western military observer said. 'It's always a big risk.

A lot of breakthroughs that Russia has had have happened during Ukrainian RiPs, where they identify a RiP is happening and they can attack at the right time.'[35]

The battle around the village of Ocheretyne in Donetsk in April 2024, which resulted in an important Russian breakthrough, is the most well-known example, but it is not unique. There are different stories about what happened. Some said unit accounts of the positions they held were inaccurate, others that a unit pulled out, giving up its position, before the relief unit came in. Others talk of 'really bad' adjacent unit coordination. Either way, inaccurate battlefield information helped the Russians to attack successfully. More generally, if Ukrainian commanders in neighbouring areas have not been clear about boundaries and troop positions, the Russians will sometimes succeed in moving between Ukrainian areas of responsibility (AORs) and attacking Ukrainian units from the flank, where they are more vulnerable.

Poor reporting is exacerbated if soldiers feel bad decision-making is killing them or if commanders do not value their lives. The Battle of Bakhmut, say soldiers, was an example of this. This city of 70,000 was originally part of Russian plans for a major 'pincer' movement in eastern Ukraine. After the collapse of Russian positions in Kharkiv in the north, the 'pincer' lost its top half and Bakhmut became little more than a pointless trial of strength, soaking up tens of thousands of lives. During the battle, some Ukrainian units held two sets of maps. Map number one was the actual combat situation, so when a building or a position was lost, it would be recorded. A second map was prepared for reporting to higher command, which would not always have accurate information. Instead, it would generally report a stable situation. 'If they did report that they had lost a building, they would be ordered to take it back,' a soldier told me. The soldier mimicked the instruction that would be received: 'You! Three-man sniper team, go take that building back that we have literally just seen a platoon [twenty-five to thirty soldiers] of Russians go into.' He paused, recollecting such orders, and then continued: 'They were being ordered to do stupid things, so they didn't report it.' Only when an entire block was lost and the situation was irretrievable would an accurate assessment be sent to higher command.

This fear of reporting bad news is linked to the fears of senior officers of being sacked or demoted for battlefield failures. One observer told me:

> If they acknowledge a lost position, that leadership might get fired, so it creates this culture where they will not acknowledge the lost positions. Higher leadership will not understand this and then sometimes send units to a position to rotate with someone who's not there. And then guys get killed. And it's been a problem … not acknowledging things accurately.[36]

Next, several senior and middle-ranking officers and observers have told me that planning does not seem to work well above the brigade level. This is widely, if privately, acknowledged. Why is a matter for debate. Perhaps because Ukrainian politicians, prior to 2022, wanted to cut military costs and so convinced themselves that there was no real threat of large-scale invasion or that the era of mass warfare was over. Perhaps they did this so that military equipment could be sold to Russia and other states. Perhaps all this was aided by Russian-inspired attempts to undermine Ukraine's ability to defend itself. Either way, planning and leadership work at brigade level and below, especially with more modern and well-trained brigades, but less so above it. Soldiers say that the two layers above the brigade level, the Operational Tactical Group and Operational Strategic Group, have not appeared to deliver like they should have, made worse by the turnover of senior officers at those levels. Some of those officers were not only too senior to have significant ground experience during the 2014 invasion but were also products of Soviet-era thinking in the Ukrainian armed forces – they were *Sovkies*, as some Ukrainians have nicknamed them. Ukraine's best officers often sit at the brigade level, mixing youth with experience of ground war, staff roles and leadership.

There is a sense that reform has stalled in some areas and is not being pushed as hard as it should be in others. At the beginning, military bureaucracy came second to repelling the invaders; command had to be delegated so that soldiers could react to the immediate threat. Volunteers helped the army to think in different ways. Professional officers become more open to ideas, open to changes in structure, even digitalising some of their operations. Since then, some commanders have brought back 'Soviet' bureaucracy and paperwork has replaced digital filing. One officer joked to me that he had checklists for checklists.

Ukraine inherited a Soviet army, which had been substantially modernised after 2014 but was still a Soviet army, poorly configured with aging kit, underinvestment and, in places, poor or stymied leadership. It had been hollowed out and corrupted as a matter of policy by the Russian state. Whilst parts of the Ukrainian Army, especially National Guard and HUR-supported units, have forged a remarkable new path, not all have reformed at the same pace. After 2014, Ukraine did not take all the opportunities offered by NATO states for training and developing a truly modern armed force. Soldiers joke that 'a big Soviet army [Russia] defeats a little Soviet army

[Ukraine]'. Ukraine has to be substantially better across the board to survive against a Russian Army that is willing and able to accept casualties of near ten to one.

At the strategic level, there is a school of thought that argues that Ukraine did remarkably well in saving Kyiv, but it should have done better. Whilst it did defeat Russian forces, Russia faced too little opposition in the south of the country. Soldiers have raised significant questions over the preparations by Ukraine for invasion. One Ukrainian intelligence source told me, 'According to our national defence plan, we should have two and a half very capable, usually airborne or marine, brigades specifically to be ready to face Russian invasion from Crimea. And we didn't have those brigades.' Likewise, we see the defence of Kyiv as little short of a miracle, in part because Western governments assumed that Kyiv would be unable to prevent the Russian advance. However, some Ukrainians in positions of authority and knowledge question why Ukrainian forces at the time did not do substantially better. One, with links to secret agencies and the military command, bluntly said, 'Ukraine had a supremacy in numbers … against the formations used for the invasion – that's why, considering the quality of troops and the means they had in February of 2022, the damage to Russia could have been much greater.'

RUSSIAN STRENGTHS

Despite relentless criticism in the Western media, one should be wary of dismissing Russian military or political capability. There is resilience in the state and the military, even at the expense of its long-term future. 'The longer the war goes on, the better they get,' one Western expert told me.[37]

One of the Russian regime's fundamental strengths is its ability to sustain the Ukraine War despite losses unequalled outside the First and Second World Wars. Experts who assumed that the current casualty rates would have been politically or militarily unsustainable have been proven wrong. Thus far, Russia has been willing to endure casualties, regardless of the reasons.

The casualty figures for this war are staggering. Some 1,200 Russian soldiers were being killed or wounded every day in May 2024, according to the UK Ministry of Defence.[38] This figure has increased since then. Russian forces suffered 80,000 casualties in September and October 2024.[39] November 2024 then became the worst month for Russian casualties since the start of the war, with the average daily loss rate reaching 1,523.[40] By December, Ukrainian assessments were running at over 750,000 Russian dead and injured since 2022. One can be sceptical of the Ukrainian figure and even that of the UK MoD, but the mayor of Moscow himself cited a figure of 600,000 Russian wounded to various degrees.[41] In April 2025, General Christopher Cavoli, United States European Commander, estimated 790,000 Russian dead and injured in testimony to Congress.[42] Even more stark, these figures suggest that 2 per cent of all Russian men aged between twenty and fifty will have been killed or badly wounded in the Ukraine War.[43]

Yet where are the protests? Some of Russia's men have left the country, especially after the first partial mobilisation, yet the state is still capable of recruiting the numbers to serve thus far. They recruit 25,000 to 30,000 a month, enough to replenish the ranks of the dead and wounded and provide the roughly 300,000 or so personnel per year that Putin's regime needs to sustain the war, despite the stream of articles in Western media over the past eighteen months predicting a dearth of recruits.[44] As Cavoli said in his testimony, despite the casualty rates, the Russian Army 'is reconstituting and growing at a faster rate that most analysts had anticipated' and was now 'larger than it was at the beginning of the war'. This is the first major war where Russia has not had mass conscription. The arrival of North Korean troops has taken at least some of the pressure off Russian recruiters, as has the arrival of fighters from the Yemeni Houthis, Nepal and elsewhere. In 2024, it was Ukraine that had a shortfall of soldiers.

Similarly, the levels of Russian equipment losses are extraordinarily high. Open-source tracking has recorded 1,830 instances of Russian equipment being destroyed, equivalent to the loss of five divisions' worth of armoured vehicles and tanks, on the Pokrovsk front alone from October 2023 to October 2024, including 539 tanks and 1,020 APCs and infantry fighting vehicles. From April 2024 to April 2025, Russia has lost 3,000 tanks, 9,000 combat vehicles of various descriptions and 13,000 artillery systems, yet 'is on pace to replace them all'.[45] These extraordinary losses have been sustainable. A year or two ago, most Western observers would have concluded that Russia would struggle to continue this war with such losses, yet as NATO Secretary-General Mark Rutte acknowledged in December 2024, 'Russia is reconstituting its forces much quicker than we had anticipated. They are learning fast from the battlefield.'[46]

Western commentators rarely, if ever, talk about the will of Putin the dictator to see this operation through – yet will, military or political, is a critical part of warfare, especially when the state is geared up to fulfil the will of the Russian leader. The war has allowed Putin to strengthen a power base that is now almost completely unchecked. He has more power over the Russian state than any dictator since Stalin and more unchecked power than any man on the planet. The war has enabled Putin to achieve a major goal, to reshape Russian identity as one virulently opposed to the Western enemy. On some levels, the war is already a success for the Russian leader. And with casualties approaching 1 million, how will anyone tell that society that it was all for nothing?

The Russian state has evaded sanctions with reasonable success despite some Western voices predicting the collapse of its economy. Indeed, its economy was expected to grow faster than any G7 economy in 2024, although by the end of that year it was looking more vulnerable to inflation and the affordability of a protracted war.[47] Firms in the EU are responsible for breaking EU sanctions on an industrial level and without censure, routing exports to Russia via Kyrgyzstan, Kazakhstan, Georgia and Armenia.[48] A shadow fleet of tankers, some of them Greek, exports illicit Russian oil in the tens of millions of barrels per month.[49]

Russia's economic leaders and oligarchs have bought into the war because they have little choice. They are also reliant on war spending. After Russian companies lost Western contracts, they have been more closely incorporated into the military-industrial complex. Western commentators who predicted disaster for the Russian economy due to this new militarisation forget that Russia's economy was a militarised economy until the 1990s. The influence of the war can be seen at the regional level too, with regional governors receiving increased funding for police and security agencies – up by more than half in 2023.[50] The regime is showing determination and resilience, even at the cost of the lives of a large number of its citizens.

Since the disaster of 2022, Russia has been rebuilding its army. It is adapting its tactics, techniques and procedures. In engineering and electronic warfare, Russia may be outperforming Ukraine. The many hectares of land mines and deep, defensive trenches prepared by Russian forces in early 2023 were central to defeating Ukraine's much-signalled 2023 counter-offensive. At a tactical level too, Russian troops dig in by hand within hours of taking a position and build strong points around the terrain. In terms of electronic warfare, Ukrainians are finding a partial, invisible electronic shield along Russian lines and even some Western missile systems are being disrupted in their final stages.

If the two greatest determinants of war are manpower and artillery rate of fire, Russian forces remain dominant. Ukraine must offset this disadvantage with better tactics, better leadership, better defensive positions and better use of technology on land, air and sea – and many fewer casualties. Ukraine innovates, but Russia steals that innovation and uses its military-industrial base to mass produce. Whilst Ukraine uses multiple drone systems as a result of its drone cottage industry, Russia produces fewer designs but in larger numbers, making supply and use easier.

Russian forces, like Ukrainians, are using tanks differently and trying to hide them better. They are also using quad bikes and motorcycles to move quickly in the lethal 'drone zone'. The mass use of glide bombs may yet change the course of the war by physically destroying the Ukrainian Army or psychologically terrorising its people, although electronic warfare measures introduced in late 2024 appear now to be successfully diverting them from their targets, if not from hitting a generalised area. The intense spoofing of GPS to hinder Russian targeting is the reason why phones do not give accurate locations in eastern cities.

THE EVOLUTION OF 'MEAT ASSAULTS'

Perhaps the most startling and grotesque tactics used in the war have been the Russian meat assaults. Ukrainian soldiers tell me they became evident during the battle for Bakhmut. The first time I heard the term, I misheard it. I thought Ukrainians were using the word *mestnoye* (local). No, I was corrected – it was *myasnoi* (meat). They have also been called Storm-Z attacks, named after the penal colony units sent to fight in Ukraine. Ukrainians say that these 'meat assaults' were pioneered by the Wagner Group. The attacks began with Russians being driven at the point of a gun to assault Ukrainian positions. They have evolved into repetitive, small-scale assaults, sometimes integrated with artillery and drones. They are inflicting casualties on Ukrainians and achieving some success on the battlefield.

Initially, Ukrainian units faced with meat assaults believed they were successfully repulsing them, assuming that the 50 per cent or more casualty rates per assault would force Russian forces to stop using them. Slowly, it dawned on them that the casualties were not an issue and that the assaults would continue regardless of Russian casualties until Ukrainian positions were overrun. One Ukrainian commander, who came across the tactic for the first time in the battle for Bakhmut, told me, 'They were just constant. In the beginning, we killed a lot of the enemy but then we were losing territory anyway … but still killing people.' He described how, repetitively and rhythmically, wave after wave of Russian penal colony troops came at the Ukrainians' positions in small groups: 'Five or six move. We kill three, two make it. Next, again five or six men. They move. We kill three, two make it. They reinforce and move to the next stage, until they get to six. They try to advance. They move. We kill three, two make it.'[51]

This continued until the Russians finally assaulted the Ukrainian trenches. If successful, Russian troops would move to the next position. Failure would mean a new wave of Russian 'soldiers' would start the process again, stepping over the bodies of the dead because senior Russian commanders would order the same assaults on the same positions via the same routes.

'Our weapons were being chewed up,' the commander told me in reference to his troops' overheated weapons.

Many others had the same experience. Call sign Segar inflicted dozens of casualties. He was a member of an 82 mm mortar team in Bakhmut. Positioning himself around blocks of flats so that his mortar, which fires at a minimum angle of 45 degrees, could shoot out but tanks and some artillery, which have a much flatter trajectory, couldn't fire back in, he and his team killed between thirty and forty Russian Storm-Z prisoner/soldiers on his first fire mission.

The meat assaults have sometimes been referred to as 'human wave' attacks, but they are not the same. These are not large-scale assaults like those executed by Chinese forces in Korea or Soviet forces in Stalingrad. They are endlessly repetitive, consistent, small-scale attacks, effectively 'fire team' assaults, comprising four or six men moving as swiftly as possible to secure a position or storm a trench. Whilst their lives are expended cheaply, their actions pin-point Ukrainian positions for drone and artillery targeting and also wear down Ukrainian soldiers, who are faced with hour upon hour of hitting them. When Ukrainians make mistakes, run low on ammunition or simply the lack the numbers to defend their lines, Russian meat assaults prevail.

However bestial, there is some logic to Russian actions. 'What is the better option?' Rob Lee, senior fellow at the Foreign Policy Research Institute, asked. 'If you bring up a company of armour, it'll probably be destroyed by UAVs and other things. If you operate in platoons, it's a bigger target too.' A four- or six-man team moving quickly presents a problem for defenders. 'Small teams are harder to counter, and they can be successful because they also do a better job of concealing themselves.'[52]

Given casualty rates of 50 per cent or more, why do Russian soldiers accept this? Do they believe Putin's words and the strength of the cause or, once engaged, do they fight due to fear of murder, jail or humiliations such as rape? All the evidence points to exceptionally low morale amongst Russian soldiers, certainly in expendable infantry units, which flies in the face of Western assumptions that getting troops to fight requires high morale. There are dozens of videos of Russian troops being filmed committing suicide rather than attack Ukrainian positions. There are many videos of Russian troops bitterly complaining about the saturation of the skies above them, with Ukrainian drones landing sometimes directly on their colleagues. Yet one should not underestimate the effect of twenty years of propaganda on Russians, either by enforcing and repeating a consensus or by at least preventing alternative opinions from being expressed. Whilst those on Telegram can air opinions, the majority of Russians, especially the elderly, get their news from state broadcast channels, which have for years pumped out the message that Ukraine has been taken over by extremists.

We know what soldiers have been told to believe because pocket-sized leaflets have been found on some of them. Professionally designed in black, red and white for starkness, the eight-sided leaflet explains why they are being sent into battle. Two copies were given to me when I spent time with the Tsunami unit in eastern Ukraine in the late summer of 2023.

'Ukraine is a terrorist state,' the leaflet exclaimed in capital letters. Below, through a shattered-glass effect, there is the picture of an elderly man holding his face in anguish whilst others crouch behind him, seemingly in fear of a Ukrainian artillery strike. 'After the Maidan of 2014, Ukrainian authorities that seized power were willing to do anything to keep it, including outright terror,' the leaflet went on. At the bottom left of every page was the letter Z, in white with fuzzy edges on a stark black background. The following pages described how the Ukraine regime was criminal, how it had oppressed civilians in the Russian puppet Donetsk and Luhansk Republics, how it humiliated Russian-language speakers and how it ran secret prisons under the control of the SBU and nationalist extremists. The leaflet ended by saying that the time for partnership had ended in the 2000s and for diplomacy in the 2010s. 'Today, weapons speak for us. The time for peaceful decisions is no more.'

It is clear that once in the army, escaping is extremely dangerous. As I heard from Russian PoWs, escapees will be brutally punished or killed, whilst on the battlefield, squad leaders will shoot soldiers who run away. In other cases, soldiers might lose their benefits if they refuse to advance, may be thrown into pits as punishment or may be raped. For whatever reason, most, once on the battlefield, choose to march towards their own slaughter. However degrading it might be for individual soldiers, the meat assaults have enabled a slow Russian advance across eastern Ukraine. It's not only that Russia has a manpower advantage; it's that they're able to use that advantage in ways Ukraine would not.

CHAPTER 14

STORIES FROM THE FRONT: KHARTIIA'S FRONTLINE ROBOTS AND ACHILLES'S COTTAGE INDUSTRY

'Follow the drone.'

– Note dropped from an Achilles Brigade drone to a Russian soldier who asked to be taken prisoner[1]

In the late summer of 2024, Khartiia made a small but important step, not only for Ukraine but for the future of war. The unit automated a section of their active front line, removing humans and replacing them with land and air drones. It wasn't a long piece of the line, just a few hundred metres, but it was 'manned' by machines moving on land and in the air. Khartiia, and Ukraine as a whole, are using technology to counter Putin's grotesque meat assaults. The unit's commanding officer Ihor Obolenskyi, call sign Kornet, was blunt in his reasoning: 'If we don't change, we'll die. Our nation will die.'[2] Since then, other limited but groundbreaking operations have taken place, expanding the use of land drones as fighting machines.[3]

What's happening in Ukraine is the evolution towards automated war – war by smart machines, controlled, at a distance, by humans. It is being driven by units such as Khartiia, originally formed as a small Ministry of the Interior unit by Kornet with the backing of a wealthy businessman. The unit has grown into a brigade of several thousand men and women. Kornet's aim is to pull their human soldiers to the second and then third lines of defence, perhaps 1 and then 2 kilometres back from 'line zero', the most forward of the frontline positions, and then let the machines do more of the work and take more of the risk. That way, troops, often highly trained or specialist, are not just sitting ducks for Russian glide bombs, drones and artillery shells, and they can be used for other tasks, such as assaults.

Khartiia's automation is just part of a bigger battle to forge an army where robots and brainpower take the pressure off a front line that may be hot or semi-hot for years. Few expect any ceasefire with Russia to be lasting. Moscow, Kornet says, is going to be a generational threat to Ukraine: 'We will have a permanent enemy. We will be like Israel. That's why we must prepare and build a new army.' The question is, can enough of the Ukrainian Army innovate fast enough and will drones be able to take the place of humans or reduce their presence enough to be able to withstand the daily waves of Russian assaults?

Already, Khartiia's soldiers, like elsewhere on the front, are supported by reconnaissance drones on permanent guard. If a Russian attack gets to the unit's soldiers on the front line, something will have gone wrong. Above and ahead of Khartiia are reconnaissance drones on a 'carousel' of three for every section on Khartiia's front line, which stretches over 12 kilometres. At any time one drone is up, one is down and one is being prepared. Russian attacks thus far have resulted in near 100 per cent loss in kit and soldiers, as Ukrainian drones spot an advancing enemy and destroy it with kamikaze drones. Detonations on the weakly protected Russian tank turrets cause a chain reaction that 'cooks' the shells stored around the turret and results in a devastating explosion, which throws the 12-tonne Soviet tank turret 100 feet into the air and vaporises anyone in the tank.

I meet Kornet in one of his bases. His team have asked me not to say where. Kornet initially retired from Ukraine's armed forces in 2019 after nearly two decades of service, though he feared war was coming. His final job was as deputy head of NATO integration, of which he says there was precious little happening: 'It is not just a shame, it's a crazy shame, because NATO and the US and Canada and the guys from Great Britain came to try to teach us. We were not ready. We took our country too cheaply.'

After retiring, he would still meet up with his old command team, but whilst he wanted to plan for the coming conflict, they wanted to socialise. 'I wanted to discuss problems so that we would be ready. My team were thinking, "Colonel, why are you doing this. We're friends, let's drink."' Putin's infamous 2021 essay on the historical unity of Russia and Ukraine signalled, said Kornet, the start of the campaign. But many Ukrainians didn't want to hear it. To exemplify the point, he reached to remember a film title where a comet was hurtling towards earth and compared that to Ukraine's unwillingness to confront the danger it faced. 'Did you know that Hollywood film? What's its name?' He tried to recollect the name of the actor. 'Leonardo di Caprio! *Don't Look Up*!' he exclaimed. 'This is our story.'

In culture and practice, the Ukrainian Army is moving away from its Soviet past. Some regiments are moving faster than others. Whilst some units sell themselves on raw machismo or sex appeal, Khartiia recruitment adverts sell the unit on brainpower and NATO standards. The implicit message is, we will do more to keep you alive.

The profile and popularity of a unit tends to be based on a number of factors, over and above individual leadership or advertising. First, there are units with an ideological basis, especially if they can trace their roots back to 2014. This includes the strongly nationalist Azov Brigade. Their anti-Russian stance is seen to be vindicated. Azov's fame in fighting in 2014, and again in Mariupol in 2024, generated headlines here and around the world. It is arguably for this reason that Putin continues to hold Azov soldiers prisoner and refuses to hand them back. Second, there are units in Ukraine, as with every society, which generate an elite *esprit de corps*, such as marines, paratroopers and special forces. Third are those units associated with particular regions, which are seen to carry the reputation of their home with them, such as the 100th Mechanized Brigade from Volyn or the 'Edelweiss' 10th Mountain Assault Brigade from the edge of the mountainous western region of Transcarpathia. Finally, in this war there are those units which have tended to have the best training, generally meaning to NATO standard, with the equipment to match, such as Ukraine's 3rd Storm Brigade or Khartiia.

Apart from Russia, Ukraine has the largest and most battle-hardened army in Europe. To understand where it is heading, one needs first to understand the difference in culture and processes between the Soviet Union and NATO. Khartiia's men argue that the USSR's military planning processes were unfit for the modern age; officers and soldiers were discouraged from showing initiative, bullying was rife and training was poor. Call sign Acoustic, an officer in Khartiia, explained. In the Soviet Union, he said, strategic operational planning was done in Moscow. The 'empire' could not allow for any critical thinking and obviously no mission command could give initiative to more junior ranks. Soviet military culture saw senior commanders plan, even to the smallest detail, a culture rooted in the scientific approach to warfare. It may have been helpful once, but it was not now. Officers in the chain of command would implement the order without question. By contrast, in the Western school, according to Acoustic, 'the commander gives his intent and then the staff makes decisions and comes up with a plan. And because they're part of this planning process, they're able to then show some further initiative.'[4] It was like, he said, comparing a science with an art.

Additionally, the Soviet Army was built on a 'prison' culture: 'on fear, on deprecation, on punishment for initiative,' Acoustic explained. 'You would need to fear your commander more than the enemy and you would need to do exactly what you are being told, contrary to mission command.' The Western idea of mission command, as a reminder, is where a commander gives his intent and his officers show initiative and leadership to work up plans to achieve that intent. That's why, especially in the first year or year and a half of the war in Ukraine, so many Russian generals were killed. Their need to micromanage meant they had to be close to the front line. They could not or would not trust their subordinates, who would not or could not show initiative. Fearing your commander more than your enemy may also explain why Russian soldiers still fight to the death. If they don't, there is a good chance that they will be killed by their own side.

Whilst all units in Ukraine have moved on from that system, it was the starting point. The first invasion in 2014 changed many things. It showed Russia as an enemy, it forced Ukrainians to fight for their country and it gave combat experience to a new generation.

Before that, however, commanding officer Kornet remembers his fellow officer cadets at college mocking him when he wanted to learn about military theory. 'When I started to read books, they said, "Be like us, do sport, shout at the soldiers, that's all. It's not important to be reading."' He still finds some cultural resistance now to the idea of drones 'manning' the front line. Some generals, he said, believed that 'the land is not ours unless a soldier is standing on it'.

Khartiia, which had the luxury of starting from scratch, developed its own culture directly from the US Light Infantry Field Manual. Fostering a culture of responsibility at junior levels was key. 'We realised that by the time British, US or other officers even got to military schools like Sandhurst or West Point, they already have a good understanding of some critical thinking, analytical skills, good understanding of teamwork and group dynamics,' Kornet says. 'They know how to provide feedback. At their worst, Soviet officers were taught only to recite.' And whilst the conditions are very different from assumptions made about the way NATO fights its wars, Kornet argues that the principles can still apply: good planning, good training, innovation and devolved responsibility in a meritocratic army.

Data and tech support the regiment, and it is eye-opening for me to see and understand how war is changing. We are in an eastern Ukrainian city and I'm heading to the brigade's operations room. The ops room is underneath a multi-storey 1950s industrial building. It's night, with no streetlights around us and low cloud. It's pitch dark. We give a password to a civilian guard and he opens a pair of uneven metal gates, through which we walk across a wet tarmac courtyard. The building itself is abandoned and throws a shadow so dark it is difficult to see where the courtyard ends and the building starts. The light from our torches shines off the puddles. I feel as if I am walking across a desolate film set, perhaps the backdrop for Batman's Gotham City. At the end of the courtyard, we give another password and more metal doors open to wide concrete stairs, leading down to a basement. Our steps echo off painted brick walls. At the bottom, the glow from half a dozen side rooms illuminates the long basement corridor. At the far end is the ops room.

We walk in. It is warm and light. There are at least fifteen people in the room and screens on three out of the four walls; it measures maybe 12 meters by 8. Underneath the screens are banks of desks, which also sit in the centre of the room. But what I notice above all is the sheer number of video feeds. Not counting individual PCs, there are seventy-three active feeds, most showing live drone video footage. When I was in a relatively sophisticated ops room targeting ISIS in Iraq in the middle of the 2010s, there might have been a dozen screens. The amount of visual information coming from a 15-kilometre section of front line is daunting.

My attention turns to a large data screen, 2 metres across by 1 metre down. It is showing, on a red bar chart, the 'kills' for the past month. Out of a total of 208 recorded Russian dead, sixty-five were killed by Khartiia's kamikaze drones and sixty-four by its bomber drones. This figure is way ahead of mortars, historically the biggest killer on the conventional battlefield, and other artillery and small arms fire. If the seventy-three video feeds represent the extraordinary increase in visual information coming into an ops room, the casualty data represents the epoch-changing evolution in infantry warfare caused by infantry-level drones. It occurs to me that in close battle with Russian troops, who are increasingly arming themselves with drones too, NATO infantry soldiers would be all but defenceless on a drone-saturated battlefield. Imagine troops equipped with traditional weapons but then having to deal with 1,000 slow-flying grenades floating about their heads.

If Khartiia is an example of a unit set up 'by the book' and founded by military officers, the Kraken Regiment comes from a more rough-and-ready background, but its evolution is no less valuable. Its founder is Kostya Nemichev, call sign Brather.

I wanted to talk to Brather because he's been fighting the Russians since 2014, and in doing so, he's fought the propaganda, political and paramilitary war. He's fought street battles with Russian provocateurs and *titushki* in the early months of 2014. From there, he served with the Azov Brigade in Mariupol in 2015. Before the full-scale invasion of 2022, he and his closest comrades set up Kraken, backed by Ukraine's HUR, to support the defence of Kharkiv. As an Azov offshoot, Kraken has the same hardened reputation. 'The guys who have been fighting since 2022 are a match for any professional soldier,' said Brather.[5] Some of their operations have involved work behind enemy lines, akin to Second World War-style resistance operations. They have a reputation for high-risk operations. There is a bounty on Nemichev's head, with his picture in every Russian police department in the border territories.

His tactics have evolved with the style of conflict being fought. After 2022, Kraken became mechanised thanks almost entirely to 'trophy' kit captured from the Russians during a series of battles in 2022 – though thanks to the drone threat, these are less useful than they were two years ago. 'We started the war in pick-ups. We evolved to armoured vehicles; now we're back on foot,' says Brather. 'Nothing is standing still. Everything is development. Action and counter action. The person who stands still, well, he loses.' He's served in the cauldron of Bakhmut too, where his men first experienced the relentless meat assaults.

Before 2014, Brather led a group of football fans ('ultras') following the Ukrainian Division 1 team FC Metalist Kharkiv. His life as an accidental revolutionary started during the 2014 protests, when, as an eighteen-year-old, he saw 'grannies and teachers' being roughed up by thugs employed by local politicians. 'There was a specific problem in Kharkiv,' he explained. Younger people had gone to the main 'Maidan' protests in Kyiv. Those who remained were often older folks or those unable to defend themselves. 'Those grannies and teachers were getting beat up. We were under a strong Russian "wing",' Brather said, referring to the powerful influence of pro-Kremlin forces in the Russian-speaking city. He and his fellow football fans set up a 'democracy guard' several dozen strong to provide protection for those civilians who remained.

Kharkiv at the time was controlled by politicians linked to organised crime and infiltrated by Russian agencies and agents of influence. At its heart was Kharkiv mayor Hennadiy Kernes. Rumour has it that Kernes was paid $1 billion dollars to deliver Kharkiv for the Russian regime as part of the 2014 'curated' coups. The amount was almost certainly untrue, even if the intent was not. When, for whatever reason, he failed, Chechen assassins allegedly acting for the FSB shot him several times. He survived, but his health never recovered and he died in December 2020. Despite allegations of skullduggery and treachery, Kharkivites remained loyal to him.

By February and March 2014, whilst much of Kharkiv looked on, fearful for the future, two rival camps had been established. The two groups started to seize buildings. Brather and his team, working at the request of the Kharkiv regional governor rather than the city's politicians, had occupied the regional administrative building and attempted to hold it against a concerted campaign. 'From March 2014, they [pro-Russian groups] started bussing in supporters. Kharkiv received about forty buses from Kursk and Belgorod regions alone,' says Brather. 'They brought in paid *masovka* [extras] and *zavadela* [cheerleaders] who assaulted our buildings.' Overwhelmed, they were beaten back by Russian activists and then arrested by the local police, despite promises of amnesties.

Eventually, Ukrainian authorities brought order to the city using loyal special forces from Vinnytsia in central-west Ukraine, who cleared the government buildings of the pro-Russian thugs. After weeks of chaos, the pro-Russian demonstrations died out, in part thanks to a march of 5,000 led by FC Metalist fans. After Kharkiv was saved, Brather, with a small number of colleagues, joined the Azov Brigade and fought in the retaking of the southern port city of Mariupol.

Roll on six years, and by the spring of 2021, Brather, like other military entrepreneurs, saw war coming. He cited two 'combat indicators'. The first, clearly, was the military build-up. 'When Russia started massing forces, we already knew what we were going to deal with,' he says. The second was the equally important Russian information campaign 'I want to live with Belgorod', which started from the spring of 2021 and focused on Kharkiv city's relationship with nearby Russian cities such as Belgorod. It was the local narrative that would help justify the invasion. Brather explained, '"I want to live with Belgorod. I have my sister there, my friends, my relatives, my brothers." This [narrative] started pouring into the Ukrainian media.' In response to the military threat, he and his comrades started to train. 'We were sharing experiences, delivering lectures – we got about 5,000 people through our training.' In response to the propaganda and psychological threat, he organised a 'Kharkiv is Ukraine' march, attended, he says, by 7,000 people. 'No flags, apart from the national, Ukrainian flag.'

As the situation worsened and the invasion date drew nearer, he reached out to HUR. Kharkiv, it was already assumed, was a lost city. Military recruitment centres shut and the government pulled out. Whilst most Ukrainian military stayed in position, some left and a small number did so by siding with the Russians. The day before the Russian invasion, Brather was in Kyiv talking with Ukraine's secret services and pleading for weapons. He was given 200 Kalashnikovs. A concerted effort produced another 1,500 weapons with ammunition, begging and borrowing where they could from other units. They set up a headquarters hours before the war began.

By 27 February, the Russians, with some resistance, had broken into the outskirts of Kharkiv, advancing between two Ukrainian brigades. Kraken was building up an intelligence picture, thanks to residents sending in videos. Additionally, they had captured a Russian subversive group and had discovered Russian plans. 'They had five targets,' he explained. 'The oblast [county] administration, the city administration, the SBU, the police HQ and the radio and TV tower.' It was, in other words, an old-school coup.

They knew one group of Russian forces had gone to ground in an empty school. He made a call to the SBU and asked to borrow a tank. It arrived that evening. 'We destroyed the school and everyone in it.' In the process, they seized several Russian vehicles. Working with and supporting loyal Ukrainian units, they pushed the Russian troops steadily back through a series of engagements. A pattern followed. In every 'contact' (skirmish or battle), Brather's men would seize Russian kit, generally five to ten pieces in every engagement, and use it to build up their own armoury. He jokingly compares it to the lend-lease programme, when the US armed Britain and other Allied nations during the Second World War. 'Thanks to Russian lend-lease, we became a fully-fledged brigade,' he laughs.

Some of Kraken's work is highly sensitive, as it has taken place behind enemy lines. Ukraine's way of war is not only innovative but also creative, and it includes sabotage and assassination in the occupied territories and now inside Russia too. The closest comparison to this in the English-speaking world is the Special Operations Executive, who worked to drive resistance operations in Nazi-controlled Europe during the Second World War. In the current war, this work is led by the Ukrainian HUR. An example of HUR's otherwise secret work is the sabotage of a Russian warship, organised with the Russian Legion, a unit composed of Russians who have chosen to serve with Ukraine. The sabotage was conducted by Hoha, a Russian serviceman from a Ukrainian background. I met him at a secret location in Kyiv, where he told me his story.

Hoha had tried resigning from the Russian armed forces on several occasions, but each time he was refused. 'I was looking for ways not to be involved in killing people, to not be a Russian soldier,' he told me.[6] Out of frustration and anger, and at high personal risk to himself, he contacted the Russian Legion and HUR. He discovered that his Russian navy vessel the *Serpukhov*, a Buyan-class corvette, was to be transferred from the Baltic to the Caspian Sea, making the voyage down the Volga River. Although the *Serpukhov* was not large, it carried cruise missiles, which were to be fired into Ukraine after the ship had reached its position in the Caspian. HUR planned Operation Rybalka (Fisherman) to sabotage the vessel. The vessel's radio room not only housed its communications systems but also its codes and targeting data. 'Without it, the ship cannot perform its duties – cannot fire, go to sea, or assume combat duty. Nothing can be done,' Hoha told me. One Sunday afternoon, when only half the crew were on the ship, he set light to the communications room, destroying the ship's ability to function. He got out fast – as he was on duty, his role would be obvious. 'I ran. I've never run that fast before.' HUR smuggled him out to Ukraine, where he now serves with the Russian Legion.

• • •

Khartiia and Kraken both represent different routes to the same idea of an army reformed in war. The first route saw a unit set up by professional soldiers applying US doctrine 'off the shelf' as its founding culture and processes. The second model saw football fans self-organising and establishing processes and a fighting culture through action and reaction against the enemy – from street fighting to regular war.

By contrast, the Achilles Battalion is an example of a third route – civil volunteers developing a specialist unit – in this case, drones – and then attracting people with skills sets in electronics and computing. Achilles was originally a volunteer company in the Kyiv territorial defence forces, serving in battles around Kyiv in 2022. The unit and many of its soldiers transferred to the Kharkiv front and were offered the role of a specialist drone unit with the 92nd Assault Brigade, one of those units which advertises that it is trained to NATO standards. They were upgraded to a battalion at the beginning of 2024, taking their name from their founder, Kyiv city councillor Yuriy Fedorenko, call sign Achilles. Achilles Battalion is now arguably the best drone unit in the Ukrainian armed forces, with a hit rate of 60–70 per cent, much higher than the typical 40 per cent.

In an action made famous on social media, one of Achilles's drones took a surrender from a Russian soldier who begged not to be bombed. A note was dropped to the soldier reading 'Follow the drone'. Under fire from his own side, the Russian soldier was led to the Ukrainian lines and to safety.[7]

I am visiting Achilles because they are one of the units that exemplify the battle for technological advantage. After the disaster of 2022, Russia has worked hard to catch up. For Ukrainians now, gains on the battlefield are more difficult to come by and the tussle over tactics is constant. Therefore, a new culture that drives innovation is critical to survival. Call sign Dev, short for Developer, goes backwards and forwards between the battlefields of eastern Ukraine and his unit's tech hub, based in what looks like a detached, run-down house in the suburbs of a frontline town. Dev is working on the latest iterations of drones. He is the chief technical officer for Achilles.

He's perfecting the weapons of 2025 – two in particular to help Achilles overcome the growing Russian capability in electronic warfare. Dev is working to develop drones that can lock onto a target, as well as fibre optic drones. The first enables a drone pilot to identify and fix a target in its site, at which point the drone will home onto its target regardless of any interference. The second allows drones to overcome electronic warfare by being linked to base with a super-thin fibre optic cable, perhaps 2 mm across, with a range of 10 km. Of the two, Dev is especially excited by the fibre optics, although there are trade-offs. 'It's great tech. The drones can hit the target and EW [electronic warfare] can't cope with it. The problem is the price; 10 km of fibre optic cable is more expensive than the drone,' he says. 'It also creates an additional weight issue, so it's best used with bigger drones.'[8]

Dev shows me around. In the building we are in, the drones are assembled and made ready for war. In the tight basement, a team of six people work. With its white desks, small table-top lights and metal-framed open shelves, it feels like a messy university technician's laboratory. Everyone here is an Achilles soldier, most of whom have already served as drone pilots. Around them are stacked-up cardboard boxes stamped with 'DRONES, FRAGILE' or 'Born in Ukraine'. There are also dozens of what look like pizza delivery boxes. The drones will be packaged in these and sent to the front for a very different sort of delivery. In a next-door office, 3D printers quietly whir, printing out additional parts for the drones. Dev talks me through the drone's construction. The 'flight controller' is in the middle of the drone, the camera at the front and the video transmitter and a receiver at the back, with an antenna that looks like a thick, short tail. A shaved-headed soldier next to us carries out electronic tests to make sure the drone has been properly made. Every time he does, a happy ringtone fires up.

If drone pilots are priority targets on the front line, the drone and bomb factories are priority targets in the rear. The house is in an anonymous part of town. Dev doesn't think they are on a Russian target list, but there is always the danger of 'spotters'. 'We'll be moving soon anyway,' he says. For the founder and commander of the unit, Fedorenko, innovation is the way to keep his soldiers alive. 'We are always trying to replace what is missing, what we do not have. So now, in comparison to the Russian Army, we are using technology to try to save people's lives. For Russia, life is cheap.'[9]

The factory produces 150 kamikaze drones per day. The battalion could use more, but it's still a good amount for a single unit. They get some funding from the Ministry of Defence, perhaps 20 per cent of what they need, and the Digital Ministry runs a regular competition for units with the best drone hit rates to give them additional support. However, 80 per cent of Achilles's drone supply is funded through businesses or donations.

Achilles was given his call sign thanks to his deputy commander, who was the Ukrainian distributor for the film *Troy*. Achilles is as high profile as military leaders get, not only because the unit's drone pilots are some of the best in the country but also because of his and his wife's political profiles – his wife is a Member of Parliament for Kharkiv. His profile helps fundraising. After the slowing down of US support in the first months of 2024, there was the painful realisation that, as he says, 'our future depends on each of us. It doesn't matter if they are civilians or military.'

Along with making drones, the teams work to improve their explosives too. I visit the unit's DIY arms factory. It's deep in a nuclear bunker underneath a dark industrial landscape of bomb-damaged factories. Call sign Yangrr (young and angry) shows me around. It's effectively a military recycling centre. They take old explosives from wherever they can and turn them into new, lethal weapons to be attached to the underside of the drones.

To enter the factory, we walk down into what looks like a small subway tunnel and past two dusty grey nuclear blast doors. A small Orthodox icon balances over the inner door, gazing over the workers. The bunker is a valuable site. A missile landed close by recently – in the darkness, Yangrr makes sure we don't slip into the crater on the way. Everyone in the bunker survived, he said, but four people outside were killed. Did the Russians know the location? Yangrr gestures with arms raised and a slight shrug of the shoulders, as if to say, 'Probably not.' The important thing, he says, is to keep focused. 'When you start dying in your head, you will probably die in real life.'[10]

Inside is an Aladdin's cave of second-hand explosives, rockets and land mines, which the soldiers of Achilles will take apart and slowly rebuild. Everywhere I look there are stacks of old and new explosives. Everything I touch seems detonatable. I begin to dread the airport explosives detector machine. There are old Soviet-era plastic explosives from anti-vehicle mines that look like large square-shaped green and white candles. The explosive is fast but not powerful, Yangrr says. To my right, I pick up a brick of a hard, dark brown substance that looks like 1930s Bakelite plastic with flecks of silvery powder – aluminium, I am told – which increases its explosive power. I see a stack of Soviet anti-tank mines – green, the size of a large dinner plate and about 6 cm thick. They are running out of these, Yangrr says, so they are taking the explosives from donated Swedish and German anti-tank mines instead. They even take explosives out of Russian glide bombs that don't detonate. 'There is nothing that we can't recycle or don't know about. We have no other choice,' says Yangrr, who before the war was a TV director and producer. He enjoys historical military re-enactment in his spare time; he has the uniforms for the US Rangers and British Royal Marines. 'The full set, mind,' he emphasises in good humour.

The unit's staple weapon is the warhead from a rocket-propelled grenade. To adapt it for drones, they remove the long, thin propellent cylinder that fires the device. It's not needed on a drone. Someone with steady hands then carefully saws the metal casing and disassembles it. The sawing is done by hand to control the temperature and minimise the risk of catastrophic reaction. A piece is unscrewed and the detonator removed. Further modifications are then made – I've been asked not to say what – but at the end of the process, in Yangrr's words, 'the casing is lighter, but the explosive is the same, so the drone can fly a few kilometres further.'

We go to the next room to see the new devices being assembled. The final weapons have wires and plastic wrapped around them. On every bomb is the date manufactured and the worker who made it.

I look at one put together by call sign Klutch (key). Unable to volunteer due to ill health, he wanted to play his role, so he was offered a job at the factory. He's a man of few words, but he's clearly proud of what he is doing.

'People aren't working for money but for an idea,' says Yangrr.

One of the people who helps put all this together and plans how these weapons will be used and by whom is call sign Avocado. Before the war, Avocado, thirty-six, was a user experience designer, working to make websites more accessible. She is quiet, articulate and exudes a slightly wan gentleness that is far removed from the cliched idea of a soldier. She's now one of the seniors in the battalion. The final ingredient in the new Ukrainian military culture, which is often overlooked when discussing conflict, is how human beings are used by armies. Achilles takes only volunteers and vets individuals not just for brawn but increasingly for brains.

'Using the right people in the right place is also how we can win,' Avocado says. 'Everything in our unit is about communication. You understand that this person can't cover for this part of the job, so we should change the place. Or you can see that this person has skills for another kind of job and we just switch those people.'[11] I ask if that was normal throughout the military. 'I haven't been part of any other regiment, but because we are from civil life, it's normal for us. As for my civil job, it was really crucial to always ask why and for what purpose. And that works in the military as well.'

Her time now is spent fighting the daily tactical battle. The drones and the bombs we saw will, within hours of their manufacture, be taken to positions, with the bombs then attached to the drone. Whilst Dev's team develops the drones and Yangrr's develops the bombs, Avocado applies the finished item to the tactical battle. 'They [the Russians] have EW [electronic warfare] systems that work and that means that we need to develop new technologies in other ways – so that's the process day after day. It's all about experimenting and finding new ways.' For that, collaboration and teamwork are vital. That work could mean drones 'free hunting' to find gaps in Russian electronic warfare cover, putting up a relay drone to provide a stronger signal or finding other ways to overcome it.

The more collaborative culture now being adopted in some, if not all, Ukrainian units is the very opposite of Russian military culture, in which human life – certainly in the meat assault infantry units – is treated as meaninglessly expendable. Day after day, Avocado and her colleagues watch, partly in disbelief, as Russian soldiers are ordered down the same tracks to assault the same positions. The soldiers, at least twenty per day, step over the previous days' dead to blindly walk into the path of Achilles's drones and munitions, which will leave most of them dead and dying. They in turn will be walked over by the next day's doomed Russian soldiers. Her words remind me of something also said by Khartiia's Acoustic: regardless of the situation on the ground, Russian troop movements seem to be micromanaged by generals with no situational awareness.

'They do not think about their infantry at all,' she says. 'They have a route and they use this route day after day, stepping on bodies, but they are still using this route. We liquidate them but they keep going, more and more.' Her quiet voice rises almost to frustration with the stupidity of her enemy. 'That's something that I cannot understand,' she exclaims. 'Seriously, find another route!'

Avocado herself spent a year on the front line as a drone pilot. She's given up a part of her life to fight the Russians – something which seems to be more poignantly felt and noted by the female soldiers with whom I have chatted. Men do not have to put off having families or family life to fight, but women do. Like many Ukrainian soldiers, she is tired but determination drives her. 'Do what you can always, and then do more than you can, and don't give up. Never, in any situation.'

The war, she says, 'took my time, definitely. But it also gave me people around me, amazing people. Also, a lot of different moral questions and rethinking my moral principles.'

What did she mean, I asked?

'I wasn't really a pacifist, but I hadn't thought I would be able to kill people.' She paused and then added, 'Obviously, I can.'

CHAPTER 15

REINVENTING BLAME: WHO LOST RUSSIA?

'Why is it that in one case white is white, while in another the same is called black? We will never agree with this nonsense.'

– Vladimir Putin[1]

Russia's break with Western states did not happen immediately. From the late 1980s to the mid-1990s, the Soviet Union/Russia was a 'status quo' power, wanting to keep the existing order and needing the goodwill of the West and the international institutions it dominated. In that brief period of hope, Moscow *did* undergo a significant change in its strategic outlook, suggesting that a nation's security culture *can* evolve.[2] Those years were an example of strategic flux as Moscow moved from confrontation to co-operation. As Marxism-Leninism waned, so did the sense of vulnerability, both physical and ideological. Sadly, this brief flowering of optimism did not prove to be permanent. It was followed in the 2000s by a sharp reversal, which may in reality have been underway from the mid-1990s. After this interregnum, Russia has again returned to a strategic worldview in which the West is perceived with profound distrust.

Exactly when did the break with the West take place and why?

Experts such as Tracey German cite 1999 as the key year, whilst distinguished geopolitics expert Dmitri Trenin cites 2006.[3] Ukrainian interviewees point to the early to mid-2000s. Whatever the answer, Putin's 2007 Munich speech, in which he attacked the US's 'uncontained hyper use of force' and NATO expansion as a 'serious provocation' was a clear point of departure.[4] But were there times when different actions could have resulted in different outcomes, or were the Kremlin's strategic ambitions, especially in relation to controlling its post-Soviet neighbours, simply unachievable in the post-communist world? Was this all inevitable, or could different behaviours on the part of the West have changed things?

NATO AND EU EXPANSION AND THE BOMBING OF SERBIA

A series of events from the late 1990s to the mid-2000s, namely the expansion of NATO and the EU and the bombing of Serbia, poisoned the relationship with the Kremlin – at least in hindsight.

Despite Russian objections, from the mid-1990s onwards, the Clinton administration and its European allies pushed for NATO expansion into central and eastern Europe. Initial enlargement brought the Czech Republic, Hungary and Poland into NATO in 1999. US diplomat George Kennan, then ninety-four, who helped to build the original 1940s framework for containment of the Soviet Union, was clear as to the outcome. 'I think it is the beginning of a new cold war,' he told *New York Times* columnist Thomas Friedman. 'I think the Russians will gradually react quite adversely and it will affect their policies. I think it is a tragic mistake. There was no reason for this whatsoever. No one was threatening anyone else.'[5]

A second tranche in 2004 saw Bulgaria, Romania, Slovakia and

Slovenia join. NATO also took in the three former Soviet republics that had done the most to undermine the USSR: Estonia, Latvia and Lithuania. Worse for the Russians, the alliance began to discuss NATO membership for Georgia and Ukraine. At the April 2008 NATO summit in Bucharest, France and Germany opposed the plan for fear of alienating Russia, and so whilst an immediate path to membership was not offered, vague commitments were made to future progress. Russian deputy Foreign Minister Alexander Grushko called the commitments, however unlikely they were to be fulfilled, a 'huge strategic mistake'. He went on to say they would have serious consequences for pan-European security.[6]

Concurrent with tensions over NATO expansion, NATO states had bombed Serbia between March and June 1999 during the Kosovo conflict. Serbia was partitioned, with its province of Kosovo placed under UN control. Kosovo eventually declared its independence from Serbia on 17 February 2008, nearly a decade later. Serbia was Russia's closest ally outside the Soviet Union. The attack and the annexation of Kosovo significantly altered Russia's view of the post-Soviet world and its place in it, poisoning much of the Russian political class against the West. As Putin later said, 'We remember 1999 very well. It was hard to believe, even seeing it with my own eyes, that at the end of the twentieth century, one of Europe's capitals, Belgrade, was under missile attack for several weeks, and then came the real intervention.'[7]

By partitioning Kosovo from Serbia and later recognising its independence, European nations put the interests of a small province ahead of those of their former main adversary, the world's most heavily nuclear-armed state. A tactical Balkan nice-to-have was placed above the overwhelming strategic goal of keeping Russia engaged, not enraged.

In this action, the UK and other states drove a coach and horses through the one international principle that had held since the Second World War: territorial inviolability. The then UK Foreign Secretary Robin Cook claimed that it would be the last chapter in the demise of Yugoslavia; in fact, it became an opening chapter in the new Cold War with Russia. At the time, I and others wrote that Putin would use this precedent to dismember countries on Russia's own borders because 'by tinkering with the map of Europe we risk the Russians doing the same in their own back yard'.[8] Russian Foreign Minister Sergei Ivanov said it opened 'a Pandora's box'.[9] And so it did, beginning with the partition of Georgia later that year and of Ukraine a few years after that. For those in any doubt about its importance, Putin made specific reference to the Kosovo partition, in relation to the annexation of Crimea, in October 2014: 'I do not understand why people living in Crimea do not have this right [to self-determination], just like the people living in, say, Kosovo.'[10]

In the early 2000s, Russia had hoped to build an alliance with the EU, in part to diminish the US's role in Europe. However, the Kremlin eventually came to see the EU as an equal threat to that of NATO. The 2013 crisis, which ultimately led to the first invasion of Ukraine, was driven by the Kremlin's attempts to block the EU–Ukraine Association Agreement. The Kremlin feared that the agreement would pull Ukraine out of Russia's economic and political sphere of influence and into that of the EU. The late Henry Kissinger, one of the great thinkers of international affairs, said that both the US and Europe failed to understand the impact the EU treaty would have on Russia. When asked if the West had a responsibility for escalation, he replied, albeit with hindsight, 'Yes, I am saying that.' He continued: 'Europe and America did not understand the impact of these events, starting with the negotiations about Ukraine's economic relations with the European Union and culminating in the demonstrations in Kyiv.'[11]

Over and above these events, I believe that the potential consequences of these actions were overlooked because Western leadership, believing that the long Cold War with Moscow was over, did not understand or accept that their actions could be seen as malign or threatening. This misunderstanding was underpinned by very different views of international relations – a clash of state cultures – on both sides. Broadly speaking, the Russian government's view of the world is 'realist'. Realism sees the nation state as the central component in international relations, which is itself marked by enduring competition in a relatively anarchic and harsh world. Realism is about control and about spheres of influence. By contrast, the dominant Western view of the world is liberal internationalism, which stresses international co-operation and working, through global institutions, to achieve liberal democracy and human rights. Russia and the Western states were speaking different languages.

John Mearsheimer, a Western critic of Western policy towards Russia, writes, 'In essence, the two sides have been operating with different playbooks: Putin and his compatriots have been thinking and acting according to realist dictates, whereas their Western counterparts have been adhering to liberal ideas about international politics.'[12] Because of this, Mearsheimer argued that the US and its allies provoked a major crisis over Ukraine. After first failing to understand Russia's concerns, Westerners were ultimately dismissive of them, believing, in Mearsheimer's words, that 'the logic of realism holds little relevance in the twenty-first century'.[13]

The Russian state, over time, came to believe liberal internationalism was the vehicle by which a hypocritical West masked its self-interest. In the words of US academic Michael Mandelbaum,

Russia believed that 'American promises were not to be trusted and that the West would take advantage of a weak and accommodating Russia.'[14]

Putin and his ruling group believed that NATO and the EU were vehicles for the West to secure its continued dominance over Russia and take historic Russian lands – now newly independent states – and 'flip' them to the West. The realists came to see liberal internationalism as a vehicle with which to undermine Russian authoritarianism and a means to interfere directly in the internal affairs of other nations through ideas such as the responsibility to protect, established at the 2005 UN World Summit following Rwanda and other genocides. Liberal internationalism, in Russia's eyes, was actually liberal imperialism.

This accusation was boosted by the interventionist agenda at the time, led by British Prime Minister Tony Blair from 1997. Whilst he may have been superficially right to argue, as he did in his now-famous Chicago speech in April 1999, that it was counter-productive to 'let' Pakistan develop as it did or 'let' thousands die in Bosnia – as if 'letting' these things happen was a casual choice and the right to intervene was a given – we are still living with the aftermath of that poorly thought-out period of militarily and ethically messy liberal interventionism, which produced a partitioned Serbia, an embittered Russia, strategic failure in Iraq and later in Afghanistan.[15] The post-Cold War world of the 1990s was imperfect, but liberal interventionism may have made it worse.

When NATO and the EU expanded, internationalist Western elites didn't perceive it as a threat to anyone and couldn't understand anyone who did. Russian elites did perceive it as a threat and couldn't understand anyone who didn't. In October 2014, Putin bitterly argued that the US 'and its satellites' imposed solutions. 'This group's ambitions grew so big,' he said, 'that they started presenting the policies they put together in their corridors of power as the view of the entire international community.'[16]

The Libyan civil war was the final breach. To prevent the slaughter of Libyan protesters who were rising up against the Gaddafi regime in 2011, UK and French warplanes struck Libyan positions. Russia did not veto a United Nations resolution, allowing NATO military action. Yet as the summer of 2011 drew on, it became increasingly clear that the British and the French believed that the only way to solve the humanitarian situation was to depose Gaddafi – 'regime change', in other words. Putin, then Russian Prime Minister, accused the West of being on a 'crusade' and said it showed Russia was right to boost its military.[17] As well as sensing another 'betrayal' at the hands of the West, the Russian state lost out financially on a $4 billion arms contract and a $1.5 billion rail contract to build a line between Sirte and Benghazi. Putin specifically referenced Libya in his grievances when he justified the invasion of Ukraine in February 2022, saying the 'illegitimate use of military force against Libya, the perversion of all decisions of the UN Security Council on the Libyan issue' led to that country's collapse, as it became a 'hotbed of terrorism, humanitarian catastrophe and mass migration'.[18]

The final piece of the jigsaw of Russian anger may be an emotional one. Did the West's alleged 'dismissal' of Russia, its diminution of Russia's sense of purpose and place, provoke an emotional and psychological response from the Kremlin that helps to explain its hostile stance?

The Kremlin's deep antagonism towards the Western world may also be driven by the West's failing to give Russia what scholar Andrei Tsygankov calls an honourable or special status within the West.[19] Tsygankov argues that Russia's historic sense of 'honour' is rooted, to an extent, in being a part of the Western world and defending its core values: 'As long as it feels sufficient recognition and reciprocation from Western capitals, Moscow is prepared to act in concert with its significant other.' When the relationship fails, Moscow retreats into isolation, rejection or hostility.

For example, both after the defeat in the Crimean War in the mid-nineteenth century and the loss of the Cold War in the late twentieth century, Russia declared a 'turn to the east' with a renewed focus on Asian relations and Russia's Eurasian, rather than European, identity. This is evidence that Russia's own identity is heavily influenced by the success or failure of its relationship with the Western world and that the relationship, for better or worse, is a core part of its political identity. Was this latest rejection of Europe, combined with the retreat into an authoritarian state dominated by secret agencies, an attempt to escape Russia's sense of 'unbearable … inferiority'[20] or what Tsygankov called its 'wounded pride'?[21]

WHERE DOES THE TRUTH LIE?

So, did the West 'lose' Russia? We will never have a counterfactual history, but ultimately the question is: if Western states had done more to keep Russia on board, could they have succeeded in keeping the peace in Europe? Although Western nations did make mistakes, sometimes significant ones, I question whether Russia's aims were ever realistic. Fundamentally, there was a painful disconnect between aspiration and reality following the collapse of the USSR. In the 1990s, Russia slipped from being one of two superpowers to being a temporarily impoverished country with a middling economy, which, apart from arms and oil, produced goods few wanted. It had become a state which, to paraphrase Pyotr Chaadayev, existed only as a cautionary tale for others. Yet it retained a quasi-imperial mindset and had neither come to terms with its totalitarian past nor felt the need to do so. It also had an extraordinarily influential secret police, a violent political culture intermingled with organised crime and thousands of nuclear weapons.

Russia was, frankly, too proud to engage on the same terms as its former satellites. In a prescient piece written in 2006, Dmitri Trenin articulated Russian frustrations. Russia, he said, was 'only willing to consider joining the West if it was given something like co-chairmanship of the Western club – or at the very least membership in its Politburo.'[22] Russian leaders baulked at following the same rules as the former Soviet republics. Russia wanted a great power powwow with the US, France, Britain and Germany; what it got was a seat between Romania and Slovakia in what it saw as a series of toothless international talking shops.

Western nations did try to find a role for Russia within the Western construct, but perhaps the partnerships on offer were neither strong enough nor deep enough nor flattering enough. Whilst former Warsaw Pact states were only too happy to once again become part of a pluralistic world free of Soviet control, this change was significantly more challenging for Russia itself. 'Despite all of the talk about Russia's integration into Western institutions, the project was stillborn from the beginning,' writes Trenin. 'It was just a matter of time before that reality became obvious to both sides.'[23] Former US ambassador to NATO Robert Hunter states that both the West and Russia gave up on finding a better role for Russia in the early years of this century. Hunter helped negotiate the NATO-Russia founding act, designed to give Russia a sense of place with, if not within, the NATO alliance. The treaty, he said, enabled Ukraine to benefit from Western co-operation but left its status open until an effort had been made to create a 'constructive' place for Russia within the European security system. In Hunter's words, 'The west, and then Mr Putin, lost interest in finding that place.'[24]

I don't doubt that there is some truth in these arguments, but the heart of the matter is this: when Russian governments talk of a new 'security framework' or gaining 'respect' from the West, what is implied is a recognised sphere of influence for Russia that allows the Kremlin free rein in former Soviet states. Putin and Yeltsin before him have both dressed that up in terms of promoting stability and the need to protect Russian citizens abroad – the same citizens whose rights Russia arguably does very little to protect inside its borders but seems exceptionally keen to defend when they are in neighbouring states – but the message is clear. Russia wanted control over its former Soviet neighbours and influence over eastern Europe too. That was clear from the mid-1990s, when Decree 940, issued on 14 September 1995, effectively rejected the full independence of most former Soviet states and gave the Russian state the right the interfere in those states – what it called the 'near abroad'.[25]

However, there is a painful reality for the Kremlin. As soon as countries have choice, they choose to leave Russia's sphere of influence. They want the wealth, freedom and security offered by the Western umbrella of the EU and NATO. Russia lacks an 'offer' built on attraction rather than coercion – one of the reasons why the country has redeveloped its tactics and tools of integrated warfare, so that it can force its neighbours to acquiesce to its demands. In Ukraine, Putin's real agenda went even further than his demands elsewhere. He did not accept the right of Ukraine and Ukrainians to exist separately from Russia. And whilst this reality has taken time to reveal itself fully, even in 2008 Putin told then President George W. Bush 'Ukraine is not a country'.[26] Russia's turn to authoritarianism and the invasions of Ukraine in 2014 and 2022 cannot simply be blamed on the breakdown of Russia's relationship with the collective West. They are a manifestation of a Russian imperialist mindset and Putin's refusal to accept Ukraine's independence. Putin's ultimate aim is and has been the absorption of both Ukraine and Belarus into an East Slavic union state.

What if the West had agreed to grant Russia, in an outbreak of Kissinger-like *realpolitik*, a sphere of influence? Would that have made a difference? I do not believe so, as such a decision would have been morally wrong and impractical.

First, the morality. I hear from time to time people saying 'let Putin have Ukraine', as if countries are 'ours' to give away and as if 40 million Ukrainians are unthinking pawns or have no opinion over the direction of their country. We do not have the right to trade away the rights of nations who wish to make their own choices about their futures. Nor do we have the power to do so. Second, the practical difficulty. To 'give' Russia free rein in former Soviet states would be a recipe for political chaos and violence because many in those states would be in near-permanent opposition to Russian influence and the corrupt politicians that the Kremlin would have installed. It would lead to instability and at best a series of frozen conflicts, along with repression and political arrests. A new, unstable iron curtain would run from Kaliningrad to Moldova along the border of the old Soviet Union.

Third, the facts do not stand up to Russian claims. With regards to NATO expansion, on 9 February 1990, US Secretary of State James A. Baker and then Soviet leader Mikhail Gorbachev agreed that NATO would not extend past the territory of East Germany. The agreement was made only in relation to Germany and was linked to German reunification. John Lough, from Britain's Royal

Institute for International Affairs, reports that as part of the final deal agreed between Gorbachev and then German leader Helmut Kohl, no NATO forces apart from Germany's could be permanently deployed in eastern Germany, with no deployment of nuclear weapons. 'Gorbachev neither asked for nor was given any formal guarantees that there would be no further expansion of NATO,' Lough states.[27]

At that point, the Soviet Union and the Warsaw Pact 'alliance' of Soviet satellite states of eastern Europe still existed. By 1995, neither the Warsaw Pact nor the Soviet Union existed. The situation had changed dramatically. Poland and other nations of eastern Europe were adapting from communism to market economics and were building functioning, law-governed democracies. As part of their progression, they wanted to join NATO and the EU. NATO, at various times in its history, had taken on new members. At the request of eastern European countries, NATO membership was discussed, leading to the first eastern Europe influx in 1999. Claims made since that support the Russian position owe more to ignorance or self-interest, such French President Macron's statement in Russia in 2018. He claimed that NATO had failed to comply with the 'obligations we had taken on, and this caused certain fears, quite reasonable ones'. He then pitched for Russia and France to lead a new European security 'architecture'.[28]

Not extending NATO would probably have sounded its death knell. It would also have made states more vulnerable to Russian aggression in the future. NATO and EU membership allowed those eastern European states to develop within a secure economic and defence framework. It helped make them prosperous, safe and free. Denying central and eastern Europe NATO membership to placate the Kremlin would have given Moscow a veto over those nations that it had only recently been repressing. Such a veto was unrealistic. It would also have broken the treaties that Moscow had signed – twice in the 1990s it committed to recognising the freedom of states to choose their own security, in the Charter of Paris in November 1990 and in the NATO-Russia Founding Act in 1997. Russia itself accepted NATO membership was spreading east.

There was a case for refusing the Baltic republics membership. This was more powerful, given that they had been part of the USSR, had been part of the old Russian Empire and had many ethnic Russians living there. However, unless Russia's development had been miraculously different, the one thing that has saved the Baltic states from ethnic bloodshed has been NATO membership. The leaders of those states do not doubt this. So, whilst Russia became angry, it was angry because it could no longer threaten to invade or actually invade the Baltic states without risk. NATO membership has, at least in the Baltic republics, probably prevented conflict. That does not mean that Russia may not try provocations there in future.

There was muted protest from Russia regarding both influxes of new members. Sir Malcolm Rifkind, the UK's Defence Secretary and later Foreign Secretary between 1992 to 1997, told me, 'There was no suggestion by Yeltsin that the expansion of NATO to Central and Eastern Europe would destroy the prospects for Western-Russian co-operation.' Regarding NATO enlargement, Rifkind added, 'on balance they [the Russians] would have preferred that it didn't happen. They were much more upset about the Baltic states, but they recognised that the Baltic states were different [because they'd been invaded by the Soviet Union when it was allied to Nazi Germany].'[29]

Was NATO an excuse for Russian anger when the real driver of the Ukraine crisis was the EU? NATO stopped expanding in the 2000s; the EU did not. The EU's eastern partnership idea came together in 2008. It was designed as a vehicle for closer trade with the former Soviet republics in Europe and the Caucasus. It was denounced by the Kremlin as an attempt to create a sphere of influence. However, given that Russian spokesmen often accuse others of the very things the Russian state is doing, the accusation hints at concerns that the Kremlin's own attempts to build a sphere of influence would be undermined by the EU's wealth and trade dominance. Whilst it is easy to criticise the high-handed arrogance of the EU's expansionist ideologues, the organisation was reacting to the demands of the governments in former Soviet republics for closer ties and an improved trading regime, especially given that most of these states were diversifying away from Russia and other Soviet states and towards richer European markets.

The Russians have some justification for complaint, though, for EU thoughtlessness may have given the Kremlin a false sense of assurance. In 2000, at the EU/Russia summit, both the EU and Russia prepared documents looking ahead to the next decade. The Russian document 'Russian Federation's Medium-term Strategy for developing relations with the European Union' specifically made reference to the need to respect Russia's special relationships with the former Soviet republics and not attempt to hinder the economic integration of the CIS. The EU welcomed the document seemingly without reading it, because when the Ukrainians complained about its content, both to the EU Commission as well as to representatives of nation states such as the UK, no one appeared to be aware of what had been accepted. So, when the EU launched its Eastern Partnership, the EU Commission had either forgotten what it had agreed with Russia, ignored it or no longer believed it to be relevant.

Kissinger's recommendation that the EU treaty should have been the subject of discussion with Moscow might therefore have had some relevance. But even if the EU had sought to discuss the issue with Russia, what would have happened? What rights did Russia have to veto treaties between other parties, especially given its commitment to recognise the choices made by other states? We also know that whilst it was bitterly objecting to Western interference, it was doing everything in its power to dominate Ukraine's government. Effectively, it was demanding the West not interfere with its own plans to interfere and that the West not engage, and certainly not peacefully compete, in Russia's backyard.

Regarding the role of colour revolutions, Trenin argued that both the US and Europe supported this kind of 'regime change' in Ukraine and Georgia – 'regime change' being the language used at the time in Moscow to mean taking those countries out of Russia's sphere of influence and into that of the US.[30] Mearsheimer also asserts that there was a battle for influence of Ukraine. He reported that the US National Endowment for Democracy (NED) funded sixty projects in the country between 1991 and 2013, spending some $6 billion. After Moscow's man Yanukovych won the 2010 election in Ukraine, the NED 'stepped up its efforts to support the opposition and strengthen the country's democratic institutions'.[31]

But again, what were the options? We knew that people and states wanted to move out of Russia's sphere of influence, even when, as in Ukraine's case, they regarded Russia and Russians in a broadly positive light. It *is* NED's role to fund democratic initiatives and democracy in Ukraine was important for the stability of Europe. It was clearly a corrupt country in need of more transparent and more accountable government. Even if NED and others had 'stood back' to allow Putin to impose a Russian model of government on Ukraine, do we really think that the Ukrainians would have passively accepted it, given that even the SBU spy agency refused to clamp down on the 2004 demonstrations against their own government? Whilst Ukraine's civil society *was* helped by Western states, the growth of civil society was a powerful development within Ukraine, not something imposed on it by a scheming West.

Furthermore, the 2003–4 Orange Revolution and the 2013–14 Revolution of Dignity would have happened anyway. Ukraine's revolutions were a genuine reaction to Russian 'palace coups'. Yes, in the 2013–14 street protests, a 'violent mob putsch', in the words of one English commentator, overthrew an elected leader.[32] That is true. It is also true to say that tens of thousands of Ukrainian protesters were in a desperate battle to save their country from being handed over to Russian control. The Russians complained not because they were defending democracy or the rule of law but because they thought they had successfully corrupted and bought the country, only for Yanukovych, despite being surrounded by Russian FSB Fifth Directorate advisers, to cut and run.

Additionally, there are other claims made by the Kremlin that weaken its case. First, there has been a tendency for it to portray Russia as the victim of the machinations of others, yet in the former Soviet republics the Kremlin has used a wide variety of tools to destabilise and undermine nascent governments. Second, Putin has presented the Cold War as a time of balance, if not harmony, thanks to the certainty of the bipolar world. It wasn't. It was a time of fear, of Soviet aggression in Western Europe and the brutal oppression of the nations of central Europe, as well as savage wars in the developing world. The bipolar world was a world in which half of Europe was in Russian chains. In 2005, Putin described the collapse of the USSR as the biggest geopolitical catastrophe of the century.[33] His 'catastrophe' was everyone else's liberation.

The Kremlin has whipped itself into a frenzy of near hysteria about NATO's expansion. Yet a series of measures were taken to assuage the Russians, including not deploying NATO forces in new member states, not placing missile defences on land and establishing the NATO-Russia Council. It was only after the 2014 invasion of eastern Ukraine that NATO developed a forward presence, with the creation of four multinational battalion-sized battlegroups in Estonia, Latvia, Lithuania and Poland, led by the UK, Canada, Germany and the US respectively. Following the invasion of Ukraine in February 2022, NATO added four more, in Bulgaria, Hungary, Romania and Slovakia. These amounted to eight battalions in total. By contrast, Russia had 110 battalion tactical groups – the approximate Russian equivalent – when it invaded Ukraine.[34] Even after 2022, the idea that NATO was threatening Russia has no basis in fact and existed only in the minds of Putin and his acolytes to justify the attack on the Ukrainian nation. Because of the extraordinary scale of that project, the lies told around it to buttress it are of a greater scale too.

Yes, there were Western mistakes. There was naivety in the 1990s. Mearsheimer's criticism that 'elites in the United States and Europe have been blindsided by events only because they subscribe to a flawed view of international politics' is, in my opinion, true, because liberal internationalists simply didn't credit any other worldview with any relevance or respect. Western policy-making too often became a narcissistic reflection of the 'moral superiority' of their governments. The partition of Serbia and the unravelling of the inviolate nature of borders was a significant strategic error. From 2007, we were clearly in denial about the direction of Putin's leadership and did too little either to defend ourselves against the coming storm or try to mitigate it. The states of the Western alliance urgently need to relearn the art of strategy. We underestimated the harm done to Russian society by totalitarian socialism. Whilst many Russians would have preferred a more open government, the Russia that evolved under Putin's leadership – in part, a reaction to the chaos of the 1990s – was one that was, for better or worse, rooted in the authoritarian culture of that society. It was a form of governance accepted, if not actively supported, by millions of Russians.

However, when Putin blames the West for his 'defensive' war in Ukraine, that is almost certainly a smokescreen for what he would have done sooner or later. He didn't act before 2022 because Russia did not have the capability to do so, hence the need for hybrid, integrated war. Anything that supported Ukrainian independence or deepened Ukraine's relationship with NATO or the EU would have been opposed, not because it threatened Russia but because it threatened Putin's ultimate aim of an East Slavic union state, uniting Ukraine, Belarus and Russia. In an era of human rights, Russian realism demanded the right to dominate others. Fundamentally, Russia wanted to keep the West out of its sphere of influence until it had the power to dominate it once more. It could either do that with Western connivance or by making the West an enemy again. It chose the latter.

Again, there is some truth when Mearsheimer says that 'it is the Russians, not the West, who ultimately get to decide what counts as a threat to them'.[35] But if the reaction is disingenuous, unrealistic and hysterical, the voice becomes negated. If you have an agenda to subvert the independence of a country that you accuse others of subverting, it is difficult to carry the lie with any credibility over time.

Even if the West had not supported Ukraine in any way, Ukrainians would not have agreed to be 'handed over' to Russia as if they were nothing more than geopolitical chattel. Many would always have fought. The surprise for the West in 2022 was how many and with what level of determination.

Fundamentally, Russia's 'realism', both about itself and Ukraine, was never realistic.

CHAPTER 16

WHAT IS TO BE DONE?

'It's terrible to lie in chains,
To rot in dungeon deep,
But it's still worse, when you are free
To sleep, and sleep, and sleep.'

EXTRACT FROM TARAS SHEVCHENKO,
'THE DAYS GO BY', 1845

One serving female soldier I talked with compared the global response to the Russian invasion of her country to a frightening experience in her youth. Whilst she was a student, a man sexually assaulted her. He pinned her to the glass double doors of her student hostel and tried to rape her. This was in a public place. The hostel porter saw what was happening and walked towards the door, but instead of helping or even just opening the door, the concierge took out the key, locked it and walked away.

'There was a feeling of helplessness. You are being raped and no one is helping, just observing to see whether you survive or not,' the soldier – who, for obvious reasons, did not wish to be named – told me. She fended the attacker off herself.

This is how many in Ukraine feel three years after an invasion in which conventional wisdom didn't expect them to last three days.

Yet they fight on. Western support has been extensive at times but also sporadic, designed more so that Ukraine doesn't lose rather than for it to win. One soldier, despairing but not wanting to seem ungrateful, observed, 'Each time we fight as a last stand and they give us just enough so we do not die.'

So, what is to be done? At the time of this book going to print, it is unclear whether I am writing about an ongoing conflict, a conflict that is about to end or one experiencing a temporary pause. It may be that Vladimir Putin changes to focus once again on primarily non-military tools as he did from 2005 to 2013. Either way, the points here remain valid.

UKRAINE

Ukraine will be at peace, as best it can whilst living next door to Putin's Russia, when it can defend not only its borders but also its society against Russia's new way of war. Its struggle is both external and internal: external against the threat from Russian armies, internal against the insidious threats from non-military tools of warfare.

On the battlefield, Ukraine is developing its own way of war. Its 'centre of gravity' is in problem-solving creativity using machines to counter Russia's manpower and equipment advantage. It uses technology to offset mass. 'The strength of the Ukrainians is in innovation. Give them sticks and sh*t and they will come up with a drone or whatever,' one special forces soldier told me. 'Most of the battlefield innovations that you see generally come from the Ukrainians, which the Russians then copy.' Many of Ukraine's units are evolving to mix Western standards with Ukrainian inventiveness – Khartiia's robots and Achilles's drones are proof of that. It goes without saying that the levels of courage of Ukraine's soldiers have been humbling to see. Their Herculean task has been beyond anything faced by the West since the Second World War.

However, as a way of war, countering Russian armies is not enough. When the 'traditional' element of military war ends, through exhaustion or ceasefire, Putin will prioritise the non-military forms of conflict – political warfare, active measures, subversion, call it what you will – which he has used against Ukraine since 2005 and which he is currently aggressively using against Georgia and Moldova. Ukraine needs to win both the *voina* (war) and the *bor'ba* (struggle) to survive in any meaningful form.

Ukrainians, therefore, need a vision for their future. They know that they are on a journey, although most do not know the destination. People have declining faith that corruption is being fought successfully. This affects their willingness to serve their country. Zelensky gave the nation its roar, to paraphrase Winston Churchill, but he needs to show how Ukraine will no longer be susceptible to those insidious vulnerabilities of which Russia has taken advantage. It was Ukraine's voluntary society that saved it, not the political state. That political state needs to tackle corruption and organised crime. Meeting basic Western standards in judicial independence, tax collection or transparency is not a case of jumping through the hoops that others demand but part of an integrated defence. A corruptible state is, as the Kremlin has repeatedly shown, a vulnerable state. A successful Ukrainian way of war therefore needs to counter subversive, political warfare as well as the direct military threat.

Ukraine will not be offered NATO membership in the near future, not least because the US conceded this to Putin before peace talks even began. Ukrainians believe NATO membership will make

Ukraine safe. It will not; nor would EU membership. Both will incite Putin further and put Ukraine in greater danger. It is dishonest for politicians from NATO or EU states to hold out the hope of NATO membership whilst there is a war on its territory. It is highly unlikely that pro-Russia Hungary or Slovakia or other NATO nations nervous about the war would vote to support Ukraine's entry. EU membership, if it ever comes, may also be years away. We should remember it was the EU treaty of 2013 that sparked the original 2014 invasion.

The answer to Ukraine's physical defence lies not in treaties that won't be honoured but in the hard grind to transform the country's army and society to repel future Russian attacks. Ukraine should, however, have membership of NATO in everything but name, as well as NATO advisers, support and guarantees concerning arms supply and support in the areas of comms, satellites, intelligence etc.

Work in Ukraine includes the continued development of layered physical defence, such as deep trenches of the kind that the country lacked but Russia built from late 2022 onwards, and a mobile and layered air defence that covers the major cities and industries as well as front lines. Those front lines could, by 2030, be largely manned by land and air drones. Ukraine's defence will have to be flexible, diffused and able to withstand surprise attack, with supply lines in neighbouring NATO countries, out of range of Russian missiles. Its military culture will have to be relatively 'flat' (non-hierarchical, with power of action delegated as low as possible), which it already is in many of the better units, so that small teams and junior commanders can fight quickly with initiative if military comms are destroyed, as they did in the defence of Kyiv. Like Lithuania, its citizens must be constitutionally free to fight as soon as Russian troops cross the border, in case the Kyiv government is compromised (as

Lithuania's was during the 1940 Soviet invasion and Ukraine's was in 2013). Like Israel's army, Ukraine's will need to continue to be heavily integrated into society, thus creating a militarised democracy – not an easy thing to achieve – with a sizeable core professional army and a large reserve that is regularly trained. This is a return to the military culture of the Cossacks of the Zaporizhzhian Sich before Muscovite domination, with a section of the population permanently on guard over the people. Service should be seen as part of the responsibilities of adulthood. Putin will always be asking, 'How much do you want your independence?' The answer must be clear. Successful deterrence deters. Weak deterrence doesn't. The West could do with relearning that lesson too.

What of the Russian language? Many Ukrainians now refuse to speak Russian out of moral choice. Some believe that not speaking Russian, almost forgetting the language, prevents Putin's regime from 'getting into their brains,' as one Ukrainian friend told me. Given the weaponisation of language, religion and culture, this argument is understandable. It is also wrong. It alienates a minority who are loyal Ukrainian patriots but happen not to speak Ukrainian well. I have been told of Russian-speaking soldiers injured fighting for Ukraine who have been given such a hard time by (non-fighting) Ukrainians over their use of language that they have quit the army in disgust. Russian-speaking Ukrainians should not have their patriotism questioned due to their language choice, especially when they are fighting for those who are not.

Rather than see the Russian language as Ukraine's Achilles heel, better to see it as its secret weapon: not Putin's way into the Ukrainian soul but Ukraine's way into the Russian mind. To suggest this is painful for Ukrainians and frankly unpopular. Because of this war, Ukrainians not only hate the Russian regime but now, in large part, hate Russians too. They see Russians as Putin's willing executioners of Ukrainians. They view Russians in the same way as Britons, Americans and others, twice in the last century, viewed Germans during and immediately after the two world wars. But nations and people move on. The Russian regime is the enemy, not its language. Ukrainians should weaponise the Russian language against the Russian regime. The strongest cultural weapon Ukrainians have is that they speak Russian and Russians do not speak Ukrainian. Ukraine should establish a Russian-language station aimed not only at those in the east and south, especially the elderly who still speak Russian, but also to beam and broadcast at Russians themselves. Ukraine should work with the BBC World Service to help set up such a channel. One day, Ukraine and Russia will have to move on from this vile war. A major Russian-language channel, aimed at Russians, will slowly help Ukraine to win the war and eventually help to win the peace that will follow. It will be Ukraine's first defence in future wars. Ukraine cannot bring down Putinism with its arms, but it could do with its broadcasts.

RUSSIA AND THE WEST

Taking the long view of this conflict, Russia will not be at peace with Ukraine, the West or itself whilst Putin and the Slavophiles rule. Putin has made clear he is in long-term conflict with the West, regardless of any temporary thawing under Trump. Whilst the Russian dictator himself is a vital factor in this, it is not just about one man. It's about the culture that produced him: the all-powerful, criminalised secret state, the mindset of the *siloviki* security elite and a historical outlook of aggressive, xenophobic Slavophilia that seeks enemies within and without, that celebrates prejudice and authoritarianism over the rule of law and which glorifies blind obedience over questioning intelligence.

Combined with this is a security culture that exaggerates threat and seeks defence of its borders not through an ordered world but through intimidating others, as happened during the Cold War. An extreme, Slavophile Russia is one that feels secure only when others do not. It is neither a recipe for a stable Europe and a stable world, nor a recipe for a stable Russia. Russia will make peace with itself, Ukraine and the West only when Westernisers and Slavophiles in Russia find common ground with each other and when Russia again sees itself as part of the West. It will be at peace when it ceases to be an empire and learns to live within its borders as a (very large) multi-ethnic nation.

Putin has set Russia back at least a decade, maybe half a century, just as the Bolsheviks set the Russian Empire back decades by leading it down the path of totalitarian socialism. Since 1917, Russia has been a political disaster, both for itself and for those around it. We are still living with the consequences. Western nations need to start working now with those Russians they can work with to develop a better alternative to Putin's xenophobic nationalism, even if this is a thankless task for many years. At some point, Russia will turn, albeit reluctantly and resentfully, back to the West.

Until there is change, which may take years or decades, we need to accept that we are in a new 'cold' conflict (or whatever one's favoured term is). This cold conflict is less stable than the previous ones and it is more dangerous for that reason. It began in 2007, when Putin broke with the West. I do not know if Western policy could have deterred Putin's invasion of Ukraine, but relentless Western weakness across the years emboldened Putin and probably persuaded him that the West would not support Ukraine. Ukraine's own internal divisions and disbelief at the true danger it faced didn't help either.

In the meantime, we should be mindful of Russia's nuclear arsenal but not intimidated by it. Appeasing nuclear blackmailers makes the world more dangerous and nuclear war more likely. If Iran, North Korea and China see Russian threats working, they will do the same. Our future will be abandoned to tyrants who threaten us with destruction. It will be the end of the West, the cold dawn of a more dangerous and unstable world of nuclear threat and counter-threat. In that case, more nations will rush to develop nuclear weapons and nuclear conflict somewhere will likely only be a matter of time.

UKRAINE'S ALLIES

As long as Ukraine is in military conflict with Russia, NATO states must increase their rate of weapons flow, either by direct supply or by investment in the Ukrainian arms industry – and probably both. The more Ukraine holds back the Russian tide on the battlefield and even reverses it, the stronger its position will be in negotiations – the more it will be able to force Putin to negotiate and the less it will have to concede. The weaker it is, the more Putin will fight and intimidate, the less likely he will be to talk. Trump's temporary halt on supplies and intelligence sharing in March 2025 only weakened Ukraine and emboldened Putin. It will not help a lasting settlement and will make any such settlement more difficult to reach.

NATO must also understand how Russia will negotiate in both current and future peace talks. The Kremlin does not see negotiation as part of a peace process where people find common ground but as part of the process of conflict.

Putin's attempted manipulation of President Donald Trump has three aims. First, to use the US leader to force Ukraine to make concessions Russia cannot win by force on the battlefield. Second, as a by-product, to weaken Ukraine's internal cohesion so that it becomes more difficult for that society to resist Russian aggression, physical, virtual or psychological. Third, to divide the West and weaken the alliance between the US and European nations.

Former Democrat-appointed US ambassador to Moscow Michael McFaul argues that Putin couldn't care less about Trump: 'He is just using him to control Ukraine, divide NATO, and weaken America.'[1]

Prior to the start of the talks, the US administration gave the Kremlin a number of major concessions, in addition to ruling out NATO membership for Ukraine. Trump's Attorney General, Pam Bondi, ordered the shutting of the FBI's Foreign Influence Task Force, designed to counter illicit influence in US politics, especially Russian. She also shut down the task force KleptoCapture, a group set up to 'strain the finances of wealthy associates of Russian President Vladimir Putin and punish those facilitating sanctions and export control violations'.[2] USAID projects were also shut, including those helping to support Ukraine's energy systems after repeated Russian strikes.[3]

Soon after and in short order, then Defense Secretary and former Fox TV host Pete Hegseth halted US cyber operations against Russia. The US also withdrew from an international group investigating leaders responsible for the invasion of Ukraine.[4] Putin's spokesman Dmitry Peskov said of the change in policy that the 'fragmentation of the collective west has begun'.[5]

Yet despite these concessions and the damaging White House meeting between Trump and Zelensky in February 2025 that appeared to harbinger a breakdown of support, as of May 2025, it appears that Putin may have overplayed his hand. Since February, Zelensky's Ukraine has regained the diplomatic initiative. Putin, by stringing out negotiations and – thus far – refusing meaningful ceasefires, has shown himself unwilling to stop the war.

Putin is not interested in negotiating a peaceful settlement. His regime does not want to live in harmony with Ukraine; it wants to destroy it. It invaded Ukraine to achieve just that aim. Russia had the offer of a militarily neutral Ukraine for years to come during negotiations in 2022 and refused it. Arguably, Putin cannot agree to peace without the destruction of Ukraine because in doing so, he will endanger his position. The longer this war continues, the more difficult it becomes for a regime that has escalated to war to return to any sort of peace. An economic and political reckoning is due at some point and therefore, as long as Putin can afford it, fighting may be better than talking. To reverse Churchill's maxim, to 'war-war' may be better than to 'jaw-jaw'.

What Ukraine must do is clear: continue to fight up to the point of any ceasefire. During the negotiations, it must continue to assume further conflict will take place and plan for a resumption of the war, in whatever guise it comes. Further, Ukraine and the West should assume that any cessation of hostilities is because the Kremlin has decided to pocket its territorial 'winnings' whilst it works out how to make further progress through political or military conflict. Negotiations are not an end to this war for the Kremlin, just a pause to switch to different tactics and tools. It may use provocations to make Kyiv look as if it is breaking the ceasefire or it may actually return to war to win further territory (as it did in Abkhazia in Georgia in the 1990s). As one Ukrainian soldier told me, 'We have already have the experience of "negotiations" with Russians at Ilovais'k and Debal'tseve,' referring to broken ceasefires in these cities in 2014, which led to the deaths of hundreds of Ukrainian soldiers.

There is significant danger for Ukraine in a bad peace. This will be understood by Russia, but it may not be understood by Ukraine's Western allies. Giving up territory to Russia permanently will put Ukraine's leadership under severe pressure and may break the cohesion of Ukrainian society. Many soldiers have told me that freezing boundaries is one thing, but giving up land permanently without the offer of NATO or EU membership is a step too far. They will ask, 'What have we fought for? What have our comrades given their lives for?' Such an outcome could spark civil conflict within Ukraine. This will be what Putin wants. At its worst, tens of thousands could leave the front lines and turn on their own government. Western governments could destroy the country they claim to want to protect. Putin will only agree a ceasefire if he has to or if he believes that course of action will help him achieve his goals. Neither does Putin want peace with the West. His regime, as Lilia Shevtsova argues, is dependent on the creation of enemies. He is arming for more conflict, not less.[6]

In relation to Ukraine's defence economy, Western firms need to increase their partnerships to develop Ukraine's own defence base. That way, Ukraine can more easily afford to defend itself whilst reducing dependency on the West. Additionally, Western money can go further, especially if it comes from interest on frozen Russian assets. Even parts of the US military-industrial base have been struggling to keep pace with the scale of the war and the speed of change. Ukraine's defence economy needs to be self-sustaining and preferably integrated into the Western defence complex. This will be in the Western interest too. Ukraine's drone and missile technology experience will also be highly valuable for NATO states.

Western support is not only important in itself; it has a direct effect on Ukrainians. Polls shows that Western support is a motivating factor in Ukrainians' willingness to fight.[7] First, when they see they are being supported by the West with weapons, it gives them greater confidence and a higher willingness to serve. Second, the more NATO-standard training a unit has had, the more popular a unit is and the more Ukrainians wish to serve in it.

On the operational and tactical level, the Ukrainian armed forces still need to develop junior tactical leaders for the army, corporals and sergeants. 'Everyone gets excited about drones and no one thinks about the infantry,' one military adviser told me. Ukraine needs to develop what the British Army calls Junior Brecon, the infantry-section command course, to give Ukraine's tactical leaders, corporals and sergeants, as well as junior officers, the skills they need to make battlefield decisions. In addition, Western training regimes need to be improved. Five weeks of basic training is not long enough – although this is at Ukraine's request – and training must incorporate Ukraine's battlefield learning over the past three years. Much of the training has been done without battlefield drones, the single most defining element of the current war. As one soldier told me, commenting on NATO courses, 'They are taught, "There are drones." That's fine, but hell, you need to train day and night how to take cover from them!'

WESTERN RESPONSES TO RUSSIA'S NEW TOTAL WAR

Ukraine is, as we have seen, the main target for Russian total war. However, the Kremlin also considers itself to be in conflict with the West. NATO military training regimes need to incorporate the lessons of the Ukrainian war with extreme urgency. Militaries are notoriously slow to learn, hence the saying that they are always fighting the last war. It is vital we do so if we are to deter Russia and avoid other conflicts in eastern Europe, most dangerously in the Baltic republics.

The purpose of this book is not to declare whether Russia's new total war is effective or not but to understand it. In some ways, it can be seen to be highly flexible and tactically brilliant in its attempt to integrate power. And if Russia did get Trump into the White House in 2016, this will be seen as the greatest espionage achievement in history. At the least, it very likely destroyed Hillary Clinton's campaign. One can equally make a case that Putin's new total war has been a strategic disaster for Russia and will eventually endanger the integrity of the state. Regardless of whether the war is successful or not, however, it is designed to confront NATO and the EU. It is designed to defeat us. It is also a template for how authoritarian states will attack democracies. So, we need to study it, understand it and work out how to counter it. Being dismissive of it achieves nothing but threatens our future.

UK defence intelligence claimed in 2023 that it will 'likely take five to ten years for Russia to rebuild a cohort of highly trained and experienced military units'.[8] This is nonsense. The Russian Army that started the war will not be the Russian Army that finishes it. At the end of this war, the army that Russia retains will be a generation ahead of any NATO force in the use of infantry drones and tactical electronic warfare. It will have equipped itself with those drones in the quantity and quality able to overwhelm any NATO adversary. It will have an army of brutalised, war-tested men and a huge amount of kit. Its electronic warfare capabilities may be able to disrupt Western missile systems. As Polish experts Agnieszka Bryc and Maria Domańska have written, if Putin and his advisers conclude that NATO Article 5, the pledge of joint defence against Russian aggressions, is losing credibility, 'they will be strongly tempted to conduct a limited military operation on NATO's Eastern Flank despite Russia's relative conventional weakness'.[9]

What might that look like? Russian GRU military intelligence might stage provocations in the Baltic republics, of the kind in which it is highly skilled. Such events might begin with political protests, violence and perhaps the use of drones launched by an 'unknown' paramilitary, political or terror group against Baltic NATO service personnel. After days of chaos, Putin may claim that Nazis in the Baltics were oppressing Russians. Russian special forces, dressed up as local volunteer paramilitaries, might take a foothold in one or more ethnic Russian areas in the Baltic states, especially Latvia or Estonia. Putin will present NATO with some kind of ultimatum: either award special status to ethnic Russians in the Baltics or he will incorporate the territory into Russia. Move against those volunteer paramilitaries and risk direct confrontation and potentially nuclear war. Given we have already let Putin shape our reaction through his nuclear threats, such an ultimatum would split NATO. Hungary, Greece and possibly Spain, Portugal and Germany might baulk immediately. As soon as NATO states seek negotiation, Putin's integrated war will have succeeded in its final purpose – breaking NATO's credibility and with it, the military unity and supremacy of the West. Let's remember the Russian dictator's aims: destroy Ukraine, remake Russia and break NATO and the West.

To avoid this, it is not only Western kit that needs updating but military practice too. The Western model of using drones as an expensive replacement for jets and fighter bombers is, at least in part, history. Drones are now flying grenades, hovering above the infantry. As one Ukrainian military adviser bluntly told me, 'Thanks to drones and technology, Western doctrine is outdated.' The ubiquity of drones and the response to them, such as physical or electronic protection, has changed war. Within two years, every squad, if not every soldier, will have their own drone. Within five years, the infantry soldier's primary weapon may not be their personal weapon but half a dozen lightweight 'cannister' FPV drones, which will be carried by every soldier in their day sack and when launched will be linked by machine learning. Ground drones will be incorporated too. Both will stream feeds into a soldier's ballistic eye wear, which will be linked to higher-level headquarters. Drones will develop tactical reconnaissance, help defend infantry positions and develop targets. They will support patrolling and, linked with larger drones held at company and battalion level, may be the primary weapon in any contact with the enemy. The human presence on the battlefield will be reduced but made much more powerful. These are just some of the areas in which technology has been racing forward and will continue to do so, aided by AI. As William Burns and Richard Moore, heads of the CIA and MI6 respectively, said in a joint article:

> Ukraine has been the first war of its kind to combine open-source software with cutting-edge battlefield technology, harnessing commercial and military satellite imagery, drone technology, high and low sophistication cyber warfare, social media, open-source intelligence, uncrewed aerial and seaborne vehicles and information operations – as well as human and signals intelligence – at such incredible pace and scale. Most of all, it has underlined the imperative to adapt, experiment and innovate.[10]

This is likely to leave the Western arms industry with a profound problem. Drones are now produced in Ukraine for less than the price of a NATO-specification 155 artillery shell at around $1,500 to $2,500, compared with a shell at $3–5,000 per item (plus the gun to fire it). The immediate future is a battlefield saturated with expendable drones. Given how much more expensive drones are in the West than for Ukraine or Russia, the Western defence industry model is going to struggle to be economically viable. Can Western nations afford expendable drones for $60,000 per item – their current price – when their enemies will produce them for many times less? And armies without enough drones and protection against them will be the mobile equivalents of the infamous Maginot Line, which failed to protect France in the 1930s.

There are a myriad of other issues. Safe rear areas in operational theatres are probably a thing of the past, unless accompanied by powerful physical and electronic defences. Without assured protection, military headquarters will need to be spread out or placed out of theatre, which will put pressure on communications and the credibility of a military command that is distant from its soldiers. For naval forces, the proliferation of naval drones is a profound threat. Ukraine, a state without a navy as such, chased Russia's fifty-ship fleet to the far side of the Black Sea. A few dozen Ukrainian speedboats painted grey and packed with explosives, navigational services and electronics triumphed over a superficially formidable navy. In the process, they reopened the Black Sea and enabled over 3,300 cargo ships to sail out of Odesa from August 2023 onwards, down the western edge of the Black Sea, amounting to £20 billion worth of exports, including over 30 million tonnes of grain exports.[11] That is an extraordinarily efficient use of resources for a very significant effect. This conflict is changing not only the nature of modern war but the economics of it too.

None of this precludes the continued importance of courage and integrity in soldiers. As Burns and Moore rightly point out, technology has been deployed 'alongside [the] extraordinary bravery' of the Ukrainian soldier.[12]

PROTECTING AGAINST NON-MILITARY CONFLICT

If finding a political consensus to defend against traditional military threats is difficult, to do so against forms of war that many do not consider part of traditional conflict is more difficult still. How do Western nations fight non-military conflict such as cyber hacking, physical sabotage and relentless disinformation?

First, and most importantly, the free world of Western nations needs to rethink definitions of warfare to better protect their populations. The binary definition of war and peace, never very useful, is finished. We are in a period of protracted geopolitical competition and conflict. Our adversaries seek to divide, demoralise and defeat us using forms of non-traditional conflict in their own right or as a shaping precursor to violence. Without the spur of physical conflict, however, we are failing to accept the reality of non-military tactics – look, for example, at German dependence on Russian gas even after 2014 or current Western supply-chain dependency on China. A common definition of non-military conflict and with it a common understanding of how power is used against free states is needed. This definition needs to include energy and economics, as Russia (and China) include both in their core integrated conflict strategies.

These states are also looking at new concepts of conflict and warfare that are beyond Western thinking. Russia's military thinkers continue to study this and the weapons they believe will be necessary. Before he died, General Slipchenko wrote that in this era, the targets may not be human beings but the systems that support an adversary's society or at least enable its functioning.[13] The tools of this era of conflict may be energy fields, climate control, biological modifications, quantum computers and nanotechnology. This thinking around 'indirect' warfare, based on destroying the basis of modern life, explains the close interest that Russia (and China) have in undersea pipelines and cables and in cyberattacks, the outcomes of which may not be truly apparent for years. How much malware has been placed on Western systems, ready for a cyber-Pearl Harbor? This form of warfare may render a society unable to defend itself, even if it wanted to. We are reacting to it slowly and hesitantly and in some senses even going backwards. As of spring 2025, the US had shut down offensive cyber operations against Russia.[14]

In the past decade, the UK has developed a cross-government approach towards Russia. However, modern governments, due to their size, still have a tendency to over-silo and at worst, to produce policies that are contradictory. EU states develop sanctions against Russia, which EU firms then flagrantly violate by routing exports via third countries such as Kyrgyzstan, Kazakhstan and Armenia. Countering integrated whole-state conflict should be the responsibility of political, intellectual and military leadership, but this is difficult in the West, due not only to the unpopularity of politicians as a class but also to the inexperience of modern politicians in grasping integrated conflict. Meanwhile, Russian information operations continue to have an effect in Europe and the US. Republican Michael McCaul, head of the US House Foreign Affairs Committee, has said that Russian propaganda had 'infected a good chunk of my party's base'.[15] The same process is happening in continental Europe, with multiple reports warning of the effects of Russian disinformation campaigns and the targeting of politicians across the EU and in the UK too.[16] Hungary and Slovakia have both elected pro-Russian leaders.

What else can we do? I would suggest these measures.

First, the UK needs to establish a National *Strategy* Council. The UK, along with the wider Western family of nations, needs a long-term strategy to deal with Russia and other authoritarian powers, as we did during the Cold War with the USSR and the Warsaw Pact alliance. Our policies are short-termist and reactive. Democracies are different from authoritarian states: we cannot, we should not, use power in the same way. Russia and other authoritarian states do not have foreign policies that Britain, the US or others should admire or copy, but we should understand that when power is (ethically) integrated behind a clearly defined strategy, it goes further and achieves more. British and indeed Western power is too often less than the sum of its parts because global engagement has come to be divided between so many competing departments, and those strategies do not cohere with domestic policy as a single view of a problem. In the winter of 2024, the UK government accepted that the world was becoming more dangerous whilst at the same time trying to relinquish British sovereign territory in the Indian Ocean due to the Foreign Office's 'decolonisation' agenda. This is an example of incoherent thinking.

Second, the UK should beef up the BBC World Service to become the global champion against authoritarian propaganda and disinformation. We need to prioritise the defence of our democracies. Despite the service being the single most powerful tool of broadcast soft power in the media world, it has been the subject of endless government cuts due to money-saving.

Third, Western nations must be far more mindful of energy and trade dependency. Western governments should publish annual statements on this topic. Our adversaries will encourage dependency on their energy and economic supply chains, as Russia did and as China is doing. To overcome this, we need first to understand the problem. Therefore, each NATO nation, starting with the US, UK and Germany, should produce an annual statement of trade dependency on authoritarian states, in the hope that it will spark a debate on how to reduce that dependency.

Fourth, we need regular public updates from a collective of Western intelligence agencies to show how non-military tools of warfare are being used against democracies. These need to come from credible agencies – the CIA, MI5 and MI6 and the French, German and other EU equivalents, especially including the Baltic states, where subversion will be particularly aimed. Estonia already produces such an annual report.

There is a final additional ingredient, one which is difficult to deliver. Westerners need once again to have faith in our values. The weaker we are, the more sidetracked by internal battles, the less our focus will be on defending our values and our future. The more we disappear down the rabbit holes of internal debate, the weaker and less able our societies will be to resist the physical and cognitive threat presented by authoritarian states intent on fuelling and feeding division. Western democracies are the best hope for the future of humanity. But we need to relearn our love for that which made us great.

The twenty-first century will witness a battle for the future of humanity between open and closed societies and the visions of humanity that they represent. Ukraine is, for now, the front line in that coming global battle. The US and its allies still represent the path of freedom. Putin's Russia and its allies, be they the mullahs of Tehran or the communists of Beijing, represent an axis of authoritarianism. For the West to survive, it must arm itself, psychologically and physically, to win.

EPILOGUE: WILL PUTIN USE NUCLEAR WEAPONS?

'The Russians still plan and practice for surviving and conducting tactical nuclear battle.'

– Lester W. Grau and Charles K. Bartles[1]

I spent the evening of 21 November 2024 with air defence teams north of Kyiv. We were expecting a busy night shooting down Shahed drones aiming for Kyiv. It was quiet, eerily quiet the soldiers told me. Later on, we found out why. The day before, the US had allowed US and UK missiles to be fired into Russian territory. In response, Putin had chosen to launch a hypersonic ballistic missile into Dnipro city in southern Ukraine. This time, it didn't have a nuclear warhead to obliterate the city and the 900,000 souls who live there, but the message was clear: I can be the destroyer of cities.

It was not the first time Putin had threatened nuclear war and it was unlikely to be the last. On the February day of his fateful invasion of Ukraine in 2022, he addressed the Russian people. Looking directly into the screen and with an air of visceral menace, he forewarned Western nations with an implicit threat to destroy them using nuclear weapons should they attempt to intervene:

> No matter who tries to stand in our way or all the more so create threats for our country and our people, they must know that Russia will respond immediately and the consequences will be such as you have never seen in your entire history. No matter how the events unfold, we are ready ... I hope that my words will be heard.[2]

Were Putin's words empty threats designed to deter Western intervention or was his warning real? Nuclear use is an issue wrapped in uncertainty, ambiguity and fear. Russia may have come close to using these weapons once already, in the autumn and winter of 2022 when Russian positions were collapsing around Kharkiv and Kherson. US intelligence suggested Moscow might have been planning to do so. If Ukraine had broken Russian lines, especially if it had pushed to Crimea, the CIA estimated that the chance of Putin ordering the use of tactical nuclear weapons might rise to 50 per cent or more.[3]

At the same time, Russia began information-shaping operations. Then Russian Defence Minister Sergei Shoigu warned his opposite numbers in the US, UK, France and Turkey that Ukraine could use a 'dirty' bomb – a cheap nuclear device able to spread radiation over a wide area, which would kill through radiation poisoning as much as blast. This may have been a psychological ploy – a form of reflexive control – to unnerve Western governments into thinking that Russia *was* considering doing just that. The true aim of such an operation would be for the UK, US and France to press Ukraine not to undertake further offensive operations, thus giving Russian forces space to regroup. In the end, the crisis passed.

We will never know for sure if Putin will use nuclear weapons until such a time as he does, but what is clear is that the threat to do so is a significant element in Russian psychological warfare and pugnacious propaganda. Western fear of escalation has made Western support to Ukraine more hesitant and has slowed reaction times due to a sense of caution over the Russian threat. Nuclear blackmail works.

• • •

Nuclear weapons are not separate from Russian integrated warfare but part of Russia's theory of strategic deterrence, which encapsulates nuclear, conventional and non-military force. Russia's nuclear arsenal is the largest in the world and has recently been modernised. As of early 2024, the Russian arsenal has roughly 5,580 warheads (others report 5,977) with 1,112 in storage.[4] The US, by contrast, has just over 5,000 warheads, of which 1,336 are awaiting dismantlement.[5] Britain and France have a much smaller number of warheads.

Of more immediate relevance to the Ukraine War are the 1,500 smaller-yield, tactical nuclear weapons – battlefield nuclear weapons. The Bulletin of Atomic Scientists says these are more difficult to assess due to the dual-use nature of the delivery systems – that is, they can fire both conventional and nuclear weapons. In addition,

> many of Russia's non-strategic nuclear weapons are several decades old, and there is a high degree of uncertainty regarding how many of these weapons remain active, are slated for retirement, and will be replaced with newer versions. The picture is further complicated by the sheer number of non-strategic warheads that Russia is estimated to possess.[6]

For a declining power such as Russia, its nuclear arsenal provides a comfort blanket of global status whilst other elements of its military forces decline, especially relative to other major states. Russia's military doctrine states that nuclear weapons are an 'important factor in preventing the outbreak of nuclear war and major conventional wars'.[7] Outside doctrine, there has long been a dangerous fetishising of ideas linking the Russian Orthodox religion with the possession of nuclear weapons to protect Russian statehood. This narrative sees Russia's nuclear arsenal and Russian Orthodoxy as the 'sword and shield' – the so-called 'atomic orthodoxy'– against the Antichrist, which the same ideologues suggest is the US and NATO.[8] The sword and the shield are coincidentally also the symbols of Putin's old KGB and now the FSB. At a press conference in 2007, Putin was asked about the future of Orthodoxy as well as Russia's nuclear strategy by a journalist from Sarov, the city near where Russia's first nuclear weapon was tested. He replied that both Russian Orthodoxy and nuclear weapons create the conditions for internal and external security of the country.[9] Whilst these apocalyptic notions may sound ludicrous, it is a view accepted by many in the armed forces and secret services.[10]

Nuclear weapon use, however, depends not only on doctrine but also on how that doctrine is interpreted by individuals whose state of mind is unknown. The 2014 military doctrine gives two grounds for employing nuclear weapons: in response to their use by others or when the existence of the Russian Federation is threatened. The 2020 document 'State Principles in the Sphere of Nuclear Deterrence' repeats these and gives two additional grounds for strategic nuclear weapon use. First, if Russia is facing an imminent nuclear attack. Second, if the country's armed forces are about to lose control of their nuclear arsenal by, for example, multiple conventional precision strikes on Russian nuclear and command and control facilities or perhaps even a successful cyberattack. This stems from Russia's 'persistent fear' that the US (or China) will succeed in neutralising the country's nuclear arsenal.[11]

Both these innovations are dangerous in themselves and under circumstances of global tension, might spark accidental use. First, hypersonic missiles mean reaction times are now shorter than ever, so the potential for error under pressure is greater. Second, Russia's nuclear warning systems now appear, according to a 2003 study, to be semi-automated, with junior decision-makers removed. On at least one occasion in previous decades, a decision-maker in that chain of command has helped to avert the launch of nuclear missiles. In 1983, Stanislav Petrov failed to report a potential US missile attack, which turned out to be a system malfunction. Separately, naval officer Vasily Akhipov refused to use nuclear torpedoes during the 1962 Cuban Missile Crisis after the captain of his submarine believed that a new world war had already started. In both cases, the initiative, judgement and moral courage of the officers was criticised by Moscow and damaged their careers.

In October 2024, Putin made further updates to the use of nuclear weapons. Of a series of changes, the most important was that attacks by non-nuclear states (read Ukraine) backed by nuclear powers (read the US, the UK or France) will be considered by Russia to be a joint attack. Belarus was also included under the Russian nuclear umbrella if attack by conventional weapons jeopardises that state.

These changes, which are under review, were introduced in a decree published as an immediate response to the use of US, UK and French missiles fired by Ukraine into Russia in November 2024.

But how useable does the Russian leadership believe nuclear weapons to be, especially those tactical, low-yield nuclear weapons designed to destroy smaller targets rather than cities? Again, there are mixed signals, but the *theoretical* nuclear-use thresholds do appear to move dependent on the decade. In the 1990s and early 2000s, Russia lagged years behind the US in the development of precision cruise missiles carrying conventional warheads. It felt *theoretically* vulnerable to attacks by these precision weapons, which could have knocked out large parts of its nuclear arsenal, at least on land. As mentioned, the 1999 bombing of Russian ally Serbia was a shocking moment for Russia's political classes, and reinforced a sense of vulnerability, especially given Serbia's helpless inability to fight back against NATO's destruction. In these circumstances of Western interventionism and military superiority, Russia would have lacked a robust conventional response and so may have had to fall back on nuclear weapons. These concerns were reflected in Russia's 2000 military doctrine, which allowed the use of nuclear weapons in 'situations that are critical to the national security of the Russian Federation'.[12] In doctrine at least, this could be interpreted as a lowering of the nuclear-use threshold.

Since then, Russia has developed cruise-missile technology, used extensively in Syria. The country is arguably significantly less reliant on nuclear weapons now because it has a broader range of more powerful conventional tools. The 2014 doctrine arguably reflected this by tightening the grounds upon which nuclear weapons could be used compared to the 2000 doctrine.

However, this assessment is complicated by historic underestimation of Moscow's readiness to use these weapons. In February 2024, the *Financial Times*, quoting secret Russian documents from between 2008 and 2015, reported that Russia's threshold for nuclear weapon use had been lower than publicly admitted.[13] Soviet-era military planning documents, left behind in East Germany and made public after the Cold War, showed that the Soviets were far more ready to use nuclear weapons than had been thought likely. Additionally, in military exercises – an important indicator of how armies plan and think about fighting – according to Lester W. Grau and Charles K. Bartles, 'the Russians still plan and practice for surviving and conducting tactical nuclear battle'.[14] Tactical nuclear weapons are used at early or mid-stages of military exercises, unlike in NATO wargames, when, if they are used at all, it is generally at the end of the exercise. For the Russians, tactical nuclear weapons are dealt with as serious but useable weapons of war, lacking the sense of apocalyptic calamity with which they are treated in the West.

What is clear is that nuclear warheads are critical in Russia's information war. The primary purpose of nuclear threat is for the Russian regime to dissuade Western nations from supporting Ukraine. The Kremlin wants to create doubt in the minds of policy-makers as to where Russia's red lines are and fear in the minds of the public.

The Kremlin's information machine has relentlessly stoked fears of nuclear conflict and the nuclear destruction of the West. These take a variety of forms but often involve threats on popular Russian TV shows. In 2015, Putin propagandist Dmitriy Kiselev stood in front of an image of an orange mushroom cloud and explained to Russian viewers that Russia is the only nation on earth that can turn the US into 'radioactive ash'.[15] Since then, nuclear boasting and intimidation have become regular, almost daily, occurrences on Russian TV.

Whilst Putin rarely speaks directly about nuclear weapons – he has done so less than half a dozen times – his acolytes and supporters issue threats on behalf of the regime. Former President Dmitri Medvedev is one of the most regular and hysterical voices. He claims the existence of human civilisation would be threatened by Russia's loss in Ukraine.[16]

Ukrainians continue to insist that the Kremlin is bluffing and uses nuclear blackmail only to preserve its declining power. One Ukrainian secret agency source told me that Ukraine's allies were scared by the 'weird' idea that Russia was looking for 'direct military confrontation with the West'. 'This is how Russia still preserves its great power status, through the fear that nobody wants to have that escalation,' they said. 'Russia just exploits that fear.' The problem for Ukraine is that there is much less appetite for risk amongst nations for whom the war in Ukraine is not a life-or-death struggle, a point noted by Medvedev. Escalation, he said, suits Russia because the Ukraine conflict is critical for its leaders, whereas for NATO and the US it is not.[17]

But would Putin use nuclear weapons – or even lethal chemical weapons such as sarin or chlorine – to regain control of the war if he felt he was losing? This is the theory of 'escalate to de-escalate'. If Russia were in danger of losing Crimea, might Putin use a tactical nuclear weapon to warn of the consequences of continuing armed conflict, as the CIA said he might?

In a 1999 edition of *Voyennaya Mysl'* (*Military Thought*), the Russian Military Academy's in-house journal, three officers presented a six-layer theory of nuclear detonations for crisis de-escalation beginning with a 'demonstration strike', a one-off strike on water. The second stage was the targeting of a poorly populated site, potentially an abandoned town. The third was a 'deterrence demonstration' on a potential military target, such as a transport hub. From there, the use escalated to an 'intimidation' strike, hitting concentrations of enemy forces to eliminate the advantage of an enemy breakthrough, in the case of Ukraine perhaps in the Kharkiv area or just to the north of Crimea. The penultimate and final stages would result in multiple tactical nuclear strikes across a theatre of operations.

In 2009, the commander of Russian strategic missile forces reportedly claimed that in any conventional conflict, Russia's ballistic missile force would ensure that an adversary would be forced to end hostilities under threat of single or multiple nuclear strikes – a clear example of the idea of Russia's strategic nuclear force being used to regain the initiative in conflict to de-escalate.[18] Whilst not doctrine, it did indicate thinking in the Russian strategic missile command.

Is there an example of escalation management in recent Russian behaviour? The answer is yes. In the non-nuclear sphere, in order to control Ukraine, Putin escalated the conflict in 2014 with a limited invasion, with separatist proxies, and then escalated again to a full-scale invasion in 2022. Russia also provoked the Georgian War in 2008. In 2008 and 2014, provocations were used as shaping operations to escalate. In 2022, the Russians ignored their own doctrine and failed to use shaping operations, with highly negative results as a consequence.

I believe that any decision to use nuclear weapons will ultimately be an emotional response, not a rational one. Behind that is a question: is the Ukraine War existential for the Russian state?

If the Ukraine War is a war of opportunistic choice, and if Russia's leaders are sufficiently self-aware to see it as that, there is no realistic chance of the use of nuclear weapons and the threat is a bluff to limit Western support. From a Western perspective, Russia's war in Ukraine only threatens the existence of an independent Ukraine, not an independent Russia. It is a war of conquest and imperial hangover. Therefore, there are no grounds for nuclear use. The threats therefore are part of Russia's long tradition of intimidatory psychological behaviour – its undiplomatic diplomacy.

However, I'd suggest that at least in part, Ukraine is not a rational issue for Putin or those closest to him. By this, I mean that his idea of the term 'existential' is different from the Western understanding of it. Ukraine is a desperate battle against the West, one that will have repercussions in Russia for decades if not centuries. And so, Ukraine is as close to being existential to the future of the Russian state as it can be. This is not only a war of survival for an independent Ukraine but also a war of survival for the idea of a Greater Russia. If Putin, who has accumulated more power than any leader since Stalin, feels that his 'concept' of Russia, which includes Ukraine and Belarus, is under threat, then the line between choice and necessity becomes blurred. Putin is fighting to regain lands 'gathered' (colonised) over a period of 400 years. He is fighting for the survival of an idea of his nation, of the greatness that was Russia. The battle will echo through time. It is a war of survival, of sorts. For this, he is already willing to stomach extraordinarily high casualties. Through state propaganda, he has also prepared the Russian people to expect war, including nuclear war. A depressingly high percentage of Russians think it is coming. The Ukrainian towns he is taking have been obliterated, so he seems to care little about the condition of the land he is 'regathering', only that it is not going to Ukraine or the West. Would he irradiate parts of Ukraine to deny the land and towns to NATO's 'Nazi puppets' in Kyiv? Probably not, but it is not an impossibility.

'Once a fight is seen as a war of survival rather than a war of choice,' to use the words of one *New York Times* analyst, 'the leap to discussing the use of nuclear weapons is a small one.'[19] Above all, the choice becomes one which is less rational and more fraught with the historical and emotional baggage that Putin carries.

If he were to use nuclear weapons, my guess is that he would test a tactical nuclear weapon, after which their use would be sudden, dramatic and without warning, as previous escalations have been, in order to retain the element of surprise.

There are other dangers that may present more of a long-term threat. In Russia's determination to keep its conventional supply of shells and drones, what nuclear or missile secrets is it sharing with states such as Iran and North Korea? The next global conflict may not directly start as a conflict between major states but as one between their allies or proxies. Additionally, there is a greater danger now of an accidental Russian launch, given the dramatically high state of tensions between Russia and NATO, the shortened decision-making times and the removal of humans from the lower levels of decision-making.

As of the time of writing, Russia is making progress on the battlefield and bombing Ukraine's energy supply and cities to destroy morale. Currently, it is slowly succeeding. As long as that remains the case, there is no immediate nuclear decision point. Should Russia be on the verge of losing its puppet regimes in eastern Ukraine or face an invasion of Crimea, then the world will find out if Russia's nuclear bluff is just that or if Putin will once again dramatically escalate to regain control of the situation.

NOTES

CHAPTER 1

1 Solomiya Khoma, interview with author, 29 August 2024, Kyiv.
2 Solomiya Khoma and Serhii Kuzan, interview with author, 29 August 2024, Kyiv.
3 Senior Ukrainian military intelligence officer, interview with author, 18 September 2017, Kyiv.
4 Valeri Gerasimov, 'Tsennost Nauki v Predvidenii', *Voyenno-Promyshlennyy Kuryer*, 27 February–5 March 2013, http://vpk-news.ru/sites/default/files/pdf/VPK_08_476.pdf (accessed 1 June 2015).
5 Russian Federation, 'Voyennaya Doktrina Rossiyskoy Federatsii', 25 December 2015, http://kremlin.ru/events/president/news/47334 (accessed 5 March 2017).
6 Whilst Ludendorff brought the term 'total war' to a wider audience, it was first used by sociologist Hans Freyer in *Der Staat* (Leipzig: Ernst Wiegandt, 1926). See Jan Willem Honig, 'The Idea of Total War: From Clausewitz to Ludendorff', in Andreas Herberg-Rothe, Jan Willem Honig, Daniel Moran (eds), *Clausewitz: The State and War* (Stuttgart: Franz Steiner Verlag, 2011), p. 39.
7 Alya Shandra, interview with author, Kyiv, 14 February 2017.
8 Agnieszka Bryc and Maria Domańska, 'Russia in the Trenches of Cognitive Warfare', *New Eastern Europe*, 27 September 2024, https://neweasterneurope.eu/2024/09/09/russia-in-the-trenches-of-cognitive-warfare/ (accessed 27 September 2024).
9 The Kremlin has presented colour revolutions as a powerful form of indirect warfare where mass street protests, controlled by external Western forces, aim to overthrow governments. See Tracey German, 'Harnessing Protest Potential: Russian Strategic Culture and the Colored Revolutions', *Contemporary Security Policy*, vol. 41, no. 4, 2 May 2020, p. 541 and 'Russia and the "Color Revolution": A Russian Military View of a World Destabilized by the US and the West', *Center for Strategic and International Studies*, 28 May 2014, http://csis.org/files/publication/140529_Russia_Color_Revolution_Summary.pdf (accessed 16 February 2021).
10 William J. Burns, 'Spycraft and Statecraft', *Foreign Affairs*, March/April 2024, https://www.foreignaffairs.com/united-states/cia-spycraft-and-statecraft-william-burns (accessed 23 May 2025).
11 John Willerton, 'Searching for a Russian National Idea: Putin Team Efforts and Public Assessments', *Demokratizatsiya: The Journal of Post-Soviet Democratization*, vol. 25, no. 3, summer 2017, pp. 209–34.
12 Articulated in Norbert Eitelhuber, 'The Russian Bear: Russian Strategic Culture and What it Implies for the West', *Connections: The Quarterly Journal*, vol. 9, no. 1, 2009, pp. 1–28.
13 Frank Gardner and Suzanne Leigh, 'Russia on Mission to Cause Mayhem on UK streets, warns MI5', BBC News, 8 October 2024, https://www.bbc.co.uk/news/articles/cp8e15yr1gwo (accessed 17 December 2024).
14 'Putin Announces War for New World Order: We Approached a Very Dangerous Line', *Pravda*, 7 November 2024, https://english.pravda.ru/news/world/161107-putin-war-world-order/ (accessed 17 December 2024).
15 DPA, 'German Major General Warns of Russian Military Build-Up', Yahoo News, 18 January 2025, https://www.yahoo.com/news/german-major-general-warns-russian-085622367.html (accessed 19 January 2025).
16 Conversation with author, September 2024, Ukraine.
17 Robert Seely, 'The Truth about Russia Foreign Policy', *Wall Street Journal*, 25 October 1995.

CHAPTER 2

1 Hew Strachan, 'The Changing Character of War', Lecture at the Graduate Institute of International Relations, Geneva, Switzerland, 9 November 2006, p. 2, https://scispace.com/pdf/the-changing-character-of-war-g04nn73z3m.pdf (accessed 23 May 2025).

2 Ibid.

3 Paul Collier and Anke Hoeffler, 'Greed and Grievance in Civil War', *Oxford Economic Papers*, vol. 56, no. 4, 2004, pp. 563–95.

4 Janis Berzins, 'Russian New Generation Warfare is Not Hybrid Warfare', in Artis Pabriks and Andis Kudors (eds), *The War in Ukraine: Lessons for Europe* (Riga: University of Latvia Press, 2015), p. 43.

5 Jeremy Black, 'What is War?', Defence in Depth, Defence Studies Department, King's College London, 11 June 2018, https://defenceindepth.co/2018/06/11/what-is-war/ (accessed 10 September 2021).

6 Michael Howard, *Clausewitz: A Very Short Introduction* (Oxford: Oxford University Press, 2002).

7 Carl Von Clausewitz, *On War* (Princeton: Princeton University Press, 1976), edited and translated by Michael Howard and Peter Paret.

8 United States, Headquarters, Department of the Army, Counterinsurgency, FM 3–24 (Washington DC, Headquarters, Department of the Army, December 2006), https://irp.fas.org/doddir/army/fm3-24.pdf (accessed 9 June 2025).

9 Clausewitz, *On War*, p. 43.

10 United States 'Doctrine for the Armed Forces of the United States', Joint Publication 1 (Department of Defence, Washington DC, March 2013), p. 1–6, http://www.dtic.mil/doctrine/new_pubs/jp1.pdf (accessed 21 April 2016).

11 A 'core' definition by the *Concise Oxford English Dictionary*, eleventh edition (Oxford: Oxford University Press, 2004), p. ix.

12 *Concise Oxford English Dictionary*, p. 1627.

13 Martin van Creveld, 'Modern Conventional Warfare: an Overview', discussion paper, undated, http://www.offnews.info/downloads/2020modern_warfare.pdf (accessed 25 August 2015).

14 Kenneth Payne, 'What is Conventional Warfare', *Small Wars Journal*, 3 January 2012, http://smallwarsjournal.com/blog/what-is-conventional-warfare (accessed 22 August 2015).

15 'UCDP Definitions', Uppsala University, https://www.uu.se/en/department/peace-and-conflict-research/research/ucdp/ucdp-definitions#:~:text=An%20armed%20conflict%20is%20a,deaths%20in%20one%20calendar%20year (accessed 9 June 2025).

16 For more, see V. I. Lenin, 'Chto Delat', in *Polnoye Sobraniye Sochineniy* (Moskva: Gosudarstvennoye Izdatelstvo Politicheskoy Literatury, 1959), vol. 6, pp. 30–40 and V. I. Lenin, 'Uroki Moskovskogo Vosstaniya', in *Polnoye Sobraniye Sochineniy* (Moskva: Gosudarstvennoye Izdatelstvo Politicheskoy Literatury, 1959), vol. 13, pp. 369–77.

17 The term 'unconventional' itself was rarely defined. A 1980s US Department of Defence dictionary equates unconventional war with insurgency war, calling it a 'broad spectrum of military and paramilitary operations, normally of long duration, predominantly conducted by indigenous or surrogate forces who are organised, trained, equipped, supported, and directed in varying degrees by an external source'. See *Department of Defence US Dictionary of Military Terms* (Elstree: Greenhill Books, 1987), p. 396.

18 Robert Thompson, *Defeating Communist Insurgency* (London: Chatto and Windus, 1966); David Galula, *Counterinsurgency Warfare: Theory and Practice* (New York: Praeger, 1964); Frank Kitson, *Low Intensity Operations* (London: Faber & Faber, 1971).

19 Roger Trinquier, *Modern Warfare: A French View of Counterinsurgency* (London: Pall Mall Press, 1964), http://louisville.edu/armyrotc/files/Roger%20Trinquier%20-%20Modern%20Warfare.pdf (accessed 3 October 2016).

20 Andrew Mack, 'Why Big Nations Lose Small Wars: the Politics of Asymmetric Conflict', *World Politics*, vol. 27, no. 2, January 1975, pp. 175–200, 178.

21 Rupert Smith, *The Utility of Force: The Art of War in the Modern World* (New York: Alfred A. Knopf, 2007); David Kilcullen, *The Accidental Guerrilla: Fighting Small Wars in the Midst of a Big One* (London: Hurst and Co., 2009); Robert Johnson, *The Afghan Way of War* (London: Hurst, 2011); Rob Johnson, Martijn Kitzen and Tim Sweijs (eds) *The Conduct of War in the 21st Century: Kinetic, Connected and Synthetic* (London: Routledge Advances in Defence Studies, 2021). To that list should be added John A. Nagl, *Learning to Eat Soup With a Knife* (Chicago: University of Chicago Press, 2002) and Emile Simpson, *War from the Ground Up* (London: Hurst & Co, 2012).

22 Frank Hoffman, 'Conflict in the 21st Century: The Rise of Hybrid Wars', Potomac Institute for Policy Studies, Arlington, Virginia, December 2007, p. 35, https://www.potomacinstitute.org/images/stories/publications/potomac_hybridwar_0108.pdf (accessed 1 April 2025).

23 Hoffman, 'Conflict in the 21st Century', p. 14.

24 William S. Lind, John Nightengale, John F. Schmitt, Joseph W. Sutton and Gary I. Wilson, 'The Changing Face of War: Into the Fourth Generation', *Marine Corps Gazette*, vol. 73, no. 10, Oct 1989.

25 Thomas X. Hammes, *The Sling and the Stone: On War in the 21st Century* (St. Paul's, Minnesota: Zenith Press, 2004), p. 2.

26 Charles Krulak, 'The Strategic Corporal: Leadership in the Three Block War', *Marine Corps Gazette*, vol. 83, no. 1, January 1999, pp. 18–23, http://www.au.af.mil/au/awc/awcgate/usmc/strategic_corporal.htm (accessed 23 October 2016); Terry Terriff, 'Of Romans and Dragons: Preparing the US Marine Corps for Future Warfare', *Contemporary Security Policy*, vol. 28, no. 1, pp. 143–62.

27 Mark Galeotti, 'Hybrid, Ambiguous, and Non-Linear? How New Is Russia's New Way of War?', *Small Wars & Insurgencies*, vol. 27, no. 2, 2016, pp. 282–301, p. 287.

28 Octavian Manea, 'Hybrid War as a War on Governance', interview with Mark Galeotti, *Small Wars Journal*, 19 August 2015, http://smallwarsjournal.com/jrnl/art/hybrid-war-as-a-war-on-governance (accessed 18 April 2016).

29 Manea, 'Hybrid War'.

30 See 'Countering Gray-Zone Wars', *Parameters*, vol. 35, no. 3, autumn 2015, http://strategicstudiesinstitute.army.mil/pubs/parameters/ (accessed 31 December 2015).

31 Galeotti, 'Hybrid, Ambiguous, and Non-Linear?'

32 John Schindler, 'We're Entering the Age of "Special War"', Business Insider, 25 September 2013, http://www.businessinsider.com/were-entering-the-age-of-special-war-2013-9 (accessed 9 April 2016).

33 A term ascribed to Russian presidential adviser Vladislav Surkov. In Oscar Jonsson and Robert Seely, 'Russian Full-Spectrum Conflict: An Appraisal after Ukraine', *Journal of Slavic Military Studies*, vol. 28, no. 1, March 2015, pp. 1–22.

34 Named as such following an article written by Russian Chief of Staff Valeri Gerasimov, in which he spoke of the power of non-conventional methods of warfare. See Valeri Gerasimov, 'Tsennost Nauki v Predvidenii', *Voenno-Promishlennii Kuryor*, March 2013, http://vpk-news.ru/sites/default/files/pdf/VPK_08_476.pdf (accessed 1 June 2015).

35 Pauli Järvenpää, 'Measures Short of War', RAND Seminar held in Cambridge, https://icds.ee/en/rand-seminar-measures-short-of-war/ (accessed 23 May 2025).

36 Stephen Cimbala, 'Sun Tzu and Salami Tactics? Vladimir Putin and Military Persuasion in Ukraine', *Journal of Slavic Military Studies*, vol. 27, no. 3, 21 February–18 March 2014, p. 359.

37 Janis Berzins, 'Russian New Generation Warfare is Not Hybrid Warfare', in Artis Pabriks and Andis Kudors (eds), *The War in Ukraine: Lessons for Europe* (Riga: University of Latvia Press, 2015), p. 43.

CHAPTER 3

1 Colonel Pavlo Khazan, interview with author, Kyiv, 20 September 2024.

2 Seth J. Frantzman, *The Drone Wars* (New York: Post Hill Press, 2021).

3 Joël Postma, 'Drones over Nagorno-Karabakh: A Glimpse at the Future of War?', *Atlantisch Perspectief*, vol. 45, no. 2, 2021, pp. 15–20, https://www.jstor.org/stable/48638213 (accessed 20 December 2024).

4 Segar, interview with author, Kyiv, 19 September 2024.

5 Military News Ukraine, X/Twitter feed, 4 November 2024, https://x.com/front_ukrainian/status/1853526694545740057 (accessed 12 November 2024).

6 War Translated, X/Twitter feed, 16 March 2025, https://x.com/wartranslated/status/1901207062228422767 (accessed 16 March 2025).

CHAPTER 4

1 Isaiah Berlin, 'The Silence in Russian Culture', *Foreign Affairs*, October 1957, http://www.foreignaffairs.com/articles/71355/isaiah-berlin/the-silence-in-russian-culture (accessed 8 March 2015).

2 Richard Pipes, *Russia Under the Old Regime* (London: Penguin, 1993), p. 86.

3 Fritz W. Ermarth, 'Russia's Strategic Culture: Past, Present, and… in Transition?', Defense Threat Reduction Agency, Advanced Systems and Concepts Office, 2006, p. 4, http://fas.org/irp/agency/dod/dtra/russia.pdf (accessed 1 January 2016).

4 MediaMera, 'Putin: U Nas Yest "Starinnaya Russkaya Zabava" – Poisk Natsional noy Idei', YouTube, 11 October 2015, https://www.youtube.com/watch?v=hN_QwYvTzZI (accessed 29 March 2021).

5 Peter Duncan, *Russian Messianism: Third Rome, Revolution, Communism and After* (London and New York: Routledge, 2000), p. 2.

6 Peter Truscott, *Russia First* (London: Bloomsbury, 1997), p. 29.

7 Cynthia H. Whittaker, 'The Idea of Autocracy among Eighteenth-Century Russian Historians', *The Russian Review*, vol. 55, no. 2, April 1996, p. 171, https://www.jstor.org/stable/131835 (accessed 2 September 2021).

8 Liah Greenfeld, *Nationalism: Five Roads to Modernity* (Cambridge, MA: Harvard University Press, 1993), p. 265.

9 Piotr Chaadayev, *Philosophical Letters*, 1829, http://www.vehi.net/chaadaev/filpisma.html#_ftnref22 (accessed 10 August 2019).
10 'Mikhail Khodorkovsky: Final Trial Speech', Open Democracy, 14 December 2010, https://www.opendemocracy.net/od-russia/mikhail-khodorkovsky/mikhail-khodorkovsky-final-trial-speech (accessed 4 April 2016).
11 Whittaker, 'The Idea of Autocracy', p. 170.
12 Paul Goble, 'Dugin Says an Azerbaijan Hostile to Russia Will "Instantly Cease to Exist"', *The Interpreter*, 6 April 2014, http://www.interpretermag.com/dugin-says-an-azerbaijan-hostile-to-russia-will-instantly-cease-to-exist/ (accessed 14 August 2019).
13 Konstantin Aksakov, 'On the Internal State of Russia', 1855, http://az.lib.ru/a/aksakow_k_s/text_1855_zapiska.shtml (accessed 23 May 2025).
14 See Russian Federation, 'Pryamaya Liniya s Vladimirom Putinym', 17 April 2014, http://www.kremlin.ru/events/president/transcripts/20796/work (accessed 13 September 2021).
15 Aksakov, 'On the Internal State of Russia'.
16 Articulated by Maria Engström, 'Contemporary Russian Messianism and New Russian Foreign Policy', *Contemporary Security Policy*, vol. 35, no. 3, 2014, pp. 356–79.
17 For more on Uvarov's development of the trinity of Russian state 'ideology' in the nineteenth century, see Cynthia H. Whittaker, 'The Ideology of Sergei Uvarov: An Interpretive Essay', *The Russian Review*, vol. 37, no. 2, pp. 158–76, http://www.jstor.org/stable/128466 (accessed 20 February 2015).
18 Christopher Andrew and Oleg Gordievsky, *KGB: The Inside Story of Its Foreign Operations From Lenin to Gorbachev* (London: Hodder & Stoughton, 1990), p. 3.
19 Richard Pipes, *The Russian Revolution* (New York: Alfred A. Knopf, 1990), p. 295.
20 Yevgenia Albats, *The State within a State: The KGB and its Hold on Russia – Past, Present, and Future* (New York: Farr, Straus, Giroux, 1994), p. 90.
21 Richard W. Harrison, *The Russian Way of War*, (Kansas: University Press of Kansas, 2001), p. 27.
22 Ibid., p. 27.
23 Dietrich Geyer, *Russian Imperialism: The Interaction of Domestic and Foreign Policy 1860–1914*, translated by Bruce Little (New Haven: Yale University Press, 1987), p. 86.
24 'A Point of View: The Writer Who Foresaw the Rise of the Totalitarian State', BBC News, 23 November 2014, http://www.bbc.co.uk/news/magazine-30129713 (accessed 13 August 2019).
25 Fyodor Dostoevsky, *A Writer's Diary: Volume Two 1877 – 1881* (Evanston: Northwestern University Press, 1994), p. 1374, quoted in Kevork Oskanian, 'Russian Empire: between Historic Myth and Contemporary Reality', The Foreign Policy Centre, 24 July 2020, https://fpc.org.uk/russian-empire-between-historic-myth-and-contemporary-reality/ (accessed 29 March 2021).
26 Helge Blakkisrud and Elana Wilson (eds), *Russia's Turn to the East: Domestic Policymaking and Regional Cooperation* (Cham, Switzerland: Springer Nature, 2018).
27 In 2005, Timothy Snyder argued that Putin rehabilitated Ilyin as the Kremlin's 'court' philosopher. That year, Snyder said, he cited Ilyin in his addresses to the Federal Assembly of the Russian Federation and arranged for the reinterment of Ilyin's remains in Russia. Timothy Snyder, 'God is a Russian', *New York Review of Books*, 12 November 2019, https://www.nybooks.com/articles/2018/04/05/god-is-a-russian (accessed 6 December 2020).
28 Greenfeld, *Nationalism: Five Roads to Modernity*, p. 234.
29 Berlin, 'The Silence in Russian Culture'.
30 Ibid.
31 Ibid.
32 Nicholas Berdyaev, *The Russian Idea* (New York: The Macmillan Company, 1948), pp. 31–32.
33 Vladislav Surkov, 'Russian Political Culture: The View from Utopia', *Russian Social Science Review*, vol. 49, no. 6, 2008, p. 82.
34 Diane Chotikul, 'The Soviet Theory of Reflexive Control in Historical and Psychocultural Perspective: a Preliminary Study', PhD dissertation, Naval Postgraduate School, Monterey, California, 1986, p. 52, https://archive.org/details/soviettheoryofreoochot (accessed 31 August 2015).
35 Ibid., p. 40.
36 Daniel Rancour-Laferriere, *The Slave Soul of Russia: Moral Masochism and the Cult of Suffering* (New York: NYU Press, 1996).
37 Vladimir A. Lefebvre, *Algebra of Conscience* (Boston: Kluwer Academic Publishers, 2001), p. 21.
38 Ibid., p. 23.
39 Jerry F. Hough, 'Soviet Leadership in Transition', The Brookings Institute, Washington DC, 1980, p. 7.
40 See Vitali Tseplyaev, 'Kuklovodstvo k Deystviyu. Nikolay Patrushev – o Metodakh "Tsvetnykh Revolyutsiy"',

Argumenty i Fakty, 10 June 2020, https://aif.ru/society/safety/kuklovodstvo_k_deystviyu_nikolay_patrushev_o_metodah_cvetnyh_revolyuciy (accessed 28 November 2020); Igor Panarin, 'The Information War Against Russia: Operation Anti-Putin', speech given at the Securing Mankind's Future conference, 25–26 February 2012, Berlin, http://www.schiller-institut.de/seiten/201202-berlin/panarin-english.html (accessed 13 July 2015).

41 Ioffe Julia, 'What is Russia Today: The Kremlin's Propaganda Outlet Has an Identity Crisis', *Columbia Journalism Review*, September/October 2010, https://archives.cjr.org/feature/what_is_russia_today.php?page=all#sthash.BjLzddxf.dpuf (accessed 19 August 2019).

42 Surkov, 'Russian Political Culture', p. 82.

43 Paul B. Rich, 'Russia as a Great Power', *Small Wars & Insurgencies*, vol. 2, no. 20, 2009, pp. 276–99.

44 Vladimir Slipchenko, 'Lecture' in Makhmut Gareyev and Vladimir Slipchenko, *Future War* (Moscow: Polit.ru, 2005), p. 12, https://community.apan.org/wg/tradoc-g2/fmso/m/fmso-books/352073 (accessed 17 March 2021).

45 Eitelhuber, 'The Russian Bear', p. 27.

46 Ermarth, 'Russia's Strategic Culture', p. 4.

47 Ibid., p. 7.

48 See 'Putin Poobeshchal ne Dopustit "Tsvetnoy Revolyutsii" v Rossii', BBC Russia, 20 November 2014, https://www.bbc.com/russian/russia/2014/11/141120_russia_putin_extremism (accessed 26 November 2020); 'Putin Zayavil o Bor'be s "Tsvetnymi Revolyutsiyami" v Rossii i stranakh ODKB', rbc.ru, 12 April 2018, https://www.rbc.ru/rbcfreenews/58eddb129a7947a410ab3fdo (accessed 26 November 2020); Tseplyaev, 'Kuklovodstvo k Deystviyu'.

49 Alexander Bogomolov and Oleksandr Lytvynenko, 'A Ghost in the Mirror: Russian Soft Power in Ukraine', Royal Institute for International Affairs, London, January 2012, p. 3, https://www.academia.edu/1792446/A_Ghost_in_the_Mirror_Russian_Soft_Power_in_Ukraine (accessed 23 May 2025).

50 Duncan, *Russian Messianism*, p. 1.

51 Maria Engström, 'Contemporary Russian Messianism and New Russian Foreign Policy', *Contemporary Security Policy*, vol. 35, no. 3, 2014, p. 363.

52 Edward Lucas, *The New Cold War* (London: Bloomsbury, 2014).

53 Vladislav Surkov, 'Dolgoye Gosudarstvo Putina', *Nezavisimaya*, 11 February 2021, https://www.ng.ru/ideas/2019-02-11/5_7503_surkov.html (accessed 24 May 2025).

54 Volodymyr Chystylin, interview with author, Kharkiv, 21 September 2017.

55 Bogomolov and Lytvynenko, 'A Ghost in the Mirror', p. 3.

56 William C. Fuller, *Strategy and Power in Russia, 1600–1914* (New York: Free Press, 1992), p. 3.

57 Bogomolov and Lytvynenko, 'A Ghost in the Mirror', p. 4.

58 Mykola Riabchuk, 'Ukrainians as Russia's Negative "Other": History Comes Full Circle', *Communist and Post-Communist Studies*, vol. 49, no. 1, March 2016, p. 76.

59 For a full list as well as an understanding of its effects, see Orest Subtelny, *Ukraine: A History* (Toronto: University of Toronto Press, 1988), pp. 283, 284.

60 Alya Shandra, interview with author, Kyiv, 14 February 2017.

61 The latest scholarly research puts the total at 3.9 million, with an estimated range from 3.5 million to 7 million. See 'Holodomor: The Ukrainian Genocide', Holocaust and Genocide Studies, University of Minnesota, https://cla.umn.edu/chgs/educator-resources-opportunities/resources/holodomor (accessed 3 September 2021).

62 Chystylin, interview.

63 Mykola Riabchuk, interview with author, Kyiv, 14 February 2017; Ihor Rushchenko, interview with author, Kharkiv, 20 September 2017.

64 Russian Federation, 'Stat'ya Vladimira Putina "Ob Istoricheskom Yedinstve Russkikh i Ukraintsev"', 12 July 2021, http://kremlin.ru/events/president/news/66181 (accessed 16 July 2021).

65 Russian Federation, 'Interv'yu Pervomu Kanalu i Agentstvu Assoshieyted Press', 4 September 2013, http://kremlin.ru/events/president/news/19143 (accessed 27 March 2021).

66 Both of which had also been on occasions evolving concepts. See Cynthia H. Whittaker, 'The Idea of Autocracy among Eighteenth-Century Russian Historians', *The Russian Review*, vol. 55, no. 2, April 1996, pp. 149–71, https://www.jstor.org/stable/131835 (accessed 2 September 2021).

67 Bogomolov and Lytvynenko, 'A Ghost in the Mirror', p. 2.

CHAPTER 5

1 Panoushka, interview with author, Kramatorsk, 25 October 2024.

2 An account of my meeting with Saha also appeared in Bob Seely, 'The Russian Way of War', *Foreign*

Affairs, 24 November 2023, https://www.foreignaffairs.com/ukraine/russian-way-war?check_logged_in=1 (accessed 28 December 2024).

CHAPTER 6

1 Makhmut Gareyev and Vladimir Slipchenko, *Future War* (Moscow: Polit.ru, 2005), p. 60, https://community.apan.org/wg/tradoc-g2/fmso/m/fmso-books/352073 (accessed 17 March 2021).
2 Igor Popov, 'Voyennaya Mysl' Sovremennoy Rossii', Voina Budushchego blog, 2007, http://futurewarfare.narod.ru/theoryRF.html (accessed 20 December 2015).
3 Popov, 'Voyennaya Mysl' Sovremennoy'.
4 Stephen Blank, '"No Need to Threaten Us, We Are Frightened of Ourselves": Russia's Blueprint for a Police State, The New Security Strategy', in Stephen J. Blank and Richard Weitz (eds), *The Russian Military Today and Tomorrow: Essays in Memory of Mary Fitzgerald*, Strategic Studies Institute, July 2010, p. 24, https://archive.org/stream/TheRussianMilitaryTodayAndTomorrowEssaysInMemoryOfMaryFitzgerald/23-RussianMil_djvu.txt (accessed 14 February 2021).
5 Ibid.
6 Makhmut Gareyev, 'Struktura i Osnovnoye Soderzhaniye Novoy Voyennoy Doktriny Rossii', *Voyennaya Mysl'*, no. 3, March 2007, p. 3.
7 Gareyev, 'Struktura i Osnovnoye', p. 3.
8 V. D. Sokolovsky (ed), *Soviet Military Strategy* (New York: Praeger, 1963), p. 42.
9 Stephen R. Covington, 'The Culture of Strategic Thought Behind Russia's Modern Approaches to Warfare', Belfer Center for Science and International Affairs, Harvard Kennedy School, pp. 3, 4, https://www.belfercenter.org/publication/culture-strategic-thought-behind-russias-modern-approaches-warfare (accessed 2 March 2017).
10 Ibid., p. 4.
11 Tor Bukkvoll, 'Iron Cannot Fight: The Role of Technology in Current Russian Military Theory', *Journal of Strategic Studies*, vol. 34, no. 5, 2011, pp. 681–706, p. 683.
12 Ibid., p. 683.
13 Dima Adamsky, *The Culture of Military Innovation* (Stanford: Stanford University Press, 2010), p. 49.
14 Gareyev and Slipchenko, *Future War*, p. 60.
15 Gareyev, 'Struktura i Osnovnoye', pp. 4, 5.
16 Andrei Ilnitsky, 'Vybor Rossii: Razvilki, Ugrozy, Vozmozhnosti i Resheniye', Sait Andreya Ilnitskogo blog, 30 April 2021, https://amicable.ru/news/2021/04/30/19453/vybor-rossii-razvilki-ugrozy-vozmozhnosti-reshenie/ (accessed 6 May 2021).
17 Makhmut Gareyev, 'Strategicheskoye Sderzhivaniye: Problemy i Resheniya', *Krasnaya Zvezda*, 8 October 2008, http://old.redstar.ru/2008/10/08_10/index.shtml (accessed 3 April).
18 Gareyev, 'Struktura i Osnovnoye'.
19 Gareyev, 'Strategicheskoye Sderzhivaniye'.
20 'Putin Poobeshchal ne Dopustit', BBC Russia.
21 Niklas Granholm, Johannes Malminen and Gudrun Persson (eds), 'A Rude Awakening: Ramifications of Russian Aggression towards Ukraine', Swedish Defence Research Agency (FOI), Stockholm, June 2014, p. 20, https://www.foi.se/en/foi/reports/report-summary.html?reportNo=FOI-R--3892--SE (accessed 24 May 2025).
22 Tseplyaev, 'Kuklovodstvo k Deystviyu'.
23 Vladimir Slipchenko, *Voyny Novogo Pokoleniya – Distantsionnyye i Bezkontaktnyye* (Moscow: Olma-Press, 2004), pp. 32–4.
24 Slipchenko, 'Lecture', in Gareyev and Slipchenko, *Future War*, p. 20.
25 Vladimir Slipchenko, 'K Kakoy Voyne Dolzhny Gotovitsya Vooryzhennyye Sily', *Otechestvennyye Zapiski*, vol. 8, no. 9, 2002, https://strana-oz.ru/2002/8/k-kakoy-voyne-dolzhny-gotovitsya-vooruzhennye-sily (accessed 5 April 2021).
26 Bukkvoll, 'Iron Cannot Fight', p. 695.
27 Sergei V. Anchukov, 'Voina i Strategiya', *Samizdat*, http://zhurnal.lib.ru/a/anchukow_s_w/woinast.shtml (accessed 4 April 2021).
28 Makhmut Gareyev, 'Struktura i Osnovnoye Soderzhaniye Novoy Voyennoy Doktriny', *Voyenno-Promyshlenyy Kuryer*, 24 January 2007, https://vpk-news.ru/articles/4824 (accessed 4 September 2021).
29 Andreĭ Kokoshin, 'O Revolyutsii v Voyennom Dele v Proshlom i Nastoyashchem', *Otechestvennyye Zapiski*, vol. 5, no 26, 2005, https://strana-oz.ru/2005/5/o-revolyucii-v-voennom-dele-v-proshlom-i-nastoyashchem (accessed 17 April 2021); Andreĭ Kokoshin, 'Sem' Syurprizov Irakskoy Voyny', *Nezavisimaya Gazeta*, 7 April 2003, https://www.ng.ru/world/2003-04-07/1_surprise.html (accessed 22 September 2021).

30 Bukkvoll, 'Iron Cannot Fight', p. 702.

31 Galeotti, 'Hybrid, Ambiguous, and Non-Linear?', p. 289.

32 S. G. Chekinov and S. A. Bogdanov, 'O Kharaktere i Soderzhanii Voiny Novogo Pokoleniya', *Voyennaya Mysl'*, no. 10, 2013, http://dlib.eastview.com/browse/doc/37494481 (accessed 11 October 2016); S. G. Chekinov and S. A. Bogdanov, 'Asimmetrichnye Deystviya po Obespecheniyu Voyennoy Bezopasnosti Rossii', *Voyennaya Mysl'*, no. 3, 2010, pp. 13–22; S. G. Chekinov and S. A. Bogdanov, 'The Strategy of Indirect Approach: Its Impact on Modern Warfare', *Military Thought*, vol. 20, no. 3, 2011.

33 Chekinov and Bogdanov, 'O Kharaktere i Soderzhanii', p. 18.

34 Scott Shane, 'What Intelligence Agencies Concluded about the Russian Attack on the U.S. Election', *New York Times*, 6 January 2017, https://www.nytimes.com/2017/01/06/us/politics/russian-hack-report.html?smid=em-share (accessed 16 March 2024).

35 Chekinov and Bogdanov, 'O Kharaktere i Soderzhanii', p. 20.

36 Vladimir Putin, 'Rossiya i Menyayushchiysya Mir' *Moskovskiye Novosti*, 27 February 2012, https://er.ru/activity/news/putin-rossiya-i-menyayushijsya-mir_76109 (accessed 24 May 2025).

37 Joseph Nye, *Soft Power: The Means to Success in World Politics* (New York: Public Affairs, 2004), p. x.

38 Putin, 'Rossiya i Menyaushchiysya Mir'.

39 Y. N. Baluevsky and M. M. Khamzatov, 'Globalizatsiya i Voyennoye Delo', *Nezavisimoye Voyennoye Obozreniye*, 8 August 2014, https://nvo.ng.ru/concepts/2014-08-08/1_globalisation.html (accessed 12 February 2021).

40 Andrei Ilnitsky, 'Vybor Rossii: Razvilki, Ugrozy, Vozmozhnosti i Resheniye', Sait Andreya Ilnitskogo, 30 April 2021, https://amicable.ru/news/2021/04/30/19453/vybor-rossii-razvilki-ugrozy-vozmozhnosti-reshenie/ (accessed 6 May 2021).

41 Katri Pynnöniemi and Minna Jokela, 'Perceptions of Hybrid War in Russia: Means, Targets and Objectives Identified in the Russian Debate', *Cambridge Review of International Affairs*, vol. 33, no. 6, 2020, pp. 828–45, p. 836.

42 *Handbook of Russian Information Warfare*, Research Division, NATO Defense College, November 2016, p. 3, footnote 1, http://www.ndc.nato.int/news/news.php?icode=995 (accessed 15 March 2017).

43 'Retired Colonel to Remain under Arrest on Terrorism Charges', Russian Legal Information Agency, 21 June 2012, http://rapsinews.com/judicial_information/20120621/263532047.html (accessed 18 August 2017).

44 'Russia's Supreme Court Cuts Jail Term for Coup Plotters', Sputnik, 19 July 2013, https://sputniknews.com/russia/20130719182314503-Russias-Supreme-Court-Cuts-Jail-Term-For-Coup-Plotters/ (accessed 18 August 2017).

45 Vladimir Kvachkov, *Special Forces of Russia* (Voyennaya Literatura, 2004), section 3.1, http://militera.lib.ru/science/kvachkov_vv/index.html (accessed 14 February 2017).

46 Ibid.

47 Ibid.

48 Ibid.

49 Makhmut Gareyev, 'Otstaivaya Natsional'nyye Interesy', *Voyenno-Promyshlennyy Kuryer*, https://vpk-news.ru/articles/3744 (accessed 4 April 2021).

50 Makhmut Gareyev, 'Strategicheskoye Sderzhivaniye: Problemy i Resheniya', *Krasnaya Zvezda*, 8 October 2008, http://old.redstar.ru/2008/10/08_10/index.shtml (accessed 3 April).

51 Ibid.

52 Makhmut Gareyev, 'Predchuvstvovat Izmeneniya v Kharaktere Voyny', *Voyenno-Promyshlennyy Kuryer*, 29 March 2013, http://vpk-news.ru/articles/16089 (accessed 5 May 2016).

53 Makhmut Gareyev, 'Voina I Voyennaya nauka na sovremennom etape', Tsentr Strategicheskoy Konyunktury, 27 March 2016, http://conjuncture.ru/os_vpk_27-03-2013_3/ (accessed 4 May 2016).

54 Timothy L. Thomas, 'Russia's Reflexive Control Theory and the Military', *Journal of Slavic Military Studies*, vol. 17, no. 2, 2004, p. 237.

55 Diana Chotikul, *The Soviet Theory of Reflexive Control in Historical and Psychocultural Perspective: A Preliminary Study*, Naval Postgraduate School, Monterey, California, 1986, https://archive.org/details/soviettheoryofreoochot (accessed 6 Jan 2015).

56 Norbert Wiener, *Cybernetics* (Cambridge, Massachusetts: MIT Press, 1965), p. 11.

57 Chotikul, *The Soviet Theory of Reflexive Control*, p. 6.

58 M. D. Ionov, 'Psikhologicheskiye Aspekty Upravleniya Protivnikom v Antagonisticheskikh Konfliktakh (Refleksivnoye Upravleniye)', *Refleksivnyye Protsessy*, no. 1, 1994. p. 37–45.

59 Thomas, 'Russia's Reflexive Control Theory', p. 70.

60 Timothy L. Thomas, 'The Mind Has No Firewall', *Parameters*, vol. 28, no. 1, spring 1998, pp. 84–92.

61 Elizabeth McLaughlin and Conor Finnegan, 'US Officials still Stumped on Mystery Illnesses in Cuba, Open

Door to "Viral" or "Ultrasound" Cause', ABC News, 9 January 2018, http://abcnews.go.com/International/state-department-fbi-differ-source-mysterious-alleged-attacks/story?id=52233492 (accessed 10 January 2018).

62 Patrick Oppmann and Laura Koran, 'Senate Holds Hearing on Cuba "Sonic Attacks"', CNN, 9 January 2018, http://edition.cnn.com/2018/01/09/politics/senate-cuba-sonic-attacks-hearing/index.html (accessed 10 January 2018).

63 United States, 'An Assessment of Illness in U.S. Government Employees and their Families at Overseas Embassies', *The National Academies Press*, National Academies of Sciences, Engineering, and Medicine, Washington, DC, 2020.

64 Andreas Umland, 'Aleksandr Dugin's Transformation from a Lunatic Fringe Figure into a Mainstream Political Publicist, 1980–1998: A Case Study in the Rise of Late and Post-Soviet Russian Fascism', *Journal of Eurasian Studies*, vol. 1, no. 2, July 2010, pp. 144–52.

65 Paul Goble, 'Dugin Says an Azerbaijan Hostile to Russia Will "Instantly Cease to Exist"', *The Interpreter*, 6 April 2014, http://www.interpretermag.com/dugin-says-an-azerbaijan-hostile-to-russia-will-instantly-cease-to-exist/ (accessed 14 August 2019).

66 Alexander Dugin, 'Fascism – Borderless and Red', undated, http://my.arcto.ru/public/templars/arbeiter.htm#fash (accessed 16 September 2021).

67 Goble, 'Dugin Says an Azerbaijan Hostile to Russia Will "Instantly Cease to Exist"'.

68 Charles Clover, 'Dreams of the Eurasian Heartland: The Re-emergence of Geopolitics', *Foreign Affairs*, March–April 1999, https://www.foreignaffairs.com/articles/asia/1999-03-01/dreams-eurasian-heartland-reemergence-geopolitics (accessed 25 May 2025).

69 Gareyev and Slipchenko, *Future War*, p. 67.

70 Ibid., p. 67.

71 Andrei Kokoshin, 'O Revolyutsii v Voyennom Dele v Proshlom i Nastoyashchem', *Otechestvennyye Zapiski*, vol. 5, no. 26, 2005, https://strana-oz.ru/2005/5/o-revolyucii-v-voennom-dele-v-proshlom-i-nastoyashchem (accessed 17 April 2021).

72 Russian Federation, 'Pryamaya Liniya s Vladimirom Putinym', 17 April 2014, http://www.kremlin.ru/events/president/transcripts/20796/work (accessed 13 September 2021).

73 Granholm, Malminen and Persson, 'A Rude Awakening', p. 30.

74 Russian Federation, 'Meeting with Members of the Valdai International Discussion Club', 14 September 2019, http://eng.kremlin.ru/transcripts/9031#sel=26:1,26:73 (accessed 18 August 2019).

75 Vladimir Putin, 'Prime Minister Vladimir Putin's Article for *Nezavisimaya Gazeta*', Archive of the Official Site of the 2008–2012 Prime Minister of the Russian Federation Vladimir Putin, 23 January 2012, http://archive.premier.gov.ru/eng/events/news/17831/ (accessed 9 August 2021).

76 Jeanne L. Wilson, 'The Legacy of the Color Revolutions for Russian Politics and Foreign Policy', *Problems of Post-Communism*, vol. 57, no. 2, 2010, p. 30.

77 Yevgenia Albats, 'In Putin's Kremlin, It's All about Control', *Washington Post*, 12 December 2004, https://www.washingtonpost.com/wp-dyn/articles/A56847-2004Dec11.html (accessed 23 January 2021).

78 Jardar Østbø, 'Securitizing "Spiritual-Moral Values" in Russia,' *Post-Soviet Affairs*, vol. 33, no. 3, 2017, pp. 200–216.

79 David Johnson, 'Russia's Approach to Conflict: Implications for NATO's Deterrence and Defence', NATO Defence College, research paper no. 111, 2015, https://www.ndc.nato.int/news/news.php?icode=797 (accessed 30 January 2021).

80 David Satter, *The Less You Know, the Better You Sleep* (New Haven: Yale, 2016).

81 Aleksandr Ostrovsky, *The Invention of Russia: The Journey from Gorbachev's Freedom to Putin's War* (London: Atlantic Books, 2015), p. 307.

82 Lilia Shevtsova, 'Novyy Mirovoy Poryadok Vladimira Putina', Carnegie Moscow Center, 11 May 2014, https://carnegie.ru/2014/05/11/ru-pub-55766 (accessed 25 November 2020).

83 Ibid.

84 Blank, 'No Need to Threaten Us, We Are Frightened of Ourselves', p. 24.

85 Russian Federation, 'Strategiya Natsional'noy Bezopasnosti', 31 December 2015, article 14, p. 4, http://static.kremlin.ru/media/events/files/ru/l8iXkR8XLAtxeilX7JK3XXy6YoAsHD5v.pdf (accessed 16 September 2017); Russian Federation, 'Strategiya Natsional'noy Bezopasnosti Rossiyskoy Federatsii', 2 July 2021, http://static.kremlin.ru/media/events/files/ru/QZw6hSk5z9gWq0plD1ZzmR5cER0g5tZC.pdf (accessed 30 September 2021).

86 Russian Federation, 'Strategiya Natsional'noy Bezopasnosti', 2015, pp. 4–5.

87 Ibid, p. 4.

88 Russian Federation, 'Strategiya Natsional'noy Bezopasnosti', 2021, p. 3.
89 Ibid., p. 5.
90 Ibid., p. 6.
91 Ibid., p. 6.
92 Russian Federation, 'Doktrina Informatsionnoy Bezopasnosti Rossiyskoy Federatsii', 5 December 2016, pp. 5–6, http://static.kremlin.ru/media/acts/files/0001201612060002.pdf (accessed 26 February 2017).
93 Ibid., p. 6.
94 Ibid., p. 6.
95 Russian Federation, 'Voyennaya Doktrina Rossiyskoy Federatsii', 25 December 2015, http://static.kremlin.ru/media/events/files/41d527556bec8deb3530.pdf (accessed 5 March 2017).
96 Valeri Gerasimov, 'Tsennost Nauki v Predvidenii', *Voyenno-Promyshlennyy Kuryer*, 27 February–5 March 2013, http://vpk-news.ru/sites/default/files/pdf/VPK_08_476.pdf (accessed 1 June 2015).
97 Ibid.
98 Ibid.

CHAPTER 7

1 Kos, interview with author, Kramatorsk area, 26 October 2024.
2 Father Vyacheslav, interview with author, Kramatorsk area, 29 October 2024.
3 Svarshchik, interview with author, Kramatorsk area, 30 October 2024.
4 Russian prisoner of war Zayats willingly talked to me, having been given the opportunity not to. Interview with author, Kramatorsk area, 30 October 2024.
5 Ukrainian interrogator, interview with author, Kyiv, 22 October 2024.
6 Schumacher, interview with author, Kramatorsk area, 29 October 2024.
7 Khersonet, interview with author, Kramatorsk area, 27 October 2024.

CHAPTER 8

1 Senior Ukrainian military intelligence officer, interview with author, Kyiv, 18 September 2017.
2 Steve Abrams, 'Beyond Propaganda: Soviet Active Measures in Putin's Russia', *Connections*, vol. 15, no. 1, winter 2021, p. 11.
3 Liudmyla Fylypovych, interview with author, Kyiv, 26 September 2017.
4 Russian Federation, 'The Military Doctrine of the Russian Federation', press release, The Embassy of the Russian Federation of the United Kingdom of Great Britain and Northern Ireland, 29 June 2015, https://london.mid.ru/en/press-centre/gb_en_fnapr_1947/ (accessed 25 May 2025).
5 Russian Federation, 'Voyennaya Doktrina', pp. 7–8.
6 Senior Ukrainian military intelligence officer, interview with author, Kyiv, 18 September 2017.
7 Vladimir Putin, 'Byt' Sil'nymi: Garantii Natsional'noy Bezopasnosti dlya Rossii', *Rossiyskaya Gazeta*, 20 February 2012, https://rg.ru/2012/02/20/putin-armiya.html (accessed 1 April 2021).
8 Lawrence Freedman, *Strategy: A History* (Oxford: Oxford University Press, 2013).
9 Mykola Sunhurovskyi, interview with author, Kyiv, 1 March 2017.
10 Yevhen Fedchenko, interview with author, Kyiv, 15 February 2017.
11 Mykhailo Honchar, interview with author, Kyiv, 19 September 2017.
12 Shandra, interview.
13 Roman Burko, interview with author, Kyiv, 20 August 2017.
14 Fedchenko, interview.
15 Mykola Riabchuk, interview with author, Kyiv, 14 February 2017.
16 Ukrainian businessman, interview with author, Kyiv, 1 March 2017.
17 Surkov, 'Dolgoye Gosudarstvo Putina'.
18 Agnieszka Bryc and Maria Domańska, 'Russia in the Trenches of Cognitive Warfare', *New Eastern Europe*, 9 September 2024, https://neweasterneurope.eu/2024/09/09/russia-in-the-trenches-of-cognitive-warfare/ (accessed 28 September 2024).
19 Russian Federation, 'Voyennaya Doktrina', pp. 7–8.
20 Russian Federation, 'Kontseptsiya Vneshney Politiki Rossiyskoy Federatsii', 1 December 2016, paragraph 8, http://www.mid.ru/foreign_policy/news/-/asset_publisher/cKNonkJE02Bw/content/id/2542248 (accessed 14 September 2017).
21 Ibid., paragraph 9.
22 Gerasimov, 'Tsennost Nauki v Predvidenii'.
23 Ihor Rushchenko, interview with author, Kharkiv, 20 September 2017.

24 Former senior secret service director, interview with author, Kyiv, August 2017.

25 Sunhurovskyi, interview.

26 'Fake: Crucifixion in Slovyansk', Stopfake.org, 15 July 2014, https://www.stopfake.org/en/lies-crucifixion-on-channel-one/ (accessed 10 August 2020).

27 Fedchenko, interview.

28 V. I. Lenin, 'Chto Delat', *Polnoye Sobraniye Sochineniy*, vol. 6 (Moskva: Gosudarstvennoye Izdatelstvo Politicheskoy Literatury, 1959), pp. 30–40.

29 V. I. Lenin, 'Uroki Moskovskogo Vosstaniya', *Polnoye Sobraniye Sochineniy*, vol. 13 (Moskva: Gosudarstvennoye Izdatelstvo Politicheskoy Literatury, 1959), pp. 369–77.

30 V. I. Lenin., 'Detskaya Bolezn "levizny" v Kommunizme', *Polnoye Sobraniye Sochineniy* (Moskva: Gosudarstvennoye Izdatelstvo Politicheskoy Literatury, 1959), vol. 41, pp. 3–104.

31 Bob Seely, 'How Russia's Trolls and Propagandists Have Turned Soviet Disinformation into a Terrifying Art Form', *Daily Telegraph*, 16 April 2018, https://www.telegraph.co.uk/news/2018/04/16/russias-trolls-propagandists-have-turned-soviet-disinformation/ (accessed 23 June 2024).

32 Jolanta Darczewska, 'The Anatomy of Russian Information Warfare. The Crimean Operation, a Case Study', Centre for Eastern Studies, Warsaw, 2014, pp. 35–6, http://www.osw.waw.pl/en/publikacje/point-view/2014-05-22/anatomy-russian-information-warfare-crimean-operation-a-case-study (accessed 31 August 2015).

33 Peter Pomerantsev, 'Russia's Ideology: There Is No Truth', *New York Times*, 11 December 2014, https://www.nytimes.com/2014/12/12/opinion/russias-ideology-there-is-no-truth.html (accessed 30 June 2021).

34 Chris McGreal, 'Vladimir Putin's "Misinformation" Offensive Prompts US to Deploy its Cold War Propaganda Tools', *The Guardian*, 25 April 2015, http://www.theguardian.com/world/2015/apr/25/us-set-to-revive-propaganda-war-as-putin-pr-machine-undermines-baltic-states?CMP=share_btn_link (accessed 26 April 2015).

35 Alya Shandra and Robert Seely, 'The Surkov Leaks: the Inner Workings of Russia's Hybrid War in Ukraine', Royal United Services Institute, occasional paper, July 2019, https://static.rusi.org/201907_op_surkov_leaks_web_final.pdf (accessed 25 May 2025).

36 Shandra and Seely, 'The Surkov Leaks', p. 74.

37 Julian Isherwood, 'Russia Warns Denmark its Warships could become Nuclear Targets', *Daily Telegraph*, 21 March 2015, http://www.telegraph.co.uk/news/worldnews/europe/denmark/11487509/Russia-warns-Denmark-its-warships-could-become-nuclear-targets.html (accessed 25 September 2016).

38 'The Katyn Deniers', *The Economist*, 2 November 2007, http://www.economist.com/node/10049754 (accessed 18 January 2025).

39 Burko, interview.

40 Andrei Soldatov and Irina Borogan, *The New Nobility: The Restoration of Russia's Security State and the Enduring Legacy of the KGB* (New York: Public Affairs, 2010), pp. 76–86.

41 Ihar Tyshkevich, interview with author, Kyiv, 18 August 2017.

42 Ibid.

43 Mark Lipovetsky, '*Brother 2* as a Political Melodrama. Twenty Years Later, Balabanov's Film Serves to Justify War with Ukraine', Russia Post, 11 July 2022, https://russiapost.info/society/brother_2 (accessed 24 December 2024).

44 Yevhen Fedchenko, 'Kremlin Propaganda: Soviet Active Measures by Other Means', *Estonian Journal of Military Studies*, vol. 2, 2016, p. 159, https://www.kvak.ee/files/2021/10/Yevhen-Fedchenko_KREMLIN-PROPAGANDA-SOVIET-ACTIVE-MEASURES-BY-OTHER-MEANS.pdf (accessed 25 May 2025).

45 Ihor Lapin, interview with author, Kyiv, 16 August 2017.

46 Ibid.

47 Yevhen Fedchenko, interview with author, Kyiv, 15 February 2017.

48 Mykola Riabchuk, 'Ukrainians as Russia's Negative "Other": History Comes Full Circle', *Communist and Post-Communist Studies*, vol. 49, 2016, p. 81.

49 Russian Federation, 'Obrashcheniye Prezidenta Rossiyskoy Federatsii', 18 March 2014, http://kremlin.ru/events/president/news/20603 (accessed 18 January 2021).

50 Fedchenko, interview.

51 Oren Dorell, 'Leaflet tells Jews to register in East Ukraine', *USA Today*, 17 April 2014, https://eu.usatoday.com/story/news/world/2014/04/17/jews-ordered-to-register-in-east-ukraine/7816951/ (accessed 30 June 2021).

52 Anton Butsenko, 'V Rossii Obnaruzhilis Seti "Ukrainskikh" Novostnykh Saytov', dp.ru, 14 November 2014, http://www.dp.ru/a/2014/11/11/Mi_sidim_s_vami_na_odnoj/ (accessed 6 July 2015).

53 Karen Horn, 'Paranoia, Populism and Propaganda still Drive Conspiracy Theorists', 13 April 2015, http://

www.capx.co/paranoia-populism-and-propaganda-still-drive-conspiracy-theorists/ (accessed 27 April 2015).

54 Shandra and Seely, 'The Surkov Leaks', p. 39.

55 Mark Galeotti, 'Crime and Crimea: Criminals as Allies and Agents', Radio Free Europe/Radio Liberty, http://www.rferl.org/content/crimea-crime-criminals-as-agents-allies/26671923.html (accessed August 23, 2015).

56 John Dziak, in Brian D. Dailey and Peter J. Parker (eds), *Soviet Strategic Deception* (Lexington: Lexington Books 1987), p. 4.

57 Shandra, interview.

58 Interview with author (anonymity requested); Dmytro Bulakh, interview with author, Kharkiv, 20 September 2017.

59 Fedchenko, interview.

60 Burko, interview.

61 Fedchenko, interview.

62 Lapin, interview.

63 Russian Federation, 'Rossiyskaya Federatsiya Federal'nyy Zakon O Protivodeystvii Terrorizmu', 26 February 2006, http://pravo.gov.ru/proxy/ips/?docbody=&nd=102105192 (accessed 30 June 2021); Steven Eke, 'Russia Law on Killing "Extremists" Abroad', BBC News, 27 November 2006, http://news.bbc.co.uk/1/hi/world/europe/6188658.stm (accessed 29 June 2021).

64 'Viktor Yushchenko: Ukraine's ex-President on Being Poisoned', BBC News, 2 April 2021, https://www.bbc.co.uk/news/av/world-europe-43611547 (accessed 25 September 2021).

65 National Archives, 'The Litvinenko Inquiry', http://webarchive.nationalarchives.gov.uk/20160613090305/https://www.litvinenkoinquiry.org (accessed 25 June 2018).

66 Bob Seely, 'Why the Kremlin likes using poison', *The Spectator*, 6 March 2018, https://www.spectator.co.uk/article/why-the-kremlin-likes-using-poison/ (accessed 25 May 2025).

67 'Understanding the use of Kompromat in Russian Politics: An Excerpt from Alena V. Ledeneva's "How Russia Really Works"', Cornell University Press, https://www.cornellpress.cornell.edu/understanding-the-use-of-kompromat-in-russian-politics-an-excerpt-from-alena-v-ledenevas-how-russia-really-works/ (accessed 10 July 2024).

68 Ibid.

69 Julia Ioffe, 'How State-Sponsored Blackmail Works in Russia', *The Atlantic*, 11 January 2017, https://www.theatlantic.com/international/archive/2017/01/kompromat-trump-dossier/512891/ (accessed 10 July 2024).

70 Riabchuk, interview.

71 Svitlana Zalishchuk, interview with author, Kyiv, 19 August 2017.

72 Peter Pomerantsev, 'How Putin Is Reinventing Warfare', Foreign Policy, 5 May 2021, http://www.foreignpolicy.com/articles/2014/05/05/how_putin_is_reinventing_warfare (accessed 30 June 2021).

73 'Ex-Chancellor Schroeder criticizes Merkel's Russia policy', RT, 28 March 2015, https://www.rt.com/news/244909-germany-schroeder-russia-policy/ (accessed 25 September 2016).

74 United States, 'Report of the Select Committee on Intelligence, United States Senate on Russian Active Measures Campaigns and Interference in the 2016 U.S. Election', vol. 5, 10 November 2020, https://www.intelligence.senate.gov/sites/default/files/documents/report_volume5.pdf (accessed 12 June 2021).

75 Honchar, interview.

76 Zalishchuk, interview.

77 Jaffe A. Myers and Ronald Soligo, 'Militarization of Energy: Geopolitical Threats to the Global Energy System', James A. Baker III Institute For Public Policy, working paper series, Rice University, Houston, May 2008, https://www.bakerinstitute.org/research/militarization-of-energy-geopolitical-threats-to-the-global-energy-system (accessed 25 May 2025).

78 Randall Newnham, 'Oil, Carrots, and Sticks: Russia's Energy Resources as a Foreign Policy Tool', *Journal of Eurasian Studies*, vol. 2, no. 2, 2011, pp. 134–43, p. 134.

79 Alexey Miller's interview with *Der Spiegel* magazine, transcript, 3 January 2011, https://www.gazprom.com/press/news/miller-journal/2011/108096/ (accessed 30 June 2021).

80 Karen Smith Stegen, 'Deconstructing the "Energy Weapon": Russia's threat to Europe as a Case Study', *Energy Policy*, vol. 39, no. 10, 2011, pp. 6505–13.

81 Irwin Stelzer, 'Energy Policy: Abandon Hope All Ye Who Enter Here', Hudson Institute, white paper, summer 2008, p. 17, http://www.npolicy.org/article_file/Energy_Policy-Abandon_Hope_All_Ye_Who_Enter_Here.pdf (accessed 25 September 2021).

82 Alex Barker and Peter Spiegel, 'Brussels Accuses Gazprom over Stranglehold', *Financial Times*, 22 April

2015, http://www.ft.com/cms/s/0/dec104ce-e8d1-11e4-b7e8-00144feab7de.html#axzz3al61h4Xv (accessed 21 May 2015).

83 'Statement of OAO "Gazprom" with Respect to the Adoption of "Statement of Objections" by the European Commission under the Antitrust Investigation', 22 April 2015, http://www.gazprom.com/press/news/2015/april/article224444/ (accessed 21 May 2015).

84 Shale Horowitz, *From Ethnic Conflict to Stillborn Reform: the Former Soviet Union and Yugoslavia* (Texas: A&M University Press, 2005), p. 118.

85 Steve Gutterman, 'Russia Halts Lithuanian Dairy Imports before EU summit', Reuters, 7 October 2013, https://www.reuters.com/article/us-russia-lithuania-dairy-idUSBRE99604Y20131007 (accessed 30 June 2021).

86 'Russia Tightens Screws on Ukraine with Candy Imports', *Moscow Times*, 5 September 2014, https://www.themoscowtimes.com/2014/09/05/russia-tightens-screws-on-ukraine-with-candy-import-ban-a39083 (accessed 30 June 2021).

87 Stephen Grey, Tom Bergin, Sevgil Musaieva and Roman Anin, 'Comrade Capitalism: Putin's Allies Channelled Billions to Oligarch Who Backed Pro-Russian President of Ukraine', Reuters, 26 November 2014, http://www.reuters.com/investigates/special-report/comrade-capitalism-the-kiev-connection/ (accessed 21 May 2015).

88 '"Chornomornaftohaz" (Black Sea Oil and Gas Company) Collects an Evidence Base for Three International Courts Against Russian Federation', Ukrainian Federation of Employers of the Oil and Gas Industry, 20 September 2018, https://frng.org.ua/en/novyny/chornomornaftohaz-zbyraie-dokazovu-bazu-dlia-trokh-mizhnarodnykh-sudiv-proty-rf (accessed 30 June 2021).

89 'Nakaz XXV Vsemirnogo Russkogo Narodnogo Sobora "Nastoyashcheye i Budushcheye Russkogo Mira"', Russkaya Pravoslavnaya Tserkov, 27 March 2024, http://www.patriarchia.ru/db/text/6116189.html (accessed 15 July 2014).

90 Martin Fornusek, 'SBU Detains Priest of Kremlin-Linked Church over Selling Arms', *Kyiv Independent*, 26 September 2023, https://kyivindependent.com/sbu-detains-priest-of-kremlin-linked-church-over-selling-arms/ (accessed 14 July 2024).

91 Jardar Østbø, 'Securitizing "Spiritual-Moral Values" in Russia', *Post-Soviet Affairs*, vol. 33, no. 3, 2017, p. 201.

92 Gleb Bryanski, 'Russian Patriarch Calls Putin Era "Miracle of God"', Reuters, 8 February 2012, https://www.reuters.com/article/world/russian-patriarch-calls-putin-era-miracle-of-god-idUSTRE81722Y/ (accessed 25 May 2025).

93 'Putin: "Pod Vashim Predstoyatel'stvom" Russkaya', *Russkaya Narodnaya*.

94 Riley Bailey, Christina Harward, Angelica Evans and George Barros, 'The Russian Orthodox Church Declares "Holy War" Against Ukraine and Articulates Tenets of Russia's Emerging Official Nationalist Ideology', Institute for the Study of War, 30 March 2024, https://www.understandingwar.org/backgrounder/russian-orthodox-church-declares-"holy-war"-against-ukraine-and-articulates-tenets (accessed 14 July 2024).

95 Nick Reynolds and Jack Watling, 'Ukraine Through Russia's Eyes', Royal United Services Institute, 25 February 2022, https://rusi.org/explore-our-research/publications/commentary/ukraine-through-russias-eyes (accessed 29 July 2024).

96 'Nakaz XXV Vsemirnogo Russkogo Narodnogo Sobora "Nastoyashcheye i Budushcheye Russkogo Mira"', Russkaya Pravoslavnaya Tserkov, 27 March 2024, http://www.patriarchia.ru/db/text/6116189.html (accessed 15 July 2014).

97 James Sherr and Kaarel Kullamaa, 'The Russian Orthodox Church: Faith, Power and Conquest', International Centre for Defence and Security and the Estonian Foreign Policy Institute, December 2019, pp. 4, 5, https://icds.ee/wp-content/uploads/2019/12/ICDS_EFPI_Report_The_Russian_Orthodox_Church_Sherr_Kullamaa_December_2019.pdf (accessed 25 January 2021).

98 Bogomolov and Lytvynenko, 'A Ghost in the Mirror', p. 11.

99 'Ukraine Conflict: Donetsk Rebels Parade Captured Soldiers', BBC News, 24 August 2014, http://www.bbc.co.uk/news/world-europe-28919683 (accessed 13 June 2021).

100 Jade McGlynn, *Memory Makers* (London: Bloomsbury, 2023).

101 Russian Federation, 'Stat'ya Vladimira Putina "Ob Istoricheskom Yedinstve Russkikh i Ukraintsev"', 12 July 2021, http://kremlin.ru/events/president/news/66181 (accessed 16 July 2021).

102 John C. Clews, *Communist Propaganda Techniques* (London, Fakenham and Reading: Cox and Wyman, 1964), p. 92.

103 Ibid., pp. 86, 87.

104 Yelena Chernenko, 'V Mire Slozhilas, Prezumptsiya Vinovnosti', *Kommersant*, 2 September 2015, http://www.kommersant.ru/doc/2014308 (accessed 11 July 2015).

105 Estonian Internal Security Service, 'Annual Review 2013', https://kapo.ee/sites/default/files/content_page_attachments/Annual%20Review%202013.pdf (accessed 25 May 2025).

106 Ibid.

107 Zalishchuk, interview.

108 Vladislava Vojtíšková, Vít Novotný, Hubertus Schmid-Schmidsfelden and Kristina Potapova, 'The Bear in Sheep's Clothing', Wilfried Martens Centre for European Studies, 2016, p. 11, https://www.martenscentre.eu/wp-content/uploads/2020/06/russia-gongos_0.pdf (accessed 27 January 2021).

109 Kim Sengupta and Andrew Osborn, 'A Lump of Rock, a Sophisticated Spying Device, and an Embassy Left Red-Faced', *The Independent*, 24 January 2006, https://www.independent.co.uk/news/world/europe/a-lump-of-rock-a-sophisticated-spying-device-and-an-embassy-left-redfaced-5336994.html (accessed 25 May 2025).

110 'Putin Sravnil Opponentov s Shakalami', BBC Russia, 21 November 2007, http://news.bbc.co.uk/hi/russian/russia/newsid_7105000/7105258.stm (accessed 23 January 2021).

111 Alexey Ivliev, 'Rossiyskiye Artisty Gastroliruyut po Gorodam Donbassa', NTV, 13 February 2016, http://www.ntv.ru/novosti/1605462/ (accessed 20 August 2017).

112 Tengiz Pkhaladze (ed.), '"Soft Power" – the New Concept of Russian Policy Towards Georgia', International Centre for Geopolitical Studies, Tbilisi, 2008, p. 108, http://www.icgs.ge/publications/Soft-Power-eng.pdf (accessed 7 July 2015).

113 Denis Dyomkin, 'Russian Orchestra, Putin's Friends, Play Syria's Palmyra', Reuters, 5 May 2016, https://www.reuters.com/article/us-mideast-crisis-russia-syria-concert-idUSKCN0XW143 (accessed 30 June 2021).

114 'Putin: Sport – eto ne "Razvlekushka"', YouTube, 27 March 2019, https://www.youtube.com/watch?v=FKVCAS3m2l4 (accessed 1 July 2021).

115 'Director General Ken McCallum gives latest threat update', MI5, 8 October 2024, https://www.mi5.gov.uk/director-general-ken-mccallum-gives-latest-threat-update#:~:text=The%20GRU%20in%20particular%20is,actions%20conducted%20with%20increasing%20recklessness (accessed 26 April 2025).

116 'The GRU: Blast puts spotlight on shadowy Russian force', BBC News, 19 April 2021, https://www.bbc.co.uk/news/world-europe-56798784 (accessed 26 December 2024).

117 'Up to 100 "Suspicious Incidents" in Europe Can Be Attributed to Russia, Czech Minister says', *The Guardian*, 4 December 2024, https://www.theguardian.com/world/2024/dec/04/up-to-100-suspicious-incidents-in-europe-can-be-attributed-to-russia-czech-minister-says (accessed 26 December 2024).

118 Cecilia Vega, 'Is Russia pursuing Putin foes abroad, going after critics and defectors on Western soil?', CBS News, 10 November 2024, https://www.cbsnews.com/news/is-russia-pursuing-putin-foes-abroad-60-minutes-transcript/ (accessed 26 December 2024).

119 Jon Richardson, 'How and why Russia is conducting sabotage and hybrid-war offensive', The Strategist, 5 November 2024, https://www.aspistrategist.org.au/how-and-why-russia-is-conducting-sabotage-and-hybrid-war-offensive/ (accessed 26 December 2024).

120 Hayley Dixon, 'Revealed: How Putin Plans to Flood West with Migrants', *Daily Telegraph*, 29 February 2024, https://www.telegraph.co.uk/news/2024/02/29/putin-russia-wagner-militia-africa-immigration-europe/ (accessed 26 December 2024).

121 Tom Sharpe, 'The US and Royal Navies Are Manoeuvring Against Russian Spy Platforms Deep Beneath the Irish Sea', *Daily Telegraph*, 15 November 2024, https://www.telegraph.co.uk/news/2024/11/15/us-royal-navy-warships-subs-russia-gugi-spy-ship/ (accessed 26 December 2024).

122 Alexander Lott, 'The Baltic Sea Cable-Cuts and Ship Interdiction: The C-Lion1 Incident', Lieber Institute, 26 November 2024, https://lieber.westpoint.edu/baltic-sea-cable-cuts-ship-interdiction-c-lion1-incident/ (accessed 26 December 2024).

123 Cachella Smith, 'Finland investigates Russia "Shadow Fleet" Ship after Cable Damage', BBC News, 26 December 2024, https://www.bbc.co.uk/news/articles/cr56l7prj2mo (accessed 26 December 2024).

124 United States, 'Russian Military Intelligence: Background and Issue for Congress', Congressional Research Service, 24 November 2020, p. 2, https://crsreports.congress.gov/product/pdf/R/R46616/6 (accessed 26 December 2024).

125 Interview with Andrei Soldatov, London, 6 August 2024.

126 United States, 'Russian Military Intelligence', p. 7.

127 Dina Temple-Raston, 'A "Worst Nightmare" Cyberattack: The Untold Story Of The SolarWinds Hack', NPR, 16 April 2021, https://www.npr.org/2021/04/16/985439655/a-worst-nightmare-cyberattack-the-untold-story-of-the-solarwinds-hack (accessed 16 March 2025).

128 Marcus Willett, 'Lessons of the SolarWinds Hack', *Survival*, vol. 63, no. 2, April–May 2021, pp. 7–26, p. 10, https://www.tandfonline.com/doi/epdf/10.1080/00396338.2021.1906001?needAccess=true (accessed 16 March 2025).

129 Bill Whitaker, 'SolarWinds: How Russian spies hacked the Justice, State, Treasury, Energy and Commerce Departments', CBS News, 4 July 2021, https://www.cbsnews.com/news/solarwinds-hack-russia-cyberattack-60-minutes-2021-07-04/ (accessed 16 March 205).
130 'Five Things to Know about the Nation-State Cyberattack on The US and West's Top Entities', HYPR, https://www.hypr.com/security-encyclopedia/solarwinds-breach (accessed 16 March 2025).
131 Zbigniew Brzezinski and Paige Sullivan (eds), *Russia and the Commonwealth of Independent States: Documents, Data, and Analysis*, Center for Strategic and International Studies (Armonk, NY: M.E. Sharpe, 1997).
132 Eduard Kulinich, interview with author, Kramatorsk, 24 September 2017.
133 'Ukrainskiye Plennyye Zvonyat Materyam', Zvezda TV, 16 August 2014, https://tvzvezda.ru/news/vstrane_i_mire/content/201408161120-78wz.htm (accessed 25 August 2020).
134 United Nations, 'Report on the Human Rights Situation in Ukraine', Office of the High Commissioner for Human Rights, 31 December 2024, p. 2, https://ukraine.ohchr.org/sites/default/files/2024-12/PR41%20Ukraine%202024-12-31.pdf (accessed 18 January 2025).
135 Ibid.
136 Susie Blann and Hanna Arhirova, '2 years after Ukrainian POW deaths, survivors and leaked UN analysis point to Russia as the culprit', Associated Press, 25 July 2024, https://apnews.com/article/russia-ukraine-pows-prison-prisoners-15561a6d5cafc5b61a1f2643009c2a2c (accessed 12 January 2025).
137 Dima, interview with author, Kyiv, 6 September 2024.
138 Petro Yatsenko, interview with author, Kyiv, 6 September 2024.
139 *The Technique of Soviet Propaganda: A Study Presented by the Subcommittee to Investigate the Administration of the Internal Security Act and Other Internal Security laws of the Committee on the Judiciary*, United States Senate, Eighty-Sixth Congress, Second Session (Washington DC: United States Government Printing Office, 1960).
140 Intelligence read-out in author's possession.
141 Bob Seely, 'Have Lammy and Starmer been played by the Kremlin over Chagos?', *Daily Telegraph*, 1 December 2024, https://www.telegraph.co.uk/news/2024/12/01/labours-chagos-deal-risks-a-return-state-on-state-war-era/ (accessed 26 December 2024).
142 Peter Dickinson, 'One Million Passports: Putin has Weaponised Citizenship in Occupied Eastern Ukraine', Atlantic Council, 17 June 2020, https://www.atlanticcouncil.org/blogs/ukrainealert/one-million-passports-putin-has-weaponized-citizenship-in-occupied-eastern-ukraine/ (accessed 19 June 2021); Neil Melvin, 'Russia's Policy of Passport Proliferation', Royal United Services Institute, 1 May 2020, https://rusi.org/commentary/russias-policy-passport-proliferation (accessed 19 June 2021).
143 'Lider Nochnykh Volkov "Khirurg": Gosudarstvo Priznalo nas Instrumentom Narodnoy Diplomatii', TV Rain, 7 May 2014, http://tvrain.ru/teleshow/reportazh/aleksandr_hirurg_zaldostanov_o_grantah_navalnom_st-387011/ (accessed 24 May 2015).
144 'Motoklub Russkogo Dukha, Motoklub Patriotov!', Night Wolves, https://nightwolves.ru/nw/about/about.php (accessed 25 September 2016).
145 Adrian Sawczyn, 'The Profitable Patriotism of Vladimir Putin's Biker Bromance', Global Voices, 19 May 2015, http://globalvoicesonline.org/2015/05/19/russia-the-profitable-patriotism-of-vladimir-putins-biker-bromance/?utm_source=Global+Voices&utm_campaign=e465bc3680-Weekly_Digest_May16_2015&utm_medium=email&utm_term=0_633e82444a-e465bc3680-290384525 (accessed 25 September 2016).
146 Ibid.
147 'Marionetki Maidana', YouTube, 4 February 2014, https://www.youtube.com/watch?v=MSxaa-67yGM&feature=youtu.be (accessed 1 February 2015).
148 '"F**k the EU": Snr US State Dept. official caught in alleged phone chat on Ukraine', RT, 6 February 2014, http://rt.com/news/nuland-phone-chat-ukraine-927/ (accessed 30 June 2021).
149 'Victoria Nuland gaffe: Angela Merkel condemns EU insult', BBC News, 7 February 2015, http://www.bbc.co.uk/news/world-europe-26080715 (accessed 1 February 2015).

CHAPTER 9

1 Interview with Dr Ivan Parkhomenko, Kharkiv, 1 September 2024.
2 Defense of Ukraine, X.com, 1 October 2024, https://x.com/DefenceU/status/1841098880068247792 (accessed 6 October 2024).
3 John Hardie, 'What we Know about Russia's New 3-Ton Glide Bomb', Foundation for Defense of Democracies, 19 July 2024, https://www.fdd.org/analysis/2024/07/19/what-we-know-about-russias-new-3-ton-glide-bomb/ (accessed 1 October 2024).
4 The higher prices quoted in the media are probably inaccurate. They are likely derived from export contracts. For more, see 'What is the Real Price of Russian Missiles: About the Cost of "Kalibr", Kh-101

and "Iskander" Missiles', Defence Express, 1 November 2022, https://en.defence-ua.com/news/what_is_the_real_price_of_russian_missiles_about_the_cost_of_kalibr_kh_101_and_iskander_missiles-4709.html (accessed 30 September 2024).

5 Interview with Dr Kyrylo Parkhomenko, Kharkiv, 1 September 2024.
6 Yevhen Vasylenko, interview with author, Kharkiv, 18 November 2024.
7 Vitali Khrystenko, interview with author, Kharkiv, 25 October 2024.
8 Serhii, interview with author, western Ukraine, 6 September 2024.
9 Dmytro Sakharuk, interview with author, Kyiv, 4 September 2024.
10 Aura Sabadus, interview with author via Zoom, 5 August 2024.
11 United Nations, 'Report on the Human Rights Situation in Ukraine'.
12 Hugh Noyes, *The Isle of Wight Bedside Anthology* (Newport: The Isle of Wight County Press, 1978), pp. 143–5.

CHAPTER 10

1 'Inside the KGB: An Interview with Retired Maj. Gen. Oleg Kalugin', CNN, January 1998, https://web.archive.org/web/20070206020316/http:/www.cnn.com/SPECIALS/cold.war/episodes/21/interviews/kalugin/ (accessed 4 July 2021).
2 Oscar Jonsson and Robert Seely, 'Russian Full-Spectrum Conflict: An Appraisal After Ukraine', *Journal of Slavic Military Studies*, vol. 28, no. 1, March 2015, pp. 1–22, p. 6.
3 F. E. Dzerzhinskogo, *Kontrrazvedyvatel'nyy slovar*, 1972, http://counterintelligence.academic.ru/442/Мероприятия_активные (accessed 4 February 2016). Thanks to Dr Steven Main for his help.
4 Andrew and Gordievsky, *KGB: The Inside Story*, pp. 7, 8.
5 Brian D. Dailey and Peter J. Parker (eds), *Soviet Strategic Deception* (Lexington: Lexington Books 1987), p. 7.
6 Vladimir Voronov, '"Zelenyye Chelovechki" Stalina' Radio Liberty/Radio Free Europe, 2 November 2014, https://www.svoboda.org/a/26670277.html (accessed 21 February 2021).
7 Dennis Kux, 'Soviet Active Measures and Disinformation: Overview and Assessment', *Parameters*, vol. 16, no. 1, 1985, p. 20, https://press.armywarcollege.edu/parameters/vol15/iss1/17/?utm_source=press.armywarcollege.edu%2Fparameters%2Fvol15%2Fiss1%2F17&utm_medium=PDF&utm_campaign=PDFCoverPages (accessed 29 September 2021).
8 Andrew and Gordievsky, *KGB: The Inside Story*, p. 71.
9 Dailey and Parker, *Soviet Strategic Deception*, p. 7.
10 Owen Bowcott, 'How Fate, and Stalin, Finally Dealt the "Ace of Spies" a Losing Hand', *The Guardian*, 7 September 2002, https://www.theguardian.com/uk/2002/sep/07/russia.artsandhumanities (accessed 5 September 2023).
11 Andrew Cook, 'To Trap a Spy', *The Guardian*, 7 October 2002, https://www.theguardian.com/world/2002/oct/07/russia.artsandhumanities (accessed 3 July 2021).
12 Richard Spence, 'Russia's Operatsiia Trest: A Reappraisal', *Global Intelligence Monthly*, 1 April 1999, p. 19, https://archive.org/details/1999-operatsiia-trest/mode/2up (accessed 18 July 2021).
13 Andrew and Gordievsky, *KGB: The Inside Story*, p. 71.
14 Victor Madeira, *Britannia and the Bear: The Anglo-Russian Intelligence Wars, 1917–1929* (Woodbridge: Boydell & Brewer, 2014), p. 159.
15 Giles Udy, *Labour and the Gulag: Russia and the Seduction of the British Left* (London: Biteback Publishing, 2017).
16 Voronov, '"Zelenyye Chelovechki" Stalina'.
17 Fletcher Schoen and Christopher J. Lamb, 'Deception, Disinformation, and Strategic Communications: How One Interagency Group Made a Major Difference', *Strategic Perspectives*, no. 11, Institute for National Strategic Studies, Washington DC, June 2012, p. 37.
18 United States Congress, Permanent Select Committee on Intelligence, 'Soviet Covert Action (The Forgery Offensive)', House of Representatives, Ninety-Sixth Congress, Second Session (Washington DC: US Government Printing Office, 1980).
19 Pavel Sudoplatov and Anatoli Sudoplatov, *Special Tasks: The Memoirs of an Unwanted Witness – a Soviet Spymaster*, with Jerrold L. and Leona P. Schecter (Boston: Little Brown and Co., 1994).
20 Ladislav Bittman, *The KGB and Soviet Disinformation* (Washington DC: Pergamon-Brassey's, 1985), p. 2; Thomas Boghardt, 'The Creation and Perpetuation of a Myth', *Studies in Intelligence*, vol. 53, no. 4, December 2009, p. 5, https://apps.dtic.mil/sti/pdfs/ADA514366.pdf (accessed 24 July 2021).
21 Bittman, *The KGB*, p. 44.
22 Christopher Andrew and Vasili Mitrokhin, *The World Was Going Our Way: The KGB and the Battle for the Third World* (New York: Basic Books, 2005), p. 507.

23 Ibid.
24 Boghardt, 'The Creation and Perpetuation of a Myth'.
25 Ibid., p. 4.
26 United States, 'Soviet Influence Activities: A Report on Active Measures and Propaganda, 1986-87', US Department of State, October 1987, p. viii, http://jmw.typepad.com/files/state-department---a-report-on-active-measures-and-propaganda.pdf (accessed 27 August 2015).
27 Ibid, p. viii.
28 Ibid, p. viii.
29 United States, *House Committee on Intelligence: Soviet Active Measures* (Washington DC: Government Printing Office, 1982), p. 31.
30 Statement of John McMahon, Central Intelligence Agency, to 'Soviet Covert Action (The Forgery Offensive)'.
31 Aleksandr Kaznacheev, *Inside a Soviet Embassy* (London: Robert Hale, 1962), p. 128.
32 Ibid., p. 130.
33 Stanislav Levchenko, *On the Wrong Side* (Washington DC: Pergamnon-Brasey's, 1998), p. 236.
34 Ibid., p. 236.
35 Christopher Andrew and Vasili Mitrokhin, *The Mitrokhin Archive: The KGB in Europe and the West* (London: Penguin, 1999), p. 310.
36 United States, US District Court for the District of Columbia, indictment, 16 February 2018, https://nsarchive.gwu.edu/document/16339-united-states-district-court (accessed 9 June 2025); United States, US District Court for the District of Columbia, indictment, 13 July 2018, https://nsarchive.gwu.edu/document/16702-indictment (accessed 9 June 2025).
37 Yuri Bezmenov, 'Lecture, 1983', approx. 11 minutes 40 seconds in, YouTube, 19 August 2017, https://www.youtube.com/watch?v=LSz_nksoYuk (accessed 23 February 2018).
38 'Former KGB Agent Explains how Elites Brainwash the Pulic [*sic*] from reality', undated interview, YouTube, 2 June 2011, https://www.youtube.com/watch?v=DAMiNTC7HOM (accessed 1 January 2016).
39 'Inside the KGB: An Interview with Retired Maj. Gen. Oleg Kalugin', CNN.
40 Ion Pacepa and Ronald Rychlak, *Disinformation* (Washington: WND Books, 2013), p. 262.
41 Ion Pacepa, 'What does Moscow have to do with the recent war in Lebanon?', National Review, 24 August 2006, http://www.nationalreview.com/article/218533/russian-footprints-ion-mihai-pacepa (accessed 1 September 2015).
42 Ibid.
43 Georgi Filin, 'Otets Terrorisma', Versiya, July 2014, https://versia.ru/general-saxarovskij-teoretik-avtokatastrof-i-razrabotchik-sekretnoj-verbovki (accessed 18 July 2021).
44 United States Congress, Permanent Select Committee on Intelligence, 'Soviet Covert Action (The Forgery Offensive)', p. 34.
45 Bittman, *The KGB*, p. 43.
46 Richard H. Shultz and Roy Godson, *Dezinformatsia*, (Washington DC: Pergamon Press, 1984), pp. 1, 2.
47 'Inside the KGB: An Interview with Retired Maj. Gen. Oleg Kalugin', CNN.
48 Yuri Bezmenov, 'Lecture, 1983', approx. 2 hours, 12 minutes and 5 seconds in.
49 Ibid., approx. 2 hours and 18 minutes in.
50 Valeri Gerasimov, 'Tsennost Nauki v Predvidenii', *Voyenno-Promyshlennyy Kuryer*, 27 February to 5 March 2013, http://vpk-news.ru/sites/default/files/pdf/VPK_08_476.pdf (accessed 1 June 2015).
51 Comment by Igor Panarin on 'Ideologiya Rossii' page, VK social media site, 19 March 2014, https://vk.com/wall-41056521_354 (accessed 2 October 2021).
52 Mette Skak, 'Russian Strategic Culture: The Role of Today's Chekisty', *Contemporary Politics*, vol. 22, no. 3, 2016, pp. 324–41.
53 Robert W. Pringle, 'Andropov's Counterintelligence State', *International Journal of Intelligence and CounterIntelligence*, vol. 13, no. 2, 2000, pp. 193–203, p. 196.
54 Robert W. Pringle, 'Putin: The New Andropov?', *International Journal of Intelligence and CounterIntelligence*, vol. 14, no. 4, 2001, pp. 545–58, p. 546.
55 Yevgenia Albats, 'In Putin's Kremlin, It's All about Control', *Washington Post*, 12 December 2004, https://www.washingtonpost.com/wp-dyn/articles/A56847-2004Dec11.html (accessed 23 January 2021).
56 Volodymyr Yermolenko, interview with author, Kyiv, 14 February 2017.
57 Vasiliy Kravets, interview with author, Kramatorsk, 22 September 2017.
58 Rushchenko, interview.
59 Roman Burko, interview with author, Kyiv, 20 August 2017.

60 Nataliya Zubar, interview with author, Kharkiv, 21 September 2017.
61 Chystylin, interview.
62 G. Isserson, 'The Development of the Theory of Soviet Operational Art in the 1930s', in Harold S. Orenstein (ed.), *Selected Readings in the History of Soviet Operational Art* (Auckland: Pickle Partners, 2016).
63 Gerasimov, 'Tsennost Nauki v Predvidenii'.
64 Ibid.
65 Ibid.
66 Kvachkov, *Special Forces of Russia*, section 3.2.1.
67 Ibid., section 3.2.
68 Andrei, A. Kokoshin, *Soviet Strategic Thought, 1917–1991* (Cambridge, MA and London: MIT Press, 1999), p. 160.
69 V. K. Triandafillov, *The Nature of the Operations of Modern Armies* (London and New York: Routledge, 2006), translated and edited by Jacob. W. Kipp, pp. 90–94.
70 Kokoshin, *Soviet Strategic Thought*, p. 160; Varfolomeyev, *Strategiya*, p 88.
71 Gerasimov, 'Tsennost Nauki v Predvidenii'.
72 Robert N. Watt, 'Feeling the Full Force of a Four Front Offensive: Reinterpreting the Red Army's 1944 Belorussian and L'vov-Peremshyl' Operations', *Journal of Slavic Military Studies*, vol. 21, no. 4, 2008, p. 677.
73 Svechin, 'Intergralnoye Ponimaniye Voyennogo Istkusstva', in Harrison, *The Russian Way*, p. 140.
74 Jacob W. Kipp, 'The Tsarist and Soviet Operational Art, 1853–1991', John Andreas Olsen and Martin van Crevald (eds), *The Evolution of Operational Art, From Napoleon to the Present* (Oxford: Oxford University Press, 2011), p. 67.
75 Hans Delbrück, *History of the Art of War Within the Framework of Political History* (Westport: Greenwood Press, 1985), pp. 439–44.
76 Harrison, *The Russian Way*, p. 130.
77 Kokoshin, *Soviet Strategic Thought*, p. 151.
78 Leon Trotsky, *Voyennaya Doktrina ili Mnimo-Voennoye Doktrinerstvo* (Petrograd: Politicheskoye Upravlenie Petrogradskogo Voennogo Okruga, 1922), pp. 9–10, http://swetschin.narod.ru/others/Trotskii_L_Military_Doctrine_or_Pseudo-military_Doctrinarism.PDF (accessed 6 December 2015).
79 Friedrich Engels, 'Conditions and Prospects of War of the Holy Alliance Against France in 1852', first published in *Die Neue Zeit*, 4 and 11 December 1914, http://hiaw.org/defcon6/works/1851/04/holy-alliance.html (accessed 5 October 2015).
80 V. I. Lenin, 'Voina i Revolyutsiya', in *Polnoye Sobraniye Sochineniy*, vol. 32, 1969, pp. 79–80, http://uaio.ru/vil/32.htm#s77 (accessed 27 November 2015).
81 *G. S. Isserson and the War of the Future, Key Writings of a Soviet Military Theorist*, translated and edited by Richard W. Harrison (Jefferson: Macfarland and Company, 2016).

CHAPTER 11

1 Ksenia, interview with author, Kyiv, 17 November 2024.
2 Rostyslav, interview with author, Kyiv, 17 November 2024.
3 Megan Gittoes, interview with author, London, 10 May 2024.
4 Vladyslav Havrylov, 'The illegal deportation of Ukrainian children is a crime organized and financed by Russian officials', Ukraine, 26 April 2024, https://war.ukraine.ua/articles/the-illegal-deportation-of-ukrainian-children-is-a-crime-organized-and-financed-by-russian-officials/ (accessed 4 November 2024).
5 Olena Barsukova, 'Putin signs a decree simplifying Russian citizenship procedure for orphans from Ukraine', Ukrainska Pravda, 20 May 2022, http//www.pravda.com.ua/eng/news/2022/05/30/7349514/ (accessed 3 November 2024).
6 Havrylov, 'The illegal deportation of Ukrainian children is a crime organized and financed by Russian officials'.
7 International Committee of the Red Cross, 'Article 49 - Deportations, transfers, evacuations', Internationa; Humanitarian Law Databases, https://ihl-databases.icrc.org/en/ihl-treaties/gciv-1949/article-49# (accessed 5 November 2024).
8 Kateryna Rashevska, interview with author, Kyiv, 1 November 2024.
9 Solomiya Khoma, interview with author, Kyiv, 29 August 2024.
10 Onysia Siniuk, interview with author via Zoom, 1 November 2024.
11 'Comment of the MFA of Ukraine on the decree of the President of the Russian Federation on simplifying the procedure for obtaining Russian citizenship for Ukrainian orphans', Ministry of Foreign Affairs of Ukraine, 31 May 2022, https://mfa.gov.ua/en/news/zayava-mzs-ukrayini-shchodo-ukazu-prezidenta-rf-pro-sproshchenij-prijom-v-rosijske-gromadyanstvo-ukrayinskih-ditej-sirit (accessed 3 November 2024).

CHAPTER 12

1 Darczewska, 'The Anatomy of Russian Information Warfare'.
2 Ibid.
3 Ibid.
4 Ihar Tyshkevich, interview with author, Kyiv, 18 August 2017.
5 Grey et al., 'Comrade Capitalism'; argued by Lapin, interview, Bulakh, interview and Riabchuk, interview.
6 Jack Watling, Oleksandr V. Danylyuk and Nick Reynolds, 'Preliminary Lessons from Russia's Unconventional Operations During the Russo-Ukrainian War, February 2022–February 2023', Royal United Services Institute, 29 March 2023, p. 6, https://rusi.org/explore-our-research/publications/special-resources/preliminary-lessons-russias-unconventional-operations-during-russo-ukrainian-war-february-2022 (accessed 26 July 2024).
7 'SBU Vykryla Ahenturnu Merezhu HRU rf, do Yakoyi Vkhodyv Narodnyy Deputat Ukrayiny (video)', Security Service of Ukraine, 24 June 2022, https://ssu.gov.ua/novyny/sbu-vykryla-ahenturnu-merezhu-hru-rf-do-yakoi-vkhodyv-narodnyi-deputat-ukrainy-video (accessed 4 August 2024).
8 Marina Litvinenko, interview with author, London, 7 August 2024.
9 Keir Giles, James Sherr and Anthony Seaboyer, 'Russian Reflexive Control', Royal Military College of Canada, October 2018, p. 17, https://www.researchgate.net/publication/328562833 (accessed 23 July 2024).
10 Answers to written questions, Kyiv, September 2014.
11 Former activist, interview with author, Kyiv, 16 September 2024.
12 'Putin Reveals Secrets of Russia's Crimea Takeover Plot', BBC News, 9 March 2015, https://www.bbc.co.uk/news/world-europe-31796226 (accessed 5 July 2021).
13 Christo Grozev, interview with author via WhatsApp, 9 August 2024.
14 Martin Hurt, 'Lessons Identified in Crimea: Does Estonia's National Defence Model Meet our Needs?', International Centre for Defence Studies, April 2014, p. 1, https://icds.ee/en/lessons-to-learn-from-crimea-does-estonias-national-defence-model-meet-our-needs/ (accessed 25 May 2025).
15 Ibid.
16 Galeotti, 'Crime and Crimea'.
17 Burko, interview.
18 United States, '"Little Green Men": A Primer on Modern Russian Unconventional Warfare, Ukraine 2013–2014', United States Army Special Operations Command, Fort Bragg, https://www.jhuapl.edu/Content/documents/ARIS_LittleGreenMen.pdf (accessed 2 October 2021).
19 Robyn Dixon, 'As NATO Talks Near, Merkel Appears to be Losing Patience with Putin', *Los Angeles Times*, 3 September 2014, https://www.latimes.com/world/europe/la-fg-germany-merkel-putin-20140904-story.html (accessed 24 July 2021).
20 Mansur Mirovalev and Denis Sinyakov, 'Russia's Crackdown on Crimea's Muslims', Al Jazeera, 25 November 2014, https://www.aljazeera.com/news/2014/11/25/russias-crackdown-on-crimeas-muslims (accessed 24 July 2021); Diane Francis, 'Putin's Crimean Crackdown Continues: Radio Free Europe Journalist Targeted', 27 June 2021, https://www.atlanticcouncil.org/blogs/ukrainealert/putins-crimean-crackdown-continues-radio-free-europe-journalist-targeted/ (accessed 24 July 2021).
21 Darczewska, 'The Anatomy of Russian Information Warfare'.
22 Konstantin Oleynik, interview with author, Kharkiv, 21 September 2017.
23 Chystylin, interview.
24 Denys Bihunov, interview with author, Sloviansk, 24 September 2017.
25 Kravets, interview.
26 Shandra and Seely, 'The Surkov Leaks', p. 45.
27 Chystylin, interview.
28 Ibid.
29 Igor Sutyagin, 'Russian Forces in Ukraine', Royal United Services Institute, March 2025, p. 4, https://static.rusi.org/201503_bp_russian_forces_in_ukraine.pdf (accessed 25 August 2024).
30 'Use of Fancy Bear Android Malware in Tracking of Ukrainian Field Artillery Units', Crowdstrike Global Intelligence Team, 22 December 2016, https://www.crowdstrike.com/wp-content/brochures/FancyBearTracksUkrainianArtillery.pdf (accessed 30 June 2021).
31 Unnamed commander, interview with author, Kyiv, 1 March 2017.
32 Liubov Tybulska, interview with author, Kyiv, 19 September 2017.
33 Robert L. Larsen, 'Russia's Energy Policy: Security Dimensions and Russia's Reliability as an Energy Supplier', Swedish Defence Research Agency, March 2006, p. 4, https://www.foi.se/rest-api/report/foi-r--1934--se#:~:text (accessed 20 July 2021).
34 Anton Grushetsky, interview with author, Kyiv, 26 September 2024.
35 Honchar, interview.

36 Fedchenko, interview.

37 Yevhen Fedchenko, 'Kremlin Propaganda: Soviet Active Measures by Other Means', *Estonian Journal of Military Studies*, vol. 2, 2016, pp. 141–70, p. 156, http://ekmair.ukma.edu.ua/bitstream/handle/123456789/11622/Fedchenko_Kremlin_propaganda.pdf?sequence=1&isAllowed=y (accessed 19 December 2020).

38 Soldatov and Borogan, *The New Nobility*, pp. 79–81.

39 S. G. Chekinov and S. A. Bogdanov, 'O Kharaktere i Soderzhanii Voyny Novogo Pokoleniya', *Voyennaya Mysl'*, no. 10, 2013.

40 For example, see this speculative piece on the use of either acoustic or microwave weapons. Julia Ioffe, 'The Mystery of the Immaculate Concussion', *GQ*, 20 October 2020, https://www.gq.com/story/cia-investigation-and-russian-microwave-attacks (accessed 11 November 2020).

CHAPTER 13

1 Mykhaylo Zabordskyi, Jack Watling, Oleksandr V. Danylyuk, and Nick Reynolds, 'Preliminary Lessons in Conventional Warfighting from Russia's Invasion of Ukraine: February–July 2022', Royal United Services Institute, 30 November 2022, p. 7, https://static.rusi.org/359-SR-Ukraine-Preliminary-Lessons-Feb-July-2022-web-final.pdf (accessed 4 January 2025).

2 Roger N. McDermott and Lt Col. Charles K. Bartles, 'An Assessment of the Initial Period of War: Russia-Ukraine 2022, Part Two', Russia Strategic Initiative, https://fmso.tradoc.army.mil/2023/2023-06-08-an-assessment-of-the-initial-period-of-war-russia-ukraine-2022-part-2-roger-n-mcdermott-lieutenant-colonel-charles-k-bartles/ (accessed 10 April 2025).

3 Hamish de Bretton-Gordon, 'Vladimir Putin's Hubris Has Finally Met its Nemesis', *Daily Telegraph*, 12 August 2024, https://www.telegraph.co.uk/news/2024/08/12/putin-hubris-nemesis/ (accessed 12 August 2024).

4 Member of Ukrainian intelligence community, interview with author, Kyiv, 27 August 2024.

5 Samuel Charap and Sergey Radchenko, 'The Talks That Could Have Ended the War in Ukraine', *Foreign Affairs*, 16 April 2024, https://www.foreignaffairs.com/ukraine/talks-could-have-ended-war-ukraine (accessed 4 January 2024).

6 Ibid.

7 Shandra and Seely, 'The Surkov Leaks'.

8 Harry Halem, interview with author, London, 26 July 2024.

9 Olga Voitovych, 'Ukraine Charges Former Head of Crimean Security Service with Treason for Spying for Russia', 3 July 2023, https://edition.cnn.com/europe/live-news/russia-ukraine-war-news-07-03-23#h_90e1c89de62951a5d3bc98b73c66ff25 (accessed 12 August 2024).

10 'Povidomlennya pro pidozru Sivkovychu V.L.', Ukrainian State Bureau of Investigations, 22 July 2022, pp. 7–9, https://www.gp.gov.ua/ua/posts/povidomlennya-pro-pidozru-sivkovicu-vl (accessed 26 July 2024).

11 Ibid., p. 8.

12 Russian Federation, 'Address by the President of the Russian Federation', 24 February 2022, http://en.kremlin.ru/events/president/news/67843 (accessed 14 December 2024).

13 Aura Sabadus, interview with author online, 5 August 2024; Michael Schwirtz, Anton Troianovski, Yousur Al-Hlou, Masha Froliak, Adam Entous and Thomas Gibbons-Neff, 'Putin's War', *New York Times*, 16 December 2024, https://www.nytimes.com/interactive/2022/12/16/world/europe/russia-putin-war-failures-ukraine.html (accessed 26 July 2024).

14 Schwirtz et al., 'Putin's War'.

15 Valerie Hopkins, 'In Video, A Defiant Zelensky Says "We Are Here"', *New York Times*, 25 February 2022, https://www.nytimes.com/2022/02/25/world/europe/zelensky-speech-video.html (accessed 15 December 2024).

16 Colonel Charles Bartles, interview with author via WhatsApp, 17 January 2025.

17 World Council of Churches, https://www.oikoumene.org/resources/image/st-andrew-orthodox-church-in-bucha (accessed 4 January 2025).

18 Fedor, interview with author, Motyzhyn, 23 September 2024.

19 Michael Kofman, 'Russian Performance in The Russo-Georgian War Revisited', War on the Rocks, 4 September 2018, https://warontherocks.com/2018/09/russian-performance-in-the-russo-georgian-war-revisited/ (accessed 4 January 2024).

20 Louisa Loveluck, 'Syrian Army Responsible for Douma Chemical Weapons Attack, Watchdog Confirms', *Washington Post*, 27 January 2023, https://www.washingtonpost.com/world/2023/01/27/syria-chemical-weapons-douma-opcw/ (accessed 20 August 2024).

21 Jack Watling, 'Russia's Callousness Towards its Own Soldiers is Undermining its Combat Power', *The Guardian*, 4 March 2022, https://www.theguardian.com/commentisfree/2022/mar/04/russias-callousness-towards-its-own-soldiers-is-undermining-its-combat-power (accessed 13 October 2024).

22 Kofman, 'Russian Performance in The Russo-Georgian War Revisited'.

23 'SBU Vykryla Ahenturnu Merezhu HRU rf, do Yakoyi Vkhodyv Narodnyy Deputat Ukrayiny (video)'.

24 Schwirtz et al., 'Putin's War'.
25 Zabrodskyi et al., 'Preliminary Lessons in Conventional Warfighting', p. 26.
26 Segar, interview with author, Kyiv, 19 September 2024.
27 Kofman, 'Russian Performance in The Russo-Georgian War Revisited'.
28 Zabrodskyi et al., 'Preliminary Lessons in Conventional Warfighting', p. 1.
29 Ibid., p. 32.
30 David Saw, 'The Rise and Fall of the Russian Battalion Tactical Group Concept', European Security and Defence, https://euro-sd.com/2022/11/articles/exclusive/26319/the-rise-and-fall-of-the-russian-battalion-tactical-group-concept/ (accessed 22 August 2024).
31 Nicholas Fiore, 'Defeating the Russian Battalion Tactical Group', Armor, US Army Fort Moore and the Maneuver Center of Excellence, 2017, https://www.benning.army.mil/armor/eARMOR/content/issues/2017/Spring/2Fiore17.pdf (accessed 24 August 2024).
32 United Kingdom Ministry of Defence, X.com, 29 November 2022, https://x.com/DefenceHQ/status/1597482502200983552/photo/1 (accessed 20 August 2024).
33 Unnamed special forces volunteer, interview with author, Kyiv, August 2024.
34 Unnamed soldier, interview with author, Kyiv, September 2024.
35 Western military observer, interview with author via Zoom, 21 September 2024.
36 Unnamed observer, interview with author via Zoom, September 2024.
37 Western expert, interview with author, Kyiv, 27 August 2024.
38 United Kingdom Ministry of Defence, X.com, 31 May 2024, https://x.com/DefenceHQ/status/1796467954907037817 (accessed 21 August 2024).
39 'Russian Offensive Campaign Assessment', Institute for the Study of War, 9 November 2024, https://www.understandingwar.org/backgrounder/russian-offensive-campaign-assessment-november-9-2024 (accessed 3 December 2024).
40 George Allison, 'Russian Casualties Reach Record Highs in Ukraine', UK Defence Journal, 6 December 2024, https://ukdefencejournal.org.uk/russian-casualties-reach-record-highs-in-ukraine/ (accessed 28 December 2024).
41 Tymofiy Mylovanov, X.com, 25 December 2024, https://x.com/Mylovanov/status/1872019982965698726 (accessed 28 December 2024).
42 United States Senate Armed Services Committee, 'Statement of General Christopher G. Cavoli, United States Army', 3 April 2025, https://www.armed-services.senate.gov/imo/media/doc/general_cavoli_opening_statements.pdf (accessed 21 May 2025).
43 'How Many Russian Soldiers Have Been Killed in Ukraine', *The Economist*, 5 July 2024, https://www.economist.com/graphic-detail/2024/07/05/how-many-russian-soldiers-have-been-killed-in-ukraine# (accessed 21 August 2024).
44 'Russia Sends Waves of Troops to the Front in a Brutal Style of Fighting', *New York Times*, 27 June 2024, https://www.nytimes.com/2024/06/27/us/politics/russia-casualties-ukraine-war.html (accessed 21 August 2024).
45 United States Senate Armed Services Committee, 'Statement of General Christopher G. Cavoli, United States Army'.
46 'To Prevent War, NATO Must Spend More', speech by NATO Secretary-General Mark Rutte, NATO, 12 December 2024, https://www.nato.int/cps/en/natohq/opinions_231348.htm (accessed 13 December 2024).
47 Faisal Islam and Hannah Mullane, 'Russia to grow faster than all advanced economies, says IMF', BBC News, 16 April 2024, https://www.bbc.co.uk/news/business-68823399 (accessed 21 August 2024).
48 Robin Brooks, X.com, 25 December 2024, https://x.com/robin_j_brooks/status/1871933375109603673 (accessed 28 December 2024).
49 Robin Brooks, X.com, 28 December 2024, https://x.com/robin_j_brooks/status/1873014916992675853 (accessed 28 December 2024).
50 'Rossiyskiye Regiony Rekordno Uvelichili Raskhody na Silovikov', 10 September 2023, https://www.moscowtimes.ru/2023/09/08/rossiiskie-regioni-rekordno-uvelichili-rashodi-nasilovikov-a106348 (accessed 21 August 2024).
51 Kostya Nemichev, interview with author, Kharkiv, 2 September 2024.
52 Rob Lee, interview with author via Zoom, 20 September 2024.

CHAPTER 14

1 Note dropped from an Achilles Brigade drone to a Russian soldier who asked to be taken prisoner. The soldier survived. See 'Ukrainian Drone Helps Wounded Russian Soldier Surrender', Militarnyi, 19 August 2024, https://mil.in.ua/en/news/ukrainian-drone-helps-wounded-russian-soldier-surrender/#google_vignette (accessed 15 March 2025).

2 Ihor Obolienskyi, interview with author, Kharkiv, 13 November 2024.
3 Joe Barnes, 'Ukraine Launches Robot-Only Assault Against Russian Troops for First Time', *Daily Telegraph*, 24 December 2024, https://www.telegraph.co.uk/world-news/2024/12/24/ukraine-launches-robot-only-assault-against-russian-troops/ (accessed 19 January 2024).
4 Acoustic, interview with author, Lyptsi front and Kharkiv, 24 and 25 October 2024.
5 Brather, interview with author, Kharkiv, 2 September 2024.
6 Hoha, interview with author, Kyiv, 5 September 2024.
7 Sofiia Syngaivska, 'Ukrainian Achilles Strike Drone Company Captures Russian Soldier Begging Not to Be Bombed' Defence Express, 10 May 2023, https://en.defence-ua.com/news/ukrainian_achilles_strike_drone_company_captures_russian_soldier_begging_not_to_be_bombed-6667.html (accessed 8 December 2024).
8 Dev, interview with author, eastern Ukraine, 19 November 2024.
9 Achilles, interview with author, eastern Ukraine, 19 November 2024.
10 Yangrr, interview with author, eastern Ukraine, 19 November 2024.
11 Avocado, interview with author, eastern Ukraine, 19 November 2024.

CHAPTER 15

1 Russian Federation, 'Meeting of the Valdai International Discussion Club', 24 October 2014, http://eng.kremlin.ru/news/23137 (accessed 8 May 2025).
2 Alan Bloomfield criticised those strategic cultural authors who took no account of the possibility of change. See Alan Bloomfield, 'Time to Move On: Reconceptualizing the Strategic Culture Debate', *Contemporary Security Policy*, vol. 33, no. 3, 2012, p. 439 and pp. 440–441.
3 Tracey German, 'Harnessing Protest Potential: Russian Strategic Culture and the Colored Revolutions', *Contemporary Security Policy*, 2 May 2020, vol. 41, no. 4, p. 548; Dmitri Trenin, 'Russia Leaves the West', *Foreign Affairs*, vol. 85, no. 4, July-August 2006, pp. 87–96.
4 Russian Federation, 'Speech and the Following Discussion at the Munich Conference on Security Policy', 10 February 2007, http://en.kremlin.ru/events/president/transcripts/24034 (accessed 20 October 2024).
5 Thomas L. Friedman, 'Foreign Affairs; Now a Word From X', *New York Times*, 2 May 1998, https://www.nytimes.com/1998/05/02/opinion/foreign-affairs-now-a-word-from-x.html (accessed 19 October 2024).
6 'Russia Criticizes NATO Pledge to Ukraine, Georgia', Reuters, 4 April 2008, https://www.reuters.com/article/world/russia-criticizes-nato-pledge-to-ukraine-georgia-idUSL03154839/ (accessed 19 October 2024).
7 Russian Federation, 'Address by President of the Russian Federation', 18 March 2014, http://eng.kremlin.ru/news/6889 (accessed 20 October 2024).
8 Bob Seely, 'We Shouldn't Have Supported Kosovan Independence', Conservative Home, 15 April 2008, https://conservativehome.com/2008/04/15/bob-seely/ (accessed 18 October 2024).
9 Ibid.
10 Russian Federation, 'Meeting of the Valdai International Discussion Club'.
11 Juliane von Mittelstaedt, 'Do We Achieve World Order Through Chaos or Insight?', *Der Spiegel*, 13 November 2014, https://www.spiegel.de/international/world/interview-with-henry-kissinger-on-state-of-global-politics-a-1002073.html (accessed 19 October 2024).
12 John J. Mearsheimer, 'Why the Ukraine Crisis Is the West's Fault', September/October 2014, https://www.mearsheimer.com/wp-content/uploads/2019/06/Why-the-Ukraine-Crisis-Is.pdf (accessed 21 October 2024).
13 Ibid.
14 Michael Mandelbaum, *Mission Failure: America and the World in the Post-Cold War Era* (New York: Oxford University Press, 2016), p. 73.
15 Tony Blair, 'Doctrine of the International Community', British Political Speech, http://www.britishpoliticalspeech.org/speech-archive.htm?speech=279 (accessed 20 October 2024).
16 Russian Federation, 'Meeting of the Valdai International Discussion Club'.
17 Gleb Bryanki, 'Putin Likens UN Libya Resolution to Crusades', Reuters, 21 March 2011, https://www.reuters.com/article/us-libya-russia/putin-likens-u-n-libya-resolution-to-crusades-idUSTRE72K3JR20110321/ (accessed 20 October 2024).
18 'Full text: Putin's Declaration of War on Ukraine', *The Spectator*, 24 February 2024, https://www.spectator.co.uk/article/full-text-putin-s-declaration-of-war-on-ukraine/ (accessed 20 October 2024).
19 Andrei P. Tsygankov, *Russia and the West from Alexander to Putin: Honor in International Relations* (Cambridge, Cambridge University Press, 2012), p. 5.
20 Greenfeld, *Nationalism: Five Roads to Modernity*, p. 234.
21 Tsygankov, *Russia and the West*, p. 5.
22 Trenin, 'Russia Leaves the West'.

23 Ibid.

24 Robert Hunter, 'The West has Failed to Find a Constructive Role for Moscow', *Financial Times*, 17 February 2015, http://www.ft.com/cms/s/0/528d1dcc-b6a3-11e4-95dc-00144feab7de.html#axzz3T3LCFgzW (accessed 28 February 2015).

25 Robert Seely, 'The Truth about Russia's Foreign Policy', *Wall Street Journal*, 25 October 1995.

26 Daniel Baer, 'Ukraine's not a country, Putin told Bush. What'd he tell Trump about Montenegro?', *Washington Post*, 19 July 2018, https://www.washingtonpost.com/news/posteverything/wp/2018/07/19/ukraines-not-a-country-putin-told-bush-whatd-he-tell-trump-about-montenegro/ (accessed 31 December 2024).

27 John Lough, 'Myth 03: "Russia Was Promised That NATO Would Not Enlarge"', from 'Myths and Misconceptions in the Debate on Russia', Chatham House Report, 13 May 2021, https://www.chathamhouse.org/2021/05/myths-and-misconceptions-debate-russia/myth-03-russia-was-promised-nato-would-not-enlarge (accessed 31 December 2024).

28 Russian Federation, 'St Petersburg International Economic Forum plenary session', 25 May 2018, http://en.kremlin.ru/events/president/news/57556 (accessed 31 December 2024).

29 Interview with author, 21 October 2024, London.

30 Trenin, 'Russia Leaves the West'.

31 Mearsheimer, 'Why the Ukraine Crisis Is the West's Fault'.

32 Christopher Hitchens speaking on 'The Great European Disaster Movie: Newsnight Debate', *Storyville*, BBC Four, Sunday 1 March 2015.

33 Claire Bigg, 'World: Was Soviet Collapse Last Century's Worst Geopolitical Catastrophe?', Radio Free Europe/Radio Liberty, 29 April 2005, https://www.rferl.org/a/1058688.html (accessed 23 October 2024).

34 Seth Jones, 'Russia's Ill-Fated Invasion of Ukraine: Lessons in Modern Warfare', Centre for Strategic and International Studies, 1 June 2022, https://www.csis.org/analysis/russias-ill-fated-invasion-ukraine-lessons-modern-warfare (accessed 20 October 2024).

35 Mearsheimer, 'Why the Ukraine Crisis Is the West's Fault'.

CHAPTER 16

1 Michael McFaul, X.com, 7 March 2025, https://x.com/McFaul/status/1897881105044586931 (accessed 7 March 2025).

2 Andrew Goudsward, 'Trump Administration Disbands Task Force Targeting Russian Oligarchs', Reuters, 6 February 2025, https://www.reuters.com/world/us/trump-administration-disbands-task-force-targeting-russian-oligarchs-2025-02-06/ (accessed 6 March 2025).

3 Giovanna Coi and Dato Parulava, 'USAID freeze opens door to Russian influence in Eastern Europe', Politico, 25 February 2025, https://www.politico.eu/article/usaid-freeze-russia-influence-eastern-europe-georgia-ukraine-moldova-belarus-ngo-media/ (accessed 6 March 2025).

4 Glenn Thrush, 'U.S. to Withdraw From Group Investigating Responsibility for Ukraine Invasion', *New York Times*, 17 March 2015, https://www.nytimes.com/2025/03/17/us/politics/trump-ukraine-invasion-accountability.html (accessed 17 March 2025).

5 Max Seddon, 'Kremlin Says Western Unity is Falling Apart after Oval Office Row', *Financial Times*, 3 March 2025, https://www.ft.com/content/8604ecd8-84ed-4469-b329-5707b0977a6c (accessed 6 March 2025).

6 'German Major General Warns of Russian Military Build-Up', Yahoo News, 18 January 2025, https://www.yahoo.com/news/german-major-general-warns-russian-085622367.html (accessed 19 January 2025).

7 Ibid.

8 Ministry of Defence, X.com, 30 December 2023, https://x.com/defencehq/status/1741026561258573901?s=61&t=5OgErnUu7LB8CUQGljFbXQ (accessed 19 May 2025).

9 Agnieszka Bryc and Maria Domańska, 'Russia in the Trenches of Cognitive Warfare', *New Eastern European*, 9 September 2024, https://neweasterneurope.eu/2024/09/09/russia-in-the-trenches-of-cognitive-warfare/ (accessed 11 May 2025).

10 Bill Burns and Richard Moore, 'Bill Burns and Richard Moore: Intelligence partnership helps the US and UK stay ahead in an uncertain world', *Financial Times*, 7 September 2024, https://www.ft.com/content/252d7cc6-27de-46c0-9697-f3eb04888e70 (accessed 15 October 2024).

11 Michelle Nichols, 'Ukraine on Track to Export all 2023 Grain, says Britain', Reuters, 13 February 2024, https://www.reuters.com/markets/commodities/ukraine-track-export-all-2023-grain-says-britain-2024-02-13/ (accessed 30 December 2024).

12 Burns and Moore, 'Bill Burns and Richard Moore: Intelligence partnership helps the US and UK stay ahead in an uncertain world'.

13 Lester Grau and Charles Bartles, 'Russian "New Generation Warfare"', Powerpoint slide deck.

14 Julian E. Barnes, David E. Sanger and Helene Cooper, 'Hegseth Orders Pentagon to Stop Offensive

Cyberoperations Against Russia', *New York Times*, 2 March 2025, https://www.nytimes.com/2025/03/02/us/politics/hegseth-cyber-russia-trump-putin.html (accessed 15 March 2025).

15 Molly Olmstead, 'With Republicans Like These, Who Needs Russian Propaganda?', *Slate*, 20 April 2024, https://slate.com/news-and-politics/2024/04/ukraine-russia-congress-johnson-republicans-marjorie-greene-putin-propaganda.html (accessed 25 May 2025).

16 Jakob Hanke Vela, 'FBI Dossier Reveals Putin's Secret Psychological Warfare in Europe', Politico, 5 September 2024, https://www.politico.eu/article/fbi-dossier-reveals-russian-psy-ops-disinformation-campaign-election-europe/ (accessed 23 October 2024).

EPILOGUE

1 Lester W. Grau and Charles K. Bartles, *The Russian Way of War: Force Structure, Tactics and Modernization of the Russian Ground Forces* (Fort Leavenworth, KS: Foreign Military Studies Office, 2016), p. 321, https://www.armyupress.army.mil/portals/7/hot%20spots/documents/russia/2017-07-the-russian-way-of-war-grau-bartles.pdf (accessed January 31, 2023).

2 Russian Federation, 'Address by the President of the Russian Federation', 18 March 2014, http://kremlin.ru/events/president/news/20603 (accessed 18 January 2021).

3 David E. Sanger, 'Biden's Armageddon Moment: When Nuclear Detonation Seemed Possible in Ukraine', *New York Times*, 9 March 2024, https://www.nytimes.com/2024/03/09/us/politics/biden-nuclear-russia-ukraine.html (accessed 16 August 2024).

4 Hans M. Kristensen, Matt Korda, Eliana Johns and Mackenzie Knight, 'Russian Nuclear Weapons, 2024', Bulletin of the Atomic Scientists, 7 March 2024, https://thebulletin.org/premium/2024-03/russian-nuclear-weapons-2024/#post-heading (accessed 17 August 2024); 'Fact Sheet: Russia's Nuclear Inventory', Center for Arms Control and Non-Proliferation, 15 September 2022, https://armscontrolcenter.org/fact-sheet-russias-nuclear-inventory/ (accessed 17 August 2024).

5 'America's Nuclear Weapons Arsenal 2024: Annual Overview', Federation of American Scientists, 7 May 2024, https://fas.org/publication/nuclear-weapons-2024/ (accessed 19 August 2024).

6 Kristensen et al., 'Russian Nuclear Weapons, 2024'.

7 Russian Federation, 'Voyennaya Doktrina Rossiyskoy Federatsii', 25 December 2015, http://static.kremlin.ru/media/events/files/41d527556bec8deb3530.pdf (accessed 5 March 2017).

8 Ibid., p. 369.

9 Engström, 'Contemporary Russian Messianism', pp. 368, 369.

10 Irina Borogan and Andrei Soldatov, 'Putin's Security Forces Find God', Centre for European Policy Analysis, 9 February 2023, https://cepa.org/article/putins-security-forces-find-god/ (accessed 26 July 2024).

11 Cynthia Roberts, 'Revelations about Russia's Nuclear Deterrence Policy', War on the Rocks, 19 June 2024, https://warontherocks.com/2020/06/revelations-about-russias-nuclear-deterrence-policy/ (accessed 18 August 2024).

12 Nikolai Soko, 'Russia's 2000 Military Doctrine', NTI, https://www.nti.org/analysis/articles/russias-2000-military-doctrine/ (accessed 18 August 2024).

13 Max Seddon and Chris Cook, 'Leaked Russian Military Files Reveal Criteria for Nuclear Strike', *Financial Times*, 28 February 2024, https://www.ft.com/content/f18e6e1f-5c3d-4554-aee5-50a730b306b7 (accessed 19 August 2024).

14 Lester W. Grau and Charles K. Bartles, *The Russian Way of War*, p. 321.

15 Stephen Ennis, 'Russian Media Learn to Love the Bomb', BBC News, 23 February 2015, https://www.bbc.co.uk/news/world-europe-31557254 (accessed 16 August 2024).

16 'Ex-Russian President Warns of Nuclear "Apocalypse"', RT, 27 February 2023, https://www.rt.com/russia/572117-medvedev-nuclear-ukraine-apocalypse/ (accessed 19 August 2024).

17 Dmitri Medvedev, 'Yeshcho raz o Primenenii Yadernogo Oruzhiya', Telegram, 27 September 2022, https://t.me/medvedev_telegram/181 (accessed 17 August 2024).

18 Mark B. Schneider, 'Escalate to De-Escalate', US Naval Institute, February 2017, https://www.usni.org/magazines/proceedings/2017/february/escalate-de-escalate (accessed 19 August 2024).

19 David E. Sanger, 'New Nuclear Threats From Putin, Timed for a Moment of Anxiety', *New York Times*, https://www.nytimes.com/2024/02/29/world/europe/putin-nuclear-threats.html (accessed 18 August 2024).

SELECT BIBLIOGRAPHY

BOOKS

Albats, Yevgenia, *The State within a State: The KGB and its Hold on Russia: Past, Present, and Future* (New York: Farrar, Straus and Giroux, 1994).

Andrew, Christopher and Gordievsky, Oleg, *KGB: The Inside Story of Its Foreign Operations from Lenin to Gorbachev* (London: Hodder & Stoughton, 1990).

Andrew, Christopher and Mitrokhin, Vasili, *The Mitrokhin Archive: The KGB in Europe and the West* (London: Penguin, 1999).

Andrew, Christopher and Mitrokhin, Vasili, *The World Was Going Our Way: The KGB and the Battle for the Third World* (New York: Basic Books, 2005).

Berdyaev, Nicolas, *The Russian Idea* (New York: The Macmillan Company, 1948).

Bērziņš, Jānis, 'Russian New Generation Warfare is Not Hybrid Warfare', in Artis Pabriks and Andis Kudors (eds), *The War in Ukraine: Lessons for Europe* (Riga: University of Latvia Press, 2015).

Bittman, Ladislav, *The KGB and Soviet Disinformation* (London, Pergamon-Brassey's, 1985).

Bittman, Ladislav (ed.), *The New Image Makers* (London: Pergamon-Brassey's, 1998).

Cialdini, Robert B., *Influence: The Psychology of Persuasion* (New York: William Morrow, 1993).

von Clausewitz, Carl, *On War* (Princeton: Princeton University Press, 1976), edited and translated by Michael Howard and Peter Paret.

Clews, John C., *Communist Propaganda Techniques* (London, Fakenham and Reading: Cox and Wyman, 1964).

Conquest, Robert, *Harvest of Sorrow* (Oxford: Oxford University Press, 1986).

Delbrück, Hans, *History of the Art of War Within the Framework of Political History* (Westport: Greenwood Press, 1985), pp. 439-444.

Dugin, Aleksandr, *The Fourth Political Theory*, http://4pt.su/ru/content/chetvyortaya-politicheskaya-teoriya (accessed 28 December 2015).

Dugin, Aleksandr, *Osnovy Geopolitiki, Geopoliticheskoye Budushcheye Rossii* (Moskva: Arktogeya, 1997).

Dugin, Aleksandr and Katekhon, Revolutsiya, *Tampliyery Proletariata* (Moskva: Arktogeya, 1997).

Duncan, Peter, *Russian Messianism: Third Rome, Revolution, Communism and After* (London and New York: Routledge, 2000).

Dunlop, John, *The Moscow Bombings of September 1999: Examinations of Russian Terrorist Attacks at the Onset of Vladimir Putin's Rule* (Stuttgart: Ibidem-Varlag, 2014).

Frantzman, Seth J., *The Drone Wars* (New York: Post Hill Press, 2021).

Freedman, Lawrence, *Strategy: A History* (Oxford: Oxford University Press, 2013).

Fridman, Ofer, *Russian Hybrid Warfare: Resurgence and Politicisation* (London: Hurst and Co., 2018).

Galeotti, Mark, *Russian Political War* (London and New York: Routledge, 2021).

Gordievsky, Oleg, *Next Stop, Execution: The Autobiography of Oleg Gordievsky* (London: Macmillan, 1995).

Isserson, G. S., 'The Evolution of Operation Art', in *The Evolution of Soviet Operation Art 1927–1991: The Documentary Basis* (London: Frank Cass, 1995), translated by M. Orstein.

Isseron, G. S., *G. S. Isseron and the War of the Future: Key Writings of a Soviet Military Theorist* (Jefferson: Macfarland and Company, 2016), translated and edited by Richard W. Harrison.

Kaznacheev, Aleksandr, *Inside a Soviet Embassy* (London: Robert Hale, 1962).

Kokoshin, Andrei A., *Soviet Strategic Thought 1917–1991* (Cambridge, MA and London: MIT Press, 1999).

Kvachkov, Vladimir, *Spetsnaz Rossii* (Voyennaya Literatura, 2004), http://militera.lib.ru/science/kvachkov_vv/index.html (accessed 14 February 2017).

Lawrence, T. E., *Revolt in the Desert* (New York: George H. Doran, 1927).

Lucas, Edward, *The New Cold War* (London: Bloomsbury, 2014).

Lunev, Stanislav, *Through the Eyes of the Enemy* (Washington DC: Regnery Publishing Inc., 1998).

McGlynn, Jade, *The Memory Makers* (London: Bloomsbury, 2023).

Measheimer, John J., *The Tragedy of Great Power Politics* (New York: Norton, 2001).

Nye, Joseph, *Soft Power: The Means to Success in World Politics* (New York: Public Affairs, 2004).

Pacepa, Ion Mihai, *Red Horizons* (Washington DC: Regnery Gateway, 1987).

Pacepa, Ion Mihai and Rychlak, Ronald, *Disinformation* (Washington DC: WND Books, 2013).

Pipes, Richard, *Russia Under the Old Regime* (London: Widenfeld and Nicholson, 1974).

Rid, Thomas, *Active Measures: The Secret History of Disinformation and Political Warfare* (New York: Farrar, Straus and Giroux, 2020).

Romerstein, Herbert, *Soviet Active Measures and Propaganda: 'New Thinking' and Influence Activities in the Gorbachev Era* (Toronto: The Mackenzie Institute, 1989).

Seely, Robert, *Deadly Embrace: A History of Russian Chechen Relations 1800–2000* (London: Frank Cass, 2001).

Sherr, James, 'Russia: Managing Contradictions', in Robin Niblett (ed.), *America and a Changed World* (London: Blackwell, 2010).

Slipchenko, Vladimir, *Voyna Budushchego, Shestoye Pokoleniye* (Moscow: Nongovernmental Science Foundation, 1999).

Slipchenko, Vladimir, *Voyny Novogo Pokoleniya, Distantsionnyye i Bezkontaktnyye* (Moscow: Olma-Press, 2004).

Smith, Rupert, *The Utility of Force: The Art of War in the Modern World* (New York: Alfred A. Knopf, 2007).

Subtelny, Orest, *Ukraine: A History* (Toronto: University of Toronto Press, 1988).

Sun Tzu, *The Art of War* (Acheron Press, online, undated).

Triandafillov, V. K., *The Nature of the Operations of Modern Armies* (London and New York: Routledge, 2006), translated and edited by Jacob W. Kipp.

Trotsky, L., *Voyennaya Doktrina ili Mnimo-Voyennoye Doktrinerstvo* (Petrograd: Politicheskoye Upravleniye Petrogradskogo Voyennogo

Okruga, 1922), http://swetschin.narod.ru/others/Trotskii_L_Military_Doctrine_or_Pseudo-military_Doctrinarism.PDF (accessed 6 December 2015).

Tsygankov, Andrei P., *Russia and the West From Alexander to Putin: Honor in International Relations* (Cambridge: Cambridge University Press, 2012).

Tukhachevsky, Mikhail, *Izbrannyye Proizvedeniya, Tom Vtoroi 1928–1937* (Moskva: Voyennoye Izdatelstvo Ministerstva Oborony, 1964).

Zhilina, P. A. (ed.), *Istoriya Voyennogo Iskusstva* (Moskva: Voyennoye Izdatelstvo, 1986).

ARTICLES AND REPORTS

Adamsky, Dmitry (Dima), 'Cross-Domain Coercion: The Current Russian Art of Strategy', Proliferation Papers no. 54, Institut Français des Relations Internationales, November 2015, www.ifri.org/sites/default/files/migrated_files/documents/atoms/files/pp54adamsky.pdf (accessed 17 January 2021).

Arreguín-Toft, Ivan, 'How the Weak Win Wars', *International Security*, vol. 26, no. 1, summer 2001, pp. 93–128.

Bērziņš, Jānis, 'Russia's New Generation Warfare in Ukraine: Implications for Latvian Defence Policy', Policy Paper no. 2, Centre for Security and Strategic Research, National Defence Academy of Latvia, April 2014, https://sldinfo.com/wp-content/uploads/2014/05/New-Generation-Warfare.pdf (accessed 30 November 2015).

Blank, Stephen, '"No Need to Threaten Us, We Are Frightened of Ourselves": Russia's Blueprint for A Police State, The New Security Strategy', in Stephen J. Blank and Richard Weitz (eds), *The Russian Military Today and Tomorrow: Essays in Memory of Mary Fitzgerald*, Strategic Studies Institute, July 2010, https://archive.org/stream/TheRussianMilitaryTodayAndTomorrowEssaysInMemoryOfMaryFitzgerald/23-RussianMil_djvu.txt (accessed 14 February 2021).

Bogomolov, Alexander and Lytvynenko, Oleksandr, 'A Ghost in the Mirror: Russian Soft Power in Ukraine', Royal Institute for International Affairs, January 2012, https://www.researchgate.net/publication/263853878_A_Ghost_in_the_Mirror_Russian_Soft_Power_in_Ukraine_The_Aims_and_Means_of_Russian_Influence_Abroad_Series_A_Ghost_in_the_Mirror_Russian_Soft_Power_in_Ukraine (accessed 9 September 2014).

Borogan, Irina and Soldatov, Andrei, 'Putin's Security Forces Find God', Centre for European Policy Analysis, 9 February 2023, https://cepa.org/article/putins-security-forces-find-god/ (accessed 26 July 2024).

Bukkvoll, Tor, 'Iron Cannot Fight: The Role of Technology in Current Russian Military Theory', *Journal of Strategic Studies*, vol. 34, no. 5, 2011, pp. 681–706.

Chekinov S. G. and Bogdanov, S. A., 'Asimmetrichnyye Deystviya po Obespecheniyu Voyennoy Bezopasnosti Rossii', *Voyennaya Mysl'*, no. 3, 2010, pp. 13–22.

Chekinov, S. G. and Bogdanov, S. A., 'The Strategy of Indirect Approach: Its Impact on Modern Warfare', *Military Thought*, vol. 20, no. 3, 2011.

Chekinov, S. G. and Bogdanov, S. A., 'O Kharaktere i Soderzhanii Voiny Novogo Pokoleniya', *Voyennaya Mysl'*, no. 10, 2013.

Danylyuk, Oleksandr, 'The Components of Russia's Undeclared War Against the West', Royal United Services Institute, 28 January 2025, https://rusi.org/explore-our-research/publications/commentary/

components-russias-undeclared-war-against-west (accessed 1 February 2025).

Eitelhuber, Norbert, 'The Russian Bear: Russian Strategic Culture and What It Implies for the West', *Connections: The Quarterly Journal*, vol. 9, no. 1, 2009, pp. 1–28.

Ermarth, Fritz W., 'Russia's Strategic Culture: Past, Present, and… in Transition?', Defense Threat Reduction Agency, Advanced Systems and Concepts Office, 2006, http://fas.org/irp/agency/dod/dtra/russia.pdf (accessed 1 January 2016).

Fedchenko, Yevhen, 'Kremlin Propaganda: Soviet Active Measures by Other Means', stopfake.org, 21 March 2016, http://www.stopfake.org/en/kremlin-propaganda-soviet-active-measures-by-other-means/ (accessed 22 March 2016).

'Former KGB Agent Explains how Elites Brainwash the Pulic [*sic*] from reality', undated interview, YouTube, 2 June 2011, https://www.youtube.com/watch?v=DAMiNTC7HOM (accessed 1 January 2016).

Galeotti, Mark, 'The "Gerasimov Doctrine" and Russian Non-Linear War', In Moscow's Shadows, 6 July 2014, https://inmoscowsshadows.wordpress.com/2014/07/06/the-gerasimov-doctrine-and-russian-non-linear-war/ (accessed 2 September 2014).

Galeotti, Mark, 'Hybrid, Ambiguous, and Non-Linear? How New Is Russia's New Way of War?', *Small Wars & Insurgencies*, vol. 27, no. 2, 2016, pp. 282–301.

Galeotti, Mark, '"Crimintern": How the Kremlin Uses Russia's Criminal Networks in Europe', Policy Brief, European Council on Foreign Relations, April 2020, https://www.ecfr.eu/page/-/ECFR208_-_CRIMINTERM_-_HOW_RUSSIAN_

ORGANISED_CRIME_OPERATES_IN_EUROPE02.pdf (accessed 2 August 2020).

Gerasimov, Valerii, 'Tsennost Nauki v Predvidenii', *Voyenno-Promyshlennyy Kuryer*, 27 February–5 March 2013, http://vpk-news.ru/sites/default/files/pdf/VPK_08_476.pdf (accessed 1 June 2015).

Giles, Kier, 'Russia's "New" Tools for Confronting the West: Continuity and Innovation in Moscow's Exercise of Power', Royal Institute for International Affairs, March 2016, https://www.chathamhouse.org/2016/03/russias-new-tools-confronting-west-continuity-and-innovation-moscows-exercise-power (accessed 5 May 2016).

Giles, Kier; Hanson, Philip; Lyne, Roderic; Nixey, James; Sherr, James; and Wood, Andrew, 'The Russian Challenge,' Chatham House Report, Royal Institute for International Affairs, June 2015 (accessed 20 June 2016).

Hoffman, Frank, 'Conflict in the 21st Century: The Rise of Hybrid Wars', Potomac Institute for Policy Studies, December 2007, https://www.potomacinstitute.org/images/stories/publications/potomac_hybridwar_0108.pdf (accessed 25 August 2021).

Ilnitsky, Andrei, 'Mental'naya Voyna Rossii', *Voyennaya Mysl'*, no. 8, 6 August 2021, https://vm.ric.mil.ru/Stati/item/336904/ (accessed 23 August 2021).

Jonsson, Oscar and Seely, Robert, 'Russian Full-Spectrum Conflict: An Appraisal after Ukraine', *Journal of Slavic Military Studies*, vol. 28, no. 1, March 2015, pp. 1–22.

Lenin, V. I., 'What Is To Be Done?', *Lenin's Collected Works* (Moscow: Foreign Languages Publishing House, 1961), vol. 5, pp. 347–530, https://www.marxists.org/archive/lenin/works/1901/witbd/index.htm (accessed 5 June 2015).

Lenin, V. I., '"Left-Wing" Communism: An Infantile Disorder', *Lenin's Collected Works* (Moscow: Progress Publishers, 1964), vol. 31, pp. 17–118, https://www.marxists.org/archive/lenin/works/1920/lwc/index.htm (accessed 2 January 2021).

Lenin, V. I., 'Lessons of the Moscow Uprising', *Lenin's Collected Works* (Moscow: Progress Publishers, 1965), vol. 11, pp. 171–8, https://www.marxists.org/archive/lenin/works/1906/aug/29.htm (accessed 2 January 2021).

Østbø, Jardar, 'Securitizing "Spiritual-Moral Value" in Russia', *Post-Soviet Affairs*, vol. 33, no. 3, 2017, pp. 200–216.

Panarin, Igor, 'Sistema Informatsionnogo Protivoborstva', *Voyenno-Promyshlennyy Kuryer*, 15 October 2008, http://www.vpk-news.ru/articles/3672 (accessed 17 December 2020).

Pomerantsev, Peter, 'Putin's Rasputin', *London Review of Books*, vol. 33, no. 20, 20 October 2011, http://www.lrb.co.uk/v33/n20/peter-pomerantsev/putins-rasputin (accessed 27 August 2015).

Pomerantsev, Peter, 'How Putin Is Reinventing Warfare', Foreign Policy, 5 May 2014, http://www.foreignpolicy.com/articles/2014/05/05/how_putin_is_reinventing_warfare (accessed 27 August 2015).

Popov, Igor, 'Voyennaya Mysl Sovremennoy Rossii', Voina Budushchego, 2007, http://futurewarfare.narod.ru/theoryRF.html (accessed 20 December 2015).

Rácz, András, 'Russia's Hybrid War in Ukraine', Finnish Institute for International Affairs, report 43, June 2015, https://fiia.fi/en/publication/russias-hybrid-war-in-ukraine (accessed 30 November 2015).

Ryabchuk, Mykola, 'The Ukrainian "Friday" and the Russian "Robinson": The Uneasy Advent of Postcoloniality', *Canadian-American Slavic Studies*, vol. 44, no. 1–2, 2010, pp. 7–24.

Ryabchuk, Mykola, 'Two Ukraines Reconsidered: The End of Ukrainian Ambivalence?', *Studies in Ethnicity and Nationalism*, vol. 15, no. 1, 2015, pp. 138–56.

Ryabchuk, Mykola, 'Ukrainians as Russia's Negative "Other": History Comes Full Circle', *Communist and Post-Communist Studies*, vol. 49, no. 1, 2016, pp. 75–85.

Seely, Robert, 'Defining Contemporary Russian Warfare: Beyond the Hybrid Headline', *RUSI Journal*, vol. 162, no. 1, February/March 2017, pp. 40–49.

Seely, Robert, 'A Definition of Contemporary Russian Conflict: How Does the Kremlin Wage War?', Research Paper No. 15, Russia and Eurasia Studies Centre, The Henry Jackson Society, June 2018, https://henryjacksonsociety.org/publications/a-definition-of-contemporary-russian-conflict-how-does-the-kremlin-wage-war/ (accessed 24 June 2018).

Shandra, Alya and Seely, Robert, 'The Surkov Leaks: The Inner Workings of Russia's Hybrid War in Ukraine', Occasional Paper, Royal United Services Institute, July 2019, https://www.rusi.org/explore-our-research/publications/occasional-papers/surkov-leaks-inner-workings-russias-hybrid-war-ukraine (accessed 27 August 2019).

Sherr, James and Kullamaa, Kaarel, 'The Russian Orthodox Church: Faith, Power and Conquest', International Centre for Defence and Security and the Estonian Foreign Policy Institute, December 2019, https://icds.ee/wp-content/uploads/2019/12/ICDS_EFPI_Report_The_Russian_Orthodox_Church_Sherr_Kullamaa_December_2019.pdf (accessed 25 January 2021).

Shevtsova, Lilia, 'Novyyi Mirovoy Poryadok Vladimira Putina', Carnegie Moscow Center, 11 May 2014, https://carnegie.ru/2014/05/11/ru-pub-55766 (accessed 25 November 2020).

Surkov, Vladislav, 'Russian Political Culture: The View from Utopia', *Russian Social Science Review*, vol. 49, no. 6, 2008, pp. 81–97.

Surkov, Vladislav, writing under the pseudonym Natan Dubovitsky, 'Bez Neba', *Russkiy Pioner*, 12 March 2014, http://ruspioner.ru/honest/m/single/4131 (accessed 15 March 2021).

Thomas, Timothy L., 'Russian Information-Psychological Actions: Implications for US PSYOP', *Special Warfare*, vol. 10, no. 1, Winter 1997, pp. 12–19, https://community.apan.org/cfs-file/__key/telligent-evolution-components-attachments/13-14863-00-00-00-24-45-67/1997_2D00_12_2D00_01-Russian-Information_2D00_Psychological-Actions_2D00_Implications-for-U.S.-PSYOP-_2800_Thomas_2900_.pdf (accessed 20 December 2015).

Thomas, Timothy L., 'Dialectical Versus Empirical Thinking: Ten Key Elements of the Russian Understanding of Information Operations', *Journal of Slavic Military Studies*, vol. 11, no. 1, 1998, pp. 40–62.

Thomas, Timothy L., 'Reflexive Control in Russia Theory and Military Applications', *Reflexive Processes and Control*, vol. 1, no. 2, July–December 2002.

Thomas, Timothy L., 'Russia's Reflexive Control Theory and the Military', *Journal of Slavic Military Studies*, vol. 17, no. 2, 2004, pp. 237–56.

Trenin, Dmitri, 'Russia Leaves the West', *Foreign Affairs*, vol. 85, no. 4, July–August 2006, pp. 87–96.

Watling, Jack and Reynolds, Nick, 'The Plot to Destroy Ukraine', Royal United Services Institute, 15 February 2022, https://static.rusi.org/special-report-202202-ukraine-web.pdf (accessed 29 July 2024).

Watling, Jack and Reynolds, Nick, 'Ukraine Through Russia's Eyes', Royal United Services Institute, 25 February 2022, https://rusi.

org/explore-our-research/publications/commentary/ukraine-through-russias-eyes (accessed 29 July 2024).

Watling, Jack and Reynolds, Nick, 'Winter Is Coming: Russia Turns to Countervalue Targeting', Royal United Services Institute, 1 November 2022, https://www.rusi.org/explore-our-research/publications/commentary/winter-coming-russia-turns-countervalue-targeting (accessed 28 July 2024).

Watling, Jack and Reynolds, Nick, 'Meatgrinder: Russian Tactics in the Second Year of Its Invasion of Ukraine', Royal United Services Institute, 19 May 2023, https://www.rusi.org/explore-our-research/publications/special-resources/meatgrinder-russian-tactics-second-year-its-invasion-ukraine (accessed 28 July 2024).

Watling, Jack and Reynolds, Nick, 'Stormbreak: Fighting Through Russian Defences in Ukraine's 2023 Offensive', Royal United Services Institute, September 2023, https://static.rusi.org/Stormbreak-Special-Report-web-final_0.pdf (accessed 28 July 2024).

Watling, Jack, Danylyuk, Oleksandr V. and Reynolds, Nick, 'Preliminary Lessons from Russia's Unconventional Operations During the Russo-Ukrainian War, February 2022–February 2023', Royal United Services Institute, 29 March 2023, https://rusi.org/explore-our-research/publications/special-resources/preliminary-lessons-russias-unconventional-operations-during-russo-ukrainian-war-february-2022 (accessed 26 July 2024).

Watling, Jack, Danylyuk, Oleksandr V. and Reynolds, Nick, 'The Threat from Russia's Unconventional Warfare Beyond Ukraine, 2022–2024', Royal United Services Institute, 20 February 2024, https://www.rusi.org/explore-our-research/publications/special-resources/threat-russias-unconventional-warfare-beyond-ukraine-2022-24 (accessed 29 July 2024).

NEWS ARTICLES

Arkhipov, Ilya, 'Putin Says Officials Must Stop Russian "Color" Revolution', Bloomberg, 20 November 2014, https://www.bloomberg.com/news/articles/2014-11-20/putin-says-russia-must-prevent-color-revolution?embedded-checkout=true (accessed 23 January 2021).

Askai707, 'Artillerymen of Russia's 136th Motorized Infantry Brigade in the Donbass', Bellingcat, 13 November 2015, https://www.bellingcat.com/news/uk-and-europe/2015/11/13/136-brigade-in-donbass/ (accessed 1 July 2021).

Baluevsky, Yuri N. and Khamzatov, M. M., 'Globalizatsiya I Voyennoye Delo,' *Nezavisimoye Voyennoye Obozreniye*, 8 August 2014, https://nvo.ng.ru/concepts/2014-08-08/1_globalisation.html (accessed 12 February 2021).

Bartosh, Aleksandr, '"Model" Upravlyayemogo Khaosa – Ugroza Natsional'noy Bezopasnosti Rossii', 12 July 2013, *Nezavisimoye Voyennoye Obozreniye*, https://nvo.ng.ru/concepts/2013-07-12/4_chaos.html (accessed 26 January 2021).

Bartosh, Aleksandr, 'Gibridnyye Voyny v Strategii SSHA i NATO', *Nezavisimoye Voyennoye Obozreniye*, 10 October 2014, https://nvo.ng.ru/concepts/2014-10-10/1_nato.html (accessed 26 January 2021).

Bellingcat Investigation Team, 'FSB Team of Chemical Weapon Experts Implicated in Alexey Navalny Novichok Poisoning', Bellingcat, 14 December 2021, https://www.bellingcat.com/news/uk-and-europe/2020/12/14/fsb-team-of-chemical-weapon-experts-implicated-in-alexey-navalny-novichok-poisoning/ (accessed 24 September 2021).

Bellingcat Investigation Team, 'Origin of Artillery Attacks on Ukrainian Military Positions in Eastern Ukraine Between 14 July

2014 and 8 August 2014', Bellingcat, 17 February 2015, https://www.bellingcat.com/news/uk-and-europe/2015/02/17/origin-of-artillery-attacks/ (accessed 8 April 2016).

Berlin, Isaiah, 'The Silence in Russian Culture', *Foreign Affairs*, October 1957, http://www.foreignaffairs.com/articles/71355/isaiah-berlin/the-silence-in-russian-culture (accessed 21 December 2015).

Chubais, Anatoly, 'Missiya Rossii v XXI Veke', *Nezavisimaya Gazeta*, 1 October 2003, http://www.ng.ru/ideas/2003-10-01/1_mission.html (accessed 9 September 2017).

Gareyev, Makhmut, 'Otstaivaya Natsional'nyye Interesy', *Voyenno-Promyshlennyy Kuryer*, 14 December 2005, https://vpk-news.ru/articles/3744 (accessed 4 April 2021).

Gareyev, Makhmut, 'Strategicheskoye Sderzhivaniye: Problemy i Resheniya', *Krasnaya Zvezda*, 8 October 2008, http://old.redstar.ru/2008/10/08_10/index.shtml (accessed 3 April 2021).

Gareyev, Makhmut, 'Voina Bez Sroka Davnosti', *Voyenno-Promyshlennyy Kuryer*, 13 May 2015, http://vpk-news.ru/articles/25172 (accessed 28 December 2015).

Gareyev, Makhmut, 'Predchuvstvovat' Izmeneniya v Kharaktere Voyny', *Voyenno-Promyshlennyy Kuryer*, 29 May 2013, http://vpk-news.ru/articles/16089 (accessed 17 March 2021).

'Inside the KGB: An Interview with retired KGB Maj. Gen. Oleg Kalugin', CNN, January 1998, https://web.archive.org/web/20070206020316/http:/www.cnn.com/SPECIALS/cold.war/episodes/21/interviews/kalugin/ (accessed 24 April 2018).

Panarin, Igor, 'Sistema Informatsionnogo Protivoborstva', *Voyenno-Promyshlennyy Kur'yer*, 15 October 2008, http://www.vpk-news.ru/articles/3672 (accessed 17 December 2020).

'Putin Poobeshchal ne Dopustit' "Tsvetnoy Revolyutsii" v Rossii',

BBC Russia, 20 November 2014, https://www.bbc.com/russian/russia/2014/11/141120_russia_putin_extremism (accessed 26 November 2020).

Putin, Vladimir, 'Russia: The Ethnicity Issue', *Nezavisimaya Gazeta*, 23 January 2012, http://archive.premier.gov.ru/eng/events/news/17831/ (accessed 25 May 2025).

Putin, Vladimir, 'Byt' Sil'nymi: Garantii Natsional'noy Bezopasnosti dlya Rossii', *Rossiyskaya Gazeta*, 20 February 2012, https://rg.ru/2012/02/20/putin-armiya.html (accessed 1 April 2021).

Putin, Vladimir, 'Rossiya i Menyayushchiysya Mir', *Moskovskiye Novosti*, 27 February 2012, https://er.ru/activity/news/putin-rossiya-i-menyayushijsya-mir_76109 (accessed 25 May 2025).

GOVERNMENT PUBLICATIONS AND DOCTRINES

Chairman of the Joint Chiefs of Staff, 'The National Military Strategy of the United States of America', 2015, http://www.jcs.mil/Portals/36/Documents/Publications/2015_National_Military_Strategy.pdf (accessed 25 August 2015).

'Director General Ken McCallum Gives Annual Threat Update 2021', Security Service MI5, https://www.mi5.gov.uk/news/director-general-ken-mccallum-gives-annual-threat-update-2021 (accessed 28 September 2021).

Estonian Internal Security Service, 'Annual Review 2013', https://kapo.ee/sites/default/files/content_page_attachments/Annual%20Review%202013.pdf (accessed 22 May 2025).

George F. Kennan, 'The Long Telegram', 22 February 1946, https://nsarchive2.gwu.edu//coldwar/documents/episode-1/kennan.htm (accessed 6 February 2021).

The Litvinenko Inquiry, 'Report into the Death of Alexander Litvinenko', January 2016, https://www.litvinenkoinquiry.org/

files/Litvinenko-Inquiry-Report-web-version.pdf (accessed 29 November 2016).

Russian Federation, 'Voyennaya Doktrina Rossiyskoy Federatsii', 25 December 2015, http://static.kremlin.ru/media/events/files/41d527556bec8deb3530.pdf (accessed 5 March 2017).

Russian Federation, 'Kontseptsiya Vneshney Politiki Rossiyskoy Federatsii', 1 December 2016, http://www.mid.ru/foreign_policy/news/-/asset_publisher/cKNonkJE02Bw/content/id/2542248 (accessed 14 September 2017).

Russian Federation, 'Strategiya Natsional'noy Bezopasnosti Rossiyskoy Federatsii', 31 December 2015, http://static.kremlin.ru/media/events/files/ru/l8iXkR8XLAtxeilX7JK3XXy6Y0AsHD5v.pdf (accessed 16 September 2017).

Russian Federation, 'Doktrina Informatsionnoy Bezopasnosti Rossiyskoy Federatsii', 5 December 2016, http://static.kremlin.ru/media/acts/files/0001201612060002.pdf (accessed 26 February 2017).

Russian Federation, 'Strategiya Natsional'noy Bezopasnosti Rossiyskoy Federatsii', 2 July 2021, http://static.kremlin.ru/media/events/files/ru/QZw6hSk5z9gWq0plD1ZzmR5cER0g5tZC.pdf (accessed 30 September 2021).

Russian Federation, 'Vladimir Putin Otvetil na Voprosy o Stat'ye Ob Istoricheskom Yedinstve Russkikh i Ukraintsev', 12 July 2021, http://kremlin.ru/events/president/news/66181 (accessed 16 July 2021).

Russian Federation, 'Stat'ya Vladimira Putina 'Ob Istoricheskom Yedinstve Russkikh i Ukraintsev', 12 July 2021, http://kremlin.ru/events/president/news/66181 (accessed 16 July 2021).

Select Committee on Intelligence, United States Senate, 'Russian Active Measures Campaigns and Interference in the 2016 U.S.

Election', volumes I–V, 10 November 2020, https://www.congress.gov/congressional-report/116th-congress/senate-report/290/1 (accessed 12 June 2021).

United States Department of Defence, 'Doctrine for the Armed Forces of the United States: Joint Publication 1', https://www.jcs.mil/Portals/36/Documents/Doctrine/pubs/jp1_ch1.pdf (accessed 21 April 2016).

United States Department of State, 'Soviet Influence Activities: A Report on Active Measures and Propaganda, 1986–87', Department of State publication 9627, August 1987, http://jmw.typepad.com/files/state-department---a-report-on-active-measures-and-propaganda.pdf (accessed 27 August 2015).

ACKNOWLEDGEMENTS

Thank you to all those who have assisted throughout the writing of this book, including those who agreed to be interviewed not only for the book but also for my PhD on contemporary Russian warfare. In total, nearly 150 individuals agreed to be interviewed.

Additionally, I would like to thank the following Ukrainian military units and individuals associated with them: Achilles, Kraken, Khartiia, Tsunami, the 92nd Brigade, Kyiv Territorial Volunteer Defence Force, 31 unit (Gagauz and Veronika), Sarmat, Kos, the 56th Brigade, Dragon School, Odesa Air Defence, former and current members of the General Staff, as well as officers from Ukrainian military intelligence and the secret service in Zaporizhzhia, Odesa and elsewhere. Thank you to Ed Brown and Andrea Belloli for their insightful suggestions and initial proofreading. Thanks also to Jade, Andrii from Kraken, Jimmy Rushton and Denys Glushko from Kharkiv. Furthermore, I would like to thank InformNapalm, StopFake, EuroMaidan Press and many other Ukrainian organisations that have helped.

My thanks also go to my PhD supervisor Professor Tracey German from the Defence Studies Department at King's College London, my examiners Rob Johnson and Rory Cormac, to Biteback Publishing for commissioning the book and to Catriona Allon for editing.

INDEX